WITHDRAWN

The Italian World
of English Renaissance
Drama

The Italian World of English Renaissance Drama

Cultural Exchange and Intertextuality

Edited by
MICHELE MARRAPODI

Associate Editor
A. J. HOENSELAARS

DELAWARE

Newark: University of Delaware Press
London: Associated University Presses

© 1998 by Associated University Presses, Inc.

All rights reserved. Authorization to photocopy items for internal or personal use, or the internal or personal use of specific clients, is granted by the copyright owner, provided that a base fee of $10.00, plus eight cents per page, per copy is paid directly to the Copyright Clearance Center, 222 Rosewood Drive, Danvers, Massachusetts 01923. [0-87413-638-5/98 $10.00 + 8¢ pp, pc.]

PR
129
.I8
I78
1998

Associated University Presses
440 Forsgate Drive
Cranbury, NJ 08512

Associated University Presses
16 Barter Street
London WC1A 2AH, England

Associated University Presses
P.O. Box 338, Port Credit
Mississauga, Ontario
Canada L5G 4L8

The paper used in this publication meets the requirements
of the American National Standard for Permanence of Paper
for Printed Library Materials Z39.48–1984.

Library of Congress Cataloging-in-Publication Data

The Italian world of English Renaissance drama : cultural exchange and
 intertextuality / edited by Michele Marrapodi ; associate editor,
A.J. Hoenselaars.
     p.   cm.
  Includes bibliographical references (p.   ) and index.
  ISBN 0-87413-638-5 (alk. paper)
  1. English drama—Italian influences.   2. English drama—Early
modern and Elizabethan, 1500–1600—History and criticism.
3. English drama—17th century—History and criticism.
4. Literature, Comparative—English and Italian   5. Literature,
Comparative—Italian and English.   6. Influence (Literary, artistic,
etc.)   7. Renaissance—England.   8. Italy—In literature.
9. Intertextuality.   I. Marrapodi, Michele.   II. Hoenselaars, A.
J., 1956–   .
PR129.I8I78   1998
822'.309–dc21   97-20907
                                                                CIP

PRINTED IN THE UNITED STATES OF AMERICA

052198-33

Contents

Acknowledgments

No critical discourse is ever born in isolation: it owes its existence to a great number of related ideas, profiting from the experience of the past and the teaching of both "old" and "new" scholarship on either side of the Atlantic. The kind and extent of the various influencers, too numerous to be listed here, can be discerned from the bibliographical section appended to the volume. I would specifically acknowledge the encouragement and criticism of those colleagues and friends who have enthusiastically shared the fortunes of the project from the outset, or participated in an international conference on the theme of the volume held at the University of Palermo in June 1995. I am particularly indebted to David Bevington, Ronnie Mulryne, Robert Miola, Louise George Clubb, Keir Elam, Alessandro Serpieri, Marcello Cappuzzo, Silvana Sciarrino, Attilio Carapezza, and Peter Dawson. I wish to thank Susan Brock of The Shakespeare Institute, Stratford-upon-Avon, for her customary kindness and efficiency shown to me on many occasions. I am also grateful to the anonymous readers of the Press for their positive and constructive responses. Special thanks are finally due to the Italian Consiglio Nazionale delle Ricerche (CNR) and the University of Palermo for providing generous financial assistance at various stages.

Michele Marrapodi
Stratford-upon-Avon,
June 1996

Prologue

MICHELE MARRAPODI

IN Shakespeare's *Julius Caesar,* the comments of Cassius and
Brutus on the assassination of Caesar have been much quoted:

> *Cassius.* How many ages hence
> Shall this our lofty scene be acted over
> In states unborn and accents yet unknown!
>
> *Brutus.* How many times shall Caesar bleed in sport,
> That now on Pompey's basis lies along
> No worthier than the dust![1]

Scholars have often regarded these lines as a cue for Shakespeare's metatheatrical reflection on his own art and the theater
in general. For Anne Barton the passage serves "to glorify the
stage," to reveal a peculiar Shakespearean attitude quite uncommon among other contemporary playwrights, and to emphasize
how "It is in the theatre that the noble actions of the world
are preserved for the instruction of future generations."[2] In a
methodology that inspires systematic investigation of the idea
of the play, Barton's response to these intriguing lines has remained unchallenged. A different perspective, however, is obviously possible: instead of looking to the future, we may go back
to the past and see the fall of Caesar against the background of
history and theatrical conventions. From this viewpoint, we may
notice the conspirators' reference to a well-worn subject of
moral *exempla,* inscribed in the *De casibus* tragedy tradition
that was fashionable throughout the Elizabethan period. In that
line of transmission, Brutus stands as the archetypal betrayer
and Caesar as the victim of his own greatness. In his *Divina
Commedia,* Dante equates Brutus's and Cassius's punishment
to that of Judas Iscariot, placing them all in the champing
mouths of the three-faced Lucifer, "Lo 'mperador del doloroso
regno" ("The emperor of the woeful realm").[3] The murderous
actio, which Cassio calls "our lofty scene," was, in fact, fre-

quently rehearsed in didactic drama. "I did enact Julius Caesar. I was killed i'th' Capitol. / Brutus killed me,"[4] boasts Polonius in *Hamlet* and, in the same play, the Prince can ponder on the death of kings and comment ironically:

> Imperious Caesar, dead and turn'd to clay,
> Might stop a hole to keep the wind away.
> O that that earth which kept the world in awe
> Should patch a wall t'expel the winter's flaw.
>
> (5.1.206–209)

I have taken Barton's authoritative critique into consideration because it exemplifies the ambiguity inherent in any serious attempt to bridge the gap between ancient and modern thought: on the one hand, the reader's claim for liberty to construct and deconstruct the text at will, in accordance with her/his views and critical experience; on the other hand, the necessity to place the text in a tradition of other texts and cultures. By adopting the first procedure we are exposed to the danger of accommodating the text to personal taste and aesthetic values; with the second we incur the risk of losing the literary thread of a native culture in a complex network of motifs and patterns. In other words, although the romantic myth of the originality of the poet is definitively debunked, it seems today that the critic's major task is still to make the old Eliotian distinction between tradition and individual talent. Questions like these come especially into focus in considering such historical figures as Caesar and Brutus, Antony and Cleopatra, Troilus and Cressida, Ulysses, or Coriolanus, all dramatized in the Shakespeare canon, whose lives were highly popular in the Renaissance and easily accessible in a considerable number of works, chronicles, and plays, in the original as well as in translation, ranging from Homer and Plutarch to Dante and Boccaccio, from medieval literature to Elizabethan drama. This long-established tradition has marked out a well-trodden path along which cultural exchange has united Italy and the classical world to England and the rest of Europe, and the blending of themes and traditions has proved particularly fertile. The circulation of learning (or "social energy" in Stephen Greenblatt's terminology) has led to the wider field of imitation, borrowing, and adaptation, including the notion of reception in its double aspects of compliance and resistance.[5] Thus, cultural exchange, cultural difference, and cultural contrast are all related concepts that hark back to Aristotle and

Greek philosophy and reach Shakespeare's age via the humanist approach to art of early modern England.

Various examples can be called to mind to illustrate the effects of intercultural discourse between literatures. One instance is the rapid spread of Italian *novelle* throughout Europe, providing an impressive bulk of translations and imitations, which had a profound influence upon English dramaturgy. From Boccaccio, Bandello, Cinthio, and others, the *novella* passed on, directly or through French adaptations, to Painter's *Palace of Pleasure* and his English successors, whose "tragical histories and tales" constituted the basic plots for many Elizabethan tragedies. Within this process of textual transmission the phenomenon of resistance played an important role, appropriating the moral of the narratives to a national culture with distinctive social and religious principles. Elizabethan schoolmasters advocated the study of Plautus and Terence. Terence's style was particularly praised and his works were frequently translated or imitated for didactic purposes, but through this practice a much stronger moralizing attitude emerged, quite alien to the constitutional levity of the original. As Madeleine Doran pointed out, "The result was a 'Christian Terence,' extremely interesting because it shows the tradition of classical comedy combining with the tradition of the religious drama to produce a strong movement towards realism."[6]

Other telling instances can be drawn from the intertextual analysis of theatrical forms and structures. The use of the prologue provides a significant case in point. The practice of beginning a play with a formal address to the audience goes back to Greek and Latin New Comedy, originating from the choral opening of Greek early theater. The function was mainly expository, centering on the presentation of the argument and characters. This part playing directly addressed to the audience was delivered either in soliloquy or dialogue, in the latter case involving two or more protatic speakers. Even when the heading "Prologue" was not specified, as in Plautus's *Mercator,* the opening soliloquy or dialogue carried the necessary information of the regular prologue. Shakespeare's *The Comedy of Errors,* based on Plautus's *Menaechmi* and probably on Warner's translation (which the dramatist might have read in manuscript), owes to Gower's *Confessio Amantis* Egeon's initial tale of the tempest that causes the splitting up of the family. Yet the motif of the shipwreck is to a certain extent foreshadowed by Prologus's scripton in *Menaechmi* (not included in Warner's translation) of the abductor's alliterative death by water: "ingressus fluvium rapidum ab urbe haud longule, / rapidus raptori pueri subduxit pedes / abstraxitque hominem in maximam malam crucem" (while he was trying to ford a rapid stream quite near the city, the rapids rapt the feet of the boy's abductor from beneath him and swept him off to perdition).[7] Whereas the Plautine prologue customarily ends by courting the audience's attention and applause, Terence's use of the prologue is more frequently self-commendatory and polemical, defending the play from detractors and rivalry alike. In both, the device serves to create a more intimate audience involvement and sympathetic participation, although it spoils the illusion of realism. The latter effect may explain why Shakespeare's tragedies do not contain prologues, but impart necessary information to the audience by means of indirect speech reports, such as Horatio's narration of the causes of the war in *Hamlet,* or the witches' choral opening in *Macbeth.* The seven Shakespearean or partly Shakespearean plays with prologues (*Romeo and Juliet, 2 Henry IV, Henry V, Troilus and Cressida, Pericles, Henry VIII,* and *The Two Noble Kinsmen*) mainly present a classical construction of mixed type, obeying diverse dramaturgical needs, ranging from exposition of the subject matter to spatial and/or temporal identification, from the necessity to provide a narrative link with the antecedent or the previous play to the metatheatrical function of audience involvement. And since the terms prologue and induction were used almost interchangeably in the Elizabethan age—the prologue in *2 Henry IV* is headed "Induction" in the Folio—we may include *The Taming of the Shrew* in our list of plays with prologues, whereby the induction offers associations with a number of contemporary plays of strong Italianate coloring, from Jonson to Marston and Middleton.[8]

Plautus's and Terence's prologues share many characteristics of the inductive pieces, especially in relation to pretense and theatricality, and in such stock elements as "the wanton who sits on the stage, the noisy lictor, the officious usher, the sleeper, slaves, nurses with crying babies, and talkative housewives," all recurring features of both Italian and Elizabethan drama.[9] From *Every Man Out of His Humour* (1599) to *The Magnetic Lady* (1632), Jonson is undoubtedly the most prolific dramatist to make use of this kind of metatheatrical inset. Most of his inductive and prologuelike pieces resemble Roman antecedents and show various links with Italian drama in the ingenious participation in the ongoing action of the actors, members of the audience, and even the author himself, as in the *"Apologetical Dialogue"* appended to the conclusion of *Poetaster* (1601).[10] In Alessandro Piccolomini's *L'Amor costante* (1536), a Spaniard comments on the staging of the performance, converses with the prologue speaker, and is involved in the mise-en-scène "perché aviam de bisogno d'uno che facci meglio un capitano" (because we need someone who plays a captain's role better).[11] The rich catalog of Italian cinquecento comedy provides, in fact, a wide variety of prologues of Plautine and Terentian derivation with frequent grafting from the proems of the *Decameron,* having an introductory, polemic, or mixed character. The speaker or presenter is endowed with a strong clownish nature, capable of lively language games by which he addresses the audience directly, usually attempting to differentiate his speech from classical models.[12] Ariosto's prologue in *Cassaria* (1508) aims to graft a new comedic form onto Italian material:

> Nova comedia v'appresento piena
> Di varii giochi, che né mai latine
> Né greche lingue recitarno in scena.[13]

> [I am presenting you a new comedy full
> Of various intrigues, which never either Latin
> Or Greek tongues did recite upon the stage.]

Yet the same prologue imitates Prologus's speech in Terence's *Andria* and presents the argument using the very words of *Phormio* (Prologus, 24–26) and *Hecyra* (Prologus 2, 1–2). The rest of the comedy, albeit not borrowed from any specific Roman play, is Terentian in spirit, as is almost all Ariostan theater. Ariosto's Terentian world, in both themes and characterization, appears explicitly in the polemical mode of the prologues and in the declared strategy to adopt a *contaminatio* of plots and situations. In the opening of *I Suppositi* (1509) Ariosto frankly admits his indebtedness to Plautus's *Captivi* and Terence's *Eunuchus,* pointing out, however, "sì modestamente però che Terenzio e Plauto medesimi, risapendolo, non l'arebbono a male, e di poetica imitazione, più presto che di furto, li darebbono nome" (in such a modest proportion that the self-same Terence and Plautus, this known, would not get angry, and would call it not theft but poetic imitation).[14] The Prologus of the second production of *La Lena* (1529), presenting two new scenes appended as a "coda" to the conclusion, complains about the judg-

ment of the severe old critics "che sempre disprezzano / Tutte
le fogge moderne, e sol laudano / Quelle ch'al tempo antico si
facevano" (who always despise all modern solutions, and praise
only those in vogue in the ancient time).[15]

In the same way, the prologue speaker of Francesco Belo's *Il
Pedante* (1529) addresses the spectators directly, with hilarious
reference to some of them, boasting ironically about the novelty
of the comedy and concluding with the conventional Plautine
request for attention and silence. Aretino's prologues are of
lively linguistic inventiveness, such as the one spoken by "Istrione" in *Il Marescalco* (1527, published 1533), which introduces
the argument by mocking the types and roles of the actors, the
spectators, and the art of the theater itself; and that used in
Cortigiana (1525), which deals with the play's argument and
authorship by way of a dialogue between a "Forestiere" and a
"Gentiluomo." Of all Italian prologues, Giordano Bruno's *Candelaio* (1582) contains what must be the most extraordinary example. With its multiple distinction into caudate sonnet,
dedication, argument, antiprologue, and proprologue and its
exuberant verbal virtuosity, it represents a strong subversive
challenge to all accepted conventions; Bruno's irreverent anti-
moralism expresses the most vivid case of Italian "radical" comedy, opening the path to satirical drama and affecting the
linguistic ability of many witty characters of the Elizabethan
stage.[16]

Despite the obvious cultural differences between Italian and
Elizabethan dramatists, "poetic imitation" is at the heart of Renaissance theatrical practice. From the satire of *Poetaster*
(1601), set in ancient Rome, to the sharp realism of such London ironical plays as *Bartholomew Fair* (1614) and *The Staple
of News* (1626), Jonson's inductions and prologues seem to possess a strong Brunian spirit in the way they criticize society on
all levels, from orthodox learning to the greed for wealth and
power. In Webster's induction to Marston's *The Malcontent*
(1604), the actor William Sly, in the part of a spectator, sits on
a stool and talks with a tire-man and other players about the
fortunes of the comedy with frequent bawdy puns and topical
allusions to the rival Blackfriars company. Echoing the oxymo-
ron of the title, Sly and Condell refer to it as "a bitter play," a
tragicomedy, which "'tis neither satire nor moral, but the mean
passage of a history; yet there are a sort of discontented crea-
tures that bear a stingless envy to great ones" (induction, 51–
54).[17] This kind of comical satire is akin in spirit to Bruno's

Candelaio, and to the witty game of oppositions that inspires his epigraphic motto "In tristitia hilaris, in hilaritate tristis," resembling the one at the end of the speech "To the Reader," "Sine aliqua dementia nullus Phoebus," and the general use of mottoes in Marston's play. Indirect allusion to Bruno is evident in Sly's reference to "the art of memory" (induction, 102) which might recall Bruno's earliest memory work, *De umbris idearum,* published in London in 1582, and his opposition to the Ramist doctrines of memory.[18]

Contemporary critical theory has paid particular attention to the complex subject of the relationship between texts and between author and reader. Relying on Pseudo-Longinus and his modern interpreters, Harold Bloom has launched his reception-oriented criticism based on an agonistic revisionism of the past, involving an Oedipal confrontation between father-poets and their successors, which has, unfortunately, tended to lead to an undue emphasis on the reader's own views and experience over the author's intertextual creativity.[19] One way of looking at Bloom's anxiety-of-influence theory is to regard it as a provocative attempt to overcome the inadequacies of traditional criticism founded on positivistic source studies. *Quellenforschung,* to give this critical approach its formal title, argues that every literary work draws of necessity on a previous text, absorbed through deliberate authorial choice and direct reading, and produces an interplay of borrowings and verbal echoes. By contrast, comparative literature studies have profited from the investigation of cultural traditions, refusing the limitations of too linear a heritage and replacing the monistic concept of source with a wider typology of archetypal models that the author's work adheres to—and identifies with—within a chain of transmission. The idea of source can therefore carry the meaning of a multiplicity of possible cultural relations, connected by common ancestry, varying from direct knowledge of the original text to indirect borrowing via translations, rewritings, and contaminations with other texts or genres.

In this line of research other methodological proposals have provided a more radical twist. New critical approaches, ranging from Michael Bakhtin's notion of the dialogical nature of the narrative text to the idea of plurality of texts suggested by Roland Barthes and, further, to a new focus on discursivity of the literary work applied by Julia Kristeva in the semiotic field, have produced challenging perspectives of the manifold potentialities of the text.[20] Drawing on Bakhtin's concept of "dialogism," Julia

Kristeva coined the term "*intertextualité*" in the late 1960s; it has since become a fashionable critical trend grouping together a number of different categories.[21] The theory of intertextuality, which I like to call the "Darwinian" theory of literary heredity by common ancestry, examines the text within the dynamics of the multiple cultural intersections that coexist in the text itself, identifying it with a particular tradition. In the aesthetics of intertextuality, the romantic idea of the originality of the poet is thus replaced by his creative ability to combine, even unconsciously, diverse themes, models, types, and structures in an ingenious *ars combinatoria*. Louise George Clubb, who has coined the term "theatergram" to indicate recurrent theatrical microstructures, finds in the *contaminatio* the felicitous reworking of patterns and situations from different texts giving rise to the principle of complication, the technique of multiple intrigue.[22] This entire process becomes intelligible through the mediation of intertextuality as a reading custom, involving both author and critic in an exclusive cooperative, though not neutral, relationship.[23] The editors of a recent anthology have indicated two "axes" of intertextuality in order to emphasize the involvement of the reader: "Both axes of intertextuality, texts entering via authors (who are, first, readers) and texts entering via readers (co-producers), are ... emotionally and politically charged; the object of an act of *influence*, whether by a powerful figure (say, a father) or by a social structure (say, the Church), does not receive or perceive that pressure as neutral."[24] In the dynamics of intertextuality, comparison between texts belonging to the same or different ages and countries has opened up a new horizon of research and understanding.

The multifaceted concept of intertextuality, understood as a composite weaving of cultural, thematic, and literary relations, is the main concern of the present collection of essays. Although the nature of intertextuality is far from being univocal, the contributors in their assessment of the aims and uses of intertextuality have confined themselves to the specific field of Italian cinquecento literature, taking the "Italian" component of Renaissance theater or prose as an "intertext" for comparison with the English equivalent. Those contributions where "intertext" belongs to a cultural construct deriving from the ideas of a specific author, or is rooted in a myth, a tradition, a philosophy current in Renaissance Italy—which Cesare Segre's nomenclature would enlist in the category of "interdiscursivity"—the editor has preferred to group in the section entitled "Cultural

Exchange."[25] Those essays in which "intertext" is intended in
its strict, technical sense of a literary text, a group of texts, or
even a corpus of texts of classical and cinquecento theater to be
compared with English texts, the editor has grouped in a special
section called "Intertextuality." It must be emphasized that this
volume shifts from traditional source studies, which necessarily
imply the idea of an intentional borrower, to focus instead on
the idea of intertextuality itself as a challenging field of inquiry
and as a fundamental component in the making of a play, a
component that also comprehends an unintentional process of
dramatic construction drawing from the entire body and nature
of drama as a genre. In Keir Elam's summing up of a three-day
conference from which most of the present chapters derive, this
collection "marks a move away from the 'topological' to the 'typological', . . . from the idea of the drama representing Italy in
some way, describing it, choosing Italy as a setting more or less
accurately, . . . to an idea of Italy as a kind of force of cultural
mediation, political mediation, and ideological mediation"
through the different types and different conceptions of intertextuality that are represented in this volume.[26]

A telling example of this kind of ideological force comes from
David Bevington's and Louise George Clubb's introductory chapters to part 1 and part 2, on cultural exchange and intertextuality respectively, which outline the critical path of the
subsequent chapters, adding a productive contribution to their
own topic. In reassessing the question of Italian influence in
England, Bevington focuses on George Gascoigne's *Supposes,*
translated from Ariosto's *I Suppositi* and performed at Gray's
Inn in 1566, and makes it a significant case of both Italian reception and appropriation in England. A comparison between the
choice and performance of an Italian comedy and of contemporary public productions, as well as that between Gascoigne's play
and Shakespeare's treatment of it in *The Taming of the Shrew,*
allows Bevington to isolate the original motifs of Polynesta's premarital union and the comic handling of lawyers, which must
have appeared positively challenging and refreshing to the gentlemanly spectators at Gray's Inn. Louise George Clubb's opening
chapter to the second section considers the various intertextual
perspectives adopted by common practice and in the present
collection, evaluating the usefulness of intertextuality in the
specific field of Anglo-Italian drama of the Renaissance. The
combination of musical with verbal texts in the *commedia
dell'arte,* so effectively brought to theatrical expression by Ru-

zante, has proved an invaluable occasion of intertextualities, involving literary, musical, and historical legacies. As a pliable instrument of knowledge, the intertextual discourse on drama does not provide certain answers or offer definitive conclusions: it opens the way to a more comprehensive human understanding of the arts in general.

Notes

1. *Julius Caesar,* ed. T. S. Dorsch (London: Methuen, 1965), 3.1.112–17.

2. Anne Righter (Barton), *Shakespeare and the Idea of the Play* (London: Chatto & Windus, 1962), 141.

3. Dante Alighieri, *Inferno,* canto 34, lines 28 and 61–67. *See The Divine Comedy: Inferno,* trans. Charles S. Singleton, 2 vols. (London: Routledge and Kegan Paul, 1970), 1: 362–65.

4. *Hamlet,* ed. Harold Jenkins (London: Methuen, 1982; rpt. Routledge, 1990), 5.1.206–209.

5. *See* Stephen Greenblatt, *Shakespearean Negotiations: The Circulation of Social Energy in Renaissance England* (Oxford: Clarendon Press, 1988), 1–20.

6. Madeleine Doran, *Endeavors of Art: A Study of Form in Elizabethan Drama* (Madison: University of Wisconsin Press, 1954; reprint, 1972), 162.

7. Plautus, *Menaechmi,* trans. Paul Nixon, 5 vols., The Loeb Classical Library (London: Heinemann; Cambridge: Harvard University Press, 1959), 2: 370–71.

8. *See* Clifford Leech, "Shakespeare's Prologues and Epilogues," in *Studies in Honor of T. W. Baldwin,* ed. Don Cameron Allen (Urbana: University of Illinois Press, 1958), 150–64.

9. Thelma N. Greenfield, *The Induction in Elizabethan Drama* (Eugene: University of Oregon Books, 1969), 69.

10. Ben Jonson, *Poetaster,* ed. Tom Cain (Manchester: Manchester University Press, 1995), 261.

11. Alessandro Piccolomini, *L'Amor costante* (1536) in *Commedie del Cinquecento,* ed. Nino Borsellino, 2 vols. (Milan: Feltrinelli, 1962), 1: 306.

12. *See* Alessandro Ronconi, "Prologhi 'plautini' e prologhi 'terenziani' nella commedia italiana del '500," in *Il teatro classico italiano nel '500,* Atti del Convegno dell'Accademia Nazionale dei Lincei, Quaderno no. 138 (Rome: Accademia Nazionale dei Lincei, 1971), 197–214. The peculiarity of the Italian prologue is stressed by Nino Borsellino in Nino Borsellino and Roberto Mercuri, *Il teatro del Cinquecento* (Bari: Laterza, 1973), 3–14.

13. Ludovico Ariosto, *Cassaria* (1508), in *Tutte le opere,* ed. Cesare Segre, 5 vols. (Milan: Mondadori, 1974), 4: 3.

14. Ludovico Ariosto, *I Suppositi* (1509), in *Tutte le opere,* ed. Cesare Segre, 4: 198.

15. Ludovico Ariosto, *La Lena* (1529), in *Tutte le opere,* ed. Cesare Segre, 4: 546.

16. *See* Hilary Gatti, *The Renaissance Drama of Knowledge: Giordano Bruno in England* (London: Routledge, 1989), 128–38. Gatti's stimulating book discusses the influence of *Candelaio* on *Hamlet* in particular.

17. John Marston, *The Malcontent,* ed. George K. Hunter (Manchester: Manchester University Press, 1975).

18. *See* F. A. Yates, *The Art of Memory* (London: Routledge and Kegan Paul, 1966), 260–78. On Bruno's life in England, *see* Dorothea Waley Singer, *Giordano Bruno: His Life and Thought* (New York: Greenwood Press, 1968), 26–45.

19. Harold Bloom, *The Anxiety of Influence. A Theory of Poetry* (Oxford: Oxford University Press, 1973); *Agon: Towards a Theory of Revisionism* (Oxford: Oxford University Press, 1982).

20. Michael Bakhtin, "La parola nel romanzo," in *Estetica e romanzo* (Turin: Einaudi, 1979), 67–233; *The Dialogic Imagination,* ed. M. Holquist, trans. C. Emerson and M. Holquist (Austin: University of Texas Press, 1981). Roland Barthes, *S/Z* (Paris, France: Seuil, 1970), trans. Richard Miller (New York: Hill and Wang, 1974; London: Cape, 1975); *Le Plaisir du texte* (Paris: Seuil, 1973), trans. Richard Miller as *The Pleasure of the Text* (London: Cape, 1976). Julia Kristeva, *Essays in Semiotics: Essais de sémiotique* (The Hague: Mouton, 1971).

21. Julia Kristeva, "Word, Dialogue, and Novel" (1967), trans. as *Desire in Language* in *The Kristeva Reader,* ed. Toril Moi (Oxford: Basil Blackwell, 1986; New York: Columbia University Press, 1986). *See* Heinrich F. Plett, "Intertextualities," in *Intertextuality,* ed. Heinrich F. Plett (Berlin and New York: Walter de Gruyter, 1991), 3–29.

22. Giambattista Della Porta, *Gli Duoi Fratelli Rivali / The Two Rival Brothers,* ed. Louise George Clubb (Berkeley: University of California Press, 1980), 32–34; and Louise George Clubb's *Italian Drama in Shakespeare's Time* (New Haven: Yale University Press, 1989), 1–26.

23. *See* Umberto Eco, *Lector in fabula: La cooperazione interpretativa nei testi narrativi* (Milan: Bompiani, 1979), trans. as *The Role of the Reader: Explorations in the Semiotics of Texts* (Bloomington, Indiana University Press, 1979; London: Hutchinson, 1981); *I limiti dell'interpretazione* (Milan: Bompiani, 1990), trans. as *The Limits of Interpretations* (Bloomington: Indiana University Press, 1990).

24. *Intertextuality: Theories and Practices,* eds. Michael Worton and Judith Still (Manchester: Manchester University Press, 1990), 2.

25. Cesare Segre, "Intertestuale/interdiscorsivo: Appunti per una fenomenologia delle fonti," in *La parola ritrovata: Fonti e analisi letteraria,* ed. Costanzo Di Girolamo and Ivano Paccagnella (Palermo: Sellerio, 1982), 15–28. Reprinted as "Intertestualità e interdiscorsività nel romanzo e nella poesia," in *Teatro e romanzo: Due tipi di comunicazione letteraria* (Turin: Einaudi, 1984), 103–119.

26. Keir Elam, "Round Table: Conclusion," in *Il mondo italiano del teatro inglese del Rinascimento: relazioni culturali e intertestualità,* ed. Michele Marrapodi (Palermo: Flaccovio Editore, 1995), 111.

The Italian World
of English Renaissance
Drama

Part One
Cultural Exchange

Cultural Exchange: Gascoigne and Ariosto at Gray's Inn in 1566

DAVID BEVINGTON

IF we examine the process of cultural exchange between Italy and England over the course of the Elizabethan and Jacobean reigns, as the present collection of essays enables us to do, we can perhaps begin to look for patterns of transition. The complex dialogue of intertextual relationships between these two countries was certainly anything but monolithic and stationary. However much certain stereotypes may have tended to persist, political and social considerations in both countries were constantly in flux, with the result that the perceptions of readers and viewers were colored by shifting ideological obsessions. Other countries of Europe, and indeed of more remote parts of the world, increasingly became part of a complex exchange of which Anglo-Italian relations represented only a fraction. Class and gender differences among English readers and spectators prompted varying responses to Italian texts. Changing religious ideologies markedly affected the temperaments of the English as they responded to what they variously saw as cultural importation or invasion. For the English of the sixteenth and early seventeenth centuries, there was not one Italy; there were many Italies.

I should like to propose a kind of trajectory path for the era of the English "high" Renaissance, roughly from the early years of Queen Elizabeth's reign to the time of the Caroline court. At the start of this period, Italian influence in England, by no means an entirely new thing, still shows the delights of newness and discovery; although resistance is discernible, more sophisticated members of the English cultural scene are able to enjoy the shock of newness, the unsettling challenge implicitly offered to English customs and mores, the enlargement of perspective attainable through a view of another culture designed and executed on a high level of artistic creativity. That enthusiasm per-

sists into the late Elizabethan period, but under increasing
conflict, with growing alarm over Italy's supposedly deleterious
effect on English values. (France was also held to blame.) In the
Jacobean years, these anxieties gain intensity through dismay
and cynicism about the perceived decline in morality at James
I's court, with the result that some dramatists and poets turn to
those Italian texts that speak most eloquently on matters of
double-dealing, hypocrisy, and internecine struggles for political
power. The drama, increasingly aimed at courtly audiences even
if "publicly" performed, capitalizes on the sensationalism of such
material even while it tempers that materialism with a Protestant and even a Puritanical moralism of perspective. During the
reign of Charles I, however, at least some dramatists and other
writers find receptive audiences for a return to some kind of
idealization of Italian cultural values. This is not the innocent
curiosity about newness of the early English Renaissance, to be
sure, but rather a sentimentalization of themes of love and
honor that accords with the tragicomic writing of Beaumont and
Fletcher and anticipates the heroic drama of the Restoration.
The trajectory does not return to its origins; trajectories never
do. Instead, the pattern is one that suggests an increasing loss
of contact with reality in the Caroline court, one that will eventually lead to civil war and the closing of the theaters in England.

The beginning of this process can be seen with a special clarity
in a work such as George Gascoigne's *Supposes,* translated from
Ariosto's *I Suppositi* (prose version acted in 1509, later put into
verse), and presented at Gray's Inn in 1566. Of special interest
is the matter of its reception among the courtly and intellectual
set in London in the early Elizabethan period. First, however, I
should like to sketch out where matters will go from here, as
the issue of cultural exchange is pursued in the present volume
of essays.

In Michele Marrapodi's investigation of a journey "From Narrative to Drama: The Erotic Tale and the Theater," we are shown
the indebtedness of Renaissance English theater to literary archetypes that extend back through Ariosto, the anonymous
author of *Gl'Ingannati,* Boccaccio, and others to Menander,
Plautus, and Terence. The motif of twin brothers offers a fine
opportunity for exploitation of the potentially erotic premise of
mistaken identity, such as we see developed in Shakespeare's
The Comedy of Errors. Bernardo Dovizi of Bibbiena's *La Calandria* (1513), with its bawdy motifs in the vein of Boccaccio, inspired a host of imitators that look forward to Falstaff's role as

lover of two women in *The Merry Wives of Windsor.* Bibbiena's true source is the *Decameron,* with its themes of twins and transvestism. The "lock-out motif," so successfully used in *The Comedy of Errors,* finds its antecedents in Plautus and in Italian neoclassical comedy. The bisexuality of Viola in *Twelfth Night* has a long history in thc Italian theater (especially *Gl'Ingannati*) as well as in Italianate fiction. Machiavelli's *La Mandragola* (1518) and *Clizia* (1525) are splendid examples of a "radical" theater, ones that later dramatists would find fascinatingly controversial. Shakespeare's *All's Well That Ends Well,* derived from a tale by Boccaccio, is analogous to Francesco Belo's *El Beco* (1538) and its stratagem of the exchanged woman in bed. To see *All's Well* as part of a gradual process of cultural exchange is to move toward clarification of its "problematic" nature, as Louise George Clubb has also pointed out.

Similarly, our understanding of the substitution of the lover in Shakespeare's *Measure for Measure* needs to be pursued not simply in isolated comparison with its chief source, George Whetstone's adaptation (*Promos and Cassandra,* 1578) of a tale from G. B. Giraldi Cinthio's *Hecatommithi* (1565), but in the larger context of cultural exchange that involves Machiavelli, Aretino, Giordano Bruno, and many others. The seriousness of Shakespeare's exploration of the morality of institutions owes much, whether directly or at some remove, to Italian radical theater and to the effects of the Counter-Reformation (again as suggested by Louise George Clubb). Themes of constancy in love link *Romeo and Juliet* to Arthur Brooke's translation of Bandello, and through that connection to a rich tradition of the "wondrous woman" in a play like Raffaello Borghini's *La Donna costante* (1589). Domestic tragedy, as dramatized by Thomas Heywood in *A Woman Killed with Kindness* (1603), goes back to Bandello (in William Painter's translation) and thus to the whole complex of Italian erotic narrative in fiction and drama. So too with Philip Massinger's *The Maid of Honour* (ca. 1625), James Shirley's *Love's Cruelty* (1631), and John Ford's *Love's Sacrifice* (1630). As Stephen Greenblatt urges us to consider, the "textual traces" of Renaissance Italian culture in Shakespeare and other English dramatists derive from a vast number of converging heterogeneous traditions and ideologies. These varying cultural forces are the essential subject of the present book.

As Mariangela Tempera observes, the Procne myth became a significant subject of Elizabethan drama and art as early as 1566, when James Calfhill's now lost translation of Gregorio Corraro's

Procne or *Progne* was performed on 5 September at Christ Church, Oxford, in the presence of Queen Elizabeth. Responses to that story tell us much about Elizabethan fascinations with Seneca, that staple of humanistic education, and with Ovid, who also gives an account of the Procne story in his *Metamorphoses*. The story is at once savage in its pagan fury and tragically serious. Sensational in its account of the ravishment of Philomela by her brother-in-law Tereus and of Procne's revengeful plot to induce Tereus to eat his own child, the story transcends its police-blotter narrative through stately language, philosophical speculations on the curse inflicted on humankind by the gods, and choric reflection on the interplay of character and fate.

The story is of course from classical mythology, and the sources in which Elizabethan readers found it were generally Roman. To what extent do Elizabethan attitudes toward Italy potentially impinge upon their retelling of the Procne myth? This question is not easy to answer. A narrative of political intrigue and instability, duplicity, rape, and mutilation invites parallels between ancient Rome and Renaissance Italy that are not especially unique or compelling. Nonetheless, a drama making use of the Procne story, like Shakespeare's *Titus Andronicus,* can play up horrors like those associated in the popular Elizabethan imagination with sixteenth-century Italy. The special emphasis on the theme of *scelus novum* noted by Tempera, encouraging dramatists and audiences alike to seek ways of outdoing any preceding work in newly invented horrors, puts a premium on grotesqueries of violence and ingenuity of revenge method that are compatible with what came to be viewed as "Italianate" murder or revenge. The genre to which *Titus Andronicus* belongs may well have encouraged the novel devices of torture and murder found in plays of succeeding years: *The Revenger's Tragedy, Women Beware Women, The White Devil,* and the like, most of which are explicitly Italianate in setting. *Titus Andronicus,* by employing motifs found in classical mythology, provides tragic grandeur and a kind of universality that are well suited to the earlier years of the English high Renaissance, before cynicism and metatheatrical emphasis on cunning artistry darken the view of what English culture might absorb from the south of Europe. Poems on analogous subjects, like Shakespeare's *The Rape of Lucrece,* similarly dignify the tragic design of their revenge plots by their use of a classical mode and ancient Roman sources.

Viviana Comensoli's argument about the uses of music in

Othello points similarly to a constructive and admiring view of what at least part of the Italian Renaissance had to offer a northern nation like England. The setting of act 1 is Venice, renowned throughout Europe as the world's greatest republic. Although Iago's villainy does work with a devastating cleverness that might seem Italianate to a viewer predisposed to such a condemnatory view, Shakespeare employs few of the more garish devices associated with the defamatory cliché. And, although tragic self-deception and misunderstanding are central to the plot, the destabilizing forces at work are partly attributable to Othello's African heritage and his status as an outsider in Venice, however senior in rank and dignity. Venice itself seems well governed. The Duke or Doge resists any racial insinuations in his evaluation of Othello as a husband for Desdemona, even if her father and Roderigo give ample evidence of racial bias among the city's presumably all-white population. Order is restored at the end of the play in the name of the Venetian state; the tragic loading of Othello's bed is a pitiable spectacle, but it is not one that implicates the social hierarchy.

Moreover, as Comensoli points out, *Othello* makes positive use of classical truisms about the humanizing power of music, and of Castiglione's defense of the importance of the liberal arts to an orderly hierarchical society. As perhaps in the case of *Titus Andronicus,* the fusion of classical and Italian models reinforces the idea of Italy as the true and original heir of the greatness of that country's classical past. The musical theory derives from Pythagoras (a Greek), as transmitted through various classical and medieval sources and ultimately embodied in *The Book of the Courtier.* Music can promote active virtue, in Castiglione's view, and is thereby commensurate with social hierarchy and the concentration of power in the hands of an elite. Othello's failure to listen attentively to music and to appear in any scene of which music is a part marks him as sharing this defect with Cassius in *Julius Caesar* and others who hear no music. Especially when he has bid farewell to "the shrill trump, / The spirit-stirring drum, th' ear-piercing fife," Othello is out of tune with the harmonies that ideally should govern the Venetian state and its great general.[1] Even at its relatively late date, *Othello* (c. 1603–1604) embodies a largely positive image of Italian culture and politics.

A. J. Hoenselaars's essay on Machiavelli's *Belfagor* deals with a more malign and defamatory insinuation about Italy: the equation of that country's brilliant political theoretician with the devil. The equation, to be sure, is not new in the plays of the early seventeenth century that Hoenselaars studies; it emerges prominently in the prologue to Marlowe's *The Jew of Malta* (c. 1589–1590), though in a passage of studied irony and in a play so fraught with unsettling paradoxes as to suggest an admiring fascination on Marlowe's part for the very figure of Machiavelli that he employs in an ostensible diatribe against diabolical and Italianate villainy. I would not wish to argue that admiration for the Italian Renaissance gave way in any orderly, chronological fashion to disillusionment in the early Stuart years: conflicting and contradictory attitudes coexisted throughout essentially all of this period. Marlowe was by no means the first to equate Machiavelli with the devil, even if he did so in a wry manner. Still, the darker view does seem to grow with an intensity that is fueled by disillusionment with the English court, at first with the last years of Elizabeth and then with the reign of her successor.

Hoenselaars's argument is that the image of Machiavelli as devil flourished in England because it found there such a fertile love of devilry that had come in part from Germany and Denmark, as well as from native English traditions. Hoenselaars points to Thomas Dekker's *If This Be Not a Good Play* and *2 Honest Whore,* to Ben Jonson's *The Devil Is an Ass,* the anonymous *Grim the Collier of Croydon,* and *The Devil and the Parliament* as evidence of the widespread equating of Machiavelli with the prince of darkness. The phenomenon renders likely Hoenselaars's contention that English dramatists knew Machiavelli's *novella Belfagor,* with its Parliament of Hell and its motif of the devil coming to earth in order to establish whether marriage there is a curse—whereupon, having linked himself in wedlock to a shrew, the devil is persuaded that marriage is indeed a curse. Machiavelli has become a construct of the English imagination, both man and devil, a historical figure and a legend, a serious writer and a dangerous joker. No figure equals Machiavelli in the English imagination of the period as it confronts and demonizes a cultural influence increasingly blamed for much that was thought to be amiss in English culture itself.

The crisis of public dismay at the venery and corruption of the Italianate Englishman is nowhere more evident than in Ben Jonson's *Volpone* (1605–1606). Michael Redmond reads this play against the backdrop of Philemon Holland's advice to the English to guard against any fondness for Rome, no matter how great the cultural tradition of that city may once have been.

Holland is at pains to discourage travel to Rome and to other Italian cities, because of the threat that such exposure poses to English religious, political, and sexual mores. Roger Ascham and Thomas Nashe are among others who join in a dismal chorus of anxious warning. The application of all this to *Volpone* is to be found in the subplot, where Sir Politic Would-be and his wife and Peregrine are English tourists in Venice. In addition, the density of allusions to Italianate works throughout *Volpone* brings the entire play into focus. Jonson's ambivalent fascination with Italy is not limited to *Volpone*: it is part of his difficult relationship with Inigo Jones, and of his undertaking to transform *Every Man in His Humour* from an Italianate setting in the Quarto text to an English setting in the Folio of 1616.

In *Volpone* itself much of the satire is directed at Sir Politic Would-be for his fatuous meddling, his cultural parochialism, his complacency, his interminable meddling, his uxorious willingness to travel in order to please his wife's humor, and so on. Like many Englishmen of his time, Sir Pol is obsessed with the "ebbs / And flows of state" in Italy.[2] He professes to be an expert on the political philosophy of "Nick Machiavel" (4.1.26). His wife affects an acquaintance with the poetry of Petrarch, Tasso, Dante, Guarini, Ariosto, Aretine, and Cieco di Hadria (3.4.79–81), thus calling attention to a long-standing tradition in England of emulating Italian works. She is not interested solely in her appearance, despite all the satirical energy directed at imported fashions in dress: Jonson is interested in her reading habits and her penchant for adulatory imitation. Peregrine, meantime, as the satirist figure in the subplot, helps to give a literate perspective on the discourse of the Italianate Englishman, invoking the support of divine order for his view that God has fitted English bodies to an English climate. The mocking of literary aspirations is like that of John Donne and Joseph Hall. Jonson's inveighing against the discourse of the Italianate Englishman is of a piece with much satirical concern in the early years of the seventeenth century.

Thomas Middleton shows how the public theater of the Jacobean era could combine a satirical presentation of the jaded Italian court with a moral perspective heavily flavored by the kind of Puritan ethic that Middleton's London audience came to expect from him. J. R. Mulryne points out the importance of a Florentine setting to a play such as *Women Beware Women,* a setting that has been too often ignored or underdeveloped in criticism about the play. Florence is presented and transformed in such a way as to comment implicitly on English courtly politics while losing none of its applicability to the commonplace English view of that city, renowned for being the home of Machiavelli.

When we come to John Ford's last plays, on the other hand, especially to *The Fancies Chaste and Noble* (1636–1638) and *The Lady's Trial* (1638–1639), we arrive at a sentimentalization of Italy that is thoroughly attuned to the self-adoring view of the Caroline court. As Lisa Hopkins persuasively argues, Ford's late reformulations of English stereotypes about Italy depart visibly from what Hopkins calls the "Italian cut-works" of Webster and the "sophisticated poisons" of Middleton's Florence. These formulations are no less distant from Ford's own earlier endorsement of familiar and defamatory stereotypes, as presented in the violence of Parma and the court of Pavia in *Love's Sacrifice* (ca. 1632) and *'Tis Pity She's a Whore* (1629–1633). In the theatrical world of late Ford, the women are honorable and chaste, while men of the cloth turn out to be saints rather than corrupted cardinals. Hopkins argues for a resemblance between the story of Adurni in *The Lady's Trial* and that of the husband of Saint Catherine of Genoa.

Clearly, in Hopkins's view the motivations for these shifts in Ford's attitudes toward Italy are not hard to find. The court of Charles I and Henrietta Maria fell increasingly under the spell of the Continent and the Roman Church. Ford's own family and circle enjoyed a firsthand knowledge of Italy. With such a familiar and loving acquaintance with Italy on the part of the Caroline court came the kind of fatal self-fascination and willingness to believe in Neoplatonic and neoclassical mythologies aimed at bolstering the self-flattering image of that court. The paintings of Rubens and Van Dyke, the masques in the style of Inigo Jones, the Palladian architecture—these achievements, once indicative of what the Italian Renaissance could offer England in the way of cultural enlightenment and sophistication, were in danger of becoming subsumed into the increasing loss of contact with social reality that, under Charles and Henrietta, went out of control.

Let me now return from endings to beginnings and to the early Elizabethan period, where, as I hope to indicate briefly, a play like George Gascoigne's *Supposes* could indicate what was new, stimulating, fresh, and usefully iconoclastic in Italian dramatic literature as seen from the point of view of the English intelligentsia in and around London.

Supposes is a translation from Ariosto's comedy in spirited, colloquial Elizabethan prose. It follows the original closely in a number of ways. Act and scene divisions are of the "Continental" sort, as in the later publication of plays by noted classicists like John Lyly and Ben Jonson, with names grouped at the head of each scene. The five-act structure is sturdily neoclassical, moving in a single plot from exposition through comic complication and misunderstanding to eventual clarification. Marginal notes point out the various "supposes" or illusory situations upon which the plot depends, or poke fun at lawyers; at one point, for example, when the crafty lawyer Cleander is plotting his next move, a marginal comment expresses the view that "*Lawyers are never weary to get money.*"[3] Character types are recognizably neoclassical: the adventuresome and financially strapped young hero (Erostrato) and his resourceful clever servant (Dulippo), the parasite (Pasiphilo), the savvy young woman (Polynesta) and the duenna who arranges her assignation (Balia), the heroine's careworn father (Damon), the businesslike father of the young hero (Philogano), the pantaloon (Cleander) who is a rival suitor for the hand of the heroine, an old trot of a woman servant (Psiteria), a cook (Dalio) and other household lackeys, and so on. The printed text is not a script for actors but a record of a single performance in 1566 at Gray's Inn, set down in a carefully prepared text presumably for the edification of those gentlemen who had seen the production and others who might like to acquire an Italianate comedy in English translation. A final stage direction, "*Et plauserunt*" (*They applauded*), in the past tense, reinforces other impressions that the printed version is a literary transcript of a play performed on a single occasion.[4] Some other stage directions, though by no means all, are in Latin: "*Erostra[to] et Du[lippo] ex improviso*" (*enter unexpectedly,* 2.4.34), or "*Pasiphilo restat*" (*remains onstage,* 1.2.183).

What did the lawyerly and courtly group of Inns of Court members who saw this play in 1566 think of it as an example of Italianate comedy? Clearly the occasion was expensive in comparison with the public theater, where repeated performances, usually by itinerant actors doubling parts and employing minimal props, with opportunities for collecting offerings from spectators, provided an economy of scale that the Inns of Court drama deliberately eschewed. Plays were part of those inns' celebration of holidays, and could be gargantuan in their penchant for conspicuous consumption. To mount an entire production for a single performance before a select audience was to make a kind of statement about Gray's Inn as a place of patronage of the arts among discerning gentlemanly viewers. What kind of Italian art, then, did the members of Gray's Inn choose to patronize on this occasion?

We do not have direct testimonial as to what the members of the audience felt about *Supposes*. We do have the play, however, with the implication that it was performed as set down in the existing text. Under those circumstances it is interesting to ask what Gascoigne did not change from his original. Shakespeare, in adapting *Supposes* to his Bianca-Lucentio plot in *The Taming of the Shrew,* changed quite a lot for what he took to be the inclinations of his London public theater audience and in response to his own artistic and perhaps ethical preferences as dramatist. Gascoigne changed essentially nothing, other than to provide colloquial English for the Italian dialogue. He and his audience at Gray's Inn were evidently content to have the play pretty much as Ariosto conceived it.

We can also compare this nifty neoclassical comedy with the sorts of plays that public audiences were seeing in London in a more parochially English vein. Many such plays that have survived from the 1560s are moralities, often with a distinctively Protestant and Calvinist flavor. The contrast between what public audiences saw and what the members of Gray's Inn arranged for their own amusement is striking.

William Wager's *The Longer Thou Livest the More Fool Thou Art* (c. 1559–1568), for example, is a Calvinist morality that centers on the saga of one Moros, or Fool—transparently a representative of incorrigible Catholic ignorance clinging to benighted superstition. Corrective abstractions like Discipline, Piety, and Exercitation can do nothing with Moros, for his life is given over wholly to Idleness, Incontinence, and the Seven Deadly Sins. Moros's suitable reward at last is administered by God's Judgment and Confusion. The virtuous characters lament the "canker pestilent" that "of late days" is "corrupting our realm to our utter decay" in a scene that is undisguisedly London and England. The implication is that England's new Protestant regime cannot afford to be sentimental about the Catholics dangerously in England's midst.

Enough Is as Good as a Feast (c. 1559–1570), also by Wager, pits Worldly Man against Heavenly Man in a similar showdown between Catholic vice and Protestant virtue, with similarly edifying results; Satan carries off Worldly Man on the devil's back to an infernal reward, leaving Contentation and Enough to comfort the triumphant Heavenly Man.[5] Thomas Preston's *Cambises* (c. 1558–1561) makes clear its dislike of that Persian king's tyranny through the trumpet call of various abstractions like Commons' Cry, Commons' Complaint, Proof, and Trial, while the king's villainy is made evident through his association with Cruelty, Murder, Venus, and Cupid. John Pickering's *Horestes* (1567) uses the story of Orestes' execution of his mother as an object lesson on the need for firm proceeding against tyrants, with palpable application to the threat represented by Mary, Queen of Scots. *The Peddler's Prophecy* (anonymous, c. 1561–1563) inveighs against meddlers from Spain and other non-Protestant countries who contaminate English customs with their corrupt fashions; so many Jews, Russians, Turks, Tartars, Anabaptists, Epicureans, and other libertines have infiltrated London that an honest person can no longer find a landlord who does not demand exorbitant rent. In the anonymous *King Darius* (published in 1565), Constancy, Equity, and Charity celebrate at last the discomfiting of Iniquity, Partiality, Importunity, and others of the unrighteous.

Moral ambiguity is similarly lacking in *Like Will to Like* (1562–1568), Lewis Wager's *The Life and Repentance of Mary Magdalene* (c. 1550–1566), and still others. Public drama of the 1560s was generally concerned with what was widely perceived as the Catholic menace and also the decline of English moral values, such as generosity, decency, cleanness, loyalty, and conservative attachment to what it meant to be English. The two problems were seen as integrally related: Catholic countries like Italy, Spain, and France were perceived as the ubiquitous source of every kind of decadence.

In a city generally obsessed with fears of cultural invasion, to judge by its surviving popular drama, the production of Ariosto's comedy in translation could not be a neutral event expressing mere scholarly or humanist curiosity about a culture to the south of England. The event, by definition, made a bold statement or at least posed some irreverent questions. Let us consider first the matter of sexual mores.

Polynesta, the female protagonist of *I Suppositi* and of Gascoigne's English translation, is a resourceful and cool young lady. Attracted to the young Erostrato, who has disguised himself as a servant (Dulippo) in her father's household in order to be near the woman he adores, Polynesta has rewarded Erostrato's attentions by taking him as her lover. The first scene of conversation between Polynesta and her duenna, Balia, is far more than an exposition of the risqué situation upon which the play's plot will depend; it is, in terms of the sexual mores that seem to have prevailed in England at the time, a disarmingly frank discussion of how the affair came about. Both Polynesta and Balia understand the need for secrecy. The nurse is worried about the seeming fact that Polynesta is sleeping with a "poor servant" of her father's, but that does not mean that Balia has attempted to hinder the liaison; to the contrary, she appears to have been active in abetting the two lovers to come together. "Whom may I thank but gentle nurse," interjects Polynesta, "that continually praising him, what for his personage, his courtesy, and, above all, the extreme passions of his mind—in fine, you would never cease till I accepted him" (1.1.33–44). Polynesta sardonically suggests that Balia's greed was a motivating factor: the young man has filled her purse "with bribes and rewards." To Balia's rather maudlin insistence that she thought only of how charitable it would be to "help the miserable young man whose tender youth consumeth with the furious flames of love," and that she now regrets her decision to have done so, Polynesta wittily retorts with understandable skepticism to this pretended reluctance: "Who first brought him into my chamber, who first taught him the way to my bed but you?" (lines 53–68). Still, Polynesta is not really angry with Balia, and does of course need her to facilitate the comings and goings of her lover, and so she discloses to Balia the secret that will make the affair seem all right: the supposed Dulippo is in fact Erostrato, a gentleman who came from Sicily to study in Ferrara (where the action is located throughout) and fell so violently in love with Polynesta that he "cast aside both long gown and books and determined on [her] only to apply his study," taking the disguise of his own servant (lines 124–32).

This is a remarkable scene to be appearing on the English stage in the 1560s. Polynesta is in control, aware of what she is doing, in love but also calculating. The trick she is playing on her father Damon seems justified by his intent to marry her off to the rich but contemptible Cleander, "an old doting doctor," a "buzzard" and "bribing villain" (1.3.113–15) who, at sixty, is perhaps three times her age. The father is, in other words, "more desirous of the dower than mindful of his gentle and gallant daughter" (2.2.8–10). Such blocking figures are a staple of neoclassical comedy, of course, and survive into many an English romantic comedy like *A Midsummer Night's Dream* and *The Two Gentlemen of Verona,* but the cool resourcefulness of Polynesta in outwitting her father is something we do not find in Shakespeare's Hermia or Sylvia.

Similarly, Juliet's close relationship with her Nurse in *Romeo and Juliet* features much of the intimacy we see in *Supposes* (or in many a *novella* or *fabliau*), and a good deal of bawdy implication in the conversations of the Nurse that distantly reminds us of Balia, but Juliet is very far from having a premarital affair with Romeo. Her love for him demands marriage, and indeed the tragic plot hinges on that fact. Romeo's question to her in the garden after they have met—"O, wilt thou leave me so unsatisfied?"—may well hint at a physical desire in Romeo that might prompt him to seek pleasure first and examine the consequences later, but he fully accepts the implied gentle rebuke in her answer ("What satisfaction canst thou have tonight?"), and gladly joins with her in a scheme of secret marriage.[6] Repeatedly in his comedies and other plays like *Romeo and Juliet* that deal with young love, Shakespeare's plots turn on the necessity of avoiding premarital entanglement for the young ladies who are to be his heroines.

Supposes is of course the source for Shakespeare's Bianca-Lucentio plot in *The Taming of the Shrew,* and it is through Shakespeare's expurgations of premarital sex that we can see most clearly the English mode of publicly endorsed morality that *Supposes* eschews. Shakespeare's Bianca, like Polynesta, is faced with a choice between an unwelcome old, rich wooer (Gremio) and a seeming servant in disguise (Lucentio), and with a father whose main interest seems to be the dowry settlement, but Bianca does not sleep with Lucentio. Her father's chief worry is whether he can find a husband for Bianca's sister, Katherine. Damon, by contrast, grieves bitterly at the loss of his daughter's chastity to a seeming servant, one who has been sent "from the depth of hell-pit" to "be the subversion of me and all mine." "O Polynesta," he apostrophizes her in soliloquy, "full evil hast thou requited the clemency of thy careful father!" (3.3.15–71). Damon's sorrow is all the more anguished because he sees that he must blame himself also for being too socially ambitious in his hopes for her. Like most children, Polynesta "cutteth the parents' throat with the knife of inward care" (lines 105–6). Damon's soliloquy is potentially tragic in its intensity of sorrow, and is prevented from being fully so only by our realization that the bad situation is merely illusory. Far more than Shakespeare allows in his comedy, *Supposes* creates poignant drama out of parental fears of sexual experimentation.

The comic premise of the play protects us as audience from undue concern, then. At the same time, it allows Polynesta to establish a kind of sexual independence that is remarkable for its cosmopolitan and matter-of-fact tone. Polynesta makes no apologies for her premarital union, and seems to be under no need to make one. If her sexual choice turns out all right in the end, since Erostrato is after all a gentleman, the fact is that she has still entered into sexual partnership with him long before there could be any hope of marriage. I am not offering a moral judgment on this circumstance, but rather pointing out that the play seems to take Polynesta's sexual independence for granted.

To an English audience familiar with the kind of homilies I have described in the popular drama of the 1560s, the play's lack of moral concern must have seemed astonishing. Polynesta is the play's heroine; she is Erostrato's prize. She is not profligate, but she is, in the context of the English theater, sophisticated. Not until Shakespeare's portrayal of Cressida in his *Troilus and Cressida* (1601–1603) does the English theater give us another woman protagonist who is at least partly sympathized with for her having an affair with the man she loves, and Cressida's story is notoriously problematic. Chaucer had portrayed her with sensitivity and understanding, but the common English view of premarital sex would not leave her alone; in Henryson's *The Testament of Cresseid* (early sixteenth century), Cresseid, deserted by Diomede, curses the gods and dies a leper. Plautus's Roman comedies, with their courtesans and businesslike sexual encounters, were partly known to the English schoolboys but in only in the expurgated and allegorized fashion of *Ovid moralisé*. Polynesta stands alone in English Renaissance comedy. Simply by being who she is, Polynesta makes a remarkable statement. We do not know what the gentlemen of Gray's Inn said to one another as they left the performance in 1566, but we can say that the mere fact of production acknowledged and sponsored a comic masterpiece of Italian Renaissance that was both foreign and challenging.

In a similar fashion, the handling of lawyers in *Supposes* provides a kind of urbane, iconoclastic wit that the lawyers of Gray's Inn must have found novel at the least. Shakespeare expunges all of this in *The Taming of the Shrew*: Gremio, the unwelcome older wooer of Bianca, is a type out of Italian comedy or the *fabliau,* to be sure, but that type is the pantaloon, rich and ridiculous in his pretensions to a young wife, rather than a grasping shyster. Ariosto's and Gascoigne's Cleander, on the other hand, is a "miserable, covetous wretch" (1.3.1) whose parsimoniousness is legendary and whose "provision is as scant as may be" (lines 8–9). He takes the occasion of saints' days as his excuse not to feast his guests (1.2.156–57). The feigned Dulippo makes "sport" with this "gallant" by pretending to inform him, for his own good, of what the parasite Pasiphilo says of Cleander: that he is "the miserablest and most niggardly man that ever was," that his guests are "like to die for hunger" while Cleander himself eats heartily, that he coughs and spits continually. "Yet further," continues Dulippo in fabricating but only mildly exaggerating the sorts of things Pasiphilo does in fact say about Cleander, "he saith your armholes stink, your feet worse than they, and your breath worst of all." When Dulippo ventures to report that Pasiphilo has accused Cleander of being "bursten in the cods," that is, ruptured in the testicles, Cleander hotly replies, "O villain! He lieth! And if I were not in the street thou shouldest see them." This indecent suggestion of sexual exposure to a younger man prompts a charge of a further sexual perversity: "And," says Dulippo, "he saith that you desire this young gentlewoman as much for other men's pleasure as for your own" (2.4.131–62). Worse still are Cleander's vindictiveness and corruption as a lawyer.

No wonder that a marginal aside is able to conclude: "*Lawyers are never weary to get money*" (5.5.75–78). The portrayal and the antilawyer jokes are not truly hostile to the legal profession, however. The jokes are for the lawyers of Gray's Inn, after all. Cleander is an instance of what we call "roasting," as on the occasions when the National Press Club in Washington, D.C., yearly puts on skits of the current presidential administration and expects the occupants of the White House to attend with smiles on their faces attesting to their being good sports. Then as now, jokes against lawyers are told most of all by the lawyers themselves.

The fun is of a familiar sort, but it is also of a sort that is hard to find elsewhere in the English drama of the early Elizabethan period. The gentlemanly spectators at Gray's Inn evidently found both the sexual gamesmanship and the flippant sarcasm about lawyers refreshing, perhaps a bit bizarre at times, but in any case different from what they encountered in more parochial art and literature. No Elizabethan playwright tried to reproduce these features in English drama, not at least until the heyday of the boys' companies after 1598 and the development of a coterie drama attuned to Italian sophistication and appreciative of its implications for a courtly English culture.[7] That development will be a part of the story that unfolds in the following chapters.

Notes

1. *Othello*, 3.3.367–68. Quotations are from David Bevington, ed., *The Complete Works of Shakespeare* (New York: HarperCollins, 1992).

2. *Volpone*, 2.1.104–5. Quotations are from C. F. Tucker Brooke and N. B. Paradise, eds., *English Drama, 1580–1642* (New York, 1933).

3. *Supposes*, 5.5.75–78. Quotations are from C. R. Baskervill, V. B. Heltzel, and A. H. Nethercot, eds., *Elizabethan and Stuart Plays* (New York: Holt, 1934).

4. *See* my *From "Mankind" to Marlowe: Growth of Structure in the Popular Drama of Tudor England* (Cambridge: Harvard University Press, 1962), 37.

5. I discuss these plays in my *Tudor Drama and Politics: A Critical Approach to Topical Meaning* (Cambridge: Harvard University Press, 1968), 127–55.

6. *Romeo and Juliet*, 2.2.125.

7. Alfred Harbage, *As They Liked It: An Essay on Shakespeare and Morality* (New York: Macmillan 1947, reprint Harper Torchbooks, 1961), and *Shakespeare and the Rival Traditions* (New York: Macmillan, 1952).

From Narrative to Drama: The Erotic Tale and the Theater

MICHELE MARRAPODI

CRITICISM, as Stephen Greenblatt has provocatively suggested, is a sort of "story-telling."[1] One might argue—certain of the approval of the doyen of American New Historicism—that literature, as an artistic expression, belongs to the same category. If every form of creative writing, be it exegetic or literary, can be classified within this definition, it is justifiable to begin this chapter by commenting on two stories that seem paradigmatic of the general content of the present collection: the one modern, but with an air of antiquity; the other ancient, but with a surprising element of modernity. The action of the first fable, if such we may call it, goes back to a certain night, a few years ago:

> A young woman is wakened by her boyfriend's identical twin, who needs to speak to his brother. She tells him that her boyfriend will not be back until late that night and returns to sleep. But after a while the twin knocks again and when the woman opens the door, half asleep, he gets into her bed. In the darkness she mistakes the twin for her boyfriend and has no objection to his invitation to make love. When she recognizes her mistake the following morning, she realizes she has been deceived and reports the matter to the police. Ironically, though, the twin is not accused of rape, but simply of sexual misconduct, as no force was used during the intercourse.

This brief anecdote, which might on a first acquaintance seem to come from an anthology of erotic *novelle,* is in fact the summary of an actual event which occurred in New York on the night of 26 August 1993. The twin brothers were Lenny and Lamont Hough, and the details were reported in the English tabloid paper, *The Sun,* by Caroline Graham, who gave the victim's verbatim account: "I was still half asleep when we started making love with the lights out and I couldn't tell the difference. He even started talking like Lenny. . . . [T]hey are so similar in every way." The reporter treats the entire incident with a touch of humor, adding ironically by way of a conclusion: "Now Lamont of Roosevelt, New York, has been charged with sexual misconduct. He could not be accused of rape because no force was used, police said. . . . The brothers are no longer on speaking terms."[2]

Significant about this tale of sexual abuse, involving an exchange of twins, is that all elements of the story are literary archetypes. Similar passionate stories of substitute or transvestite lovers and mistaken identity, heightened by the erotic use of mockery, belong to the genre of Greek and Latin New Comedy (from Menander to Plautus and Terence). They were then taken up by Boccaccio and may be found in many narrative and theatrical works by Italian and other Renaissance authors, including of course the plays of Shakespeare and his contemporaries. If we examine the diegetic content of the news item more closely, we may discern in the sequence of events a cross between two different comedic traditions that were generally kept apart in the history of literature: the *topos* of the twin brothers and the theatergram of the bed-trick, i.e., the substitution of the lover in the darkness. In the closest analogous context, Plautus's *Menaechmi*—the most popular comedy in the Renaissance with numerous performances and imitations—twin brothers, separated by destiny and reunited after a number of years, are mistaken in their respective roles by the wife of the local twin, until in the end all is resolved in the recognition scene. The felicitous formula, received by Plautus from Greek antecedents, is related to Terence's comedy, which also presents cases of exchanged identity which lead to misunderstanding and deception, and in which the comic movement toward recognition is disciplined in the three phases derived from Aristotle of *protasis* (exposition), *epitasis* (complication), and *catastrophe* (resolution).[3] In the *Decameron* the use of exchanged identity is more elaborate and more oriented toward explicit erotic developments. Here the *beffa* of the bed-trick either serves for the triumph of male satisfaction, as in the case of Ricciardo Minutolo (3.6), or is inverted to the man's discomfiture.[4] In the tale of the parish priest of Fiesole (8.4), the protagonist, who thinks he is sleeping with the fair widow with whom he has fallen in love, is in fact in bed with the woman's ugly maid, and in the morning has to endure the scorn of her brothers and the bishop. Both of these solutions offer diegetic variations of great dramatic effectiveness that are frequently found in modern theater.[5] In cinquecento *commedia erudita,* the first expression of the comic genre founded on imitation of the classics, the narrative syntax is complicated by the technique of *contaminatio,* with which different theatergrams, taken from separate classical plays, fuse together to make the *fabula* composite and unpredictable. The plurality of the dramatic situations thus explains the creation of the multiple plot, which brings cinquecento comic theater closer to Elizabethan and Jacobean dramaturgy. *La Calandria* (1513) by Bernardo Dovizi from Bibbiena, based on Plautus's *Menaechmi* and *Casina,* is full of bawdy motifs in the manner of Boccaccio and also has an extremely original prologue, totally extraneous to the main diegesis, which gave rise to a long series of imitations and disputes between playwrights of the day.[6] This autonomy of the prologue—which supersedes the proposal of mediation between old and new advanced by the young Ariosto (*Cassaria, Suppositi*), drawing abundantly on the prose of Boccaccio—is another anticipation of the Jacobean bourgeois comedy.[7] Bibbiena's comic invention consists in the increase in the number of errors thanks to the use, in the main plot, of twins of different sex who cross-dress as their opposites, thus generating a series of misunderstandings not devoid of a subtle erotic flavor. In the subplot, the motif of the foolish husband who has himself taken into the house of his beloved in a trunk, in the hope of lying with her, comes from Boccaccio and is echoed to some extent in Falstaff in *The Merry Wives of Windsor* (3.3) and in the character of Iachimo in *Cymbeline* (2.2). Despite the classical derivation, the true source of *La Calandria* is the *Decameron,* which Bibbiena uses in the creation of the motif of the *beffa* and the construction of the language, skillfully succeeding in combining the theatergram of the substitution of the lover in the darkness with the theme of twins and transvestism, which gives rise to the erotic content of the episode. In 4.2 the female Lidio, who is pretending to be male, goes "*in forma di donna*" to Calandro's wife, Fulvia, who is in love with the twin brother. Here is how Fulvia despairs when she believes that her lover has been transformed into a woman by the necromancer Ruffo:

O il cielo o il peccato mio o la malignità dello spirito che stato si sia, non so; ma una volta voi avete, oimè!, di maschio in femina converso Lidio mio. Tutto l'ho maneggiato e tocco: né altro del solito ritrovo che la presenzia in lui. E io non tanto la privazion del mio diletto piango quanto el danno suo; ché, per me, privo si trova di quel che più si brama.[8]

[I know not if it be the fault of heaven, or my sin, or the malignity of the spirit; but you have, alas, transformed my Lidio from male to female. I have handled and touched him all over: and I find nothing of that which I was wont to find in him. And I do not mourn the loss of my delight so much as his own loss: for I think he now lacks that which is most desirable.]

The character in question is Lidio's sister, Santilla, who impersonates a boy in female attire who has been changed into a woman by Ruffo's magic. Thus we have the paradoxical situation of a woman pretending to be a man pretending to be a woman. To complicate this roundabout of true and presumed crossdressing, we have the affirmation of the servant Fannio who passes off his mistress Santilla for a hermaphrodite capable of using at pleasure either the male or the female sex.[9] If we recall that boy actors played female roles in Elizabethan theater we can imagine the degree of erotic confusion generated by the multiple crossdressings.[10]

In *The Comedy of Errors,* the narrative line is taken from Plautus's *Menaechmi* and *Amphitruo;* Shakespeare's contribution is to multiply the possibility of error (by introducing a second pair of twins) and to transfer the action entirely to Ephesus, a city dedicated to Diana, and known to Elizabethans from John Gower's *Confessio Amantis* (book 8). Gower's work suggested not only the figure of Emilia, the wife of Egeon and subsequently abbess of the temple, but also the initial theme of shipwreck that causes the splitting up of the family.[11] Wolfgang Riehle has recently demonstrated that, in addition to the original text, Shakespeare's work presents echoes of numerous adaptations that were directly or indirectly borrowed from William Warner's translation of 1594, which circulated in manuscript before the date of printing.[12] In 2.2 the erotic complication of the Plautine plot is introduced by Adriana, the wife of Antipholus of Ephesus, who mistakes her identical twin brother-in-law, Antipholus of Syracuse, for her own husband, rebukes him for his lack of interest in her, and urges him to be more affectionate:

> How ill agrees it with your gravity
> To counterfeit thus grossly with your slave,
> Abetting him to thwart me in my mood;
> Be it my wrong, you are from me exempt,
> But wrong not that wrong with a more contempt.
> Come, I will fasten on this sleeve of thine;
> Thou art an elm, my husband, I a vine,

Whose weakness married to thy stronger state,
Makes me with thy strength to communicate.[13]

Among the Plautine themes most effectively employed by Shakespeare is the "lock-out motif," that is, the theatergram of the twin or lover locked out of his house, a twist that derives from *Amphitruo,* is taken up by Boccaccio, and is artfully adapted in the Italian theater. Shakespeare accentuates the erotic game by the attraction of Antipholus of Syracuse for Luciana, sister of the wife of Antipholus of Ephesus, while the twin servant Dromio is pursued by a fat "kitchen wench," the wife of Dromio of Ephesus (3.2). The comic tension, enhanced by the presence of two pairs of twins who alternate their appearance on stage, thus increasing the errors, skillfully reflects on the space-time structure, which is also disrupted by the contradictions of sequence, appearances, and events. The linearity of the time sequence and the spatial relationships is thus subverted and the characters, who are all involved in this unnatural process of doubling, comically accentuate—with frequent queries as to "when" a given event occurred—the degree of comic intrigue caused by the distortion of reality.[14]

In *Twelfth Night,* a maturer work, the twin *topos*—this time bisexual in type—is complicated by the false identity of Viola, who crossdresses as the eunuch Cesario. In this guise she is loved by Olivia, to whom she has to report the love of Orsino, whom she herself secretly loves. This intriguing erotic triangle is resolved by the arrival of the twin brother, Sebastian, who, after a series of misunderstandings, marries Olivia, while his sister marries Duke Orsino. Robert Miola has convincingly demonstrated how the theatergram of the lover's exclusion (the lockout motif) in *The Comedy of Errors,* derived from the Latin New Comedy, is inverted in *Twelfth Night,* in the sense that Orsino and Olivia are physically and symbolically "locked-in, entrapped in self-absorbed vanities, confused about their desires and the nature of love."[15] But although the most ancient matrix of the comedy is to be found in plots of Plautus (*Menaechmi*) and Terence (*Eunuchus*), Shakespeare closely follows *Gl'Ingannati* (1531), of the Siennese "Accademia degli Intronati," which had a prose version in the tales of Bandello (1554) and in the *Histoires Tragiques* (1571) of Belleforest. The play was performed in Latin at Cambridge in the translation of Charles Etienne's French version (1543). The probable Shakespearean derivation is also explained by the fact that *Gl'Ingannati* owes the clever idea of the

confusion of the sexes to the game of erotic deviations constructed on the rotation and not on the specularity of the twins
(as was the case in *La Calandria*);[16] the strategy of rotation
gives rise to the climate of sexual ambiguity that surrounds the
construction of the *fabula*, as testified by the character of Lelia
who, dressed as her brother, has to defend herself from the
amorous advances of Isabella:

> Io ho, da un canto, la più bella pastura del mondo di costei che si
> crede pur ch'io sia maschio; dall'altro, vorrei uscir di questa briga e
> non so come mi fare. Veggio che costei è già venuta al bacio; e verrà,
> la prima volta, più avanti; e trovarommi aver perduta ogni cosa: tal
> che forza è ch'e' si scuopra la ragia.[17]

> [On the one hand I have the finest pasture [enjoyment] in the world
> in this woman who thinks I am a man; but on the other I would
> escape from this predicament, yet know not what to do. She has
> already gone so far as to kiss me; and soon she will go yet further; I
> shall find that I have lost all; the trick must needs be discovered.]

Viola/Cesario in *Twelfth Night* is in a very similar plight, as she
has to fend off Olivia's unwanted attentions while she cannot
declare her own love for Orsino because of the male identity that
she has assumed.

> Disguise, I see thou art a wickedness,
> Wherein the pregnant enemy does much.
> How easy is it for the proper false
> In women's waxen hearts to set their forms!
> Alas, our frailty is the cause, not we,
> For such as we are made of, such we be.
> How will this fadge? My master loves her dearly,
> And I, poor monster, fond as much on him,
> And she, mistaken, seems to dote on me:
> What will become of this? As I am a man,
> My state is desperate for my master's love:
> As I am woman (now alas the day!)
> What thriftless sighs shall poor Olivia breathe?[18]

The affinity with *Gl'Ingannati* extends also to the subplot in
the common use of the comedic stock types of vanity and pre-
sumption (*alazoneia*), derived from the classical and Italian traditions, such as the parasite, the braggart soldier, and the
pedantic teacher; the Plautine matrix of twins and transvestism
is however present in many other sixteenth-century comedies.

Following the transmission line of theatergrams of cross-dressing and the bed-trick, with reference to the two time parameters that mark the development of cinquecento comedy, i.e., Bibbiena's *Calandria* (1513) and Bruno's anticomedy *Candelaio* (1582), we find two works by Nicolò Secchi (which present interesting similarities to *Twelfth Night*), *Gl'Inganni* (1562), and *L'Interesse* (1581), in which a young woman dresses as a man in order to court the woman who is loved by the man she is herself in love with. This thematic twist naturally includes Machiavelli's two major comedies: *La Mandragola* (1518) and *Clizia* (1525), the first examples of "radical" theater in the Italian cultural panorama. *La Mandragola* is an inspired blend of elements from Terence and Boccaccio, in which Boccaccio's contribution is also linguistic, being "not so much in the space of the signifier as in that of the signified, as a configuration of events, a set of motifs, or a mixing of situations."[19] Here the topic of disguise and exchange of person is realized in the *beffa* at the expense of the impotent husband who, in order to have a son, agrees to have his wife drink a potion made with mandrake and to have her lie with a passing "*garzonaccio*" (in fact the wife's suitor in disguise) who will absorb the poison and die a week after the encounter. The play's subversive nature lies not only in the irreverent subject of marital infidelity, already present in Boccaccio, but also in the complicity of the mother—the epitome of Catholic morality—who actively contributes to the realization of the plan.[20] Ambiguity from the viewpoint of social and religious convention may also be observed when the husband and mother-in-law approve of the idea that the man who is to lie with Lucrezia must die. This doctrine of the utilitaristic and pragmatic view of life is an essential aspect of Machiavelli's radically new philosophy.[21] The unconventional ideology of the play is also recognizable in the characterization of the other dramatis personae who unscrupulously bend to the situation: Lucrezia, who as if by divine Providence accedes to the union with her suitor Callimaco and willingly agrees to further encounters; and the friar, who also with hypocritical hesitancy accepts the agreement with the ingenious Ligurio who offers him a handsome reward. This satirical mode, which invests all levels of society, is amply reflected in the satirical city plays of the Jacobean bourgeois theater, including the comedies of Marston, Jonson, and Middleton. *Clizia* is derived from Plautus's *Casina,* although it differs in its scurrilous and provocative mode flouting contemporary morality. Here the theatergram of the exchanged woman

in the dark proves in the end to be a double trick at the expense
of its inventor. The first is a failure (that of Nicomaco who hopes
to possess, unbeknown to his wife, the young Clizia, whom his
son loves), while the second is turned against the lewd old man
(Nicomaco is compelled to lie with the boy Idrio, believing him
to be Clizia). The original comic matrix of inspiration is not so
much the Greek and Latin New Comedy as that "species of lay
and profane theater dressed up as a tale," the *Decameron,* plun-
dered as it was by most playwrights of the day.[22]

Casina and *Clizia* are the sources of Donato Giannotti's *Il
Vecchio amoroso* (1533), which heralds some themes of the
Shakespearean romance such as the motif of the kidnapping of
the girl and the generational conflict between father and son.
Also related to Machiavelli's two radical plays are *Il Frate* (c.
1540) by Anton Francesco Grazzini, known as Il Lasca, and *L'As-
siuolo* (c. 1549) by Giovan Maria Cecchi. In the first of these, a
three-act farce based on the sixth tale of the third day of the
Decameron, a friar, having satisfied his passion for a merchant's
beautiful wife, contrives to have the husband go to an amorous
encounter with his spouse, thinking her to be another woman
to whom he has taken a fancy. The wife's hypocritical scolding
and the friar's intervention resolve the situation, so that the
beffa of the bed-trick turns out positively. The second play, *L'As-
siuolo,* also goes back to the *Decameron* not only for its plot—
taken from the same tale of Ricciardo Minutolo (3.6)—but above
all for the atmosphere of joyous erotic frenzy surrounding the
action. This atmosphere is embodied, with popular craftiness
and Machiavellian pragmatism, in the figure of the dissatisfied
woman, neglected by her sister and her jealous husband who is
subjected to the Plautine (or Boccaccio-like) jest of exclusion
from his own home, i.e., the lock-out motif. In *El Pedante* (1529)
by Francesco Belo, taken from the story of Giletta di Nerbona
(*Decameron,* 3.9), an interesting variation of the bed-trick technique is used by a young woman to win over the husband who
refuses to love her. Compelled to adopt a disguise in order to
follow him, she makes her husband believe that she is a lover
desirous to lie with him. The man thus sleeps with his wife and
when at dawn she reveals her true identity and begs him to stab
her to death, he not only pardons the deception but decides to
continue to live with her because her action has won back his
love. The innovative style of this author leads to the disintegration of the narrative syntax, which is constantly interrupted by
short sequences of secondary or collateral events and even quite

irrelevant episodes, since "a continuous process of multiplication and opening up, as in a collection of tales, without any plan or fate to select or give shape to the action, . . . is the substance of the text and no mere accident."[23] Another work by Belo, *El Beco* (1538), presents the stratagem of the exchanged woman in bed, and in both cases the wife takes the lover's place. Once again disguises and mistaken identities are amongst the dramatic techniques most appropriate for the development of the comedic action.[24]

In the analogous Shakespearean *All's Well That Ends Well*, based on the same Boccaccio tale translated by William Painter in *The Palace of Pleasure* (1566–7), it is Helena who takes the fair Diana's place in bed in order to lie with her husband Bertram, who has spurned her:

> *Helena.* You see it lawful then; it is no more
> But that your daughter, ere she seems as won,
> Desires this ring; appoints him an encounter;
> In fine, delivers me to fill the time,
> Herself most chastely absent. After,
> To marry her I'll add three thousand crowns
> To what is pass'd already.
>
> *Widow.*   I have yielded.
> Instruct my daughter how she shall persever
> That time and place with this deceit so lawful
> May prove coherent.[25]

Thanks to a providential exchange of rings (an expedient which has its deep source in Menander via Terence's *Hecyra*) and the evidence of her pregnancy, Helena's plan succeeds; she proves that she has slept with her spouse and obtains his legitimate love, though not without teaching him a lesson. The play revolves around the fundamental Shakespearean dichotomy, centered on the moral significance of the contrasts between appearance and reality. The initial error of the aristocratic Bertram, who fails to recognize Helena's true value because of her humble origins, is equivalent to the false and hypocritical behavior of his friend Parolles, whose squalid betrayal makes him act as a foil to the discomfited Bertram. The two characters seem in fact to be associated in a single didactic-moral design, based on a subtle interplay of mirrors. It is Bertram's return to reason, thanks to Helena's example, that ultimately signals the distance between the count and his corrupt follower. The ethic of "seeming" and "being" is related to the issue of licit and illicit sexuality that is anticipated in the initial debate between Parolles and Helena on the value of virginity (1.1) and recalled in the bed-trick episode by the chaste role of Diana, which she forcibly asserts and which is recognized by the king himself in the final denouement.

> If thou beest yet a fresh uncropped flower
> Choose thou thy husband and I'll pay thy dower;
> For I can guess that by thy honest aid
> Thou kept'st a wife herself, thyself a maid.[26]

This explicit didacticism and the artificially contrived solution, according to which the repudiated wife's constancy triumphs over the ordeals to which she is subjected, have not fully convinced the critics, and the comedy has been classified among the "problem plays." As Louise George Clubb has pointed out, if *All's Well* is considered as part of a gradual process of cultural exchange, some aspects of the "problematic" nature of this play may be clarified. The essence of the theater as a mixture of genres and receptive of the evolution of society reveals a slow process of transforming archetypes, *topoi*, and theatergrams on which the play depends.[27] Thus the irreverent cynicism of Parolles—who at the end of the play seems to accept the accommodating moralism of the king of France, himself anxious to reestablish the social order of matrimony—can be better understood with reference to Boccaccio's fondness of jest, Belo's ambiguous nonconventionalism, and the satirical mode of the Italian radical comedy of Machiavelli, Aretino, and Bruno, with its subversive erotic and antimoralizing social content. "Ariosto's theater, a most evocative example of 'integrated' theater," as Giulio Ferroni has written, "is quite unlike that of Machiavelli's *Mandragola* or Bruno's *Candelaio*, which reveal a surprisingly disruptive critical force that is recognizable in the manner in which the 'public' structure is called into question and overturned."[28] Aretino's theater seems to be situated in a midway position, one that is both ambiguous and contradictory, between *commedia erudita*, strictly conforming to classical rules and motifs, and the radical trend of Machiavelli and Bruno, which breaks with tradition, disrupting hierarchical and gender roles with a powerful charge of transgressive sexuality and social satire. In *Cortigiana* (1526) Aretino produces a caricature portrait of court life in Rome and its affectations, with the

Boccaccio-like use of the *beffa* against Master Maco, who desires to become a courtier so that he may aspire to a cardinalate, and Signor Parabolano, who is in love with a young woman. Maco is instructed how to pursue vice and to invert every positive attitude of society and the court, since corruption and free language were considered to be the exclusive prerogatives of the courtier; Parabolano goes to an amorous encounter with the strumpet Togna, a baker's wife, organized by the groom Rosso and the procuress Aluigia, but Togna, dressed as a man further to complicate matters, is mistaken for the woman whom Parabolano loves. The *beffa* of the bed-trick is ironically turned by the victim into an invitation to laughter for all the characters involved (including Togna's betrayed husband), and in this way he saves his reputation. The play parodies two aspirations of the bourgeoisie of the time: erotic success and admission to court life. A more subversive intent is perhaps to be found in *Il Marescalco* (1533), a work in which the cross-dressing motif is related to the *beffa* at the expense of the misogynic protagonist, who is obliged by the count to take a wife. The whole play develops this design by means of a series of comic episodes that culminate at court in the marriage with the page Carlo dressed as a woman. The transgressive aspect lies in the fact that the revelation of the jest fully satisfies the homosexual and misogynistic tendencies of the Marescalco, who willingly accepts the union with the boy. Aretino's text is one of the probable sources of Ben Jonson's *Epicoene, or the Silent Woman* (1609). Giordano Bruno's only theatrical work, *Candelaio* (1582) contains the three main stock types on which cinquecento comedy is constructed in a sort of comical synthesis: the *senex amans* (Bonifacio), the alchemist (Bartolomeo), and the pedant (Manfurio), all of whom are equally duped because of the stupidity of their passion. The figure of the aged dotard is ridiculed by his transformation from a homosexual to heterosexual, inverting his libido from "candle-maker" to "ring-maker"; the alchemist is mocked because of his spasmodic search for the magic powder, the "pulvis Christi," which will turn everything into gold; while the pedant, as Borsellino has it, is "the most grotesque of all the incarnations of Bruno's polemical antiformalism."[29] Bruno was an opponent of Scholasticism and Aristotelianism and rails against scientific, philosophical, and religious orthodoxy, starting with the prologue, which consists of a series of irreverent and caustic darts scattered throughout its various component parts (caudate sonnet, dedication, argument, antiprologue, and proprologue), pass-

ing from the ironic genre to satire, parody, and linguistic
exuberance just for its own sake. Without any doubt, one of the
many instances of Bruno's revolutionary ideology clashing with
contemporary principles, reflecting all the subversive force of
his opinions, is to be seen in the monologue pronounced by
Vittoria. Here we find a polemical confutation of the Humanistic-
Renaissance doctrine of the *corpus mysticum* of the sovereign,
as the prince's immortal part (the body politic) is denied in favor
of the human or natural component (the body natural):

> Non possiamo non far differenza fra il culto divino e quello di mor-
> tali. Adoriamo le sculture e le imagini, ed onoriamo il nome divino
> scritto, drizzando l'intenzione a quel che vive. Adoramo ed onoramo
> questi altri dei che pisciano e cacano, drizzando la intenzione e
> supplice devozione alle lor imagini e sculture, perché, mediante
> queste, premiino i virtuosi, inalzino i degni, defendano gli oppressi,
> dilatino i lor confini, conservino i suoi e si faccino temere dall'aver-
> sarie forze: il re, dunque, ed imperator di carne ed ossa, si non corre
> sculpito, non val nulla.[30]

> [We must needs distinguish between the cult of gods and the cult of
> mortal men. We worship sculptures and images, and honor the writ-
> ten name of the divine, directing our attention to that which lives.
> We worship and honor these other gods that piss and shit, directing
> our intentions and suppliant devotion to their images and sculp-
> tures, so that through these they may reward the virtuous, elevate
> the worthy, defend the oppressed, extend their borders, preserve
> their own, and inspire fear in their enemies: the king therefore, and
> emperor in flesh and blood, if not sculpted, is worth naught.]

The bed-trick theatergram is seen in the episode where Bonifacio's wife, Carubina, meets her husband in the dark, pretending to be the courtesan Vittoria, whom he believes to be
well disposed toward him thanks to the enchantments of a
pseudomagician. This allows Carubina to inflict terrible tortures
on her husband, making him believe that she is acting under
the influence of the erotic passion produced by the magic spell.
At the same time, Carubina agrees to lie with Master Gioan Bernardo, who persuades her to abandon all moral scruples, disput-
ing the concept of honor and reputation in a manner very
similar to that of Iago manipulating Cassio in *Othello* (2.3):

> Vita della mia vita, credo ben cha sappiate che cosa è onore, e che
> cosa anco sii disonore. Onore non è altro che una stima, una riputaz-
> ione; però sta sempre intatto l'onore, quando la stima e riputazione

persevera la medesma. Onore è la buona opinione che altri abbiano di noi: mentre persevera questa, persevera l'onore. E non è quel che noi siamo e quel che noi facciamo, che ne rendi onorati o disonorati, ma sì ben quel che altri stimano, e pensano di noi.[31]

[Life of my life, I believe you know full well what is honor, and what is dishonor. Honor is but esteem, reputation; thus honor remains intact when esteem and reputation persist unchanged. Honor is the good opinion that others have of us: while this persists, then so does honor. For it is not what we are and what we do that makes us honored or dishonored but what others repute, and think of us.]

In Shakespeare the substitution of the lover has an important structural function in *Measure for Measure*. This play provides an interesting inquiry into the effects the exercise of power produces on human nature in the administration of justice and in the erotic response. Based directly or indirectly—via George Whetstone's adaptations [*Promos and Cassandra* (1578) and *Heptameron of Civill Discourses* (1582)]—on G. B. Giraldi Cinthio's *Hecatommithi* (1565), part two (8.5) and probably also on the dramatization of the same tale, *Epitia* (1583), *Measure for Measure* partially owes the "dark comedy" or "problem play" nature to the influence of the Italian theater and in particular to the model of satirical comedy that may be discerned in the writings of Machiavelli, Aretino, and Bruno, all of whom were in varying measure vigorous opponents of any form of moral, social, or religious convention. The appearance/reality contrast is immediately queried by Duke Vincentio, who, in the habit of a friar, proposes to observe the behavior of his deputy, Angelo ("Hence shall we see / If power change purpose, what our seemers be").[32] The atmosphere of the play, focused on the clash between power and sexuality, affects all social levels in a society where erotic freedom is increasingly checked by the rigor of the law. Angelo's proposal to spare Claudio's life on condition that he may lie with Isabella sets up the bed-trick trap (a purely Shakespearean invention of which there is no trace in the sources), by means of which the disguised duke proposes the substitution of Mariana, whom Angelo has refused to wed, for Isabella. Mariana will thus have the legal right to insist upon her marriage to Angelo:

Go you to Angelo; answer his requiring with a plausible obedience; agree with his demands to the point. Only refer yourself to this advantage: first, that your stay with him may not be long; that the

place may have all shadow and silence in it; and the time answer to
convenience. This being granted in course, and now follows all. We
shall advise this wronged maid to stead up your appointment, go in
your place. If the encounter acknowledge itself hereafter, it may
compel him to her recompense; and hear, by this is your brother
saved, your honour untainted, the poor Mariana advantaged, and the
corrupt deputy scaled.[33]

Thus conceived, the strategy of the exchange of women is skillfully blended into the dramatic action, setting off a string
of events that repeat the same motif of sexual union in three
different couples: Claudio-Juliet, Angelo-Mariana, and Lucio-
"wronged woman." Isabella's substitution in fact allows the
erotic union that has already occurred to be legitimated by marriage, thus bringing the Angelo-Mariana relationship in line
with the other two cases.[34] In the same way the final scene of
the revelation of the duke is ably linked to the arrival of the
veiled Mariana, who discloses Angelo's deception, and the successive reappearance of Claudio, thought to be dead. The appear-
ance/reality contrast is thus based, as in *Much Ado about
Nothing,* on the disguise technique, even if in this play it acquires a strong metatheatrical component due to the duke's disguise, which persists throughout the play, creating in the
character an ambiguous mixture of intention and expectancy,
of observation and complaisance.[35] It is no coincidence that
Shakespeare's use of the bed-trick in *All's Well That Ends Well*
and in *Measure for Measure* is accompanied by the development
of a serious social concern that obliquely involves the morality
of institutions and the behavior of the prince or duke and his
court. It is difficult to say to what extent this significant development is due to direct acquaintance with the radical theater of
Machiavelli, Aretino, and Bruno or, as suggested by Louise
George Clubb, to the effects of the Counter-Reformation on Italian *commedia grave,* but there is no denying the common
themes, motifs, and forms of the two schools of dramaturgy.

2

The site of the second story, narrated long before the first but
with a decidedly more modern diegetic content, is Prato. In
those days Prato was a city governed by a male-dominated law
that prescribed that any woman caught by her husband in flagrant adultery should be burned to death. The plot is as follows:

A husband returns home early and discovers his wife in the arms of a young man. He controls his first impulse to punish the guilty lovers and denounces his wife for the sin she has committed. Summoned before the judge the following day, the woman is advised by friends and family to deny committing adultery. Even the judge, smitten by her beauty and her noble manner, hopes that she will deny the charge. The woman however confirms the accusation, but denounces the iniquitous character of a law that condemns to death by fire only wives, who, being women, can satisfy many men. She requests that her husband be asked if she has ever denied him her affection. Her husband having testified that she has always accepted his every whim, the woman asks the judge what she was supposed to do with what her husband left over, throw it to the dogs? This astute response provokes the merry approval of all present; the judge modifies the law so that wives may be punished only if they are unfaithful for gain, and acquits the wife, while the puzzled husband leaves the court.

This story is clearly a synthesis of the seventh tale of the sixth day of the *Decameron,* which in the English translation of 1620 recounts the episode in the following vivid words: "Madam Philippa, being accused by her Husband Rinaldo de Pugliese, because he tooke her in Adulterie, with a yong Gentleman named Lazarino de Guazzagliotri: caused her to bee cited before the Judge. From whom she delivered her selfe, by a sodaine, witty, and pleasant answer, and moderated a severe strict Statute, formerly made against women."[36] The theme of the sixth day, as governed by Elissa, is the ability of an accused person to use artful language to rebut a charge by providing "a sudden, unexpected and discreet answere, thereby preventing losse, danger, scorne and disgrace, retorting them on the busi-headed Questioners."[37] The success of the *novella*, with its erotic overtones, is attested by a whole series of references in a number of cinquecento plays. One of the clearest examples is the almost literal quotation by Togna in Aretino's *Cortigiana,* when she is accused by her husband of adultery:

Arcolano. Ahi crudelaccia, perché m'hai tu tradito?
Togna. Che vuoi ch'io faccia di quel che mi avanza, che io lo gitti ai porci?[38]

[*Arcolano.* Oh cruel woman, why hast thou betrayed me?
Togna. And what am I to do with what is left to me, throw it to the pigs?]

Herbert G. Wright's important monograph on Boccaccio's influence in England does not report any theatrical derivation from this *novella*.[39] However, many thematic contacts and contrasts are possible if we observe the intertextual dynamics in the light of recurrent dramatic microstructures. From this viewpoint, with regard to the topic of the lady on trial, it is possible to relate two typological lines to the narrative syntax of the tale: the theatergram of the slandered woman and that of the assertive woman. The two situational developments are copiously represented in Anglo-Italian Renaissance theater, both separately and blended in a single paradigm. The figure of the lady on trial is part of the more serious and problematic climate of the *commedia grave,* which is characterized by loans from the tragic genre that replace the classic *topos* of fate and whorish fortune with the Counter-Reformation belief in the intervention of Providence. The first of these thematic fields includes the character of the constant woman who remains faithful to her husband despite being repudiated or driven from home. The prototype for this characterization is *L'Amor costante* (1536) by Alessandro Piccolomini, a theoretician and the founder of the Siennese "Accademia degli Intronati," who constructs a play *à thèse* on constancy in love which in the end will be rewarded by Providence. The whole play, including the prologue, is structured in metatheatrical terms. The characters often address the audience directly in a rhetorical game that underlines and amplifies the scenic fiction and the explicit didactic message, as is the case in the final comment of the maid Agnoletta:

> Imparate, donne, da costei a esser costanti nei pensier vostri; e non dubitate, poi. Imparate voi, amanti, a non abbandonarvi nelle miserie e soffrir le passioni per fin che venghino le prosperità.[40]

> [Learn from her, o ye women, to be constant in your thoughts; and then do not doubt. And learn, o ye lovers, not to abandon yourselves to misery but suffer passion until prosperity shall come.]

In *La Pellegrina* (1564) by Girolamo Bargagli the main leitmotiv is the conflict of love that prevents the union of two pairs of lovers, whose difficulties intersect and in the end are resolved. The *eiron,* the stock character who resolves the situation, is the young Drusilla who, dressed as a pilgrim, is searching for her betrothed, Lucrezio, whom she believes to be unfaithful (a motif that foreshadows Helena's courageous search in *All's Well*). Lucrezio, himself believing Drusilla to be dead, has reluctantly promised to wed another young lady. Drusilla's arrival resolves the misunderstanding and is like a reward for Lucrezio's faithfulness. The theatergram of constancy in love blends here with the theme of the "wondrous woman" whose extraordinarily strong faith enables her to overcome all the snags of fortune, as Drusilla herself testifies at the end of the play, when she can finally abandon her disguise,

> Entriamo, ché non veggo l'ora di gittar giù affatto quest'abito, ché ora è finito il pellegrinaggio, ora è ottenuta la grazia, ora sono adempiti i voti![41]

> [Let us go in, for I cannot wait to doff this habit, now that my pilgrimage is done, grace has been given, and my vows are fulfilled!]

La Donna costante (1589) by Raffaello Borghini is not dissimilar in content. This play is based on the type of conflict between families that Shakespeare used in *Romeo and Juliet*. The heroine Elfenice is obliged to renounce Aristide, who believing that he has killed her cousin is compelled to flee. Several years later Aristide returns and learns that his beloved is dead. But in fact Elfenice has feigned death in order to be able to seek Aristide. The final encounter stresses the motif of the lovers' faith being rewarded. After further reversals, concluding in a trial scene with the recognition of the various characters and the reconciliation of the family members, the young couple can finally marry. To this theme Louise George Clubb has devoted a convincing chapter that associates the characterization of the wondrous woman with the spiritual ideals of Christian doctrine. In these comedies, she writes, love is elevated

> to the rank of grace and providence, and the commonplace of feigned death and burial is used as more than an example of cleverness: it is a wonder of steadfastness signifying the right human action that cooperates through love in the stability of the Unmoved Mover, who is the source of love and of the providence that controls the mutability of fortune.[42]

Subsequent derivations from the same theme include Annibale Caro's *Gli Straccioni* (1543–45), Sforza Oddi's *commedie gravi*—particularly *Erofilomachia* (1572) and *I morti vivi* (1576)—and Giambattista Della Porta's *Gli duoi fratelli rivali* (1601). These plays are directly or indirectly based on the theatergrams of apparent or presumed deaths and of the lady on trial, which lead to Shakespeare's Hero in *Much Ado about Nothing* and ultimately to Hermione in *The Winter's Tale,* by way of Desdemona's calvary in *Othello* and the slandered Imogen in *Cymbeline*—all representations of women brought to trial by the arrogance of male power. The female type that emerges from these characterizations is often a saintlike or Christlike figure that through the use of religious images or metaphors expresses a positive symbology of eros directed at the recovery and salvation of man.[43] The various roles of wife and daughter in Shakespeare's romances—Thaisa and Marina, Hermione and Perdita, Imogen and Miranda—are clearly derived from the archetype of the wondrous woman. As the relationship with Shakespeare's theater has already been carefully analyzed by Louise George Clubb, I will attempt here to trace a few further points of reference with some later Stuart plays. It should be noted first of all that the most interesting intertextual links are to be found in the sentimental tragedies and the tragicomedies, in which the narrative line of the *novella* adapts more naturally to the canons of the tragic genre and the Puritan decorum of the age. The explicit and provocative transformation of the adulterous Madonna Filippa into a fiery and victorious feminist is in fact the prerogative of Boccaccio and his taste for surprise and the transgressive treatment of eros.[44]

An interesting case of thematic contact and contrast with the *novella* may be discerned in the domestic tragedy *A Woman Killed With Kindness* (1603) by Thomas Heywood, a double-plot play drawn, particularly as regards the subplot, from Bandello through Painter's translation in *The Palace of Pleasure.* The main plot dramatizes the sentimental story of a wife caught in the act of adultery by her husband, who ordains that she shall live far from her home and children. Only when she dies does she finally obtain her husband's pardon and the salvation of her soul. The subplot revolves around the figure of a man who compels his debtor to sell him his sister but who is then so struck by the girl's honesty that he repents his evil act and takes her to wife. In mirrorlike manner, the two women reflect the dual image of a single didactic example, since the adulteress redeems her sin by letting herself starve to death, obeying the need for moral catharsis required by the play. By this gesture the adulterous wife is identified with Mary Magdalene, the redeemed prostitute, and associated with the idea of the wondrous woman as incarnated in Susan, the other female protagonist, who to save her honor is prepared to commit suicide. If the "judgement" to which Anne Frankford in *A Woman Killed With Kindness* is subjected finds an appropriate response in the rhetoric of the woman's behavior, the dramatic effectiveness of the public trial in the "Arraignment of Vittoria" in *The White Devil* (1612) lies in the adulteress's verbal defence, the aim of which is to assert the perfidy of her accusers and tortures. Through Vittoria's words Webster denounces the iniquity and partiality of a tribunal where prosecutor and judge are one and the same person and where erotic transgression becomes a metaphor of the "Italian" vice of the court, involving all the characters and identifying itself with the corruption of power.[45]

> if you be my accuser
> Pray cease to be my judge, come from the bench,
> Give in your evidence 'gainst me, and let these
> Be moderators: my lord cardinal,
> Were your intelligencing ears as long
> As to my thoughts, had you an honest tongue
> I would not care though you proclaim'd them all.[46]

The defensive harangue delivered by Vittoria, who from defendant turns plaintiff, places her in the category of the assertive woman who assigns to the illocutionary power of her language the difficult task of defying a patriarchal and misogynist male-dominated society, as she herself ironically observes: "O woman's poor revenge / Which dwells but in the tongue" (3.2.283–84). Jonathan Dollimore has identified in the motif of the assertive woman the denunciation of a process of exploitation of women, which is expressed as a form of affirmation of power, "the issue of men's domination of women being put alongside men's domination of men."[47] Dollimore associates the ideology of male power in *The White Devil* with a short sequence in *The Comedy of Errors* in which Adriana beats Dromio of Ephesus (2.1), venting on the guiltless servant her anger at man's domination of woman. Iago in *Othello* is possibly the clearest case of a character with a vision of life in which man's exploitation of woman is equated to man's exploitation of man. It is no coincidence that this play presents the significant psychomachia between Emilia and Desdemona on the temptations of adultery, which the lady swears to reject also "for all the world" in contrast with her servant's opinion, and the parallel scene between Othello and Iago on the acceptance of jealousy in which the Moor swears to revenge and asks for "some swift means of death"

(3.3.484).[48] In the scene in question, against the ultrafeminist Emilia's utilitarian view Desdemona sets her own testimony of love and faith, for the victory of which over Iago's perverseness she will in the end sacrifice her life.

> *Emil.*   Let husbands know,
> Their wives have sense like them: they see, and smell,
> And have their palates both for sweet, and sour,
> As husbands have. What is it that they do,
> When they change us for others? Is it sport?
> I think it is: and doth affection breed it?
> I think it doth. Is't frailty that thus errs?
> It is so too. And have not we affections?
> Desires for sport? and frailty, as men have?
> Then let them use us well: else let them know,
> The ills we do, their ills instruct us so.
> *Des.* Good night, good night: God me such usage send,
> Not to pick bad from bad, but by bad mend!
>
> (4.3.93–105)

As the heroine's chastity imitates the sacred love vows of the constant woman, Emilia's opposite view follows the theatergram of the libertine *balia* (like Shakespeare's nurse in *Romeo and Juliet*) that is exemplified in Ariosto's *I Suppositi* (1509), Della Porta's *La Fantesca* (1592), or in the figure of Giglietta in *La Pellegrina* (1.2):

> Eh, la parte de' mariti si è per cirimonia. I mariti, ben sapete, non sono altro che fattori e guardiani degli innamorati. I mariti fanno loro le spese, i mariti lor fanno le vesti; gli impacci, i rimbrotti, i fastidi che portan seco le donne son tutti de' mariti, i piaceri, i vezzi, le docezze tutte toccano agli amanti.

> [Eh, the husbands' role is only appearance. Husbands, you know, are but servants and protectors of their wives' lovers. Husbands buy their wives' shopping and provide for their dresses. The nuisances, complaints, and problems all belong to husbands; the pleasures, caresses, and sweetness all belong to lovers.]

Castiza in *The Revenger's Tragedy* (1607), in her refusal of the invitation to indulge in illicit sexual encounters proffered to her by the court and by her own mother (2.1), is constructed on the same model of the wondrous woman, although Desdemona's rhetoric contains a subtle assertive will that operates along the amplifying axis of Christian theological language, as opposed to the attenuative, metalogical will of Iago's idiolect, which is based instead on the tropes of negation and suspension.[49]

Philip Massinger's tragicomedy *The Maid of Honour* (c. 1625), set in fourteenth-century Sicily, tackles the moral question of the relationship between honor and love, religion and passion, and the exercise and ethics of power. The source is the story of Camiola and Rolando related by Boccaccio in *De claris mulieribus* and taken up in the thirty-second *novella* of the second volume of Painter's *The Palace of Pleasure,* where the plot is thus summarized:

> A Gentlewoman and Wydow called Camiola of hir owne minde Raunsomed Roland the Kyng's Sonne of Sicilia, of purpose to haue him to hir Husband, who when he was redeemed vnkindly denied hir, agaynst whom very Eloquently, she Inueyed, and although the Law proued him to be hir Husband, yet for his vnkindness, shee vtterly refused him.[50]

The play revolves around the strong characterization of the fair Camiola, who ransoms her lover from imprisonment and receives the promise of his hand in marriage, only to find that he casts her aside to marry the duchess Aurelia. In act 5 Camiola receives the news of Bertoldo's betrayal (as Roland is called in the play) and resolves to present herself at court to claim the fulfillment of the marriage contract the young man signed when he was ransomed. Before the king of Sicily, Camiola accuses Bertoldo and succeeds in exacting marriage, but when the priest appears to celebrate the wedding, great is the surprise when the woman takes the veil and marries the Church.

> This is the marriage! this the port! to which
> My vowes must steere me, fill my spreading sayles
> With the pure wind of your devotions for me,
> That I may touch the secure haven, where
> Eternal happinesse keeps her residence,
> Temptations to frailty never entring.[51]

Camiola begs that those who have offended her may be pardoned and, relinquishing earthly goods, she seeks refuge in spiritual peace. Her behavior is praised by all present, as they admire her noble nature and concertedly attribute to her the title of "maid of honor." It is clear that Massinger wished to produce a play of striking effect revolving around a woman endowed with great moral qualities who was capable of pardoning her detractors and desirous of setting them an example of Christian virtue. Camiola's humble condition also sets an ironic contrast between the corruption of the court, the powerful and their favorites, and the moral integrity of a girl of lowly origin but one who is capable of immense human understanding for the weaknesses of others. Massinger's treatment of Camiola virtually turns her into a saint, willing to assist and pardon even those who have slighted her, as for example the king's favorite, Fulgentio. To Bertoldo, who has betrayed her love, she says,

> You have been false once. And if
> When I am married (as this day I will be)
> As a perfit signe of your attonement with me
> You wish me joy, I will receive it for
> Full satisfaction of all obligations
> In which you stand bound to me.[52]

Eubella, in James Shirley's *Love's Cruelty* (1631), is certainly constructed on the same moral characterization as Camiola. Eubella tenaciously pits her chastity against the duke of Ferrara's attempts at corruption and in the end redeems the perverseness of his nature. A harsh contrast is provided by the other female figure in the play, the adulteress Clariana, who seduces her husband's best friend, under the impulse of an uncontrollable, cynically perverse desire. As she herself confesses to her lover, "What makes a maidenhead the richer purchase, think you? But I am married, and my husband is your friend."[53] Shirley's play is related by a series of situational contacts and contrasts to Thomas Middleton's *Women Beware Women* (c. 1621), a tragedy that develops the idea of the erotic seduction of power and on the fascination of illicit and transgressive sexuality. Middleton's influence is in fact plainly visible in many Italianate plays of the Stuart period, which center on strong female characterizations and the search for striking variations on the theatergram of the adulterous woman.

In John Ford's *Love's Sacrifice* (1630) the Duchess Bianca is killed by the duke of Pavia because she shamelessly admits to him her love for his favorite Fernando, to whom she has not, however, conceded the grace of her bed owing to a hypocritical pseudo-principle of conjugal fidelity:

> I know what you would say now;
> You would fain tell me how exceeding much
> I am beholding to you, that vouchsaf'd

Me, from a simple gentlewoman's place,
The honour of your bed: 'tis true, you did;
But why? 'twas but because you thought I had
A spark of beauty more than you had seen.
To answer this, my reason is the like;
The self-same appetite which led you on
To marry me led me to love your friend:
O, he's a gallant man! if ever yet
Mine eyes beheld a miracle compos'd
Of flesh and blood, Fernando has my voice.[54]

Even considering the dramaturgical requirement for a new twist in an amply exploited dramatic situation, Bianca's confession would seem to express a conscious need to assert the female identity that matches that expressed by Boccaccio's Madonna Filippa and foreshadows the more sophisticated view of woman that was to emerge in the Restoration theater.

Another play by Shirley, *The Lady of Pleasure* (1635), presents an interesting case of an adulteress in the character of Lady Aretina, whose wantonness is clearly hinted at in her name. Determined to take advantage of her arrival in town, as she declares in the opening scene, to devote herself to amusement and pleasure, Aretina with the aid of the procuress Madam Decoy contrives a stratagem worthy of Boccaccio in order to enjoy the favors of an attractive man, Master Alexander Kickshaw, without however being recognized. The man is prevailed upon to believe that he is the victim of the spells of a witch, who in the guise of a young woman is awaiting his services in the dark. Aretina thus achieves the double aim of the satisfaction of her desires without being betrayed by her chosen lover.

> *Aretina.* I blush while I converse with my own thoughts:
> Some strange fate governs me, but I must on;
> The ways are cast already, and we thrive
> When our sin fears no eye nor perspective.[55]

The bitter consequences of the remorse and sense of guilt that begin to work on the adulteress's conscience, in the end radically modifying her initial attitude toward conjugal fidelity, determine a process of repentance that with skillful psychological analysis leads to Aretina's return to the holy values of matrimony.

If the figures of Bianca and Aretina, albeit with their considerable contradictions, repeat the rhetorical model of the assertive woman, the candor of Spinella in *The Lady's Trial* (1638), Ford's last work, proposes the image of an Italian woman rich in moral values that exalt the traditional feminine qualities of purity, constancy, and fidelity in love. Unjustly accused of adultery, the heroine leaves the court, setting up a rhetoric of absence that obliges the other characters to reflect upon her true qualities, and allowing her at the same time to observe how she is condemned by her detractors or defended by her admirers. With its happy ending, the Italian world presented in the play does not reflect the customary climate of corruption and violent crime of so much Italianate drama, but instead shows an entirely positive dimension that involves all the characters, including the taciturn Adurni, who declares Spinella's innocence, and the noble Auria, who never doubts his wife's fidelity. Faced with the accusations made by his friend Aurelio, who in good faith advises him to take his revenge for Spinella's alleged adultery, Auria—inverting the stereotype of the vindicative Italian—replies,[56]

> Revenge! for what, uncharitable friend?
> On whom? let's speak a little, pray, with reason.
> You found Spinella in Adurni's house;
> 'Tis like he gave her welcome—very likely;
> Her sister and another with her; so!
> Invited, nobly done; but he with her
> Privately chamber'd:—he deserves no wife
> Of worthy quality who dares not trust
> Her virtue in the proofs of any danger.[57]

Ford is an able manipulator of Shakespeare's theater. In *The Lady's Trial* the object of the playwright's attention is *Othello,* which is used to contruct a reversed plot based on the characterizations of the Moor (Auria), Desdemona (Spinella), and Iago (Aurelio). At the center of the play we do not find the tragic consequences of jealousy, but, on the contrary, the values of trust and constancy between spouses, which are exalted despite the adversity of fate and the treachery of man. In the trial scene, Spinella's defense derives its peculiar strength from the affirmation of qualities and values that are interpreted as "masculine" by Auria and are related to the amplifying rhetorical model of the assertive woman:

> *Auria.*   Said ye, lady,
> "No kindred, sister, husband, friend"?
> *Spinella.*   Nor name;
> With this addition—I disclaim all benefit

Of mercy from a charitable thought;
If one or all the subtleties of malice,
If any engineer of faithless discord,
If supposition for pretence in folly,
Can point out, without injury to goodness,
A likelihood of guilt in my behaviour,
Which may declare neglect in every duty
Requir'd, fit, or exacted.
Auria.　　　　　High and peremptory!
The confidence is masculine.[58]

The Lady's Trial thus offers an admirable synthesis of the two typological trends identifiable in the thematic developments of Boccaccio's *novella*: on the one hand it infuses with new dramatic energy the motif of the trial of a slandered woman, and on the other it reveals the surprising rhetorical qualities of a wife that are necessary for the characterization of the assertive woman, such as are found in numerous female figures in Tudor and Stuart drama, from Shakespeare's Hero, Desdemona, Hermione, and Imogen, to Webster's Vittoria Corombona and the duchess of Malfi, and finally, through the mediation of Middleton, Massinger, and Shirley, to the women in the theater of John Ford.

In his description of the polysemous cultural potentialities present in what he calls "the textual traces" of Renaissance literature, and in particular of Shakespeare's works, Stephen Greenblatt affirms the principle that they are determined by an infinity of different factors derived from the convergence of cultures, traditions, and ideologies underlying the cultural heritage of that particular society and epoch:

> The textual traces that have survived from the Renaissance and that are at the center of our literary interest in Shakespeare are the products of extended borrowings, collective exchanges, and mutual enchantments. They were made by moving certain things—principally ordinary language but also metaphors, ceremonies, dances, emblems, items of clothing, well-worn stories, and so forth—from one culturally demarcated zone to another. We need to understand not only the construction of these zones but also the process of movements across the shifting boundaries between them.[59]

These heterogeneous characteristics, which thrive on the ideological clash of different cultures, constitute a "circulation of social energy" with which the author or dramatist is bound to come into conflict, indirectly setting up an activity of negotiation between his own art and the social or political hierarchy of power of a "totalizing society," as was that of Renaissance England. Greenblatt carries his theory so far as to classify the ways and the stylistic and linguistic processes by which this continuous "cultural exchange" between author and society progresses, using terms like "appropriation," "purchase," and "symbolic acquisition." This is not the place to enter into the pertinence of Greenblatt's theory, the interest and utility of which cannot be denied, but one can certainly affirm that thanks to his considerations intertextual dynamics may be better understood and research extended to hitherto unexplored fields and areas that allow the concept of intertextuality to blend and integrate with the anthropologically more ample concept of interdiscursivity and interculturality in the European Renaissance.

Notes

1. Stephen J. Greenblatt, *Learning to Curse: Essays in Early Modern Culture* (London: Routledge, 1992), 1–15.

2. Caroline Graham, "I Was Fooled into Sex by Lover's Twin," *The Sun,* 28 August 1993, 15.

3. Frances Muecke, *Plautus "Menaechmi"* (Bristol: Bristol Classical Press, 1987), 6–7 and ff. The structure of Terence's comedy, borrowed from the Aristotelian construction of tragedy, was adopted and theorized by sixteenth-century theoreticians. *See* particularly G. B. Giraldi Cinthio, *Discorso intorno al comporre delle commedie e delle tragedie* (1543), in *G. B. Giraldi Cinzio: Scritti critici,* ed. Camillo G. Crocetti (Milan: Marzorati, 1973), 169–224.

4. Cf. Giovanni Boccaccio, *Decameron,* ed. Vittore Branca, 2 vols. (Milan: Mondadori, 1985). *See also* 7.7. The device of the bed-trick is found in Plautus's *Amphitruo* and *Aulularia* and Terence's *Hecyra.*

5. On the comedy as a genre *see* Northrop Frye, "The Argument of Comedy," *English Institute Essays* 1948 (New York, 1949), 58–73 and *Anatomy of Criticism. Four Essays* (Princeton: Princeton University Press, 1951). On the relationship between the Italian and Elizabethan-Jacobean theater, *see* Leo Salingar, *Shakespeare and the Traditions of Comedy* (Cambridge: Cambridge University Press, 1974) and his *Dramatic Form in Shakespeare and the Jacobeans* (Cambridge: Cambridge University Press, 1986); Louise George Clubb, *Italian Drama in Shakespeare's Time* (New Haven: Yale University Press, 1989); J. R. Mulryne and Margaret Shewring, eds., *Theatre of the English and Italian Renaissance* (Basingstoke: Macmillan, 1991); Robert S. Miola, *Shakespeare and Classical Tragedy: The Influence of Seneca* (Oxford: Oxford University Press, 1992), and *Shakespeare and Classical Comedy: The Influence of Plautus and Terence* (Oxford: Oxford University Press, 1994).

6. The prologue in question, written for an unknown comedy, is traditionally associated with *La Calandria. See* Nino Borsellino and Roberto Mercuri, *Il teatro del Cinquecento* (Bari: Laterza, 1973), 14; *Commedie del Cinquecento,* ed. Nino Borsellino, 2 vols. (Milan: Feltrinelli, 1967), 2: 18–22.

7. Among the most suggestive examples of the prologue in English Renaissance theater, besides the famous "frame" of Shakespeare's *The Taming of the*

Shrew, see especially the Induction written by Webster in *The Malcontent* (1604) by John Marston and that in Francis Beaumont's *The Knight of the Burning Pestle* (1607).

8. Quotation from the edition by Guido Davico Bonino, *Il teatro italiano. La commedia del Cinquecento,* 3 vols. (Turin: Einaudi, 1977), 1: 67. All English translations, unless otherwise specified, are my own.

9. The androgynous motif in Santilla is however due to the girl's manifest aspiration to be a man, the better to move in the male-dominated society of the age. *See* on this point Roberto Alonge, *Struttura e ideologia nel teatro italiano fra '500 e '900* (Turin: Edizioni Stampatori, 1978), 9–31.

10. For a typology of the comic situations offered by the strategies of doubling in cinquecento theater, *see* Giulio Ferroni's lucid analysis "Tecniche del raddoppiamento nella commedia del Cinquecento", in *Il testo e la scena. Saggi sul teatro del Cinquecento* (Rome: Bulzoni Editore, 1980), 43–64.

11. Cf. Leo Salingar, *Shakespeare and the Traditions of Comedy,* 59–67; M. Marrapodi, "L'odissea di Pericles," *The Blue Guitar* 7–8 (1984–87): 118.

12. Wolfgang Riehle, *Shakespeare, Plautus and the Humanist Tradition* (Cambridge: D. S. Brewer, 1990), 279–83. See also Robert S. Miola, *Shakespeare and Classical Comedy. The Influence of Plautus and Terence,* 11ff. Possible references in *The Comedy of Errors* to Italian comedy and in particular to *commedia grave* have been noted in Louise George Clubb's fundamental work *Italian Drama in Shakespeare's Time,* 49–63.

13. *The Comedy of Errors,* ed. R. A. Foakes (London: Methuen, 1962), 2.2.168–76.

14. See to this regard Giulio Ferroni, "Il sistema comico della gemellarità," in *Il testo e la scena,* 65–84.

15. Robert S. Miola, *Shakespeare and Classical Comedy. The Influence of Plautus and Terence,* 41. The thematic inversion of the lock-out motif is recalled in the jest at the expense of Malvolio, whose physical confinement by Sir Toby Belch "suggests the spiritual incarcerations of Orsino and Olivia, their closed worlds now given concrete stage representation in Malvolio's cell" (45).

16. *See* Giulio Ferroni, "Tecniche del raddoppiamento nella commedia del Cinquecento," 63. According to Ferroni, the erotic plot is constructed not by specularity, but by rotation of the characters, who "follow and flee each other for many different reasons. [. . .] The escape from this rotation, in itself insuperable, is achieved by the appearance of Lelia's twin, Fabrizio, whose chance meeting with Isabella is sufficient to resolve all relationships" (63–64).

17. *Gl'Ingannati,* 2.6, in *Il teatro italiano. La commedia del Cinquecento,* ed. Guido Davico Bonino, 2: 131.

18. *Twelfth Night,* eds. J. M. Lothian and T. W. Craik (London: Methuen, 1975), 2.2.26–38.

19. N. Machiavelli, *Mandragola, Clizia,* ed. Gian Mario Anselmi and "Presentazione" by Ezio Raimondi (Milan: Mursia, 1984). The definition is by E. Raimondi, 9–10. By the same critic, *see* the important volume *Politica e commedia. Dal Beroaldo al Machiavelli* (Bologna: Il Mulino, 1972), especially pp. 173–264.

20. *See* to this regard Gratiana, Castiza's mother, in *The Revenger's Tragedy,* 2.1, by Thomas Middleton, in which there is possibly a derivation from *La Mandragola.*

21. On the "radical" ideology of Machiavelli's theater, *see* Giulio Ferroni's

"Mutazione" e "riscontro" nel teatro di Machiavelli e altri saggi sulla comme-dia del Cinquecento (Rome: Bulzoni Editore, 1972). According to Ferroni,

> Laughing [. . .] at the social, moral, and religious values of the Florentine bourgeois class, descending as far as possible into the "low life" of the comic world, the sage finds a more than merely literary accord with external "nature" and with the "times," rediscovering the active value of laughter, of comic invention, of the mocking smirk, of that aspect of humanity which tradition was wont to keep hidden and almost to condemn. (116).

Ferroni's essay, together with other important contributions on Machiavelli's theater and prose, is now included in *Machiavelli and the Discourse of Literature*, eds. Albert Russell Ascoli and Victoria Kahn (Ithaca: Cornell University Press, 1993), from which this quotation is taken.

22. The phrase is Nino Borsellino's in N. Borsellino and R. Mercuri, *Il teatro del Cinquecento*, 12. *See also* Nino Borsellino, "*Decameron* come teatro" and "Aretino e Boccaccio: conclusioni sulla scrittura scenica del Cinquecento," in *Rozzi e Intronati: esperienze e forme di teatro dal 'Decameron' al 'Candelaio'* (Rome: Bulzoni Editore, 1976), 13–50 and 213–28 respectively.

23. Clelia Falletti, "Il comico non integrato e la frantumazione degli statuti," in *Il teatro italiano nel Rinascimento,* eds. Fabrizio Cruciani and Daniele Seragnoli (Bologna: Il Mulino, 1987), 294.

24. In the subplot of John Marston's *The Insatiate Countess* (1613), derived from Bandello and from the twenty-sixth novel of Painter's *Second Tome* (1567), a double bed-trick is played by two wives to defend themselves from the attempts at seduction by each other's husbands. They safeguard conjugal integrity by means of a reciprocal interchange of beds: "we two will climb over our garden-pales, and come in that way [. . .] and thus wittily will we be bestowed, you into my house to your husband, and I into your house to my husband" (2.2.70–74). *See* J. Marston and Others, *The Insatiate Countess,* ed. Giorgio Melchiori (Manchester: Manchester University Press, 1984), 26–30.

25. *All's Well That Ends Well,* ed. G. K. Hunter (London: Methuen, 1959), 3.7.30–39.

26. *Ibid.,* 5.3.321–24.

27. Louise George Clubb, *Italian Drama in Shakespeare's Time,* 1–26.

28. Giulio Ferroni, *Le voci dell'istrione. Pietro Aretino e la dissoluzione del teatro* (Naples: Liguori, 1977), 13.

29. Nino Borsellino and Roberto Mercuri, *Il teatro del Cinquecento,* 54.

30. Giordano Bruno, *Candelaio,* 4.1. in *Il teatro italiano. La commedia del Cinquecento,* ed. Guido Davico Bonino, 3: 218–9.

31. *Candelaio,* 5.11, p. 257.

32. *Measure for Measure,* ed. J. W. Lever (London: Methuen, 1965), 1.3.53–54.

33. *Ibid.,* 3.1.243–56.

34. *See* William Dodd, *'Misura per Misura'. La trasparenza della comme-dia* (Milan: Il Formichiere, 1979), 130.

35. *See* Agostino Lombardo, "L'onesto duca," in *Measure for Measure. Dal testo alla scena,* ed. Mariangela Tempera (Bologna: Clueb, 1992), 9–16.

36. *The Decameron,* ed. W. E. Henley, 3 vols. (London: David Nutt, 1909), 3: 129.

37. *Ibid.,* xii.

38. Pietro Aretino, *Cortigiana*, 5.25, in *La commedia del Cinquecento*, ed. Guido Davico Bonino, 2: 313.

39. *See* Herbert G. Wright, *Boccaccio in England: From Chaucer to Tennyson* (London: The Athlone Press, 1957).

40. A. Piccolomini, *L'Amor costante*, 5.9, in *Commedie del Cinquecento*, ed. N. Borsellino, 1: 423.

41. Girolamo Bargagli, *La Pellegrina*, 5.6, in *Commedie del Cinquecento*, ed. N. Borsellino, 1: 552.

42. Louise George Clubb, *Italian Drama in Shakespeare's Time*, 73.

43. For a differently orientated feminist interpretation of Renaissance theater, *see* in particular Juliet Dusinberre, *Shakespeare and the Nature of Women* (Cambridge: Cambridge University Press, 1975); Carolyn Lenz, Gayle Greene, and Carol Neely, eds., *The Woman's Part: Feminist Criticism of Shakespeare* (Urbana: University of Illinois Press, 1980); Lisa Jardine, *Still Harping on Daughters: Women and Drama in the Age of Shakespeare* (Brighton: Harvester Press, 1983); Linda Woodbridge, *Women and the English Renaissance: Literature and the Nature of Womankind, 1540–1620* (Brighton: Harvester Press, 1984); Stevie Davies, *The Idea of Woman in Renaissance Literature: The Feminine Reclaimed* (Brighton: Harvester Press,1986); Valerie Wayne, ed., *The Matter of Difference. Materialist Feminist Criticism of Shakespeare* (New York: Harvester Wheatsheaf, 1991). *See also* Hugh Grady, *The Modernist Shakespeare: Critical Texts in a Material World* (Oxford: Clarendon Press, 1991), 235–45.

44. On the subversive theme of the adulterous woman and the affirmation of female identity in the rigid Elizabethan-Jacobean patriarchal society, *see* Catherine Belsey, *The Subject of Tragedy: Identity and Difference in Renaissance Drama* (London: Routledge, 1985), especially 129–91.

45. *See* on this point Andreas Mahler, "Italian Vices: Cross-Cultural Constructions of Temptation and Desire in English Renaissance Drama," in *Shakespeare's Italy: Functions of Italian Locations in Renaissance Drama*, eds. M. Marrapodi, A. J. Hoenselaars, M. Cappuzzo, and L. Falzon Santucci (Manchester: Manchester University Press, 1993), 49–68.

46. John Webster, *The White Devil*, ed. John Russell Brown (Manchester: Manchester University Press, 1977), 3.2.225–31.

47. Jonathan Dollimore, *Radical Tragedy: Religion, Ideology and Power in the Drama of Shakespeare and His Contemporaries*, 2d ed. (New York: Harvester Wheatsheaf, 1989), 241.

48. *Othello*, ed. M. R. Ridley (London: Methuen, 1971). 4.3.93–105.

49. *See* Michele Marrapodi, "Let her witness it," *Nuovi Annali della Facoltà di Magistero dell'Università di Messina*, 2 (1984): 403–30.

50. W. Painter, *The Palace of Pleasure*, ed. J. Jacobs, 4 vols., "The thirty-second nouell," 3: 354.

51. Philip Massinger, *The Maid of Honour*, in *The Plays and Poems of Philip Massinger*, 2 vols. (Oxford: Oxford University Press, 1976), 1: 5.2.267–72.

52. *Ibid.*, 5.2.215–220. On the ethic-moral theme of the play, *see* Russ McDonald, "High Seriousness and Popular Form: The Case of *The Maid of Honour*," in *Philip Massinger: A Critical Reassessment*, ed. D. Howard (Cambridge: Cambridge University Press, 1985), 83–116; M. Marrapodi, *La Sicilia nella drammaturgia giacomiana e carolina* (Rome: Herder, 1989), 72–77.

53. James Shirley, *Love's Cruelty*, in *The Dramatic Works and Poems of*

James Shirley, eds. William Gifford and Alexander Dyce, 2 vols. (London: John Murray, 1833), 4.1., 2: 238.

54. John Ford, *Love's Sacrifice,* in *The Works of John Ford,* eds. William Gifford and Alexander Dyce, 2 vols. (London: James Toovey, 1869), 5.1., 2: 92–93.

55. James Shirley, *The Lady of Pleasure,* ed. Ronald Huebert (Manchester: Manchester University Press, 1986), 3.2.349–52.

56. *See* Katsuhiko Nogami, "The Rationalization of Conflicts in John Ford's *The Lady's Trial,*" *Studies in English Literature* 32 (summer, 1992), 341–59.

57. John Ford, *The Lady's Trial,* in *The Works of John Ford,* eds. W. Gifford and A. Dyce, 3.3., p. 55.

58. *Ibid.,* 5.2., p. 89.

59. Stephen Greenblatt, *Shakespearean Negotiations: The Circulation of Social Energy in Renaissance England* (Oxford: Clarendon Press, 1988), 7.

"Worse than Procne": The Sister as Avenger in the English Renaissance

MARIANGELA TEMPERA

Procne and the "Scelus Novum"

AT a key moment in *Titus Andronicus,* an early tragedy that is steeped in classical culture at least as much as it is in blood, the bereaved and severely tried Titus solemnly promises a horrible death to the louts who have raped and mutilated his daughter Lavinia:

> For worse than Philomel you used my daughter,
> And worse than Procne I will be revenged.[1]

Shakespeare was here engaging in a well-known rhetorical exercise, a peculiar form of imitation of classical sources that consists in declaring a model and then outdoing it. The exercise, which very often took the form of inventing a *scelus novum,* a new crime in the tradition of Seneca's theater, should not be mistaken for a sadistic pandering to the readers' and audiences' basest tastes; rather, it was a bravura performance, a new writer's homage to and competition with his predecessors. The young Shakespeare, full of theatrical talent but without the university learning that his contemporaries could flaunt in their writings, was so eager to prove his worth as an imitator of the classics that he set himself an impossible task.

While the severely mutilated Lavinia is on stage to confirm that it is quite possible to treat a victim "worse than Philomel," Titus's threat that he will act "worse than Procne" is bound to remain idle. From the wide collection of mythical examples he could have referred to, in fact, Shakespeare selected one that was generally seen to represent a complete dead end for imitators: whereas Philomela's story was repeatedly woven into Renaissance literature as a mythical explanation of the source of

71

poetry (she is the voice of the nightingale, whose sad song inspires the poet), her sister's was very seldom reclaimed and rein-
terpreted, as if writers and playwrights had quietly agreed that
she was too hot to handle. There is no doubt that Procne outdid
Medea (the evil mother) as unequivocably as Medea had outdone
Atreus (the evil uncle). Imitating Procne, therefore, was a challenge, and it would be a rare storyteller indeed who managed to
invent a character capable of outdoing her.

Greek mythology is quite explicit on the relative responsibil-
ities of its most famous evil mothers: Medea is a Colchian witch,
a stranger to Corinthian society who reacts with unprecedented
brutality when her husband forsakes her for a younger woman.
Procne is an Athenian virgin cast among barbarians as Tereus's
wife. Not only should she know better than resorting to means
of revenge as primitive as Medea's, but, the tale implies, she has
less cause to do so. Other than raping, mutilating, and imprisoning her sister, in fact, Tereus does nothing to threaten Procne's
status as his wife and queen. In assuming the role of avenger,
Procne explodes from within the fiction of wedded bliss that
Tereus had kept up after raping Philomela and selects a course
of action that will eventually bring down the family and the
state. She refuses to "love and be silent," takes revenge in her
own hands, and turns her nurturing qualities into a lethal
weapon. Her unforgivable sin is not so much the murdering of
her own child as the overreacting to her husband's escapade.
Postclassical writers avoided wrestling with this intractable
character in favor of eulogizing her sister, even if this meant
playing down sweet Philomela's very real involvement in Procne's revenge plot.

Yet, no Philomela story is complete without Procne; whatever
approach to the myth writers may choose, the two sisters depend
on each other to weave a pattern of female revenge that is unique
in literature. From Ovid to Shakespeare, via French and Italian
rewritings, the myth acquires new elements and sheds old ones,
but cannot ever completely solve the problems that it posits
on a literary scene where avenging fathers and brothers were
plentiful but an avenging sister was a dangerous oddity, so dangerous that even Shakespeare would eventually settle for a conventional solution that phased Procne out of her own myth.

The Sources: Ovid and "Ovid Moralisé"

Ovid was so deeply embedded in the culture of Renaissance
England that his direct influence on individual authors becomes

difficult to gauge.[2] Though not the only source for the Procne myth, his tale, both in Arthur Golding's translation and through its most popular French rewriting in *Ovid moralisé*, represents a mandatory point of entry for a study of versions of the Procne story in the English Renaissance. In *Metamorphoses,* the poet strays from his prevailing pattern of virgins ravished by gods to portray a particularly gruesome scene of domestic horror.[3] As always with Ovid, the tale is fast paced, with little room for moralizing, and told with a turn of phrase so economical that the task of the translators becomes almost impossible.

Pandion, king of Athens, rewards his powerful ally Tereus by giving him in marriage his daughter Procne; it should be a perfect match, but neither the wedding ceremony nor the birth of Itys is blessed by the gods. Five years later, Procne asks her husband to return to Athens and fetch her younger sister Philomela. He complies but, on seeing his sister-in-law, is overwhelmed by a sudden passion for her. In Ovid's tale, Tereus is only partially responsible for what happens next: he rapes Philomela not only because his natural lust is excited by her beauty, but also because all the men from his country are inclined to Venus. Philomela shouts her rage against a relative who, in raping her, has hopelessly confused the boundaries of the family; she will demand revenge in front of the people or, if isolated in the woods, from the gods. To silence her, Tereus cuts off her tongue, imprisons her, and tells Procne that her sister is dead. Having acquired a new voice through her weaving skills, Philomela sends Procne a tapestry that relates the entire story.[4] Procne reads and "(mirum potuisse) silet" (line 583: "She held hir peace (a wondrous thing it is she should so doe"). For a moment Procne is poised on the brink of the same silence that has engulfed her sister, but then she breaks free in words and deeds. Taking advantage of the freedom that Bacchic rituals offer women, she roams the woods and rescues her sister: "Terribilis Progne furiisque agitata doloris, / Bacche, tuas simulat" (lines 595–96: "and where the sting of sorrow which she feeles / Enforceth hir to furiousnesse, she feynes it to proceede / Of Bacchus motion"). Like a character from a Senecan tragedy, Procne is beside herself, prey to a *furor* that begets the worst actions, so much so that she dares profane the rites of Bacchus by feigning the holy frenzy and by using the religious garb to smuggle her sister into the palace. Here, while Philomela mimes her shame, Procne plots her revenge: she does not even consider taking the matter to the people or leaving it in the hands of the

gods, the socially approved options that had first been selected
by Philomela; she examines various ways of killing Tereus—
"artificem" (line 615), the culprit, says Ovid, "the worker of *our*
shame" (emphasis added) expands Golding, thus emphasizing
the concept that Tereus has disgraced both sisters. Lear-like in
her impotent rage, Procne strives for some unknown deed of
revenge: "magnum quodcumque paravi; / quid sit, adhuc dubito"
(lines 618–19: "The thing that I doe purpose on is great, what
ere it is, / I know not what it may be yet"). The tale culminates
at this point, where Procne "faces an intolerable conflict
amongst roles of sister, wife, and mother" and, against all conventions, chooses to privilege the role of sister.[5] When her maternal instinct seems to prevail and prevent her from sacrificing
her child, the final consideration that condemns Itys, this minia-
ture replica of his father, is one of pride in her own lineage and
acknowledgment of the unworthiness of her husband: "cui sis
nupta, vide, Pandione nata, marito!" (line 634: "Seest thou not /
Thou daughter of Pandion what a husband thou hast got?"). Both
sisters turn on Itys in perfect accord and act as one to the very
end: Procne stabs first, but Philomela is fast behind; together
they boil and roast the corpse, together they prepare the banquet
and break the horrible truth to Tereus.[6] If, after the meal, Procne cannot hide her cruel joy, Philomela too, on throwing Itys'
head at his father, wishes, more than ever, "that able she might
be / Hir inward joy with worthie wordes to witnesse franke and
free" (line 660). The last part of the tale is dominated by this
need of the sisters to tell Tereus their story, a need which is cut
short by the sudden metamorphosis.

Ovid "is far from composing parables or preaching sermons;
he merely tells fascinating stories; and yet, in so doing, he fur-
nishes material for many a sermon."[7] One of the earliest and
most influential of these sermons is the *Ovid moralisé,* which
attempts to reconcile Ovid's tale not only with the principles of
Christianity but also with the conventions of French medieval
romance.[8] After Procne "fut a mari donnee" (line 2223: "was
given away in marriage") by King Pandion, the story meanders
into lengthy descriptions of Tereus's visit to Pandion's court in
order to fetch Philomela and of the irresistible beauty of the
princess. Raped and mutilated, Philomela sends a girl servant
to Procne with the tale-telling tapestry. The queen "son panser
pas ne descuevre" (line 3454: "does not reveal her thoughts")
and quietly follows the servant back to Philomela's prison. The
place of the Bacchic frenzy is here taken by a folktale ruse more

in keeping with the convention of the "moralisé"; the rage is there, though, and it resurfaces unimpaired in the queen's way of gaining entry to the house: "Et Progné fiert et hurte et bote / Tant que l'uis desconfist et brise" (lines 3472–73: "And Procne kicks and hits and beats until the door gives way and collapses"). Back to the palace with Philomela, the queen despairs of finding a fitting form of revenge until Itys has the misfortune of appearing in front of her. She will kill him and serve him to the king, "Einsi puet sa seror vangier" (line 3542: "So she can avenge her sister"). The banquet is prepared with sinister care, from the detail of the beautiful white tablecloth to Procne's promise that, if Tereus agrees to come alone, "ele del tot servira" (line 3567: "She will serve him in everything"). It is this "promise of something akin to the erotic pleasure Tereus sought from Philomena" that turns the banquet into a fitting punishment for the rape.[9] The horror is further tuned down by yet another element borrowed from the popular tradition: the riddle that Procne presents to her husband when he inquires about Itys: "Partie an as dedanz ton cors / Et partie an as par defors" (lines 3620–21: "You have part of him inside your body and part outside"). In portraying the mythical queen, the author repeatedly gives to her courses of action and strategies of discourse that are more in keeping with medieval tradition than with the original mode of the tale. It is, therefore, not surprising that metamorphosis itself should be seen in a new light: no longer a means of avoiding death through change, it becomes a revenge of the gods on three people who have proved unworthy of human shape.

Chaucer and Gower: The Helpless Victim and the Woman Scorned

The material inherited from Ovid hardly vouchsafed the inclusion of the bloodthirsty sisters in a catalog of "good women," yet Chaucer chose to engage in the arduous task of turning a horror story into "a tale of the pathetic."[10] In his "Philomela," the action is dominated by a Tereus so villainous that the narrator is forced to wonder why God should create such monsters; the two sisters are portrayed as his helpless victims, steeped in tears from beginning to end. The result is a carefully sanitized version of the tale that blurs the horrible details of Philomela's rape and mutilation and cuts off entirely her cry for revenge. Not even

Chaucer, however, can completely obliterate the disruptive presence of Procne. On receiving her sister's tapestry,

> No word she spak, for sorwe and ek for rage,
> But feynede hire to gon on pilgrymage
> To Bacus temple.[11]

Her "rage" is reluctantly recorded, but has no outlet in this text; it is hinted at and then ignored, as if inconsistent with the "pilgrymage" that, quite aptly in the context of the catalog, takes the place of the Bacchic frenzy. Her silence is not a temporary pause followed by the torrent of verbal abuse that in other versions runs parallel to the action of revenge; rather, "it is as if Philomela's condition had infected the narrative": Procne does not speak another line of dialogue, silenced by the discovery of her husband's crime as effectively as Philomela was by his sword.[12] She goes to her sister's prison but Chaucer leaves them there, crying in each other's arms:

> Allas! the wo, the compleynt, and the mone
> That Procne upon hire doumbe syster maketh!
> In armes everych of hem other taketh,
> And thus I late hem in here sorwe dwelle.

> (lines 2379–82)

This is the socially acceptable response to Tereus's crime: Procne should drown her rage in a sea of tears and leave revenge to God. The moral is more pointed and in keeping with the advisory character of a tale addressed to women: "Ye may be war of men, if that yow liste" (line 2387). But Ovid's text is so famous that just by hinting at it Chaucer recalls the whole story, murders and metamorphoses included, to the mind of its readers, and of the narrator as well, since another line of advice, "Ne serve yow as a morderour or a knave" (line 2390), would only make sense if the entire story had been told; in this severely mutilated version of the myth, it simply lingers there, at the surface of the text, as one more sign of "the narrator's imperfect suppression of the unacceptable."[13]

Gower is far more faithful to Ovid, in the *moralisé* variety. He skips the omens at the wedding and the birth, and contextualizes Procne's request to see her sister in the homely atmosphere of a bedroom scene. When he grants her request,

> sche. . . . there as he lay,
> Began him in hire armes clippe,
> And kist him with hir softe lippe.[14]

While Philomela is isolated in the usual prison, Gower stays with her and explores her thoughts. From appeals to Jupiter, she turns to Procne: "if ye knewe / Of myn astat, ye wolde [. . .] do vengance / On him that is so fals a man" (lines 5759–63). She knows her sister well because, on receiving the cloth, she first cries and faints, and then she "swerth . . . It schal be venged otherwise" (lines 5794–95). Once Philomela has been stealthily introduced into her room, Procne addresses Cupid and Venus with words that invite a new, more conventional reading of her plight: she reminds the gods that Tereus's crime is unforgivable because

> I have be trewe in mi degre, . . .
> . . . .
> And never love in other place,
> Bot al only the king of Thrace,
> Which is mi lord and I his wif

> (lines 5829–5833)

Twice to blame because he "forsok" a *faithful* wife, one who had scrupulously kept her vows, Tereus should therefore experience the wrath of the gods of love. Failing that, Procne will take revenge in her own hands, and "It schal be wreke, / That al the world therof schal speke" (lines 5869–70), a promise of *scelus novum* that Gower inserts in his text imitating his source and then undermines by turning Procne's tragedy strictly into a husband-wife affair that will turn gruesome, he seems to imply, simply because Hell hath no fury "like a woman scorned." The reduction of myth to domestic tragedy is further aided by another addition to the source: Procne pleads sickness so that "sche moste hire chambres kepe / And as hir liketh wake and slepe" (lines 5873–74). In this homely context, Procne is reduced from her unique position in myth of cold-blooded avenging sister to the less threatening stereotype of the deranged housewife who kills because she is mad with sorrow.

Where Ovid expresses, in passing, a sense of the general untrustworthiness of mankind, men and women, and Chaucer advises women to beware of all men, the moral here is more complex; within the text, Procne "chitreth out in hir langage / What falshod is in marriage" (lines 6011–12), thus confirming the wholesale condemnation of all husbands already seen in Chaucer. As befits a warning from man to man, rather than man to woman, however, the main moral is focused on Tereus's punishment: "Amans" beware, because should he be inclined "To gete of love be Ravine" (line 6050), he may end up like Tereus.

Calfhill-Correr: The Sister as Avenger

On the evening of 6 September 1566, as part of the celebrations for Queen Elizabeth's visit to Oxford, "was played in the Common Hall at Christ's Church a Tragedy in Latin named 'Progne.'"[15] Like the other two contributions of the distinguished Oxford scholars to the queen's entertainment (Richard Edwards's *Marcus Geminus* and *Palæmon and Arcite*) the play is lost and can only be reconstructed through the somewhat muddled account given by John Berebock. It was, he claims, "a very fine and costly entertainment" and "the Queen and nobles were wonderfully and very exceedingly delighted."[16] A fairly conventional fare of romance and Roman history was thus followed, for the first time on record, by the staging of an episode from Ovid's *Metamorphoses,* a particularly gruesome one, hardly suitable for light entertainment.[17] The author is given as James Calfhill, a Canon of Christ Church who does not appear to have had any further contacts with the stage and who seems to have spared himself the effort of producing an original play: Berebock's synopsis "makes it highly probable that Calfhill merely adapted *Progne,* a Latin play by Gregorio Corraro, published at Venice in 1558."[18] Calfhill's source may also have been the fairly accurate translation into Italian of Correr's play that Ludovico Domenichi published in 1561 and tried to pass off as his own work.[19]

It is unfortunate that Berebock, after treating us to a vivid account of the staging of the prologue, should continue to provide a confused anthology of Ovid's verse for the rest of the play, and one, moreover, that includes the weaving episode, absent from Correr. Berebock's account of a prologue delivered by the ghost of Diomedes and interrupted by the Furies represents the strongest argument in favor of the identification of Correr as Calfhill's model. It would be surprising indeed if the two writers had independently selected the same device to introduce the main plot.

"Imitatur in hac tragoedia Senecam in Thyeste" (In this tragedy I imitate Seneca's *Thyestes*), Correr tells us in his "Argumentum." This declaration of intents is quite unnecessary: Seneca is present in every detail, from structure (the ghost, the choir, the messengers), to content (the emphasis on the *scelus novum*, the detailed description of horrors, the *furor* that drives the characters), to direct quotations.[20] Moreover, while not strictly adhering to the unity of time, Correr "made a determined if not altogether successful effort to create the illusion of a few hours passing."[21] When selecting from myth material that might be suitable for a "Senecan" tragedy, the Philomela story is an obvious choice for its immediate echoes of the *Thyestes* and *Medea* plots. It does, however, present an almost impossible challenge to the playwright in that the protagonist is soon deprived of her tongue and reduced to a silent presence that defies the laws of theater.

Accordingly, Philomela has a minor role in Correr's tragedy: since the tragedy opens with Tereus's return to Thrace, his whole visit to Pandion's palace is missing, and she is first described by him as a seasick passenger on his ship; he praises her beauty only to bemoan the sickness that has destroyed it; the rape scene and Philomela's furious verbal reaction are related by a servant; even her ingenuity has been deleted, since her tale of woe is told to Procne by the same servant. When Procne breaks into her prison, killing the guardians with the help of the other bacchantes, Philomela briefly comes to life in her sister's description, which is surprisingly naturalistic in its references to bruised arms and stinking feet. From that point onward, she is stage-directed by her sister and merely figures as a helper of the real protagonist of the play.

The betrayed wife is as much a victim as the ravished virgin; in fact, we are led to believe that she may have been ravished herself since Correr transforms Tereus from a precious ally into a victorious enemy of the Athenians and Procne from a reward amicably bestowed into a prey of war snatched by force. On hearing the news of her sister's plight, this Procne does not observe even a second of crafty silence; rather, she immediately unleashes a stream of verbal abuse that will not relent until the end of the tragedy; in finding expression for her most Senecan *furor*, Correr exploits all the resources of his first-rate classical education. He weaves into Procne's words a web of quotations so intricate and fascinating that source hunting tends to supersede interpretation as an approach to the text. This is particularly

unfortunate because one loses sight of the novelty in characterization that represents the play's greatest virtue.

Correr's Procne sees Tereus's crime as being first of all against
Pandion's line; revenge is, therefore, a family duty to be undertaken by whoever (man or woman) is in a position to do so.
Second, it is a crime against both sisters: "hic die, hic est . . . /
quo violenti *stupra* tyranni / datur ulcisci" (lines 561–63: "this is
the day we'll be revenged of the cruel tyrant's *rapes*" [emphasis
added]). The queen asks the Furies to come witness a *scelus
novum* to fit Tereus's crime and ends her invocation with the
upbeat "Femina vincat!" (line 610: "Victory to the woman!"); her
revenge will teach husbands to beware of their wives and to
think carefully before they betray them. In killing Itys she will
outdo Medea, here presented as killer and quarterer of her
brother, not as a murderous mother. After acknowledging that
grief and anger have dissolved her previous identity—"non sum
mea" (line 640: "I am not myself")—Procne engages in a painful
search for a new self: when the nurse extols the sacred duty of
the mother, she replies, in Domenichi's translation that expands
on the original:

> Ma, dimmi, che dee far sorella offesa
> sî altamente come io son?
> Dunque ella non dee curar onor, nome et vendetta?

(lines 1082–84: "But tell me, what should a sister do who has
been so deeply injured as I have? She should not care for honor,
name, and revenge?"). When the search is completed, a new
person is born: no longer wife or mother, but "tota sum (fateor)
soror" (line 753: "I confess, I am all sister"). And again, Domenichi goes further: "Tutta sorella io son, tutta vendetta" (line 1244:
"I am all sister, all revenge"). Correr's contribution to a new
reading of the Procne myth lies in his open acknowledgment of
sisterhood as a stronger bond than motherhood.

The select company at Christ Church did not witness the actual eating of the child because the killing and quartering of
Itys are related by a duly horrified messenger who, rather un-
convincingly, claims to have seen the avenger and her sister
working as one in the kitchen in a cruel parody of women's
nurturing role. The spectators, however, were treated firsthand
to Tereus's horrified discovery. When the author needs to make
Philomela's presence felt on a stage, Procne is there to give the
right order: "Philomena, pueri profer extincti caput / in ora

patris" (lines 991–92: "Philomela, present the head of the dead child to his father"). Having performed her traditional task, Philomela is phased out again: the tragedy closes on a shouting match between husband and wife that reduces the myth to the claustrophobic dimension of a domestic tragedy and leaves the characters trapped in a private hell that has no room for the relief of metamorphosis.

Pettie and Gascoigne: The Lady Procne and the Bale of Beauty

After the performance in front of the queen, the gruesome tale of Progne and Philomela returns in the hands of storytellers and poets. The year 1576 sees two versions in print, one in prose as part of *A Petite Pallace of Pettie His Pleasure,* the other in verse in George Gascoigne's *The Complaint of Philomene.*

From the very title of Pettie's tale, "Tereus and Progne," the doomed couple overshadow Philomela as protagonists of this "romanticized and psychologized version."[22] Ovid is there, but prettified almost beyond recognition. Far from being a prey of war or a reward to an important ally, the "Lady Progne" is here a young princess celebrated throughout Greece for her outstanding beauty. King Tereus falls in love with her after being visited by her image in his dreams, courts her at length, and finally conquers her. Pettie omits the evil omens that traditionally accompany the wedding ceremony and picks up the thread of their story after five years of wedded bliss, when their "most loyal love . . . through lust was turned to loathsome hate."[23] Lust makes Tereus rape his sister-in-law; when she uses her voice to curse him and threatens to appeal to her sister and to her father for revenge, he, "like a bloody butcher" maims her (62). After imprisoning Philomela, Tereus breaks the news of her death to Procne and assuages her grief with promises of devotion: "I will be to you instead of a father and a sister" (63). It is a mockery of the love that was the key note of the opening section of the tale, a fiction that encloses Procne within the walls of the palace and isolates her in the stifling embrace of a treacherous husband who claims that he can take the place of any other affection. It works, at least temporarily: his "loving words caused her somewhat to cease from her sorrow" (63).

On receiving her sister's weaving, Procne understands Tereus's guilt, "yet (a marvellous thing a woman could do so) she concealed the matter secretly, hoping to be revenged more speedily" (64–65). However, she soon translates her anger into words that denounce her husband's duplicity, but fill the *scelus novum* promise with a moralizing twist: "I can and will devise such exquisite punishment for this tyrant, that it shall fear all that come after from the like filthiness" (67). While allowing his Procne to envisage herself as an avenger with a mission, the narrator is careful to distance himself from a horrible deed that no amount of artistic manipulation—of fleshing out the rhetoric and playing down the horror—can render acceptable; in Pettie's view, Procne's stated objective of setting an example that might deter future rapists does not justify her brutality; before embarking on the last part of his narrative the author warns us that, when all is said, we will have to agree with him that "her fury exceeded his folly, and her severity in punishing, his cruelty in offending" (67).

An excruciatingly cute Itys, who has learned his "Christcross" and pesters his distraught mother for a cuddle, is rejected with an "Away imp of impiety!" which must be the worst line ever attributed to Procne (68). Pettie cuts through all the doubts, all the ambivalence that other writers had underlined in the queen, to leave her wholly without justification. The comparison between Itys and her mutilated sister, the duty to herself and to her family, all the extenuating circumstances of her decision disappear to make room for an act so repulsive that it could only be performed by a woman (and other mythical murderesses are mentioned to prove the point). In preparing the bloody banquet, Procne is helped by Philomela, but the strong emotional link between the two sisters that was so prominent in Correr's tragedy is here completely missing. The drama is presented as wholly internal to the nuclear family of Procne and Tereus to the point where, after a quick reference to the metamorphosis, the summing up reviews the case of the murderous pair and comes to the conclusion that they are equally guilty. It is a conclusion that somewhat contradicts prior statements about Procne's outdoing any man in wickedness and seems to have been added more because it offered the opportunity for a series of well-balanced phrases than because it qualifies the prior rash condemnation of Procne. As for Philomela, she has disappeared entirely from the tale, as if her story had been merely a pretext to explore the madness that turned the Lady Procne into a murderess.

From Pettie's neglect Philomela is rescued by Gascoigne,

whose *The Complaint of Philomene* (1576) tells her story within a frame that introduces the sorrowful song of the nightingale and then calls upon a personification of Nemesis to explain its meaning. With the quick, balladlike rhythm of his quatrains, Gascoigne adapts Ovid's story to the tastes of his audience by interjecting elements of popular wit; the catalog of clichés is so long that it nearly succeeds in turning the primitive horror of the original plot into an old wives' tale. In the opening lines, the "bale of beauty" motif establishes the charms of Pandion's daughters, rather than Tereus's lust, as the primary cause of all the doom that follows; it is because of her beauty that Procne attracts her Thracian suitor, while his wealth is the main reason why Pandion's "eldest daughter chosen was, / To serve this king in bedde."[24] What follows is a "lively, but rather crude poem . . .: the crucial incidents are quickened by dialogue, but also coarsened in broadside style by gory details"[25]—the goriest being the kiss that Tereus plants on Philomela's bloodied mouth after mutilating her.

Gascoigne's main objective is to universalize the story, as far as possible, to make it the occasion for a general praise of women; thus, Philomela's weaving is exhalted as an example of "womans witte, / Which sodainly in queintest chance, / Can best it selfe acquit" (192). The entire issue of voicelessness, extended from Philomela's mutilated mouth to Procne's self-control, is trivialized by a comment on the oddity of women's silence:

> O silence seldom seene,
> That women counsell keepe,
> The cause was this, she wackt hir wits
> And lullde hir tong on sleepe.
>
> (192)

Again "wit" is a key word, one that unites the sisters with womankind at large: Gascoigne is interested in enhancing what they have in common with other women, rather than what makes them unique.

After freeing her sister, Procne begins to speak with an angry voice that strikes a surprisingly original note in the context of this rather pedestrian retelling of Ovid's story: "My wrongs shall lende me lawes" (194) establishes her as a fellow victim bent on avenging herself as well as her sister. This point is most effectively made when Ovid's "quae tibi membra pudorem / abstuler-

unt, ferro rapiam" (lines 616–17: "or cut / Away those members
which haue thee to such dishonour put") is expanded into

> Or let me carve with knife,
> The wicked Instrument,
> Wherewith he, thee, *and me* abusde.
>
> (194; emphasis added)

When she conceives the idea of killing Itys, Gascoigne records
more than the usual share of doubts and second thoughts; eventually, he links her decision to an acknowledgment that women
are as honor bound as men to take revenge into their own hands.
Before surrendering to the horror of Procne's ruthless deed, he
plays up any extenuating circumstance for his avenger. Taking
his cue from Ovid's "Pandione nata" (line 634), Gascoigne weaves
into Procne's words a Medea-like awareness of being a foreigner
at Tereus's court:

> *Pandions* line (quoth she)
> Remember still your race,
> And never marke the subtil shewes
> Of any soul in *Thrace.*
>
> (196)

From this point onward, the author takes every opportunity to
oppose the sisters to Tereus as Greeks to a Thracian. But the
values of civilization that they should embody are forsaken when
Procne, aided by her sister, quarters and cooks Itys for Tereus's
banquet. At this stage, the sisters lose any sympathy the author
might have previously bestowed on them; when Procne cannot
hide "hir joy of griefe" (197) in telling the father the horrible
truth, she proves to be indeed more primitive than Medea.

In appealing to her "line," Gascoigne's Procne reminds herself
that revenge should be embraced not as an option but as a holy
duty: "You should degenerate, / If right revenge you slake" (196).
It is a statement fully in keeping with the ethos of the contemporary theatrical scene, but one that required softening and qualification in the context of the *Complaint:* when drawing the
moral of the tale, Nemesis piously states the principle that "men
must leave revenge to Gods, / What wrong soever raigne" (201).

Shakespeare and the Maiming of the Myth

Young Shakespeare was so deeply intrigued by the Philomela
myth that, around 1594, he rooted in it two completely different

works: the highly formalized "Lucrece" poem and the crude *Titus Andronicus*. "Come Philomel, that sing'st of ravishment," cries the virtuous Roman lady, determined to restore through suicide her reputation irrevocably tarnished by Tarquinius.[26] She links the very material knife that will pierce her heart to the thorn that pricks the breast of the nightingale and, constantly renewing her pain, is responsible for her melodious voice, a post-Ovidian image that appeals to poets of all ages. The rape victim will, in "Lucrece," take action against herself rather than the rapist; not surprisingly, then, the Procne side of the myth is quietly dismissed as irrelevant.

The same effacement of the avenging sister's plot operates in *Titus Andronicus,* but with more difficulty, since revenge is here a very central issue. In introducing the myth, Shakespeare cuts through all the embellishments of the romance tradition to go straight back, even physically, to Ovid's book: no nightingales and pricking thorns, but the original bleak story of rape and mutilation. By using the Philomela story as the source of a new cycle of rape and revenge, Shakespeare "reaches to outdo the Roman poet for pathos, and Seneca as well for horror."[27] In Shakespeare's openly fictitious Rome, the Philomela myth cuts across all cultural boundaries, even those one would be inclined to judge impenetrable. Romans, Goths, even the Moor Aaron, can all refer to it in a type of verbal shorthand that implies deep familiarity. It is, in fact, the strongest cultural link between the two warring factions, and so, it becomes a leitmotiv in the all-important rape scene, where it is established by Aaron's flippant forecast that Bassanius's "Philomel must lose her tongue today" (2.3.43). Even worse, it is a source of inspiration for Lavinia's rapists, who will cut off her hands as well as her tongue to prevent her from imitating Philomela's weaving. Throughout the empire, Roman education has thus become "the teacher and rationalizer of heinous deeds."[28]

From Ovid, the characters in *Titus Andronicus* learn their crimes but not their revenge. Lavinia partakes of the characteristics of both Philomela and Procne (she is presented as a virgin, but is in fact a wife; she is at the same time bashful and outspoken; she is both victim and participant in the revenge plot), but she has no sisters; she has more than the average quota of male relatives, though, and, in a world supervised by indifferent gods, revenge is, most emphatically, theirs. By materially killing the rapists, with his daughter's assistance, Titus does the right thing; his act should mark the beginning of a new cycle in the life of the Andronici, their rebirth into Roman society. But the avenging father remains hopelessly entangled in the Philomela myth, so often evoked by the characters.

When, in his madness, he boasts that he will outdo Procne's revenge, he embarks in a spiral of violence that will lead to wholesale slaughter. The secretive gloating of the mythical sisters over Tereus's solitary meal is substituted with Titus's bravura performance in front of a large audience that includes "*Emperor and Empress, with Aemilius, Tribunes, and others*" (5.3.16 s.d.); with them, we are treated to a new version of the bloody banquet, but one in which Lavinia's sudden death by her father's hand hopelessly upstages Tamora's partaking of her sons' bodies. To substitute for Procne's grief in sacrificing her own child to revenge, Titus must look elsewhere in the great storehouse of tales that is Rome's legacy to the Renaissance: "as woeful as Virginius was" (5.3.49), he ultimately resorts to claiming as his model another avenging father. Lavinia's death collapses the carefully wrought imitation of the Philomela myth; it also triggers the implosion of violence that brings down many of the protagonists, because metamorphosis cannot intervene to halt their descent into abject brutality by shifting them to another dimension.

Notes

1. William Shakespeare, *Titus Andronicus,* ed. Eugene M. Waith (Oxford: Oxford University Press, 1984), 5.2.194–95.

2. For a survey of Ovid's influence on Renaissance writing, *see* Frederick S. Boas, *Ovid and the Elizabethans* (London: Morrison and Gibb, 1947); Leonard Barkan, *The Gods Made Flesh* (New Haven: Yale University Press, 1986); Charles Martindale, ed., *Ovid Renewed* (Cambridge: Cambridge University Press, 1988); and Jonathan Bate, *Shakespeare and Ovid* (Oxford: Clarendon Press, 1993).

3. Ovid, *Metamorphoses,* ed. Moritz Haupt (Dublin: Weidmann, 1966), vol. I, book 6, lines 424–674. All quotations are from this edition; all translations from Arthur Golding's version (*The XV Bookes of P. Ovidius Naso, entytuled Metamorphosis,* 1567).

4. For the significance of this new alphabet, *see* Patricia Klindienst Joplin, "The Voice of the Shuttle Is Ours," in *Rape and Representation,* eds. Lynn A. Higgins and Brenda R. Silver (New York: Columbia University Press, 1991), 35–64.

5. Barkan, *The Gods Made Flesh,* 61.

6. For the collapsing of ritual in this mixture of cooking practices, *see* Jane O. Newman, "'And let mild women to him lose their mildness': Philomela, Female Violence, and Shakespeare's *The Rape of Lucrece,*" *Shakespeare Quarterly,* vol. 45, no. 3 (1994): 319.

7. Hermann Fränkel, *Ovid: A Poet Between Two Worlds* (Berkeley and Los Angeles: University of California Press, 1945), p. 83.

8. "'Philomena', de Chrétien de Troyes," in *Ovid Moralisé*, ed. C. de Boer, (Amsterdam: Johannes Müller, 1920), vol. 2, lines 2217–3856. For the attribution of the tale to Chrétien de Troyes, *see* Elisabeth Schulze-Busaker, "*Philomena:* une révision de l'attribution de l'oeuvre," *Romania*, vol. 107, no. 4 (1986), 459–85.

9. E. Jane Burns, *Bodytalk: When Women Speak in Old French Literature* (Philadelphia: University of Pennsylvania Press, 1993), 134.

10. Robert Worth Frank Jr., *Chaucer and "The Legend of Good Women"* (Cambridge: Harvard University Press, 1972), 140.

11. "The Legend of Good Women," in *The Complete Works of Geoffrey Chaucer,* ed. F. N. Robinson, 2d ed. (London: Oxford University Press, 1974), lines 2374–76.

12. Elizabeth D. Harvey, "Speaking of Tongues: The Poetics of the Feminine Voice in Chaucer's *Legend of Good Women*," in *New Images of Medieval Women,* ed. Eldegard E. DuBruck (Lewiston: The Edwin Mellen Press, 1989), 57.

13. Donald W. Rowe, *Through Nature to Eternity: Chaucer's "Legend of Good Women"* (Lincoln: University of Nebraska Press, 1988), 74.

14. "Confessio Amantis—Liber Quintus" in *The Complete Works of John Gower,* G. C. Macaulay ed. (Oxford: Clarendon Press, 1901), vol. 3, lines 5590–92.

15. From the English account of Richard Stephens, reprinted in Charles Plummer, *Elizabethan Oxford* (Oxford Historical Society, 1887), 203.

16. From the Latin account of Berebock translated by W. Y. Durand in his "*Palæmon and Arcyte, Progne, Marcus Geminus,* and the Theatre In Which They Were Acted, as Described By John Berebock (1566)," *PMLA*, vol. 20, no. 3 (1905): 513–14.

17. As such it was not so well received as *Palæmon and Arcyte. See* Plummer, *Elizabethan Oxford*, xxiii.

18. Frederick S. Boas, *University Drama in the Tudor Age* (Oxford: Clarendon Press, 1914), 104. The hypothesis was first formulated by Durand ("*Palæmon and Arcyte,*" 520–23) and has since gained general acceptance. *See* E. K. Chambers, *The Elizabethan Stage* (Oxford: Clarendon Press, 1923), vol. 3, 239; H. B. Charlton, *The Senecan Tradition in Renaissance Tragedy,* 2d ed. (Manchester: Manchester University Press, 1946), cxlix; David Orr, *Italian Renaissance Drama in England Before 1625* (Chapel Hill: University of North Carolina Press, 1970), 68; Joseph R. Berrigan, "Latin Tragedy of the Quattrocento," *Humanistica Lovaniensia* 23 (1973): 6; Gordon Braden, *Renaissance Tragedy and the Senecan Tradition* (New Haven: Yale University Press, 1985), 102.

The son of an influential Venetian family who assured for him the best teachers, including the famous humanist Vittorino da Feltre, Gregorio Correr (or Corraro) wrote his first and only play in 1428, when he was only eighteen. The quality of the work was such that when Giovanni Ricci first published it from an anonymous manuscript nearly a century after the death of the author, it was taken as being the original work of a classical author. For further details *see* "Introduzione," Gregorio Correr, *Progne,* ed. Laura Casarsa, *Il teatro umanistico veneto: La tragedia* (Ravenna: Longo, 1981), 99–109. This edition also contains Ludovico Domenichi's version of the play. All quotations from both tragedies derive from this edition. All translations from Latin and Italian are mine.

19. *See* John W. Cunliffe, *Early English Classical Tragedies* (Oxford: Clarendon Press, 1912), lxxix.

20. For parallels with Seneca and Ovid, *see* Wilhelm Cloetta, *Beiträge zur Litteraturgeschichte des Mittelalters und der Renaissance* (Halle: Max Niemeyer, 1892), vol. 2, 190–221. *See also* Roberto Gigliucci, *Lo spettacolo della morte* (Anzio: De Rubeis, 1994), 98–102. For the influence of Seneca on Humanist and Renaissance drama, *see* Jean Jacquot ed., *Les Tragédies de Sénèque et le théâtre de la Renaissance* (Paris: Editions du Centre National de la Recherche Scientifique, 1964); *La rinascita della tragedia nell'Italia dell'Umanesimo* (Viterbo: Centro di Studi sul Teatro Medievale e Rinascimentale, 1979); Gordon Braden, *Renaissance Tragedy and the Senecan Tradition* (New Haven: Yale University Press, 1985).

21. Marvin Herrick, *Italian Tragedy in the Renaissance* (Urbana: University of Illinois Press, 1965), 16.

22. Douglas Bush, *Mythology and the Renaissance Tradition in English Poetry* (Minneapolis: University of Minnesota Press, 1932), 37.

23. I. Gollancz, ed., *A Petite Pallace of Pettie His Pleasure* (London, Chatto and Windus, 1908), vol. 1, pp. 58–59.

24. George Gascoigne, "The Complaint of Philomene," in *The Glasse of Government . . . and Other Poems and Prose Works,* ed. John W. Cunliffe (Cambridge: Cambridge University Press, 1910), 183.

25. Götz Schmitz, *The Fall of Women in Early English Narrative Verse* (Cambridge: Cambridge University Press, 1990), 52.

26. William Shakespeare, "Lucrece," in *The Poems,* ed. F. T. Prince (London: Methuen, 1960), line 1128.

27. Albert H. Tricomi, "The Aesthetics of Mutilation in *Titus Andronicus,*" *Shakespeare Survey* 27 (1974): 17.

28. Grace Starry West, "Going by the Book: Classical Allusions in Shakespeare's *Titus Andronicus,*" *Studies in Philology,* vol. 79, no. 1 (1982): 65.

Music, *The Book of the Courtier,* and Othello's Soldiership

Aᴄᴛ three of *Othello* opens beneath Othello and Desdemona's chamber window. In keeping with the Venetian custom of greeting newlyweds with a pleasing aubade in honor of their union, Cassio requests a group of musicians to play so as to "bid 'Good morrow, General.'"[1] The interlude would have reminded Shakespeare's audience of the Venetians' high regard for music. In the fifteenth and sixteenth centuries Venice was praised throughout Europe as an international center for musical experimentation and excellence.[2] In the first printed guide to the city (1581), Francesco Sansovino noted that the esteem in which music and musicians were held had made Venice the center of musical arts:

> Dove correndo i virtuosi in questa professione, si fanno concerti singolari in ogni tempo, essendo chiarissima e vera cosa, che la Musica ha la sua propria sede in questa città.[3]

> [From the extraordinary concerts that are performed whenever the *virtuosi* of this profession assemble together, it is perfectly clear and obvious that Music has its official seat in this city.]

Music was especially important in bolstering Venice's image as an indestructible power. In 1497 the German traveler Arnold von Harff noted in his diary that on Ascension Day the Doge proclaimed Venice's naval might by "throw[ing] a golden finger-ring into the wild sea, as a sign that he takes the sea to wife, as one who intends to be lord over the whole sea," a ceremony preceded by the exquisite music of "fourteen minstrels, eight with silver bassoons, from which hung golden cloths with the arms of St. Mark, and six pipers with trumpets, also with rich hangings." The ceremony was performed in "a small stately galley, very splendidly fitted out," in front of which was "a gilt maiden," who in one hand held "a naked sword and in the other golden scales, a sign that . . . the government is still virgin and was never taken by force."[4] The ritual was originally introduced to affirm Venice's control over the northern Adriatic and gradually gained local political significance as a sign of domination.[5]

While at the outset of the sixteenth century Venice was the most powerful of the Italian states, by the last decades it was faced with the irrevocable loss of empire and deteriorating self-confidence. As Edward Muir observes, the ruling patriciate revitalized the myth of Venetian stability and harmony by "intertwining the threads of parochialism, patriotism, and the ideal of *la vita civile* to weave their own sort of republican, popular piety."[6] The emphasis Venice placed "on music and, indeed, on all of the arts," writes Jane Baldauf-Berdes, "was joined to political ideology and cultural self-dramatization by the state." Venetians found in music, and in the idealized image of a stable, harmonious republic, a means of revitalizing a popular sense of contentment. Just as the ancients had equated music with cosmic order, Venice, according to official ideology, "was an ordered cosmos. Music conquered the space between heaven and earth. . . . Venice was a place where people could be 'happy.'"[7]

The political backdrop of *Othello* paints the Venetian state as it was in actuality, that is, burdened with social and political instability. But while the play reveals disorder in the *polis,* it does not ultimately find its cause in the oppositions of a fragmented society. Instead, disorder is located in Othello, the individual who tragically deludes himself into believing that he is not Other, discordant, and savage. The play's conservative ideology is clarified in Othello's relationship to music.

Cassio calls for the musicians in the midst of the "stubborn and boisterous expedition" (1.3.230–31) of the Turks, which Othello has been charged with quelling. Ironically, the serenade requested by Cassio quickly turns dissonant. The musicians are interrupted by the sudden entrance of the Clown, who taunts them with bawdy quips and puns about their untuned "instruments":

> *Clown.* Why, masters, have your instruments been in Naples, that they speak i'the nose thus?
>
> *First Musician.* How, sir, how?
>
> *Clown.* Are these, I pray you, wind instruments?
>
> *First Musician.* Ay, marry, are they, sir.
>
> *Clown.* O, thereby hangs a tail.

(3.1.3–8)

The allusion to Naples and "speak[ing] i' the nose" is usually glossed as a double entendre referring both to a nasal sound and to the sound of one whose nose has been attacked by venereal disease (Naples was said to have a high occurrence of syphilis). The term "tail" is slang for *penis;* and "wind instrument" refers to the podex, or *ars musica.*[8] The Clown's bawdy language and the off-pitch sounds of the music provide not only an instance of comic relief but also a carnivalesque disruption of the solemn occasion that is being celebrated.[9] Noting that "most critical discussions of the play simply ignore the Clown," Leonard Prager has suggested that "the delicate aubade offered by Cassio is rejected through the medium of the Clown, whose crude quibbles center on the theme of cacophony."[10] And Lawrence Ross has argued that the Clown's dramatic function is grounded in humanist theories of music: Shakespeare draws on the concept of music as capable of blending "the elements of human nature and society." The Clown's role is therefore choric in that he informs the audience that Othello has tragically set himself "at odds with the very universe . . . [he] inhabits."[11] The episode, I will argue, not only alerts the audience to the fact that Othello is out of tune with both *musica mundana* (music of the macrocosm) and *musica humana* (music of the soul), but also confirms that in the civilized and insular world of contemporary Venice, Othello remains ontologically and socially Other.[12]

Othello's alien status in Venice is brought into relief in the Clown's startling explanation for having interrupted the musicians:

> *Clown.* But, masters, here's money for you. [*He gives money.*] And the General so likes your music that he desires you, for love's sake, to make no more noise with it.
>
> *First Musician.* Well, sir, we will not.
>
> *Clown.* If you have any music that may not be heard, to't again; but, as they say, to hear music the General does not greatly care.
>
> (3.1.11–18)

Beneath the banter, we overhear the Clown report the widely held perception in Venice that Othello does not "greatly care" for music. Mikhail Bakhtin has noted that one of the functions of clowns is "the right" not only to burlesque the conventions of good taste and decorum, but also "to betray to the public a personal life, down to its most private and prurient little secrets."[13] Yet at the same time as clowns parody and expose the status quo, it remains unchallenged. The clown or fool, contends Enid Welsford, "may easily act as a social preservative by providing a corrective" to various forms of "unruliness" so that "there is nothing essentially immoral or blasphemous or rebellious about clownage."[14] Echoing a number of commentators on *Othello,* Mary Beth Rose has observed that "Othello, a stranger and alien, founds his identity and assesses his own value in terms of his relationship to the Venetian state that has granted him membership in the community because of his exceptional abilities as a military leader."[15] Yet the Clown, by exposing Othello's dislike of music, the art form which Venetians claimed distinguished the state above others, also highlights Othello's ultimate exclusion from the culture in which he has fashioned an identity.[16]

Among the early modern texts that explore the relation of music and the liberal arts to personal and social order, Castiglione's *Il Cortegiano* offers a comprehensive treatment of the significance of music to the preservation of the orderly, hierarchical *polis.* The enormous popularity in England of *The Book of the Courtier* has been well documented. "Its influence as a model of courtly behavior," writes Raymond Waddington, was "nowhere ... more pervasive than at Elizabeth's court," and its popularity, as Joan Simon points out, was such that it "became in time almost a second bible for English gentlemen."[17] Frank Whigham has observed that *The Book of the Courtier* belongs to the genre of courtesy books governing not only the art of conduct but also "the formation or transformation of an individual or social construct (such as the state or family)."[18] In early modern England, as well as in Italy, mobility between dominant and subject classes was becoming a possibility, and membership in the elite class was becoming contingent upon actions rather than birth (Whigham, 5). *The Book of the Courtier* was especially influential on English literary and extraliterary discourses concerned with the relation of identity, and in particular of elite identity, to action.

Castiglione's commentary on the importance of the arts, and of music in particular, to the ideal Captain helps to clarify Othello's status as Other. The "principall and true profession of a Courtyer," observes Count Lewis of Canossa, "ought to be in feates of armes, ... and to be knowen among other for his hardinesse, for his acheving of enterprises, and for his fidelitie towarde him whom he serveth"; but while it behooves the ordinary courtier to aspire to "excellen[ce]" in the "arte" of "carr[ying] weapon[s]," it is not "necessarye" for him to display "so perfect a knowledge of thynges and other qualities that is requisite in a capitaine."[19] A skilful and able commander's success derives not only from his being *officioso,* that is, conscious of his duties or office, but also from his ability to join military skill with the study of music. A Captain's ability to "savour" music (119) ranks as the most important of nonmilitary accomplishments. For Castiglione and many other Italian humanists, music's relation to the sacred can enhance the soul's capacity for virtue: "it hath bene the opinion of most wise Philosophers," explains the count, "that the world is made of musick, and the heavens in their moving make a melody, and our soule framed after the very same sort, and therfore lifteth up it self, and (as it were) reviveth the vertues and force of it with musick" (89). The relation of the human and heavenly virtues elicited by music is echoed by the Milanese mathematician and music theorist, Gerolamo Cardano (1501–1576), in his meditation on the nature and order of music: "emotions in music ... consist of gentle virtues, and correspond to those more appropriate to action and also to those almost divine virtues suitable for intellectual endeavor. Accordingly, music celebrates ... moral virtues."[20]

The notion that music reflects universal harmony ("the world is made of musick, and the heavens in their moving make a melody, and our soule [is] framed after the very same sort" (89) derives from the Pythagorean theory of sound: different sounds are produced according to the length of a vibrating cord; because their length can be measured mathematically, music is grounded in numerically ordered universal relations mirroring the symmetry of the celestial sphere. Castiglione's contemporary, Franchino Gaffurio (1451–1522), who was *maestro di cappella* at the Cathedral in Milan, and whose later treatises became the standard references on music throughout the sixteenth century, clarifies the relation of music to personal and universal order.[21] Gaffurio invokes Plato's observation that "those who are endowed with virtue and distinguished mores, and are removed from baser men," find it "easy to hear harmony and universal sound."[22] That Shakespeare shares the view of music as reflective of personal and cosmic order is suggested by the numerous references in his plays to the moral, educative, and harmonizing powers of music. In *The Merchant of Venice* Lorenzo notes that a "man that hath no music in himself" cannot "be trusted" (5.1.83 and 88). Shortly before Richard's death in *Richard II,* music interrupts his thoughts, leading him to recognize the interconnection between *musica humana* and *musica mundana:*

> How sour sweet music is,
> When time is broke and no proportion kept!
> So is it in the music of men's lives.
> And here have I the daintiness of ear
> To check time broke in a disordered string;
> But for the concord of my state and time
> Had not an ear to hear my true time broke.
> .   .   .   .
> This music mads me. Let it sound no more,
> For though it have holp madmen to their wits,
> In me it seems it will make wise men mad.
> Yet blessing on his heart that gives it me!
> For 'tis a sign of love.
>
> (5.5.42–65)

About Richard's well-known soliloquy, John Long has observed that Richard's internal music is "out of tune. . . . There remains only that music which . . . is a sign of love in the highest form, *musica divina.*"[23]

Noting that Plato and Aristotle advise a man who "is well brought up" also to be "a musician," since "the force of musicke" is "to very great purpose in us," *The Book of the Courtier* recounts a number of instances in which philosophers and "excellent captaines of olde time" (90) succumbed to music's power to "revive . . . the vertues" (89). The "grave Socrates whan he was well stricken in yeares learned to playe uppon the harpe;" and Alexander the Great "was sometime so fervently styrred" with music "that . . . against his wyll he was forced to arise from bankettes and runne to weapon." Even the Lacedaemonians, "whiche were valiaunt in armes, and the Cretenses used harpes and other softe instrumentes" (89–90). A Captain's ability to hear music becomes "sufficient" not only to inspire "a custome enclyning to vertue, whiche maketh the minde more apt to the conceiving of felicitie," but also to act as "a great staie" to "civyl matters and warrelyke affaires" (90).

Notwithstanding his public role as a "noble and valiant general" (2.2.1–2), Othello has little in common with the "excellent captaines" praised by Castiglione's count. Othello's neglect of music and the arts clarifies his internalization of Venetian prejudice against his race and status. With the exception of the instances in which the military trumpet ushers Othello into Cyprus (2.1.176–77), and in which "Trumpets" honor Lodovico and other Venetian emissaries (4.2.170), Othello never appears in a scene in which music is heard. Nor is it ever suggested that Othello derives pleasure from any cultural activity other than the martial arts. As he himself admits in his speech to the Senate, "little of this great world can I speak / More than pertains to feats of broils and battle" (1.3.88–89). Othello's responses to music reveal a profound mistrust of its power. When the Herald proclaims six hours of celebration in honor of Othello and Desdemona's marriage—"some to dance. . . . All offices are open, and there is full liberty of feasting" (2.2.4–9)—Othello does not join in the celebration; instead, he advises the company, "Let's teach ourselves that honorable stop / Not to outsport discretion" (2.3.2–3). And when Othello reflects upon Desdemona's musical talents, he concedes that it is not immoral that she "sings, plays, and dances well" (3.3.199), but he qualifies the compliment by adding, "Where virtue is, these are more virtuous" (line 200). As Rochelle Smith has suggested, Othello's "qualification reveals a deeply ambiguous response to female singing," a response that gestures toward the "association of female singing with female sexuality."[24] Othello's responses to music and entertainment echo Puritan warnings about these activities. Philip Stubbs, for example, in *The Anatomy of Abuses* (1583), writes that music's seductive powers are capable of "alluring" men "to nicenes, effeminacie, [and] pusillanimitie." He also observes that "sweet Musick, at the first delighteth the eares, but afterward corrupteth and depraueth the minde."[25] Music is corrupted by its association with dancing and feasting: "as in all feasts and pastimes, dauncing is the last, so it is the extream of all other vice"; music should be "used" only for the "glory of God . . . or privatly in a mans secret Chamber or house for his owne solace or comfort, . . . but being used as it is, it corrupteth good minds, maketh them womannish and inclined to all kinde of whordome and mischeef" (Stubbs, sigs. D1 and D4). The fear that music could induce effeminacy was a commonplace of misogynist discourses, both English and Continental. In *The Book of the Courtier* this concern is voiced by the courtier L. Gaspar:

> I beleve musicke (quoth he) together with many other vanities is mete for women, and paradventure for some also that have the lykenes of men, but not for them that be men in dede: who ought not with suche delicacies to womannishe their mindes, and brynge themselves in that sort to dread death." (89)

Gaspar's fear, however, is quickly dispelled by Count Lewis, who enters into a lengthy "praise of Musicke," reminding Gaspar of "howe much it hath alwayes bene renowmed emong them of olde time, and counted a holy matter" (89).

Othello, as we have seen, does not esteem the power of music; his interests hinge strictly on the science of warfare, in which he is most skilled and with which he is most at ease.

> *Othello.* The tyrant custom, most grave senators,
> Hath made the flinty and steel couch of war
> My thrice-driven bed of down. I do agnize
> A natural and prompt alacrity
> I find in hardness.
>
> (1.3.232–36)

But it is not only Othello who constructs an identity entirely dependent on the military ethos; Venetians also perceive him strictly in terms of his accomplishments on the battlefield. When they speak of Othello in his absence, it is always in the context of his valor: "the valiant Moor" (1.3.49); "the warlike Moor Othello" (2.1.29); "the man commands / Like a full soldier" (2.1.37–38). As a city state, Venice was known for its rigid class system and for its suspicion both of *stranieri* ("foreigners") and allies. Citizenship was the birthright only of members of the nobility (the state was ruled by a hereditary class of approximately 2,500 nobles), and foreigners who resided in Venice were considered privileged.[26] Yet Venice knew how to exploit, and was well served by, *stranieri.* Despite the pervasive suspicion of outsiders, the governing class scrupulously followed the long-standing custom of treating strangers justly; it was also common practice to employ foreign soldiers and mercenaries and to appoint outsiders as military commanders, the chief reason being that the custom would help to "prevent military *coups d'état.*"[27] The status of "insider," however, was rarely conferred upon foreigners, their often notable reputations notwithstanding.

Eldred Jones has observed that in Othello's first speech (1.3.17–28) his "'services' represent the one solid prop of his confidence; they are the source of his security in Venetian society." Although Othello reminds Iago that he is descended from royalty —"I fetch my life and being / From men of royal siege" (1.2.21–22)—his ancestry "is apparently not generally known, and therefore has been of no service to him. Indeed he never invokes it during the rest of the play."[28] Whereas for Jones the reference to Othello's descent "enhance[s] Othello's stature as a tragic hero in the eyes of the audience," in that his "office and his life go hand in hand," I would suggest that his royal descent is ultimately of no importance to the Venetians, which is why he never mentions it again (Jones, 90–91). Othello's precarious identity at court is brought into relief in the Duke's revealing comment to Brabantio after Othello has defended his marriage in front of the Venetian Senate: "If virtue no delighted beauty lack, / Your son-in-law is far more fair than black" (1.2.292–93).

Othello's lack of interest in the arts sets him apart both from Venetians and from his counterparts in other plays by Shakespeare. Mark Antony, for example, cherishes the arts. When Caesar explains to Antony why the calculating and pragmatic Cassius is "dangerous" (*Julius Caesar,* 1.2.195), one of the reasons he gives is that "He loves no plays, / As thou dost, Antony; he hears no music" (1.2.203–4). Although music ranks as the most important of the arts, Castiglione's count also observes the need for "excellent capitaines" to emulate classical heroes in "joyn[ing] the Ornament of letters, with the prowesse of armes." Alexander, for example, "had Homer in such reverence, that he laide his *Ilias* always under his beddes head"; and Alcibiades "encreased his good condicions and made them greater with letters" (83). The importance of the arts had also been emphatically articulated by Guarino Veronese (1370/1374–1460), one of the most influential of the early humanists, for whom the pursuit of the "litterae" confers nobleness of spirit:

> Hominem medius fidius non esse arbitror qui litteras non diligit non amat non amplectitur, non arripiat, non sese in earum haustu prorsus immergat.[29]

> [By God, one is not human if one does not esteem highly the litterae, does not love or embrace them, is not seized by or immersed in them.]

Shakespeare's Brutus, like Antony, has a deep love of books and music. In act 4, just before the visit of Caesar's ghost, Brutus finds solace both in "the book" which he has "sought for so" (4.3.252) and in the "strain" of the lute (line 257), the instrument associated with Orpheus, which in the sixteenth and seventeenth centuries was a sign of civility and refinement. For this reason the eighteenth-century music historian Charles Burney described the lute as "the favourite chamber-instrument of every nation in Europe."[30]

In medieval discourses music is valued chiefly for its reflection of universal categories. As Ernesto Grassi observes,

> medieval thinking is above all intent on tracing back any art form to the realm of the non-historic, the eternal. One of the arts, music, gains its legitimation only insofar as it mirrors the harmony of beings and therefore the eternal and universal.

If music expresses subjectivity or relativity, that is, "something that is bound to time and space, . . . it is entitled to do so only if it tries to express human despair over the unattainability of the eternal."[31] In the early modern period the role of music as a mirror of an eternal and harmonious universe coextends with the emphasis on the relation of music to the civilizing process and to the systems of hierarchy that ideally were thought to function according to reciprocal relations. Contemporary European discourses posit an important connection between classical and medieval theories of music and the systems of class and status. By the midfifteenth century the link between music and cosmic harmony becomes contingent upon the sociopolitical need of early modern elite cultures to sustain and perpetuate an ideology of social relations based on order and hierarchy. Thus in *The Book of the Courtier* the count advises that it is essential for the ideal courtier not only to demonstrate skill in music and "understanding" of "the booke," (88), but also to avoid playing in the presence of common people: "In vauting, wrastling, running and leaping, I am well pleased if he flee the multitude. . . . The like judgement I have in musicke," (117) which "quicken[s] the spirites of the verye doers. I am well pleased (as I have saide) they flee the multitude, *and especially of the unnoble*" (119; emphasis added).

Music and letters thus define the civility of the human subject, an attribute fashioned through the pursuit of noble action at court. "I am not pleased with the Courtyer," states Castiglione's count in conversation with L. Gaspar, "if he be not also a musitien, and beside his understanding and couning upon the booke, have skill in lyke maner on sundrye instruments. . . . And princypally in Courtes" (88–89), where "musicke," as Gaspar concludes, "is not onelye an ornament, but also necessarie for a Courtyer" (91). Music is no longer an expression of human despair and longing for divinity but, according to L. Octavian, a "force" with which "to render laude and thankes unto God," for "it is a credible matter that is acceptable unto him, and that he hath geven it unto us for a most swete lightning of our travailes and vexations" (90). Because music and letters can make a person knowledgeable, wise, and temperate, they are a requisite for "*Virtus in actione,*" the quintessential goal of which is a well-regulated body politic overseen by a "Prince" who is also "inclined to vertue."[32]

In England Elizabeth I was commended for having elevated English culture through her cultivation of music. "Queen Elizabeth," wrote the Renaissance musicologist John Playford, "was not only a Lover of this Divine Science [Music], but a good Proficient herein," and Charles Burney claimed that "during the long and prosperous reign of Queen Elizabeth, . . . we never had so just a claim to equality with the rest of Europe; where Music was the most successfully cultivated, as at this period."[33] Not only do the arts in the early modern period acquire "a new equivalence with the political," argues Frank Whigham, but the artist "gains a new importance in public life—ideological celebrant as well as moral guide" (Whigham, 87). Because in early modern European courts the orderly body politic is commensurate with the concentration of hierarchy and the retention of political power, literary and musical compositions, notes Claude Palisca, "that could sway people through their feelings, whether to . . . sorrow for a deceased notable, joy upon victory, or enthusiasm for a cause, became a prime instrument for gaining or maintaining power"; letters and the "language of music," which was perceived as having "greater force than verbal rhetoric," were also employed "for this purpose" (15–16). Sir Thomas Elyot, in *The Book named The Governor* (1531), clarifies the political and ideological function of music when he advises that the "wise and circumspect tutor" to a young nobleman

> shall commend the perfect understanding of music, declaring how necessary it is for the better attaining the knowledge of a public weal: which . . . is made of an order of estates and degrees, and by reason thereof containeth in it a perfect harmony.[34]

For neo-Aristotelians and neo-Platonists, the perfection of the body politic is coterminous with the harmonious (and hierarchical) design of the human body. Within the hierarchy of the senses, the sense of hearing is the most important. In the Clown's comment that Othello "does not greatly care" to "hear music" (3.1.18 and 17) Shakespeare implicitly alludes to the primacy of hearing in Renaissance psychology, which determined hearing to be the least corrupted of the senses, and the most dependable.[35] Although Leonardo da Vinci, in his *Paragone,* had suggested that the sense of sight surpasses the others, Italian humanists for the most part argued for the superiority of hearing.[36] "Thinges that . . . are lesse in effect than the fame is of them," remarks Sir Friderick in *The Book of the Courtier,* "are for the most part of that sort, that the eye at the first sight maie geve a judgemente of them. . . . But in the conditions of menne, . . . that you see outwardly is the least part" (142). Unlike the other senses, hearing is more acute and less prone to misapprehension. The "sense of hearing," writes Cardano in his treatise *De Musica* (1574), "is more subtle than the sense of sight" because it "recognizes even smaller differences than the visual sense or any other sense" (213). For Ficino, the ear perceives imagery, and music is a type of image: "the soul receives the sweetest harmonies and numbers through the ears, and by these echoes is reminded and aroused to the divine music that may be heard by the more subtle and penetrating sense of mind"; the soul

> uses the ears as messengers, as though they were chinks in . . . [the] darkness. By the ears, . . . the soul receives the echoes of that incomparable music, by which it is led back to . . . its rightful home, so that it may enjoy that true music again.[37]

Because words, sounds, and music are all received by the soul in the form of images, there is no epistemological differentiation between them. "The meanings of words" for Ficino, writes Gary Tomlinson, "were a consequence of their place in the harmonies of the world. They were, in the broadest sense, musically determined."[38]

It has been widely observed that Othello conceives of knowledge as dependent on sight—he must, he tells Iago, see before he will doubt (3.3.204), for Desdemona "had eyes, and chose me" (line 203). Because, as James Calderwood suggests, "sight is keyed to surfaces, sight is Othello's enemy in Venice, where the color of virtue is not black but white." Othello's preoccupation with Desdemona's "external beauty, insofar as she is his property and reflects his virtues, will close the gap between his inwardly 'perfect soul' and his outwardly perfect surface."[39] Throughout the play, Desdemona is the character who is most closely connected with hearing and music: she hears Othello's words— "These things to hear / Would Desdemona seriously incline"

(1.3.147–48)—and, as Othello sarcastically notes, she is "An admirable musician! O, she will sing the savageness out of a bear" (4.1.188–89). The irony of Othello's quip would not be lost on Shakespeare's audience. It was a Renaissance commonplace that music had the effect of taming the savage: "Do ye not then deprive our Courtyer of musicke," warns Castiglione's count, "which doth not onely make swete the minds of men, but also many times wilde beastes tame" (90). Desdemona's affiliation with music provokes Othello's unconscious fear and anxiety because it reifies his own savage origins. "For noblenesse of birth is (as it were) a clere lampe that sheweth forth and bringeth into light, . . . and enflameth and provoketh unto vertue, . . . with the hope of praise" (44). Like Cassius in *Julius Caesar,* Othello "hears no music" and therefore belongs with "men as . . . be never at heart's ease" (1.2.204 and 208). In Othello's case, lack of ease stems primarily from insecurity with respect to his race—

> Haply, for I am black
> And have not those soft parts of conversation
> That chamberers have.
>
> (3.2.279–81)

Insecurity belongs to the base; grace and *sprezzatura* are the province of the true courtier (56–58).

The extensive intertextuality between *Othello* and *The Book of the Courtier* suggests that while the play exposes the conflicts and contradictions generated by the hierarchies of race, class, and status, it does not deconstruct the dependence of dominant ideologies on those hierarchies.

Notes

1. *Othello,* in *The Complete Works of Shakespeare,* ed. David Bevington, 3rd ed. (Glenview, Illinois: Scott, Foresman, and Co., 1980), 3.1.2. All subsequent quotations from Shakespeare are taken from this edition.

2. *See* Jane L. Baldauf-Berdes, *Women Musicians of Venice: Musical Foundations, 1525–1855* (Oxford: Clarendon Press, 1993), 30–42. Venice's reputation for musical excellence encompassed all aspects of music making, including publishing. Claude V. Palisca, in *Humanism in Italian Renaissance Musical Thought* (New Haven: Yale University Press, 1985), observes that "Chamber music, particularly for instrumental ensembles, received unprecedented impetus from the patronage of the Italian courts. And to supply printed parts for all this music making, Venice became the music publishing capital of the world" (5).

3. F.T. Sansovino, *Venetia città nobilissima* (1581; reprint Venice, 1698),

380; translation mine. As Baldauf-Berdes notes, Sansovino's claim for Venice "is one that apologists for other Italian cities seem neither to have challenged nor to have made on behalf of the musical culture of their own cities" (30).

4. *The Pilgrimage of Arnold Von Harff, Knight,* trans. and ed. Malcolm Letts, 2d ser., 44 (1946); reprint (Millwood, N.Y.: Hakluyt Society, 1990), 59.

5. *See* Gina Fasoli, "Liturgia e cerimoniale ducale," in *Venezia e il Levante fino al secolo XV,* ed. Agostino Pertusi, 2 vols. (Florence: L. S. Olschki, 1973), 1: 274.

6. Edward Muir, *Civic Ritual in Renaissance Venice* (Princeton: Princeton University Press, 1981), 13.

7. Baldauf-Berdes, *Women Musicians,* 34 and 42. The myth of Venice was not contained within the city; in European discourses, Venice was the most praised of Italian cities (*see* Muir, *Civic Ritual,* 23). David C. McPherson has observed that in England, Venice "was the favored Italian city" (*Shakespeare, Jonson, and the Myth of Venice* [Newark: University of Delaware Press; London and Toronto: Associated University Presses, 1990], 49). Venice was praised highly in English travelogues and guides such as Sir Lewis Lewkenor's *History and Commonwealth of Venice* (1599) and Sir Robert Dallington's *A Survey of the Great Dukes State of Tuscany in … 1596* (1605), and in Richard Knolles's *General History of the Turks* (1603). McPherson usefully illustrates that these texts, together with "Venetian polity and society" (70), would have been familiar to Shakespeare (*see* 51–90).

8. Francis Grose, *A Classical Dictionary of the Vulgar Tongue* (1785). *See also* Eric Partridge, *Shakespeare's Bawdy,* 3rd ed. (London and New York: Routledge, 1968), 219–20.

9. The episode, however, is rarely staged in modern productions, and it has been largely ignored in the scholarship on the play. Harold C. Goddard, in *The Meaning of Shakespeare,* 2d ed. (Chicago: University of Chicago Press, 1967), voices a common sentiment in calling the Clown scene "the most supererogatory" in the play (485).

10. Leonard Prager, "The Clown in *Othello,*" *Shakespeare Quarterly* 11 (1960): 94–95. Prager's discussion focuses primarily on the Clown's second appearance in act 3, scene 4, where his quibbling with Desdemona about Cassio's whereabouts (lines 1–21) also "has a jarring effect" (96).

11. Lawrence J. Ross, "Shakespeare's 'Dull Clown' and Symbolic Music," *Shakespeare Quarterly* 17 (1966): 108–9. Briefer assessments of the episode include Harley Granville-Barker's observation that it provides "relaxation before the tense main business of the tragedy begins"; Cassio "bring[s] musicians to play beneath Othello's window (a pleasant custom, and here what delicate amends!), to this being added the grosser conventional japes of the Clown" (*Prefaces to Shakespeare,* 2 vols. [Princeton: Princeton University Press, 1946–1947], 2:23); J. Dover Wilson's remark that the interlude establishes the time in which the action takes place (Introduction, *Othello,* ed. J. Dover Wilson, New Cambridge Edition [Cambridge: Cambridge University Press, 1957], xxxiii); and John H. Long's suggestion that "Shakespeare apparently wished his audience to recall that a distaste for music is an index to character" (*Shakespeare's Use of Music: The Histories and Tragedies* [Gainesville: University of Florida Press, 1971], 148).

12. In humanist theories of music, *musica mundana* refers to the principle of harmony in the macrocosm, and *musica humana* to harmony in the microcosm or human sphere.

13. Mikhail M. Bakhtin, *The Dialogic Imagination: Four Essays,* trans. Caryl Emerson, ed. Michael Holquist (Austin: University of Texas Press, 1981), 162.

14. Enid Welsford, *The Fool: His Social and Literary History* (London: Faber and Faber, 1935), 317. *See also* Anton Zijderveld's suggestion that during a clown's or fool's antic, "the veil [is] lifted for a short while," and it is "briefly demonstrated that power" can be "justified and legitimated differently or maybe not at all. But the power itself has not been really affected and its legitimation" has been "only relativized for a moment" (*Reality in a Looking-Glass: Rationality Through an Analysis of Traditional Folly* [London, Boston and Henley: Routledge & Kegan Paul, 1982], 29).

15. Mary Beth Rose, *The Expense of Spirit: Love and Sexuality in English Renaissance Drama* (Ithaca: Cornell University Press, 1988), 132.

16. Although I disagree with John Long's claim that Othello is not portrayed as monstrous, he offers the important insight that Othello's "dislike of music . . . should warn us that there are dark depths in his character, that being wrought, perplexed in the extreme, he is capable of dark and bloody deeds. The fact that the poet placed this information about the Moor's lack of musical appreciation during the consummation of the marriage (apparently interrupted by Othello's hasty dispatch to Cyprus) may not have been unintentional on his part" (*Shakespeare's Use of Music,* 148).

17. Raymond Waddington, "Elizabeth I and the Order of the Garter," paper presented to the Sixteenth Century Studies Conference, Minneapolis, 27 October 1989. Joan Simon, *Education and Society in Tudor England* (Cambridge: Cambridge University Press, 1967), 340. *See also* Daniel Javitch, *Poetry and Courtliness in Renaissance England* (Princeton: Princeton University Press, 1978), 4–5; Sydney Anglo, "The Courtier: The Renaissance and Changing Ideals," in *The Courts of Europe,* ed. A. G. Dickens (London: Thames and Hudson, 1977), 33–53; and Frank Whigham, *Ambition and Privilege: The Social Tropes of Elizabethan Courtesy Theory* (Berkeley and Los Angeles: University of California Press, 1984), 15.

18. Whigham, *Ambition and Privilege,* 26. Thomas M. Greene notes that courtesy books such as these formed an autonomous genre, which he calls the *institute* ("The Flexibility of the Self in Renaissance Literature," in *The Disciplines of Criticism: Essays in Literary Theory, Interpretation, and History,* eds. Peter Demetz, Thomas Greene, and Lowry Nelson Jr. [New Haven: Yale University Press, 1968], 250).

19. *The Book of The Courtier from the Italian of Count Baldassare Castiglione: Done into English by Sir Thomas Hoby, Anno 1561* (New York: AMS Press, 1967), 48–49. Further references to the text will be from this edition; page numbers will be designated in parentheses in the body of the essay.

20. Hieronymus Cardanus, *Writings on Music,* trans. and ed. Clement A. Miller, Musicological Studies & Documents 32 (American Institute of Musicology, 1973), 105.

21. *See* Anne E. Moyer, *Musica Scientia: Musical Scholarship in the Italian Renaissance* (Ithaca: Cornell University Press, 1992), 67–68.

22. Franchinus Gaffurius, *De Harmonia Musicorum Instrumentorum Opus,* trans. Clement A. Miller, Musicological Studies & Documents 33 (Neuhausen-Stuttgart: American Institute of Musicology, 1977), 203.

23. Long, *Shakespeare's Use of Music,* 73. In *The Great Chain of Being: A Study of the History of an Idea* (Cambridge: Harvard University Press, 1936),

Arthur O. Lovejoy traces the history of the binary opposition in Western philosophy between transcendent or absolute Being and mundane, temporal existence, and its relationship to ideas of order and chaos (*see* especially pp. 24–66).

24. Rochelle Smith, "Admirable Musicians: Women's Songs in *Othello* and *The Maid's Tragedy,*" *Comparative Drama* 28 (fall 1994): 311.

25. *"The Anatomy of Abuses" by Philip Stubbs, 1583,* Introduction by Peter Davison (New York and London: Johnson Reprint Corporation, 1972), sig. D3.

26. See Muir, *Civic Ritual,* 19; Brian Pullan, "Service to the Venetian State: Aspects of Myth and Reality in the Early Seventeenth Century," *Studi secenteschi* 5 (1964): 101; and Baldauf-Berdes, *Women Musicians,* 12–15.

27. McPherson, *Shakespeare, Jonson, and the Myth of Venice,* 73. *See also* M. E. Mallett and J. R. Hale, *The Military Organization of a Renaissance State: Venice c. 1400 to 1617* (Cambridge: Cambridge University Press, 1984), who note that the reliance on foreign soldiers, officers, and mercenaries was "the carefully calculated price of political stability." The patricians' "stance" was one of "peaceful neutrals"; "the patrician was not militaristic: responsive to his Christian duty to repel the Turk at sea he was nonetheless basically a statesman, a merchant and a patron of Church and learning" (313–14).

28. Eldred Jones, *Othello's Countrymen: The African in English Renaissance Drama* (London: Oxford University Press, 1965), 90.

29. Guarino Veronese, *Epistolario,* ed. R. Sabbadini, 3 vols. (Venice, 1915–1919), Ep. 148 (1, 244): 24; cited in Erneto Grassi, *Renaissance Humanism: Studies in Philosophy and Poetics* (Binghamton, N.Y.: Medieval & Renaissance Texts & Studies, 1988), 52; translation mine.

30. Charles Burney, *A General History of Music: From the Earliest Ages to the Present Period (1789),* with critical and historical notes by Frank Mercer, 2 vols. (New York: Dover, 1957), 2: 123.

31. Grassi, *Renaissance Humanism,* 48.

32. *Book of the Courtier,* 336. Cf. Veronese, *Ep.* 803 (2, 478): 82, for whom the "litterae" make individuals knowledgeable, and are indispensable to action: "ipsam disciplinam tibi patriam tibi parentem tibi nutricem tibi nobilitatem adoptasti et sic adoptasti, ut emineas et doctissimus antecellas; nec vero antecellere satis habuisti, nisi praecepta in actum deduxisses" (cited in Grassi, 52–53).

33. John Playford, preface, *An Introduction to the Skill of Music* (1694), 12th ed., corrected and amended by Henry Purcell, Introduction by Franklin Zimmerman (New York: Da Capo Press, 1972), 44; Burney, *A General History of Music* 2: 22. In his schematic overview of what he called the Elizabethan "world picture," E.M.W. Tillyard noted that writers and philosophers inherited the Greek notion of creation "as an act of music" reflected in the well-regulated body politic; Elizabeth's court revealed "the cosmic dance reproduced in the body politic, thus completing the series of dances in macrocosm body politic and microcosm" (*The Elizabethan World Picture* [1943; reprint, New York: Penguin, 1979], 109 and 114).

34. Sir Thomas Elyot, *The Book named The Governor,* ed. S. E. Lehmberg (London: Dent; New York: Dutton, 1962), 23 and 22–23.

35. Although John N. Wall, in "Shakespeare's Aural Art: The Metaphor of the Ear in *Othello,*" *Shakespeare Quarterly* 30 (1979): 358–66, does not consider Othello's lack of interest in hearing music, he makes the important observa-

tion that in Shakespeare's tragedies "aural misdirection . . . inevitably leads to the downfall of the deluded characters" (359).

36. Leonardo da Vinci, *Paragone,* in *The Literary Works of Leonardo da Vinci,* ed. Jean Paul Richter; commentary by Carlo Pedretti, 2 vols. (Berkeley and Los Angeles: University of California Press, 1977), 1: 84–85.

37. Marsilio Ficino, *The Letters of Marsilio Ficino,* trans. members of the Language Department of the School of Economic Science, 5 vols. (London: Shepheard-Walwyn, 1975), 1: 45.

38. Gary Tomlinson, *Music in Renaissance Magic: Towards a Historiography of Others* (Chicago: University of Chicago Press, 1993), 121.

39. James L. Calderwood, *The Properties of Othello* (Amherst: University of Massachusetts Press, 1989), 46.

The Politics of Prose and Drama:
The Case of Machiavelli's "Belfagor"

A. J. HOENSELAARS

IN the study of Italian Renaissance authors in England, few if any cases of reception seem more erratic than that of Niccolò Machiavelli and his work. Much attention has been devoted to the impact of Machiavelli's political works, their impact on English politics as well as English literature, and Mario Praz's long essay, "Machiavelli and the Elizabethans," is still useful as a critical survey.[1] The influence of Machiavelli's literary work outside Italy has also been thoroughly investigated. Machiavelli's comedy *The Mandragola* has received ample attention, as have his *Clizia,* the *Dialogue on Language,* and even *The Golden Ass.* However, his "Novella di Belfagor Arcidiavolo"—which was written between 1515 and 1520—has been largely ignored. It goes unacknowledged by Praz, and there is no reference to it in Ascoli and Kahn's ambitious and authoritative collection of essays entitled *Machiavelli and the Discourse of Literature,* nor in Kirkpatrick's more recent study, *English and Italian Literature from Dante to Shakespeare.*[2]

"Belfagor" would appear to have been neglected by critics of English literature because it reads like a well-written and somewhat flippant tale without any apparent relevance to Machiavelli's political ideas as these were received in England.[3] At least, this is what would seem to underlie Felix Raab's view of "Belfagor" as expressed in *The English Face of Machiavelli.* Raab unflinchingly states that the 1647 "Belfagor" translation—the very first translation of the *novella* into English—was "an uncontentious addition to the translations of Machiavelli's works into English."[4] J. R. Hale adopts a different stance. He notes that the story has been looted for the purpose of reconstructing Machiavelli's political views in a narrow biographical context, and Hale tries to redress the balance by stressing the story's literary and stylistic merits, as well as its relation to the private correspondence.[5] Doing so, Hale nevertheless perpetuates a reading that ignores the political impact of the "Belfagor" *novella* in the British Isles. Given this state of affairs, it is the *novella*'s political potential and relevance that will be my central concern. When employing the term "political," I am not primarily thinking of matters popular during these politicized days such as race or gender; I shall mainly be using it in its narrow and traditional sense, meaning "matters of state," or "*ragion di stato*" in the Machiavellian tradition.

Before studying the political reverberations of the *novella*, however, it seems worth recalling the other reason why the critics' interest in "Belfagor" has been faint. As the tale itself clearly acknowledges in its opening lines, it was rooted in legend. In fact, it derived from an ancient oriental folk tale. As a result, it is not the only tale of its kind to reach the reading public around the midsixteenth century. Soon after Machiavelli's *novella* first appeared in 1545 (and was included in the first collected edition of Machiavelli's *Works* of 1549), a rather comparable tale by Francisco Straparola became available as the fourth story of the second night in his *Le piacevoli notti,* published at San Luca in 1557 and in Venice in 1578.[6] Much energy has been invested in finding out which of the two authors produced the prototype *novella*, though in vain. Notably, the question of originality has blinded critics to the many essential differences between the two tales, differences that are often rather obvious and transparent enough, in the case of later renderings of the legend, to determine which of the two Italian tales functioned as the model, or whether indeed both tales exerted a formative influence together. A focus on differences rather than similarities would also seem more relevant for another reason. At around the time when these two Italian tales on the theme of "the devil takes a wife" traveled across the Alps to England, the northern Germanic variant of the tale (with England as an integral location since time immemorial) had reached London via Denmark and Germany in the guise of "Friar Rush."[7]

This confusion should not prevent one from identifying the various narrative elements at play as the southern or Mediterranean version of the "Belfagor" story developed and spread. For the present purpose of defining the political impact of the "Belfagor" tale in an English context, the focus shall mainly be on the Italian strands in an attempt to follow their tortuous tour of the British Isles. Before turning to a discussion of the political relevance of the "Belfagor" legend in Britain, a summary of the *novella* seems in order.

The story of "Belfagor" begins in Hell. Here, the devils are amazed that so many men flock to Hell, alleging that women and marriage were the cause of their misery. In a deft attempt at crisis management, Pluto calls the various courts of the infernal region together for a parliament in Hell. At this gathering, the decision is taken to investigate the misogynist claims that might ultimately give Hell a bad reputation. It is decided that one of the devils will visit earth to investigate the matter. Since there are no volunteers, the devils draw lots, and one-time archangel—now archdevil—Belfagor is picked. Belfagor is dispatched to Florence in the shape of a rich and handsome young man, named Roderigo of Castile. At Florence, he is to take a wife and live with her for ten years. Any hardships that might befall him, he has to accept.

Roderigo goes to Florence and marries Onesta, the daughter of Amerigo Donati, a noble citizen with more daughters than money. Despite the hundred thousand ducats that Roderigo lavishly spends on Onesta, the girl has a tendency to sulk. Onesta's pride, it is Belfagor's informed opinion, is greater than Lucifer's. Still, Belfagor does all he can to satisfy her. To keep the peace, the devil finances the weddings of Onesta's other sisters, and sets up the three brothers in trade, both at home and abroad. Inevitably, Roderigo is soon suspected of bankruptcy, and, fearing the consequences, he flees from the city.

Following a cross-country escape, he meets the farmer Gianmatteo del Brica in Peretola near Florence. In return for protection from his spendthrift wife and the Florentine creditors, Roderigo promises to make Gianmatteo's fortune. Gianmatteo who considers that he has nothing to lose, complies. The way to make Gianmatteo's fortune will be as follows: whenever Gianmatteo hears of a woman possessed by the devil, he may rest assured that it is Belfagor possessing her. Gianmatteo is to exorcise the devil and Belfagor will leave the victim's body so that Gianmatteo will acquire the reputation of a successful exorcist and can collect the generous payment offered by the woman's family. Their first successful act of exorcism takes place at Florence, but finding that they have not earned enough yet, the two partners-in-crime proceed to victimize the daughter of Charles, king of Naples. This leaves Gianmatteo rich, and he decides to settle in peace and quiet. Not for long, though, since Belfagor has promised that he will hurt him as much as he has helped him. One day, it becomes known that the daughter of King Louis the Seventh of France is possessed by the devil. Much against his will, the famous exorcist Gianmatteo is sent to Paris by the city government of Florence. Inspecting the patient at Paris, Gianmatteo of course recognizes the presence of Belfagor whose plan it is to have Gianmatteo sentenced to death once it turns out that he cannot cure the king's daughter. In order to rid himself of the devil forever, the wily Gianmatteo asks Louis to erect a scaffold in front of Notre Dame cathedral and to have "besides in one corner of the square at least twenty men with trumpets, horns, drums, bagpipes, flutes, cymbals and any other loud instruments." These men are to sound their instruments when Gianmatteo raises his hat.[8] On the Sunday following, the king's possessed daughter is brought onto the scaffold. In front of a large crowd, Gianmatteo whispers to Belfagor to help him, but the devil refuses. At that instant, Gianmatteo lifts his hat, and the band, now producing a deafening roar, begins to advance toward the scaffold. Asking what is going on, Belfagor is told that his wife has come to fetch him back. The mere mention of Onesta proves sufficient to send Belfagor flying back to the comforts of Hell.

In the subsequent discussion of the various manifestations of the Italian devil legend in England, two main texts will be central. The first text—often considered the earliest occurrence of the Italian legend in England—is to be found in the conclusion to Barnabe Riche's collection of stories known as *Riche his Farewell to Militarie Profession* of 1581. The other text is the neglected anonymous Civil War play known as *The Devill, and the Parliament* (1648).[9]

The earliest occurrence in England of the Italian "Belfagor" legend may be found in *Riche his Farewell to Militarie Profession* which, as the 1581 title page reads, Barnabe Riche "Gathered together for the onely delight of courteous Gentlewomen."[10] As though in an attempt to frustrate contemporary readers or to tease future scholars, the identity of Riche's source for the tale that concludes his *Farewell* is shrouded in mystery: "I will co[n]clude with a tale that maketh somethyng for my purpose. ... I haue read it so long agoe, that I can not tell you where."[11]

Riche's apology has inevitably given rise to a considerable amount of conjecture. For years, critics assumed that Machiavelli was the source, until D. W. Thompson argued a convincing case for the Straparola version of the *novella*.[12] A close look at the text suggests that if the Straparola version lies at the basis of the Riche story, Machiavelli's "Belfagor" must have provided the idea for the narrative's structuring of the topography that was, as I shall point out, the reason why it was to trigger a considerable political incident as it reached Britain. Unlike in the tale by Straparola, which has no local habitation, the devil in both the Machiavelli and the Riche version initially operates in what to the respective authors—Machiavelli and Riche—is their own geographical center, the omphalos of their readership. In the second half of the *novella*, there is an important move abroad, to a distinctly foreign location.

In Riche's rendering of the traditional *novella*, the devil, here named Balthaser, marries an English woman, Mildred, the daughter of Persinus. The main location is no longer Machiavelli's Florence but contemporary London and its immediate environment. The setting in the second half of the story as rendered by Riche is devised by substituting the Scottish capital Edinburgh for Machiavelli's Paris. At Edinburgh the devil does not possess any young woman, as in the *novella* by Machiavelli, but a male, as in the Straparola tale, where the duke of Melfi falls victim to the devil. But in Riche's version the devil does not possess a duke or an earl; he possesses the "King of Scots himself . . . with straunge and vnaquainted passions" (sig. Eei^r).

Although the Scottish king in Riche's version of the *novella* remains anonymous, King James VI was most displeased when reading Riche in 1595. His displeasure reached such heights that he had George Nicholson, in Edinburgh, bring the matter to the attention of the English ambassador, Robert Bowes. This is what the *Calendar of the State Papers Relating to Scotland* quotes from the letter of 18 June 1595: "In the conclusion of a book called 'Rich his Farewell', printed in 1594, such matter is noted as the King is not pleased with; *he says little but thinks the more*."[13]

It is not easy on the basis of the evidence available to deduce the reasons for James's response. Why did he not say as much as he thought? Knowing full well that the more explanations one can offer, the more likely it is that none of them is the right one, I believe that in view of the Scottish King's preoccupations during the mid-1590s several suggestions may safely be ventured. It is quite likely, for example, that King James's reaction was determined by the mere appearance of a devil in Riche's collection of stories.[14] Throughout the 1590s James was profoundly occupied with witchcraft. His interest really dated from

1589. This was the year of James's marriage to Anne of Denmark. A windswept journey with her across the North Sea back to Scotland had endangered the lives of the king and his new queen and had fueled James's superstition. An overcredulous James, convinced that witchcraft had been employed to prevent the arrival of Anne of Denmark in Scotland, set out to write his *Daemonology,* which was to appear two years after the incident concerning *Riche his Farewell to the Military Profession.* James's open irritation may, therefore, well have been part of his crusade against witchcraft in general; a flippant and light-hearted treatment of the matter would not further the cause. Nor would the intimation have been that the very king who meant to tackle the problem of witchcraft in his country had at one time or other been possessed by the devil himself. For in Riche's rendition of the story, it is not a king's daughter who is possessed by the devil, as in Machiavelli's *novella*; nor is it an Italian duke, as in the Straparola version, but a king. And Barnabe Riche's prose style is obviously geared to foreground this as a special issue. How else is one to interpret the emphatic statement that the devil took possession of the "King of Scots himself"? If an apparently playful allusion to living royalty in a collection of stories designed for the delight of women was enough to initiate diplomatic action of the kind described, perhaps one should look for reasons other than James's kingship alone.

The king of Scots in Riche's version of the *novella* is visited by "strange and vnaquainted passions." In this sense, Riche would freely seem to follow the Straparola tale where misogyny and sometimes violent homoeroticism seem to be reverse sides of the same coin. To illustrate this point, some passages from Straparola may be cited that leave fairly little to the imagination. Of the devil in Straparola, Pangrazio Stornello, the following is reported:

"E fattile molti drappi alla foggia che allora si usavano, e sodisfattala del tutto, da lei senza tuor commiato alcuno si parti, ed a Melfi se n'andò: *e nel corpo del duca entrato, oltre modo lo tormentava.*[15]

[After giving her many types of silken clothes for all weather conditions, and having given her everything she wanted, he left his wife without taking his leave of her, and went to Melfi where he entered the body of the Duke, whom he rudely tormented.]

When the devil's original accomplice, named Gasparin, discovers the devil in the flesh, and tries to get him out, Straparola's narrative reads:

> Il demonio, che indi quetamente si posava, nulla in quel punto li ripose, ma al duca si fattamente gonfiò la gola, che quasi si senti morire. (92)

> [The devil who was still inhabiting that body at his pleasure, did not answer him, but so strongly caused the Duke's throat to swell that he felt like he was dying.]

In view of the misogynist slant of the key *novella* and the homoerotic implications surrounding the devil's possession of the duke of Melfi, it is my belief that Barnabe Riche's choice of ruler in his rendering of the tale was an allusion to King James's unorthodox inclinations—the king's "strange and vnaquainted passions." After all, when Riche's collection of *novelle* first appeared, in 1581, the homoerotic affections of an adolescent James for his renowned cousin Esmé Stuart were a cause for profound concern both in Scotland and in England. Of course, when King James read the alleged 1594 reprint of the Riche collection, the Esmé Stuart affair safely belonged to the past. But during the late 1580s and the early 1590s it was George Gordon, the sixth earl of Huntly who could call himself King James's favorite. And was it not concerning this particular relationship between the king of Scotland and the earl of Huntly that an informant of the English government had written: "The King hath a strange, extraordinary affection to Huntly, such as is yet unremovable" (*CSP*, Scotland, X, 3).

It is by no means certain that the Huntly connection was on James's mind when *he said little but thought the more* about *Riche his Farewell*. Still, James's relations with Esmé Stuart and, later, with the earl of Huntly—even when one forsakes the theme of homosexuality—help us to arrive at the most likely reason for the king's displeasure over Riche's tale. Both Esmé Stuart and the earl of Huntly were associated with the Catholic faction at a time when James—with an eye ultimately to the English crown—increasingly tried to present himself to the world as the avowed leader of a Protestant Church. Particularly the second half of the "Belfagor" story as narrated by Riche, the part hinging on the actual exorcism of the devil, would have enjoyed a most doubtful status within the context of the Protestant theology that James was at pains to advance. "Protestant opinion," as Keith Thomas puts it in his *Religion and the De-*

cline of Magic, "viewed the practice of . . . exorcisms with considerable hostility. The Wycliffites had denounced them as sheer necromancy, and their attitude was shared by the Protestant theologians of the Reformation era."[16] The logic behind this attitude, running against the Christian Church's earlier proceedings, was that "the power to cast out devils had been a special gift, conceded on the heroic age of the early Christian Church, but no longer necessary in a time of established faith" (Thomas, 571). For a Scottish king to be represented as a faithful believer in the practice would have exceeded the bounds of propriety under any circumstances, though especially after 1586 when Queen Elizabeth had formally recognized James as her heir. James was put to severe tests to make Elizabeth believe in his efficacy as a Protestant ruler. His Catholic mother's death he had taken silently. Also, he had made sure to convert Esmé Stuart to the Protestant faith and had even considered it appropriate to have Huntly exiled for his association with the pro-Catholic, Spanish contingent. With his explicit rejection of procedures of devil exorcism as egregious popish impostures—to echo Harsnet's anti-Catholic opus of 1603—James clearly could not afford to be associated with the practice, not even in Barnabe Riche's apparently harmless fiction for cultivated gentlewomen.[17] What a difference between King James and Machiavelli. For Machiavelli the "Belfagor" *novella* had been a delightful exercise in ridiculing the idea of possession by the devil with healthy skepticism.[18] For James it was an important matter of state.

If Riche was only vaguely aware of the ramifications that his transposition in the *novella* of Florence to London and of Paris to Edinburgh would have, the collection was both his *farewell* to one profession (the military profession) as well as his decisive entry into the political sphere. All we can say for certain is that King James, for good reasons, no doubt, as a recipient virtually *drew* Riche and his tale into that political sphere. A jest's propriety continues to lie in the ear of the listener. If the king did not distort the tale as he read it first in 1595, he certainly altered its fate. George Nicholson's letter to Robert Bowes of 18 June 1595 was to lead to significant alterations in the next edition of *Riche his Farewell,* which appeared in 1606. The passage about the king of Scotland being possessed by the devil was resolutely modified. In the original version the reader had been informed about the devil who "deuised with speede to flie the Countrey, and commyng to *Douer,* thinkyng to crosse the Seas, findyng no shippyng readie, he altered his course and gat hym into *Scot-*

lande, neuer staiyng till he came to *Edenbrough,* where the Kyng kept his Court" (sig. Eei[r]). In the 1606 version, however, the devil, "finding shipping ready, . . . toke his course and gat him to *Rome,* neuer staiyng till hee came to *Constantinople.*"[19] With the Edinburgh location changed to "Constantinople," the ruler possessed by the devil was no longer the king of Scotland, but, less disconcerting while James was king of England, "the *Turke.*"

After 1581, when Riche's *Farewell* first appeared, the "Belfagor" legend was to inspire English authors, each lifting from the original Italian, or from the English predecessor, whatever they deemed fit under the prevailing political climate. William Houghton's *Grim the Collier of Croydon* (c. 1602) is unique for its lengthy opening scene with the Parliament in Hell, in which Belfagor (here named "Belphagor") is elected as the unlucky devil sent out to examine the merits of marriage in England. No less unique is the end of Houghton's play, which shows Belphagor's precipitous return to hell, where the unfortunate devil is debriefed about his disastrous marital experiences due to women's pride. There may have been artistic reasons why Houghton should have wished to expand the notion of Parliament in Hell into the play's frame. A closer look, however, reveals that it may well have been motivated by a wish not to offend Queen Elizabeth.

The misogynist, Machiavellian subject matter of the play— namely that a wife should be "a curse ordained for the world" (Baillie, 1.1.64) or that marriage had "become so great a Curse" (1.1.103)—was not a theme that Queen Elizabeth's master of the revels would have approved with enthusiasm. Hence, the playwright's peculiar effort in the final scene of the comedy to undermine the play's very thesis about women. Back in hell, Belphagor reports on his twelve-month residence in England and discourses at length about the atrocities that he has suffered at the hands of his wife. After completing his speech, Pluto diplomatically asks Belphagor in a vocabulary highly unusual for the period,

> Doth then *Belphagor* this report of thine
> Against all Women hold in general?
>
> (*Grim the Collier,* 5.3.48–49)

Belphagor will not generalize:

> Not so, great prince, for as 'mongst other Creatures,
> Under that Sex are mingled good and bad,
> There are some women vertuous, chast and true,
> And to all those the Devil will give their due.
>   (*Grim the Collier*, 5.3.50–53)

Only after bestowing on a group of women the virtues then associated with Queen Elizabeth herself does Belphagor conclude,

> But, Oh my Dame! born for a scourge to man,
> For no mortality would endure that,
> Which she a thousand times hath offered me.
>   (*Grim the Collier*, 5.3.54–56)

Ironically, in an attempt to be diplomatic vis-à-vis the ruling queen, Houghton exploded the play's very theme, which was to ascertain precisely the general applicability of the allegations made about women in the opening scenes of *Grim the Collier*. All that Houghton is left with is the suggestion that some women are virtuous, chaste, and honest, whereas others are bad, and that Belphagor simply happened to become involved with the wrong type.

Although Houghton refrained from dramatizing the possession sequences that he found in Machiavelli's *novella*, this is not to say that possession by the devil could not be staged. This is evidenced most conspicuously by the final act of Ben Jonson's *The Devil Is an Ass*. Notably, though, the possession is a fake, so explicitly introduced as a form of trickery, as indeed it is in *Volpone*. Herford and Simpson conjecture that the playwright might have been trying to placate King James, and this is not unlikely, certainly given James's response to Riche's story and his engagement with deceptive practices of witchcraft. This assumption is more than justified by the fact that when James visited Cambridge in 1615 the university presented a play containing an episode mocking the procedure of exorcism of the type that James, officially after the Church canons of 1604, sought to expose as fraudulent.[20] Jonson's play, though, has its elements that recall the Italian "Belfagor" legend—especially the sociocritical slant that distinguishes Machiavelli's tale from Straparola's—but a close analysis of the text and the fortunes of devil Pug in Jacobean London strongly suggests that the German legend known as the Friar Rush story lies behind the comedy, including even the brief scene between the devils, which also seems to have been inspired by the Friar Rush-derived Parliament in Hell that opens Thomas Dekker's *If This Be not a Good Play*. Peter Happé is appropriately cautious when he considers the possible impact of Machiavelli's *novella* on Jonson's devil play, but it is always hazardous to underestimate Jonson's reading and his art of creative metamorphosis.[21] Of course, the "Belfagor" legend rears its head in English drama less conspicuously—not in the form of a scene, or in the shape of a character, but in the occasional, brief reference, as in Francis Beaumont and John Fletcher's *The Chances*, or Thomas Dekker's *The Honest Whore*. A most creative addition may be found in *News from Hell, Hull and Halifax* by John Taylor, the Water Poet. Here, the legend has been placed on its head once again, since the devil is remembered not as an impotent emissary of Pluto but as a highly successful Don Juan whom women remember with dread.[22]

Notably, all these manifestations may be dated *before* the tale of "Belfagor" was ever translated into English.[23] All authors, if they did not copy one another, used the first collected edition of Machiavelli's works in Italian, readily available in a London reprint by John Wolfe of 1588. This could be used to show that the cultural exchange between Italy and England during the late sixteenth and early seventeenth centuries was hardly affected by the language barrier. However, one hastens to qualify such optimism by observing that an original response may be registered as soon as the first English translation appeared during the troublesome year 1647 as "The Devil a Married Man, or the devil hath met with his Match." At this time of political turmoil, the tale with its conclave of devils in hell, and its theme of the fiend outwitted by mankind, proved a potent frame of reference.

Following the translation of "Belfagor" in 1647, one witnesses the emergence of that peculiar addition to English Machiavelli lore, namely the totally ignored 1648 playlet entitled *The Devill, and the Parliament* (1648), revealing its source most clearly by occasionally adopting the very wording of the *novella* in its 1647 translation, and by taking over the characters' names from Machiavelli's *novella*, including Belphagor.[24] *The Devill, and the Parliament* is a royalist and antiparliamentarian play for four actors. These include the Devil and Mr. Parliament, as well as the Devil's servants, Artophilax and Belphagor. It opens with the master devil, singing a song addressed to his old accomplice, Mr. Parliament. The master devil states that he has exhausted his array of infernal tricks and that he will be returning to hell: "Ile aide no more, for I have done, The worst that Hell could thinke upon" (sig. A2ʳ). With his idea to return to the lower regions, comes the decision to call a parliament:

> I meane to call a Parliament in Hell, but I shall not need to hunt about my territories to summon Members from each corporation, the upper House and lower House at *Westminster* shall be law-makers for me. I have found that they in policie [the household term to brand a Machiavel] exceed me farre, yea *Æacus Minos* and *Rhad* a man thus, and all his powers of Hell, that are beside.
>
> (*The Devill, and the Parliament*, sig. A2ᵛ)

For this purpose, he calls upon Belphagor, the emissary. Belphagor, it emerges, has over the past seven years of civil war "ever been a willing friend to flie abroad with any Messenger, sent by Parliament to cease upon the persons of all those Wrot[e] for the King, whose Pens did stab Rebellion to the heart" (sig. A2ᵛ). He has spied on judges who feared to show their malcontent, churchmen compelled to aid the rebels, and "rural swains" whom Westminster has sheared "nearer then their sheep" (sig. A3ᵛ). This same Belphagor is sent to fetch Mr. Parliament, but the latter refuses to come. Following Belphagor's characteristic failure, the master devil sends Artophilax, who soon returns with the unruly Mr. Parliament on his back, Mr. Parliament, who proudly accounts for his refusal to cooperate as follows, sounding surprisingly much like Gianmatteo, the wily farmer in the *novella* by Machiavelli:

> I tell thee brother, I am now as potent, and can without thee be as devillish, as when thy selfe wert most my friend, I now am my Crafts master, and know how, to be as envious bloody, and barbarous, as thou thy selfe canst possibly invent, I can out-do thee Lucifer my master. (sig. A3ᵛ)

As a matter of fact, Mr. Parliament is uncooperative partly because he finds that the infernal company—with whom he concluded a "contract" or a devil's pact seven years ago—is no longer serving him with its original strength (sig. A4ᵛ). The master devil cuts short Mr. Parliament and declares that "*God* will no longer let the *English* Nation bee slave to [his] Command" (sig. A4ᵛ). Having said those words, the devil instructs Belphagor and Artophilax to help him tear Mr. Parliament to pieces: "each of you take a limbe my masters *Devils,* I'le beare the rest myself" (sig. A4ᵛ). Exit for hell three devils with their prey, chanting the liberation of the English nation from the old, now deconstructed Parliament.

In the preface to his 1961 translation of "Belfagor," J. R. Hale argued that the Machiavelli tale could "be looted for evidence of Machiavelli's attitude towards society and the church." He also argued that "the just and formal government of Hell [can be] . . . seen as a deliberate contrast to the arbitrary and discordant government of Florence (where Machiavelli himself had been tortured . . . for suggested implication in an anti-government plot)" (p. xiv). The political frustration thus said to be biographically contained in the *novella* may explain why the playlet entitled *The Devill, and the Parliament* was so easily employed to comment on English politics during the Long Parliament, even when there was no reference whatsoever to Machiavelli. Clearly, Mayer's long-standing claim that "Machiavelli was . . . seldom cited in popular literature by the Loyalists against the Cromwellists and *vice versa*" looks in need of modification.[25]

In this paper I have tried to demonstrate that the *novella* of "Belfagor" entered a colorful political career with Barnabe Riche's *Farewell to the Militarie Profession* and *The Devill, and the Parliament.* Also in other contemporary texts, like Houghton's *Grim the Collier* or Jonson's *The Devil Is an Ass,* political considerations played an important role as the prose text was transformed for the stage. By way of a conclusion one may say that it would be impossible to speak of even a degree of consistency in the case of these examples. Whereas in the 1580s the "Belfagor" legend was employed for a practical joke on the Stuart king, in 1648 it served to mobilize sympathy for Charles and against Parliament. But it remains ironic, of course, that the monarchic crisis that the playlet tried to defuse with utopian zeal was due, in part, to Machiavelli's other work, and *The Prince* in particular. Still, even if we cannot speak of consistency, it is beyond doubt that the Italian tale was recognized for its political potential and that the 1647 "Belfagor" text was not "an uncontentious addition to the translations of Machiavelli's works into English," as Felix Raab assumed.

Notes

I am grateful to my colleagues Paul Franssen (Utrecht University) and Frank van Meurs (University of Nijmegen) for their assistance while researching this paper. My thanks also go to Susan Brock of The Shakespeare Institute,

Stratford-upon-Avon, who has been generous with her time, and supportive as ever.

1. Mario Praz, "Machiavelli and the Elizabethans," in *The Flaming Heart: Essays on Crashaw, Machiavelli, and Other Studies in the Relations between Italian and English Literature from Chaucer to T. S. Eliot* (1958; reprint, New York: W. W. Norton & Co., 1973), 90–145.

2. *Machiavelli and the Discourse of Literature,* ed. Albert Russell Ascoli and Victoria Kahn (Ithaca: Cornell University Press, 1993); Robin Kirkpatrick, *English and Italian Literature from Dante to Shakespeare: A Study of Source, Analogue and Divergence* (London: Longman, 1995). Victoria Kahn, though, convincingly argues that the threat of "Machiavellian rhetoric" to English politics fully justified the image of the fraudulent, deceptive and cunning "Machiavel." *See Machiavellian Rhetoric: From the Counter-Reformation to Milton* (Princeton: Princeton University Press, 1994).

3. For a fruitful discussion of the interrelation between "Belfagor" on the one hand and Machiavelli's *The Prince* and *The Discourses on Livy* on the other, *see* Theodore A. Sumberg, *"Belfagor:* Machiavelli's Short Story," in *Interpretation* 19 (1992), 243–50. Sumberg's thesis is explored in greater depth by Sebastian de Grazia, *Machiavelli in Hell* (Princeton: Princeton University Press, 1989), 65 and 320–23. *See also* J. A. Rawson, "Le 'Belphégor' de Machiavel,'" in *Diable, diables et diableries au temps de la renaissance,* ed. M. T. Jones-Davies, S.I.R.I.R., 13 (Paris: Jean Touzot, 1988), 183–88.

4. Felix Raab, *The English Face of Machiavelli: A Changing Interpretation, 1500–1700,* with a foreword by Hugh Trevor-Roper (London: Routledge & Kegan Paul, 1964), 114.

5. Lord Macaulay took a very narrow view indeed when he sought to account for the plain misogyny of "Belfagor" by naming the author's marital problems. As Macaulay put it, "Machiavelli was unhappily married; and his wish to avenge his own cause and that of his brethren in misfortune, carried him beyond even the licence of fiction." *See The Works of Lord Macaulay Complete,* ed. by his sister Lady Trevelyan, 8 vols. (London: Longmans, Green, and Co., 1866), vol. 5, 68. For another, more recent reading of the women's parts in "Belfagor," eschewing the allegation of misogyny, *see* Hanna Fenichel Pitkin, *Fortune is a Woman: Gender and Politics in the Thought of Niccolò Machiavelli* (Berkeley: University of California Press, 1984), 120–21. Lucy de Bruyn argues that in the *novella* man, woman as well as the devil are burlesqued. *See Woman and the Devil in Sixteenth-Century Literature* (Tisbury: The Compton Press, 1979), 143.

6. For a useful bibliographical account, *see A Choice Ternary of English Plays: Gratiæ Theatrales (1662),* ed. William N. Baillie, Medieval & Renaissance Texts & Studies, 26 (Binghamton, N. Y.: Medieval & Renaissance Texts and Studies, 1984), 185–86.

7. Charles H. Herford, *Studies in the Literary Relations of England and Germany in the Sixteenth Century* (1886; reprint, London: Frank Cass & Co., 1966), 293–322. (The title page of the 1966 reprint erroneously reads Charles E. Herford).

8. "The Devil Takes a Wife, or The Tale of Belfagor," in *The Literary Works of Machiavelli: "Mandragola," "Clizia," "A Dialogue on Language," "Belfagor," with Selections from the Private Correspondence,* ed. and trans. J. R. Hale (1961; reprint, Westport, Conn.: Greenwood Press, 1979), 201.

9. Listed in the Thomas L. Berger and W. C. Bradford, *Index of Characters*

in English Printed Drama to the Restoration (Englewood, Calif.: Microcard Editions, 1975). *The Devill, and the Parliament: or, The Parliament and the Devill: A Contestation between them for the precedencie* ([London], 1648), wing D1216.

10. *Riche his Farewell to Militarie profession … Barnabe Riche Gentleman* (London, 1581), STC 20996a.

11. *Rich's Farewell to Military Profession, 1581,* ed. Thomas Mabry Cranfill (Austin: University of Texas Press, 1959), 205, lines 30–32. The alleged memory failure here seems typical of the seventeenth-century reception of Machiavelli's *novella* in England. Compare the address to the reader in John Wilson's *Belphegor, or The Marriage of the Devil* (1690): "Matchiavel—whether the original were his own or Straparola's, for both lived near the same time, and both played with the same story—gave me the Argument of the ensuing play." *The Dramatic Works of John Wilson,* ed. James Maidment and W. H. Logan (Edinburgh, 1874), 287.

12. *See* D. W. Thompson, "Belphegor in *Grim the Collier* and Riche's *Farewell,*" in *Modern Language Notes* 50 (1935), 99–102. *See also* Cranfill, ed., *Rich's Farewell,* 334–35.

13. *Calendar of the State Papers relating to Scotland,* ed. Markham John Thorpe, 2 vols. (London, 1858), vol. 2, *The Scottish Series of the Reign of Queen Elizabeth, 1589–1603; An Appendix to the Scottish Series, 1543–1592; And the State Papers relating to Mary Queen of Scots during Her Detention in England, 1568–1587,* 683 (italics added).

14. In the preface to his two-volume edition of the *Calendar,* Thorpe fittingly notes that King James consulted an untraced 1594 edition of *Riche his Farewell* which he thought was a first edition. *See Calendar of the State Papers relating to Scotland,* ed. Markham John Thorpe, 2 vols. (London, 1858), vol. 1, *The Scottish Series of the Reigns of Henry VIII. Edward VI. Mary. Elizabeth. 1509–1589,* xxii.

15. Giovan Francesco Straparola, *Le piacevoli notti,* ed. Giuseppe Rua (1927; reprint Bari, 1975), 1, 91 (italics added).

16. Keith Thomas, *Religion and the Decline of Magic: Studies in Popular Beliefs in Sixteenth- and Seventeenth-Century England* (1971; reprint, Harmondsworth, Penguin Books, 1973), 571.

17. For further references to James's efforts to ban exorcism, *see* Thomas, *Religion and the Decline of Magic,* 569–88.

18. *See* de Grazia, *Machiavelli in Hell,* 320–23.

19. Barnabe Riche, *Riche His Farewell to the Military Profession. Newly Augmented* (London, 1606), STC 20997, sig. Y2^v. For another example of the topographical flexibility of the *novella's* plot see the stunning illustration of *San Gimignano Exorcizes the Daughter of the Emperor,* in De Grazia, *Machiavelli in Hell,* 332.

20. Thomas, *Religion and the Decline of Magic,* 579. Still valid is the discussion by C. H. Herford and Percy Simpson in *Ben Jonson* (Oxford: Clarendon Press, 1925), vol. 2, p. 163.

21. Ben Jonson, *The Devil Is an Ass,* ed. Peter Happé, The Revels Plays (Manchester: Manchester University Press, 1994), 28. Nevertheless, one continues to feel tempted to concur with Daniel C. Boughner when he concludes his comparative analysis of Jonson's comedy and the "Belfagor" *novella* with the words, "*The Devil Is an Ass* stands as an impressive final tribute to Machia-

velli." *See The Devil's Disciple: Ben Jonson's Debt to Machiavelli* (New York: Philosophical Library, 1968), 226.

22. *Early Prose and Poetical Works of John Taylor, The Water Poet (1580–1653)* (London, 1888), 283.

23. *See* Adolph Gerber, *Niccolo Machiavelli: Die Handschriften, Ausgaben und Übersetzungen seiner Werke im 16. und 17. Jahrhundert* (Gotha, 1912–13), *s.v.* "Belfagor."

24. Compare the phrase in the English Machiavelli: "Minos and Radamanthus and the other judges of the infernal region" (Hale, 193), and the following phrase from *The Devill, and the Parliament:* "Aeacus Minos and Rhadamanthus, and all his powers of Hell, that are beside" (sig. A2ᵛ). A rather similar phrase occurs in *Grim the Collier.*

25. Edward Meyer, *Machiavelli and the Elizabethan Drama* (1897), reprinted in the Burt Franklin: Research and Source Works series, 69 (New York: Burt Franklin, *s.d.*), 169. Even the political verse quoted by Meyer on the same page recalls the Parliament in Hell of the Belfagor tale.

"I have read them all": Jonson's *Volpone* and the Discourse of the Italianate Englishman

Michael J. Redmond

> Ascham sounds that deep mistrust of the effects of ill-chaperoned travel to Italy that lingers among Anglo-Saxon peoples even to the present day.
>
> Lawrence V. Ryan, *Roger Ascham*

In studying *Volpone* it has become a standard gesture to treat the subplot of the play as a satire on the efforts of gauche English travelers to mimic Italian sophistication. David C. McPherson's recent monograph, concentrating on the experiences of the English couple in Venice, dismisses Lady Would-be and her husband, Sir Politic Would-be, as "two unskillful imitators."[1] While such an approach takes account of the derivative behavior of the Would-bes, eager to display their knowledge of the country's customs and literature, critics tend to elide the implications of Peregrine's hostility toward Italian culture. Yet, aside from the comic aspects of Ben Jonson's depiction of cultural exchange between the two countries, the susceptibility of travelers to Italian influences was a controversial issue in early modern England. From 1570 onwards, following the publication of Roger Ascham's *The Schoolmaster*, domestic writers based their endorsement of restrictions on foreign travel upon the specific need to preclude contact with Italy. The cautionary figure of the Italianate Englishman, which Ascham used to typify the "many" travelers who are supposed to have "returned out of Italy worse transformed," reflects the concern that Englishmen abroad would adopt the vices conventionally ascribed to Italy, introducing alien modes of behavior into their native country.[2] What Peregrine has in common with his less judicious compatriots, implicated with the local vices, is his reliance upon the books that he read about Italy prior to his departure from England. As Peregrine attempts to distinguish his method of travel from the practices of the Would-bes, referring to his previous reading on the subject, he draws on the arguments established within the discourse of the Italianate Englishman. By highlighting the sources of each traveler's knowledge about the country, through the sheer mass of allusions within the play to prominent authors, Jonson places the contemporary debate about travel within the context of the textual transmission of national stereotypes.

To satisfy the fascination of their compatriots with Italian culture, without exposing them to dangers of the country itself, English writers advocated reading as a textual alternative to travel. In a postscript to a translation of the works of Livy, Philemon Holland cautions his readers "who shall take delight and pleasure in reading the Romane storie above-written" against forming "a liking of the verie place, which hath affourded so many woorthy persons and rare examples."[3] As he emphasizes how "farre degenerate now are the inhabitants now from that aunchient people, so devout, so vertuous, so uncorrupt, in old time," Holland makes manifest his desire to counteract the manner in which "the love [of classical learning] hath moved many a man to undertake a voiage to Rome" (1346). He stresses that, although travelers intend "onely to see the river Tyberius, those seven hills, and the monuments remaining of that famous citie," the journey has "exceeding dangerous" consequences for their "religion, conscience and good manners" (1346). In order to ensure that his readers are not tempted to depart from England, Holland provides a survey of the ancient city "to bring Rome (as it were) home to them, even to represent unto their eye the topographie therof," so that they may "avoide the perill of that travaile" (1346). The translator's advice, attempting to restrict English contact with Italy to classical remnants that can be experienced textually at "home," marks the tension between the reverence for Italian culture fostered by an educational regime based on Latin and the demonization of contemporary Italian religious and social practices.

The obligation Holland felt to insert a passage discouraging foreign travel at the conclusion of his scholarly translation suggests the extent of the anxiety about Italian influences that pervades early modern English writing. Despite acknowledging the cultural necessity of texts derived from Roman and Italian sources, writers continually assert that exposure to the Italy of their age threatens the stability of domestic, religious, political, and sexual structures. The ease with which the native virtues of the Englishman abroad may be displaced makes certain that, as Thomas Nashe's banished earl explains in *The Unfortunate Traveller,* reading offers the only safe way of approaching Italian culture:

> What is here but we may read in books, and a great deal more too, without stirring our feet out of a warm study? . . . So let others tell you strange accidents, treasons, poisonings, close packings in France, Spain and Italy; it is no harm for you to hear of them, but come not near them.[4]

By locating the site of danger outside the borders of England, the emphasis on the hazards of travel permits the English to appropriate Italy's cultural legacy. For although the tenor of Ascham's arguments "stands in sharp contrast to the humanist idea of Italy as the legitimate heir to Roman virtue," as Andreas Mahler contends, his acknowledgment of the country's past virtues serves to exonerate the texts used in his classroom.[5] As the author of an educational treatise based on the study of classical literature, Ascham disclaims

> any private malice . . . to Italy, which country and in it, namely Rome, I have always specially honoured because time was when Italy and Rome have been, to the great good of us that now live, the best breeders and bringers-up of the worthiest men, not only for wise speaking, but also for well-doing, in all civil affairs, that ever was in the world. (60)

However, as the country's mores and manners have declined, "Italy now is not that Italy it was wont to be and therefore now not so fit a place as some do count it for young men to fetch either wisdom or honesty from thence" (62). For Ascham, then, the problem at hand consists not in the imitation of foreign models per se, but in the type of models that travel offers to his compatriots. The transformation of Italy into a textual experience promises that, with censorship mechanisms in place, the influnces that sway the English reader may be restricted to safe and orthodox discourse.

Concerns about the nature of the English relationship with Italy come to the fore in Jonson's *Volpone.* Within the subplot of the comedy, concentrating on the adventures of three English tourists in Venice, Jonson rehearses the debate about foreign travel. Through the two Englishmen abroad, Sir Politic Would-be and Peregrine, the subplot opposes the actions of an apparently stereotypical Italianate Englishman with those of a traveler who refuses to succumb to the allure of Italian decadence. While Sir Politic Would-be, who claims that "Within the first week of [his] landing" he was taken "for a citizen of Venice," embodies domestic apprehensions about exposure to Italian culture, Peregrine rejects the vices that he encounters in the city.[6] The use of the name Peregrine, a word specifically denoting "a sojourner in a strange land" (OED), raises the possibility that the character may be more representative of English travelers abroad than his foolish countryman. In his first encounter with the knight, Peregrine uses an explicit allusion to the discourse of the Italianate Englishman to describe him: "Heart! / This Sir Pol will be ignorant of nothing" (2.1.97–98). With the phrase "ignorant of nothing," the suspicious traveler repeats the exact words that Ascham uses in *The Schoolmaster* to portray "English Italians" as "busy searchers of most secret affairs" (74). Yet, apart from casting Sir Politic in terms of the stock image of an unwary traveler, Peregrine betrays here his reliance upon his previous reading. Insofar as all Jonson's travelers reenact the texts they have been exposed to, the extent to which Peregrine avoids being transformed into an Italianate Englishman is merely a function of the books he has chosen to emulate.

When considered in light of the pervasive influence of the discourse of the Italianate Englishman, Ben Jonson's assistance in the preparation of an ill-received volume of travel writing provides a valuable means of approaching the issue of intertextuality in *Volpone*. In 1611, four years after his Venetian play was printed, the dramatist became involved in the controversy surrounding the publication of *Coryat's Crudities,* a text featuring an earnest account of the beauties of Venice and the benefits of foreign travel. To help promote the work, written and self-published at great cost by his friend Thomas Coryate, Jonson contributed characters of the author to both the original book and a second organized in its defence. Coryate required Jonson's assistance because the Prince of Wales had compelled the traveler to preface his narrative with over a hundred pages (in the original edition) of "Panegyrick Verses" that actually condemn the book.[7] Prince Henry's intervention in the publication of the *Crudities* came at a time when the heir to the throne, styling himself as the champion of the anti-Catholic party at court, was becoming uneasy about James's policy of engagement with the independent Italian states. The prince was particularly opposed to the manner in which his father, eager to encourage other states to take up Venice's conflict with the papacy, was pursuing an Italian match for him.[8]

Within the prefatory material that Coryate wrote for the *Crudities,* he depicts the collection of verses demanded by Prince Henry as an intrusion within his work. What is at stake in the enforced publication of the verses, as Coryate makes clear, is control over the representation of his journey. In defending his project, the travel writer repeatedly emphasizes that he "could not give the repulse unto the Authors of the verses following to insert their lines into [his] book."[9] He attributes their inclusion to force majeure, noting that "the Princes Highnesse . . . understanding that I meant to suppresse so many, gave me a strict and expresse commandement to print all those verses," and he implores his potential readers to reserve their opinions until they have read the entire text. While prefatory material was conventionally employed to promote the publication of a new work, the verses that open the *Crudities* censure the travel writer for being heedless of the manner in which, as Robert Philips's contribution puts it, "many of our English men . . . returne home corrupted in manners and much worse then they went forth" (1:31). By privileging claims that Coryate may have absorbed "the vices of the countries through which [he] traveld," the inclusion of such arguments casts the book as a contest between competing models of travel (1:31). For although Coryate goes on to claim that "a virtuous man will be the more confirmed and settled in virtue by the observation of some vices," the verses that he was compelled to print ahead of his account emphasize the susceptibility of English travelers to dissolute Italian influences (1:408). To maintain the authority of his narrative, denying that he was corrupted by contact with Italy, he must discredit the assertions of his unwelcome detractors. Yet, aside from the subversive position that they occupy at the opening of his book, the subsequent circulation of the verses ensured that the contest was unequal. Upon publication, the official edition of the *Crudities* was immediately eclipsed by a pirated edition of the "Panegyric Verses" that "purposely omitted" Coryate's text in order to safeguard the "gentle Reader."[10]

It was a canny move by Coryate to enlist Jonson in his rebuttal of the verses. By doing so, displaying the support of a noted literary figure, he preempts efforts to compare him with the foolish English travelers who appear in *Volpone.* Jonson's contributions disclaim any connection between Coryate and Sir Politic Would-be, who had already become a byword for the wrong sort of Englishman abroad: "The greatest Politick that advances into Paules [Coryate] will quite, to go talke with the Grecian who begs there; such is humility"(1:17). Indeed, adopting the title of the traveler who resists the charms of Venice in the play, Coryate casts himself as the "Peregrine of Odcombe" at the end of his introduction to the book (1:6).

Coryate's second publication of 1611, the *Crambe,* a work refuting "the malicious censure" and "very scandalous imputations" that greeted the initial book, includes a poem by Jonson addressed "To the London Reader."[11] To preserve the travel writer from "reproofe," Jonson emphasizes the details his friend provides about foreign locales "that another should hide":

> And therefore how ever the travelling nation,
> Or builders of story have oft imputation
> Of lying . . .
>
> . . . .
>
> Poor Tom have we cause to suspect thee?
> No: as I first said, who would write a story at
> The height, let him learne of Mr. Tom Coryate.
>
> (sigs. A2v-A3r)

Through his reference to that which he "first said," Jonson may be recalling the "Character of the Author" that he provided for the *Crudities.* The title of the character, stating that it is "Done by a charitable Friend, that thinks it necessary, by this time, you should understand the Maker, as well as the worke," indicates that the dramatist was already worried about the reception of Coryate's work prior to its initial publication (1:16).

While Jonson responds to the imputations against his friend's personal integrity, Richard Badley's contribution to the collection of "Panegyric Verses" emphasizes that the problem with the *Crudities* is not the effect that Venice may have had on Coryate personally, but the influence that his book may have upon susceptible English readers:

> If Schedules of this nature had been found
> About Sir Politick, 'twold have made him swound.
>
> (1: 107)

The allusion to Jonson's dramatic character functions as a warning against unchecked writing about Italy, rather than against the threat posed by Italy itself. In worrying about the consequences of reading a book promoting the attractions of Italian culture, Badley implicitly relocates the site of the threat against the English subject to the libraries of his own country.

By offering Sir Politic Would-be as an example of the consequences of reading about Italy, Badley's verse calls attention to the importance that issues of textuality acquire within the subplot of *Volpone*. As Jonson stages domestic anxieties about Italian influences, a focus that ensured its relevance to the debate surrounding the publication of the *Crudities*, he takes care to show that the knight's departure from the boundaries of acceptible English behavior occurred prior to any foreign travel. For although Peregrine attempts to identify his compatriot according to the discourse of the Italianate Englishman, Sir Politic himself denies that his motives correspond with those conventionally ascribed to travelers:

> Yet, I protest, it is no salt desire
> Of seeing countries, shifting a religion,
> Nor any disaffection to the state
> Where I was bred, and unto which I owe
> My dearest plots, hath brought me out, much less
> That idle, antique, stale grey-haired project
> Of knowing men's minds and manners.
>
> (2.1.4–10)

Dismissing the usual grounds of tourism or religious and political dissent, the knight admits that his journey to Venice was occasioned by a "peculiar humour of [his] wife's" (2.1.11). However, Sir Politic does not merely place himself outside the parameters of the contemporary definition of travel. He goes on to attribute his "dearest plots" to the influence of "the state / Where I was bred" (2.1.8 and 6–7).

While Sir Politic makes much of his powers of "observation," as he introduces his fellow countryman to Venetian culture, he derives his self-proclaimed expertise from the representations of the area that he read at home in England (4.1.2). When he comes to offer Peregrine some advice "fit to be known / Of your crude traveller," he acknowledges that he is rehashing old "themes" (4.1.6–7 and 9). The instructions that he provides, encouraging the traveler to "never speak a truth" while in the company of strangers, conform with standard counsel about the dangers of the city and its inhabitants (4.1.17). Sir John Stradling concludes his guide to foreign travel, for example, with a specific note about the guile that visitors to "Italie and Venice" must practice:

> The men, as are inveigling underminers and deep dissemblers, whoe when they have pried into your nature, and are privie to your secrets, wil straight change their coppie, and shew themselves in their colours: against these dissemblers I know no other, or at least no better buckler, then to dissemble also your selfe ... To deceive a deceiver is no deceit.[12]

Though Stradling's depiction of Italian deceit reflects the acceptible face of English travel writing, in contrast to Coryate's enthusiastic endorsement of Italian culture, Sir Politic does not restrict himself to this sort of material. After offering precepts for travel, he quickly shifts to the more compelling issue of "*ragion del stato*" (4.1.141). He makes much of his plans to serve the council of Venice but claims that he cannot talk further about matters of policy without the "notes" that he has written on the subject (4.1.81). However, the trick that Peregrine and three English merchants arrange for Sir Politic confirms the would-be politician's reliance on previous representations of Italian statecraft. To expose the pretensions behind his compatriot's talk of "weighty affairs of state," Peregrine disguises himself as a merchant and comes to warn Sir Politic that the senate of the city plans to seize his papers (5.4.15). Here, although he has often spoken of his firsthand knowledge of plots and projects, the knight is forced to concede that he has no documents of his own: "Alas, sir, I have none, but notes / Drawn out of playbooks ... And some essays" (5.4.41–43). Instead of participating in the schemes of the Venetians, by producing his own text, Sir Politic has only been reading about them.

By tracing the sources of the knight's knowledge of "the ebbs / And flows of state," Jonson points to the explosion in domestic interest about Italian political and social practices that emerged alongside the efforts to preclude travel (2.1.104–5). Although Ascham's warnings against "plenty of new mischiefs never known in England before" contend that travel was the principal means of cultural exchange between the two countries, there was a ready market amongst his compatriots for texts detailing "the learning, the policy, the experiences, [and] the manners of Italy" (69). In a letter to Edmund Spenser (printed in 1580), reporting on the books "highly regarded of Schollers," Gabriel

Harvey ruefully concedes that his colleagues have forsworn classical and domestic authors:

> Matchiavell a great man: Castilio [Castiglione] of no small reputation: Petrarch, and Boccace in every mans mouth: Galateo and Guazzo never so happy: over many acquainted with Unico Aretino.[13]

Between them, Sir Politic and Lady Would-be manage to refer to almost all of the prominent Italian authors that Harvey mentions. Indeed, when Volpone inadvertently raises the subject of poetry, the Englishwoman offers her own extensive list of writers from the country:

> Which o' your poets? Petrarch? or Tasso? or Dante?
> Guarini? Ariosto? Aretine?
> Cieco di Hadria? I have read them all.
>
> (3.4.79–81)

The pride that Lady Would-be displays in the breadth of her reading is shared by her husband. To justify his pose as an authority on Venetian policy, Sir Politic advertises his acquaintance with the precepts of "Nick Machiavel" and states that he has "read Contarine" (4.1.26 and 40). While critics of the play have conventionally focused on the couple's lack of interpretive skills, listing the "hilariously inept" allusions, the ironies that arise as they discuss their reading are contingent upon the English audience's previous knowledge of these authors.[14] Through encouraging his compatriots to laugh at the understatement implicit in Lady Pol's comment that Aretino's pictures "are a little obscene," Jonson plays on their own familiarity with such an emblematic figure of Italian vice (3.4.97).

Despite the fears about the learning that travelers might acquire in Italy, the reading habits of the Would-bes make manifest the extent to which Italian influences have already been assimilated textually. In offering a model for her actions, Lady Would-be refers to Castiglione's *The Courtier*, rather than the Venetian courtesans:

> I would be loath to contest publicly
> With any gentlewoman, or to seem
> Froward or violent: as *The Courtier* says;
> It comes too near rusticity in a lady,
> Which I would shun by all means.
>
> (4.2.33–37)

Lady Pol's comments, as she disputes with the supposed courtesan accompanying her husband, recall the third book of Castiglione's collection of debates about courtly conduct. Within its discussion of the feminine graces appropriate to a woman of the palace, encouraging a "certain bashfulnesse" in behavior, the book includes a specific condemnation of ladies who "speake and willingly give eare to such as report ill of other women."[15] Yet, although she knows what to avoid, the Englishwoman falls well short of the ideal she is trying to emulate. For the Italian courtier, the model lady should have "above all other thinges, a certaine sweetnesse in language that may delite, whereby she may entertain all kinde of men with talke worthie the hearing" (190). The horror with which Volpone responds to Lady Pol's visits, begging her to accept that the "highest female grace is silence," underlines the inadequacy of her conversation (3.4.78).

In her references to the courtly writing that was popular during the Elizabethan period, Lady Would-be calls attention to the long-standing tradition of emulating Italian texts. For Jacobean audiences, part of the humor of the Englishwoman's literary allusions would have come from the anachronistic nature of her choice of reading material. Aside from her interest in Castiglione, a writer whose precepts for self-promotion had become associated with the competition for favor at Elizabeth's court, she admits to being an enthusiastic reader of the poets that inspired domestic writers in past "days of sonnetting" (3.4.94).[16] When she finds a copy of Guarini's "*Pastor Fido,*" Lady Pol lectures Volpone on the literary theft practiced by previous authors from her own country:

> All our English writers,
> I mean such as are happy in th' Italian,
> Will deign to steal out of this author ...
> .   .   .   .
> He has so modern and facile a vein,
> Fitting the time, and catching the court-ear!
> Your Petrarch is more passionate, yet he,
> In days of sonnetting trusted 'em with much.
> (3.4.86 and 87–94)

Her comments make manifest that, for all the efforts to preserve the boundaries separating English culture from its enemies abroad, domestic writers catering to the demands of "the court-ear" have been adopting Italian models for many years.

Lady Would-be's fascination with Italian writing suggests that critics have been too quick to accept Peregrine's contention that she came to Venice "for intelligence, / Of tires, and fashions, and behaviour, / Among the courtesans" (2.1.27–9). For although she is certainly concerned about her appearance, proudly resisting potential accusations that "The English lady cannot dress herself," Lady Pol never admits to imitating the Venetian women (3.4.34). While her position as a traveler abroad evokes the fears about English subjects adopting foreign vices, her reading habits point to the circulation of Italian texts within England. The argument that Lady Would-be "strives to adopt Italian vices for her own" overlooks the manner in which Peregrine's accusation reflects stock anxieties about the potential influence of the city's fashions upon Englishwomen.[17] In *The English Ape, The Italian Imitation, The Footesteppes of France,* a text offering the requisite attack on how the "Italian Englishman . . . prefers the corruption of a forreine nation, before the perfection of his owne profession," William Rankins condemns "the monstrous pride of some women . . . in so much that they rather seeme Curtyzans of Venyce, then Matrones of Englande."[18] Rankins asserts that, where men are seduced by the allure of Italian vices, the "godly conversation" of Englishwomen is contaminated by "apish toyes borrowed from Italian Curtezans" (25). By viewing his countrywoman within the context of such expectations, at the same time as he uses Ascham's remarks to cast Sir Politic as an Italianate Englishman, Peregrine reveals more about the domestic prejudices that shape his response to Italy than he does about her character.

The priority that Peregrine gives to notions derived from the discourse of the Italianate Englishman conforms with the instructions offered by antitravel writers during the period. For Joseph Hall, writing six years after the controversy surrounding the publication of *Coryat's Crudities,* the best protection against the dangers of Italy is for would-be travelers to "carefully foreinstruct and poise themselves" and pay special heed to "those lessons taught by the State."[19] In *Quo Vadis,* a treatise cautioning against foreign travel, Hall encourages his compatriots to read the hostile accounts of Italy provided by "learned and credible Authors" (32). Hall's formulation of textual authority, expanding on arguments already implicit in Ascham and Nashe's efforts to discourage contact with Italian culture, articulates the concerns that are at stake in the representations of reading in *Volpone* and the prefatory material to the *Crudities.* As a prominent court divine and prolific writer, Hall was well aware of the restrictions placed on the texts that were legitimately available to English readers. The printing of domestic works and the import of books from abroad was licensed by a panel of twelve clerics appointed by the archbishop of Canterbury and the bishop of London.[20] Indeed, after satires were prohibited in 1599, works by Hall himself were recalled and burned.[21] Nonetheless, as he went on to acquire more influential positions in the Stuart Church, Hall became an enthusiastic proponent of state censorship.[22] His promotion of the value of reading in *Quo Vadis,* relying upon the veto of the censor, works to militate against the emergence of further Italianate Englishmen. With the acknowledged vulnerability of domestic subjects to foreign influences, where Hall himself concedes that "few young travellers have brought home, sound and safe, and (in a word) English bodies," it becomes essential that the ideologies that foster orthodox versions of Englishness obtain a monopoly position (17).

To ensure their safety from the persuasive influences of Italian culture, Hall advises young gentlemen to restrict themselves to reading about the country. He takes care to belittle the value of personal experience: "we may well consider, what varietie of report every accident will yeeld; and that our eares abroad are no whit more credible, then our eyes at home" (38). He asserts that, with the information available in approved books, "the lessons [offered by travel] may be as well taken out at home":

I have known some that have travelled no further than their owne closet, which could both teach and correct the greatest Traveller, after all his tedious and costly pererrations, what doe we but lose the benefit of so many journals, maps, historical descriptions, relations, if wee cannot with these helps, travell by our owne fire-side? He that travells into forraine countries, talkes perhaps with a Peasant, or a Pilgrim, or a Citizen, or a Courtier; and must needs take such information as partiall rumour, or weake conjecture can give him; but he that travels into learned and credible Authors, talkes with them who have spent themselves in bolting out the truth of all passages. (31–32)

In choosing to "travell through the world of bookes" (36), Hall maintains, readers may avoid the hazards of a foreign journey:

A good book is at once the best companion, and guide, and way, and end of our journey. Necessitie drove our forefathers out of doores, which else in those misty times had seene no light, we may with more ease, and no lesse profit sit still, and inherit, and enjoy the labours of them, and our elder brethren, who have purchased our knowledge with much hazard, time, toile, expence; and have beene liberall of their bloud (some of them) to leave us rich. (34)

Yet, although Hall emphasizes the virtues of travel literature, his endorsement of reading is predicated on the policing of English texts and readers. The metaphor that the clergyman uses to depict the benefits of reading betrays the power relationships that are involved in his project: "We have heard a bird in a cage sing more change of notes, then others have done in the wilde liberty of the wood" (37). By the end of his account, Hall makes explicit his demand for enforced cultural isolation: "oh, that the hands of supreme authoritie would be pleased to locke us within our owne doores, and to keepe the keyes at their owne girdle"(88).

With the importance that early modern opponents of travel assign to the act of reading, it was inevitable that domestic texts that failed to provide the requisite condemnations of Italian culture would be received unfavorably. The contest between competing versions of foreign travel that arises in *Coryat's Crudities,* as a consequence of the intervention of the Prince of Wales, highlights the author's transgression of the orthodoxies regarding Italian culture. It is of doubtful validity to argue, with Ann Rosalind Jones, that the work caters to "the desire to hear about foreign evils already present in earlier English versions of Italy."[23] The hostile commentary that the "Panegyrick Verses" provide focuses precisely upon Coryate's failure to conform with accepted depictions of the country. For although Jones recognizes the "erotic sensationalism" that the contributors of the verses employ as they describe the travel writer, she elides the tensions surrounding the work's publication (116). These tensions may be seen by the way in which, to prevent his readers from being persuaded by the verses, Coryate provides a series of defensive footnotes that challenge their portrayal of him. For instance, where Inigo Jones accuses him of overfamiliarity with a Venetian courtesan, the traveler affixes a dissenting comment at the bottom of the page: "Beleeve him not Reader. Read my apologie in my discourse of the Venetian Cortezans, p. 270" (1:64).[24]

While many of the verses offer bawdy accounts of Coryate's encounter with the courtesan, taking advantage of the connotations that such a woman had for domestic readers, the issue at hand is the possible reception of his text. Robert Richmond's submission, drawing on the discourse of the Italianate Englishman, warns the author that he was "too curious [about] / Such places that oftentimes make most temperate men most furious":

> Say what you list, sweare and protest, for all this great Bravado,
> It will be said, at least be guest, you were the Puncks Privado,
> And so you'll lose great store of those, whose verse may give you
>   glory . . .
> . . . .
> You'le have noe such to praise you much: they will suspect the
>   wench
> Hath turned your Greeke and Latin both into a perfect French.
>   (1:51)

The final reference to a change in languages, where Coryate's classical learning threatens to be lost in favor of a tongue associated with decadent sexuality, evokes Ascham's concerns about the displacement of national characteristics. With his acknowledgment of the reservations of his fellow contributors, Richmond underlines that the so-called "Panegyric Verses" function as an oppositional presence within the book.

As he mocks the travel writer's literary aspirations, John Donne—in two poems staging domestic anxieties about disintegration—makes manifest that the controversy surrounding the book is about representation, rather than travel. To express his contempt for the work, the poet and cleric uses an elaborate conceit which compares the fate of the offending text to that of an executed criminal:

> Worst malefactors, to whom men are prize,
> Doe publique good, cut in anatomies;
> So will thy book in peeces . . .
> . . . .
> Some shal wrap pils, and save a friends life so,
> Some shall stop muskets, and so kill a foe . . .
> . . . .
> Some leav's may paste strings there in other books,
> And so one may, which on another looks,
> Pilfer, alas, a little wit from you,
> But hardly much.[25]

The verse depicts the destruction of the physical book by the hands of authority. By suggesting that the only benefit that may be obtained from Coryate's work is through the reuse of its dismembered pages, he refuses to allow that the text has any literary or social value. Although the purpose of the verse is ostensibly to promote the book, Donne states, "I am gone; / And rather than reade all, I would reade none" (1:39).

In this poem, written in the same period that his anti-Catholic works *Pseudo-Martyr* (1610) and *Ignatius his Conclave* (1611) were published, Donne predicates his criticism upon the travel writer's suspect choice of destination: "Venice vast lake thou hast seene, wouldst seeke than / Some vaster thing, and foundst a Cortizan" (1:37). He contends that the book is contaminated by its exposure to Italian decadence:

> The east sends hither her deliciousness;
> And thy leav's must embrace what comes from thence,
> The Myrrhe, the Pepper, and the Frankinsence
>
> (1:37)

Through the anticlimactic zeugma arising from the insertion of "Pepper" within his allusion to the gifts of the magi, Donne notes that there is a disturbing presence amidst the allurements of the east that Coryate's pages seek to enumerate.

Donne's second poem focuses its attack on the threat posed by Coryate's project. As the verse collapses into a mishmash of different languages, evoking the discourse of the Italianate Englishman, Donne offers a text that has become utterly corrupted by outside elements:

> In euendum Macaronicon
> Quot, dos haec, LINGUISTS perfetti, Disticha fairont,
> Tot cuerdos STATES-MEN, hic liure fara tuus.
> Es sat A MY l'honneur estre hic inteso: Car I LEAVE
> L'honra, de personne nestre creduto, tibi.[26]

A translation of the verse shows that the poet is addressing the domestic reception of the *Crudities*:

> As many perfect linguists as these two distichs make,
> So many prudent statesmen will this book of yours produce ...
> To me the honour is sufficient of being understood; for I leave
> To you the honour of being believed by no one.[27]

As the compelling attraction of foreign influences threatens to displace native learning, the text itself loses its English identity. The format of the macaronic verse, where the meaning is obscured by the multitude of tongues, portrays the implications of the manner in which Coryate's book brings the cultures of Italy and Europe to the English reader.

In considering national stereotypes, as Joep Leerssen has warned, images of foreign cultures must be seen "not as measureably (un)faithful or (un)reliable item[s] of information concerning a knowable objective reality, but rather as a textual construct."[28] Through the use of foreign languages in the second verse, calling attention to the literary conventions that govern his work, Donne offers a vision of English culture under siege. Yet, as the poet's concern about the type of books available to his compatriots suggests, the threat that the discourse of the Italianate Englishman attributes to external influences is ultimately a projection of issues being contested internally. By fashioning "an outward positive cause whose elimination would enable us to restore order, stability, and identity," according to Slavoj Zizek, ideological projects take account of the impossibility of attaining domestic consensus.[29] The safe and secure English subject that Donne and his fellow opponents of travel promise, in the absence of contact with Italy, is a fantasy scenario disguising the lack of any inherent national identity. Jonson enables us to see this in *Volpone,* where the behavior of the travelers is determined by the representations they were exposed to before their departure from England. Even Peregrine, whose function within the play is to resist the insinuations of Italian culture, resorts not to the notion of a stable centered self but to his previous reading. When the two Englishmen abroad observe the mountebank, Jonson highlights the manner in which the more reticent traveler mouths the standard condemnations of Italian vice that domestic readers were offered at home. For although Peregrine denounces mountebanks as "the most lewd imposters, / Made all of terms and shreds," he admits that his opinion is derived solely from the "discourse" provided by his "instructor / In the dear tongues" (2.2.14–15 and 2–3). In responding to the knight's query about the source of his "rules for travel," Peregrine states that he "had / Some common ones from out that vulgar grammar, / Which he that cri'd Italian to me, taught me" (2.1.112–14). The character's allusions to an Italian grammar, as Brian Parker has suggested, likely refer to the publications of John Florio, "the foremost Italian tutor in London at that time."[30] The British Library has a copy of the play that Jonson dedicated to Florio. In Florio's *Second Frutes* (1591), a text featuring a series of dialogues printed in English and Italian, there is a discussion "of divers necessarie, profitable, civil, and proverbial precepts for a travaillour."[31] With the suggestion of a possible textual source for Peregrine's views on Italian culture, albeit from a more orthodox author than those enjoyed by the foolish Would-bes, Jonson emphasizes that none of the English travelers is able to escape the influence of earlier representations of the country. Indeed, despite the extent to which his own responses are formed by books about Italy, Sir Politic goes on to criticize Peregrine's reliance upon secondhand ideas: "Why, this is that spoils all our brave bloods, / Trusting our hopeful gentry unto pedants" (2.2.115–16).

Notes

1. David C. McPherson, *Shakespeare, Jonson, and the Myth of Venice* (Newark: University of Delaware Press, 1990), 107.

2. Roger Ascham, *The Schoolmaster,* ed. Lawrence V. Ryan (Ithaca: Cornell University Press, 1967), 63. All subsequent quotations will be taken from this edition.

3. Philemon Holland, "To the Reader," *The Romane Historie Written by T. Livius of Padua,* (London: A. Islip, 1600), *STC* 16613, 1346. All subsequent quotations will be taken from this edition.

4. Thomas Nashe, *The Unfortunate Traveller and Other Works,* ed. J. B. Steane (1972; reprint, Harmondsworth: Penguin Books, 1985), 343–44.

5. Andreas Mahler, "Italian Vices: Cross-Cultural Constructions of Temptation and Desire in English Renaissance Drama," in *Shakespeare's Italy: Functions of Italian Locations in Renaissance Drama,* eds. Michele Marrapodi, A. J. Hoenselaars, Marcello Cappuzzo, and L. Falzon Santucci (Manchester, Manchester University Press, 1993), 50.

6. Ben Jonson, *Volpone,* ed. R. B. Parker (Manchester: Manchester University Press, 1983), 4.1.37, 8. All subsequent quotations will be taken from this volume.

7. *See* Michael Strachan, *The Life and Adventures of Thomas Coryate* (London: Oxford University Press, 1962), 124–25.

8. For the prince's aversion to a marriage aligning his family with either the grand duke of Tuscany or the duke of Savoy, *see* Roy Strong, "England and Italy: The Marriage of Henry Prince of Wales," in *For Veronica Wedgewood these Studies in Seventeenth Century History,* ed. Richard Ollard and Pamela Tudor Craig (London: Collins, 1986): 59–87; and Elkins Calhoun Wilson, *Prince Henry and English Literature* (Ithaca: Cornell University Press, 1946), 97–100.

9. Thomas Coryate, *Coryat's Crudities,* 2 vols. (Glasgow: J. MacLehose, 1905), 1 : 99. All subsequent quotations will be taken from this edition.

10. *The Odcombian Banquet: Dished Foorth by Thomas the Coriat, and Served in by a number of Noble Wits in prayse of his Crudities and Crambe too* (London: T. Thorp, 1611), *STC* 5810, sig. P4v. For a further discussion of this text see Strachan, *The Life and Adventures,* 134–37.

11. Thomas Coryate, *Coryats Crambe, or His Corwort Twise Sodden, And*

now served with other Macaronicke dishes as the second course to his Crudities (London: W. Stansby, 1611), *STC* 5807, sig. A2r.

12. Sir John Stradling, *A Direction for Travailers Taken Out of Justus Lipsius, and enlarged for the behoofe of the right honourable Lord, the yong Earl of Bedford, being now ready to travell* (London: R. B[ourne] f. C. Burbie, 1592), *STC* 15696, sig. C3r.

13. Gabriel Harvey, *The Works of Gabriel Harvey,* ed. Rev. Alexander B. Grosart, 3 vols., Huth Library series (1884, reprint, Ann Arbor: Xerox Reprographic Services, 1963), 1: 69.

14. McPherson, *Shakespeare, Jonson, and the Myth of Venice,* 110. *See also* John W. Creaser, "A Vindication of Sir Politic Would-be," *English Studies* 57 (1976): 502–14.

15. Baldassare Castiglione, *The Book of the Courtier,* trans. Sir Thomas Hoby, Everyman's Library (1928; reprint, London: J.M. Dent & Sons, 1974), 194, 191. All further references will be to this edition.

16. For an account of the manner in which Castiglione's reputation declined among English readers, *see* Daniel Javitch, *Poetry and Courtliness in Renaissance England* (Princeton: Princeton University Press, 1978), 131.

17. Jonas Barish, "The Double Plot in *Volpone,*" *Modern Philology* 51 (1953): 88.

18. W[illiam] R[ankins], *The English Ape, The Italian Imitation, The Footesteppes of France* (London: R. Robinson, 1588), *STC* 20698, 2, 23.

19. Joseph Hall, *Quo Vadis? A Just Censure of Travell As it is commonly undertaken by the Gentlemen of our Nation,* The English Experience, no. 740. (1617; reprint, Amsterdam: Theatrum Orbis Terrarum, 1975), 90–91. All further quotations will be taken from this edition.

20. W. W. Greg, *Some Aspects and Problems of London Publishing Between 1550 and 1650* (Oxford: Clarendon Press, 1956), 51.

21. Christopher Hill, "Censorship and English Literature," *The Collected Essays of Christopher Hill, Volume One: Writing and Revolution in Seventeenth Century England* (Brighton: Harvester Press, 1985), 34.

22. The necessity of such censorship became a prominent theme in Hall's later writing. *See* Richard McCabe, *Joseph Hall: A Study in Satire and Meditation* (Oxford: Clarendon Press, 1982), 133.

23. Ann Rosalind Jones, "Italians and Others: Venice and the Irish in *Coryat's Crudities* and *The White Devil,*" *Renaissance Drama* 18 (1987): 116. All subsequent quotations will be taken from this edition.

24. Coryate's reference to "p. 270" directs the reader to the page where his apology was printed in the 1611 edition of the *Crudities.*

25. "Panegyrick Verses," *Coryat's Crudities,* 1: 38. Donne's contributions to the *Crudities* are collected in *The Poems of John Donne,* ed. Herbert J. C. Grierson, 2 vols. (Oxford: Oxford University Press, 1966), 1: 172–74. For an account of the original publication of Donne's verses, see Ernest W. Sullivan, *The Influence of John Donne: His Uncollected Seventeenth-Century Printed Verse* (Columbia: University of Missouri Press, 1995), 58–59.

26. "Panegyrick Verses," *Coryat's Crudities,* 1: 39.

27. R.S.Q, *Notes and Queries,* 3rd ser., (1865): 145.

28. Joep Leerssen, "Echoes and Images: Reflections upon Foreign Space," *Alterity, Identity, Image: Selves and Others in Society and Scholarship,* ed. Raymond Corbey and Joep Leerssen. Amsterdam Studies on Cultural Identity. (Amsterdam: Rodolpi, 1991), 128.

29. Slavoj Zizek, *The Sublime Object of Ideology* (London: Verso, 1991), 128.

30. Brian Parker, "An English View of Venice: Ben Jonson's *Volpone*," in *Italy and the English Renaissance,* eds. Sergio Rossi and Dianella Savoia (Milan: Unicopli, 1989), 190.

31. John Florio, *Florios Second Frutes,* The English Experience, no. 157 (1591; reprint, Amsterdam: Theatrum Orbis Terrarum, 1969), 79.

Thomas Middleton, *Women Beware Women,* and the Myth of Florence

J. R. MULRYNE

Thomas Middleton's remarkable tragedy, *Women Beware Women,* stands out among the dramatist's work not least for its range of its interest in social experience and social values. Middleton's other major tragedies, *The Changeling* and *The Revenger's Tragedy* (accepting it as Middleton's)—even where they involve lower-order characters—adopt the modes and perspectives of a privileged society. The city (or civic) comedies draw their inspiration, typically, from bourgeois activities and bourgeois values. *Women Beware Women,* by contrast, consciously juxtaposes the courtly and the bourgeois, and sets ostentation against thrift, leisure against business (and "busyness"), power against industry, display against necessity. Its locations take in, on the one hand, the physical confinement of the mother's house, and on the other the spaciousness of the court (for banquet and masque), moving between the two by way of the ornamented upper-class lodgings of Livia and Guardiano. Costumes and hand-props cover the full spectrum between the necessities of the merchant poor and the fashionable garments and toys of the rich. Nor is this simply a matter of externals. The play's moral and political themes explore the interaction (and in a fragile sense the integration) of the social values and practices of a society flagrantly based on financial power. Leonard Tennenhouse has written that seventeenth-century plays represent "the staging of cultural materials, the mobilization of the political thinking of the culture" and has shown how theater "created political literacy among people who mattered."[1] My own emphasis will fall in this essay on a broader cultural rather than political literacy, though the two are ultimately indivisible. I have discussed elsewhere the play's adroitly ironic moral consciousness, which I take to be at the center of its analysis of a corrupt society.[2] Here I wish to argue that *Women Beware Women* repre-

141

sents the (English or London) cultural moment to which it belongs by a notably pervasive transculturation of its Florentine source materials, as though Medici Florence provided a cultural icon of peculiar pertinence for English self-contemplation in the second decade of the seventeenth century.

My essay draws on and complements Zara Bruzzi's chapter in this volume and should be read alongside it. I agree with Bruzzi that *Women Beware Women* addresses issues of acute moral and political concern at the court of King James, issues given particular prominence in the relationship of James with his favorites Carr and Villiers. I share her sense that Middleton's audience would recognize implicit references if not to individuals and individual occasions (such as the Carr/Howard marriage) then to the behavior patterns and moral choices of which these persons and occasions are the most evident examples. My essay differs from hers, however, in emphasizing the intercultural awareness that arises for the audience from the play's Florentine setting and from the recognition that Florence represents English social and political life in particular ways. I have also tried to locate *Women Beware Women* and its sense of Florence within the developing concerns of Middleton's theatrical art, especially in the city comedies and pageants. It is thwarting that neither Bruzzi nor I can date the play accurately, since the allusions it seems to make could, given a precise date, offer an even more secure purchase on contemporary culture in a period (between 1613 and 1622) when much was changing in English life, both at court and in society more generally. We both note, however, that many of the intertexts we enumerate cluster round the earliest years of the possible span, in particular 1613 and 1614. At the same time, it would be difficult to set aside the apparent flattering reference in act 1, scene 3 to the fifty-five-year-old James (he was fifty-five on 19 June, 1621).[3] I am tempted to guess—no more than that—that the play was first written in 1613/1614 and was revived (or first performed; there is no early record) in a slightly revised form when the topics to which it refers, and especially those connected with favorites, once more came into focus in late 1621 or early 1622, as Bruzzi argues, this time with reference to Villiers rather than Carr. My principal purpose, however, is to suggest how a theatrical recreation of Florentine events and practices provided Middleton with a way of representing English concerns at some point in the teens or early twenties of the century. This occurred not merely at court but in a society accommodating itself, largely for the first time, to a balance of authority between court and city, privileged and bourgeois.

It is no doubt simplistic to portray the major cultural divide of early modern England as that between the values of the city and those of the court. Historians today are more likely to write about the opposing discourses of court and country.[4] Simon Adams has noted indeed that relatively little attention has been paid in recent historical writing (with the exception of Robert Ashton's *The City and the Court*)[5] to the relationship between these two centers of political influence.[6] Yet in contemporary perception the exercise of power did in fact divide between court and city, a division openly confirmed by public ceremonial. Court ceremony meant in considerable part the masque, a form that has been fully studied, and I return to it for particular purposes below. As the author of city pageants, and eventually as city chronologer, Middleton was well placed to appreciate and represent the official ceremonial life of the city, as Margot Heinemann has so fully shown.[7] But the division between court and city, even in pageantry, was less than absolute. Masques (of which Middleton himself wrote three) might be presented under the patronage of city companies. The court routinely participated in civic occasions.[8] In cultural terms, the divide was, unsurprisingly, partial rather than complete. Malcolm Smuts has recently warned interpreters against regarding the culture of the Stuart court as homogeneous: "in Jacobean England one finds a remarkable assortment of urban and aristocratic, native and foreign influences converging on a court that had not yet established a dominant cultural attitude."[9] The same could be said of the cultural orientation of the city. In place of a sharp differentiation of cultural and moral viewpoints, we may see in the early seventeenth century a negotiation, and where successful an accommodation, between divergent tendencies (broadly identifiable as City and Court) as part of the process of self-fashioning undergone by early modern England. It would be possible to read *Women Beware Women* as a satiric tragedy exposing the exploitation of the merchant class (Leantio and the Mother), standing in for the city, by a powerful courtly elite. A more convincing reading, and one I should like to develop in this paper, would see the society of the play, from merchant to courtier, as possessed by a common (and eventually disastrous) ideology. Middleton, I should like to suggest, is portraying in *Women Beware Women* the full range of contemporary society in its common and interacting preoccupations and preferences.

And for this portrait, I want to argue, he finds the most convincing prototype in the social practices and structures of Medici Florence.

2

It has been widely recognized that *Women Beware Women* draws on Middleton's experience as a writer of city comedies and city pageants, a quite natural situation if the play was first written in 1613 or 1614, when Middleton was deeply engaged with these genres. What has been less fully emphasized, perhaps, is the extent to which the play inherits not only the writing skills but also the social and moral preoccupations of the comedies and pageants, and the ambivalences that attach to them, in order to develop these in a tragic mode. I shall need to identify at least the outlines of these preoccupations if I am to show why and how Middleton turned to the myth of Florence for the setting and, in an allusive or metaphoric sense, the substance of his tragedy.

It would be impossible fully to explore the comedies and pageants (Middleton's myth of London) in the space available here, and I shall have to summarize by referring to what I take to be a seminal essay on the topic by Susan Wells, an essay not fully taken up in subsequent Middleton commentary.[10] Calling on Mikhail Bakhtin's *Rabelais and His World,* Wells defines Middleton's account of the social order of Jacobean London in relation to the Bakhtinian marketplace:

> The marketplace of the Middle Ages and the Renaissance was a world in itself, a world which was one: all "performances" in this area, from loud cursing to the organized show, had something in common and were imbued with the same atmosphere of freedom, frankness and familiarity. . . . The marketplace was the centre of all that was unofficial; it enjoyed a certain extraterritoriality in a world of official order and official ideology, it always remained "with the people."[11]

Such a communal (and protected) exchange of values, economic and ideological, whether or not it ever existed in the world of fact, has become unavailable, Wells argues, to Jacobean society as Middleton's city comedies portray it. She writes,

> the marketplace is compromised, first, by becoming simply the location of exchange and profit rather than a gathering place, a common

space; second, by being circumscribed more tightly by the "official order," by losing its "extraterritorial status" and becoming more integrated with the central apparatus of government—a process which of course also increases the access to power of the most wealthy members of the merchant strata.[12]

What emerges from the city comedies is not (we may summarize) a convergent social ideology, but one of tension and conflict, a fractured society of self-directed individuals living and working within a hierarchy of authority to which they offer no more than ambivalent consent. And yet, as Wells points out, this satirical account is balanced by an equally vigorous appreciation of the marketplace as *festive. A Chaste Maid in Cheapside* (to take the culminating instance of the genre in Middleton) combines we may say a thoroughly negative account of human (and especially sexual) profligacy (and aridity) with a festive geniality that envisages social structures flourishing, however grotesquely (as in the gossips' feast), within the wealth-and-authority structures of the city. London, that is, figures in the comedies as a society balanced between celebration and satire, between openness and exploitation, between festival and greed, between the body freed ("at liberty") and the body oppressed, parodied, and distorted.

If we turn to the pageants Middleton wrote for city occasions we find them far more ideologically conservative than the comedies. At the same time, the pageants complement the positive emphases of the comedies by presenting the city, in Gail Kern Paster's words, as "an insistently benign community," one where the wealth of London is "transformed into the expression of bounty."[13] James Knowles has pointed to "the explosion in civic ceremony after 1603"—annual processions, oath takings, pageants—by means of which the city as a kind of corporate author sought to reconcile its accumulation of wealth (and authority) with its duty toward charitable giving and social concern.[14] The city—city merchants—*needed* the positive image the pageants (including Middleton's) afforded in order to combat the negative moral lexicon of avarice and self-interest that was frequently employed against them. Theodore B. Leinwand cites John Wheeler's *A Treatise of Commerce* (1601) as a representative text striving from an evidently anxious perspective (because a powerful case could be made out to the contrary) to show that "there is nothing in the world so ordinarie, and naturall unto men, as to contract, truck, merchandise, and trafficke one with an other."[15] Middleton's pageants function, in this context, as the public expression of a positive—even empowering—image for the merchant. Yet (somewhat as in Wheeler) the ambivalence associated with the comedies can be discerned as a kind of unadmitted subtext beneath the pageants' language, straining syntax and expression, and laying an implicit question mark against offered meaning. Together, pageants and comedies, we might summarize, present a portrait of contemporary London that draws almost equally on pride and rejection. Perhaps this is only to say that Middleton's representation of the City takes into itself, in pageant and comedy, the conflicting tensions of Puritan ideology, especially in regard to such terms as liberty and thrift. The creative intelligence behind *Women Beware Women* remains preoccupied with moral and social issues (greed, esteem, community, possession) that fuel the comedies and pageants, but that are now construed as issues within a more widely defined social and political order.

Perhaps I can represent the continuity between the city plays (and pageants) and the tragedy by citing one striking parallelism of language between *Women Beware Women* and Middleton's 1613 pageant *The Triumphs of Truth,* a parallelism that may serve to draw the two texts (and two genres) into significant counterpoint, rendering *The Triumphs of Truth* virtually an intertext for the tragedy's exploration of merchant values. In the pageant, London is figured as the Mother presiding over "the glory of this day,"

> To which, with tears of the most fruitful joy
> That ever mother shed, I welcome thee [the Lord Mayor]:
> O, I could be content to take my part
> Out of felicity only in weeping,
> Thy presence and this day is so dear to me.[16]

The opening words of *Women Beware Women* present the Mother, weeping, as she welcomes her merchant ("factor") son to Florence:

> Thy sight was never yet more precious to me;
> Welcome with all the affection of a mother,
> That comfort can express from natural love.
> Since thy birth-joy, a mother's chiefest gladness,
> After sh' has undergone her curse of sorrows,
> Thou wast not more dear to me than this hour
> Presents thee to my heart. Welcome again.

(1.1.1–7)

The coincidence of language is marked. What is less immediately obvious is the coincidence of values for which London and the *Women Beware Women* mother stand. As the play's first scene develops and as we hear more of the mother's attitudes and those of Leantio, it becomes evident that Middleton intends them to express a merchant outlook that puts a high premium on thrift, sobriety, and industry. Yet the temptations of status and wealth soon pervert these commitments, and both mother and son readily embrace the privileged status and lifestyle of the elite. Their play-experience almost becomes an allegory of that ambivalent conflict (including acceptance of "the central apparatus of government") that the comedies and pageants express in other terms.

It may be worth saying just a little more about how *Women Beware Women* offers a displaced account of tensions embedded in contemporary city and court relationships. Gail Kern Paster has noticed "the recurrent tension in London's centrality between acknowledging how much London owes to the king and how much the King owes to the city."[17] Writers seek to resolve the tension by strategies that range from hyperbole to commonplace. Thomas Dekker, for example, laments at the end of *The Magnificent Entertainment* (written for James's Royal Entry of 1604) that with the king's departure London "resigns her former shape and title of Citie." A prince, he says, by his very presence "hath power to turn a Village to a Citie, and to make a Citie appeare great as a Kingdom"—an urbanized version of the rural myth of Queen Elizabeth giving life to her countryside by her very presence on Progress.[18] Middleton's *The Triumphs of Truth* evokes the commonplace of the City as *camera regis*:

> This place is the king's chamber; all pollution,
> Sin, and uncleanness, must be locked out here,
> And be kept sweet with sanctity, faith and fear.[19]

The characteristic merging of moral quality and physical space, and the characteristic preoccupation, pervasive in Middleton's account of the merchant sensibility, with locked-up space as guarantee of probity, suggest just that tension by which merchant London tries to contain the meanings of kingship. In the real world (or at any rate the real world of pageantry) city and court cohabited. One of the annual oath-taking ceremonies took place at Guildhall, the other before the monarch at the court of exchequer. The elector palatine, prospective husband of James's daughter Elizabeth, attended Dekker's *Troia-Nova Triumphans.* Yet cohabitation does not confirm identity. In *Women Beware Women,* city and court are in value terms patently at odds. Leantio hides Bianca away, the duke displays her. It is perhaps worth remarking that, of the play's two ceremonial occasions, one, the "yearly custom and solemnity" (1.3.82) during which the duke and state make their way to St. Mark's Temple, is strongly reminiscent of London civic processions, while the other, the masque, represents plainly the ceremonial life of the court. It is as though Middleton wished by presenting both types of ritual to convey to his audience, however subliminally, the unequal negotiation in this play between the city and the court. However that may be, the interaction of merchant and elite is pervasive in the play, with the interaction characterized by an unstable mix of acceptance and conflict. The cameo (act 4, scene 1) of Bianca and Leantio strutting their new-found influence and wealth before each other may stand as summary of a common theme.

It is the argument of this paper that Middleton turned to Florence for the socially and politically inclusive image he needed to represent the London of his own cultural moment. The Florentine setting, fed by the references, associations, and intertexts I discuss, offered the playwright, in Barthes' words, a "situation of writing" sharply expressive of the tragic potentialities of the sociopolitical world of the city comedies, enlarged to take in court as well as city, but structured nevertheless out of common preoccupations and practices.[20] It is necessary now to say something of the ways in which Florence as an image (or myth) in the Jacobean mind provided the meanings fitting it to this role.

3

One aspect of the myth of Florence (as we may call it) is represented by the Florentine court culture of Stuart England. Zara Bruzzi, following Frances Yates, Roy Strong, Bonner Mitchell, and others, has ably summarized the Florentine influence on the literary, artistic, and ceremonial practices of the Jacobean court, especially as these relate to royal panegyric.[21] It is unnecessary therefore to dwell on the matter here, except perhaps to emphasize how closely the interest in Florence was identified with Prince Henry, whose court stood for one possible interpretation of the meaning of kingship in Jacobean England. The major historical study of Florence, Sir Robert Dallington's *A Survey of the Great Duke's State of Tuscany* (1605), was written by a gentleman of the bed and privy chamber to Henry; Henry despatched his close friend John Harington to Florence to observe and report on the extravagant Medici Festival of 1608 for the wedding of Cosimo de' Medici to Archduchess Maria Maddelena; the influential if not always satisfactory Florentine festival designer Constantino de' Servi was among Henry's entourage.[22] Altogether, in the public mind, the mode of kingship (or potential kingship) associated with Henry must have seemed to a considerable degree Florentine in character. In the shifting cross currents and uneasy adjustments of royal and parliamentary power under James, the language of the Florentine festival must have seemed a convenient symbolism for one definition of the nature of royal authority.

But there is another aspect to the myth of Florence that we may compare with the more familiar myth of Venice, and one that helps to specify the interest of Florence for a playwright much concerned with city values and practices. The myth of Venice, assiduously cultivated and distributed by the Venetian publicity apparatus, has been a good deal studied. Jean Remple, for instance, has shown how widely the myth was assimilated into English theater, tracing its literary sources principally to Gasparo Contarini's *The Commonwealth and Government of Venice* (translated by Lewis Lewkenor, 1599) and its political sources to the long Venetian service of the ambassadors Sir Henry Wotton and Sir Dudley Carleton.[23] The outlines of the Venetian myth are pretty clear: strong and just government, wealth, trade, and (as Roberta Mullini points out) a multicultural society whose civic life expressed itself notably in processions and pageants.[24] The negative shadowings of the myth are also well known through accounts of Venetian licentiousness and extravagance.[25] The glamour attaching to Venice in the English literary and theatrical imagination of the early seventeenth century, in both its positive and negative aspects, has become an accepted and well-understood part of the vocabulary of play reading.

By contrast, the myth of Florence has received much less attention, though in its festival aspects it was just as assiduously disseminated (the Medici festivals of the 1570s and after were widely publicized through festival books). Some outline account of the myth may therefore be useful here. Gail Kern Paster has traced the idealization of Florence as community and as built

environment, showing how the city was represented as the true
political and architectural heir of republican Rome, a civic community at peace with itself and enjoying the benefits of just and
even-handed government.[26] In an important essay not much
noticed by literary scholars, Donald Weinstein has amplified and
nuanced this account. Taking Savonarola as one defining figure
in the development of the myth, Weinstein writes,

> With Savonarola's teaching Florence would multiply her *imperium*
> and create the new era (*novum illud saeculum*). In Florence Christ
> reigned and the golden age had begun. Such were the dreams
> dreamed in Florence, city of hard-headed businessmen, practical
> politicians and sophisticated artists and thinkers at the turn of the
> sixteenth century.[27]

Weinstein goes on to show how this not uncommon mille-
narianism varied in its emphases with the shifting currents of
Florentine history. But the consistent element of the myth, he
demonstrates, lies in the adjusted tension between the realization of a "special destiny of leadership," expressed in the fostering of certain (rather ill-defined) high ideals, and the
establishment of a democracy capable of meeting the interests
of that "city of hard-headed businessmen." It is an achievement
that Machiavelli, for English readers the archetypal Florentine,
conceded to the civic government of the city:

> The grave and natural enmities that exist between the men of the
> people and the nobles ... are the cause of all evils that arise in
> cities. . . . Those [enmities] . . . in Rome brought the city from equal-
> ity in the citizens to a very great inequality, those in Florence re-
> duced it from inequality to a wonderful equality.[28]

Florence emerges, on this account, as the mythically perfect
example of the city-state. J. R. Hale, in his authoritative *Florence
and the Medici,* sees the myth from a historian's perspective,
returning repeatedly to the problem faced by the Medici rulers
of constructing a social and political accord that could accommodate both rank and wealth. The grand dukes (Cosimo, Francesco,
Ferdinand) were careful, he writes, "to accentuate the princely
ritual of the court" even if it meant including "trivia which
would have alienated rather than intrigued the Florentines had
not the grand dukes, like themselves, retained an active interest
in business and trade." "They remained," he adds, "bankers,
though through intermediaries."[29] Florence assumes, in all

these accounts, the characteristics of the exemplary state, solving, or at least taking on, the problem faced by most early modern societies of adjusting inherited power to the challenge of new wealth. Just such a set of problems confronted Jacobean England, in the aftermath of the profound changes that (even if some of his accounting has been questioned) Lawrence Stone has laid out so comprehensively for us in *The Crisis of the Aristocracy* and elsewhere.[30]

Women Beware Women, I suggest, employs Florence for its setting, not because Middleton wishes to present that city and its government as the ideal against which his own country can be measured—far from it, indeed almost the opposite—but because his audiences might be expected to see in a fictionalized Florence a working model of a possible future for London and England.

4

If the most obvious sense in which Florentine court culture makes itself apparent in *Women Beware Women* is the final-act masque, there is another pivotal episode that may have struck audiences as an appropriate historical parallel that can figure also as cultural symbol. The historical Duke Francesco's profound interest in "ingenious, rare and precious objects"[31] is well documented and well known. This *principe dello studiolo*[32] maintained a small closet (or *studiolo)* that, approached by way of his magnificent collection of art treasures, provided "a place for solitary musing, or to show to a few friends and favoured visitors."[33] The place of Bianca's seduction in *Women Beware Women* offers an intriguingly similar set of properties and a similar location, though displaced (we might say) to the house occupied by the favorite Guardiano, and by Livia. The circumstances of the seduction are very carefully set up, and its location emphasized:

Guardiano.   . . . the gentlewoman
          Being a stranger, would take more delight
          To see your rooms and pictures.

Livia.   Marry, good sir,
          And well remembered, I beseech you show 'em her

          .   .   .   .

> Show her the Monument too—and that's a thing
> Everyone sees not, you can witness that, widow.
>
> (2.2.271–78)

As Guardiano later reports, he duly gave Bianca the appropriate guided tour, ensuring her exposure to the influences of art:

> ... to prepare her stomach by degrees
> To Cupid's feast, because I saw 'twas queasy,
> I showed her naked pictures by the way:
> A bit to stay the appetite.
>
> (2.2.401–4)

Bianca's (apparently naive) wonder at these art treasures, and Guardiano's witty misapplication of their naturalism (what he calls their "liveliness"), intensify the atmosphere of innocence raped by privileged sophistication:

> *Bianca.*   Trust me, sir,
> Mine eye ne'er met with fairer ornaments.
>
> *Guardiano.* Nay, livelier, I'm persuaded, neither Florence
> Nor Venice can produce.
>
> (2.2.310–13)

The Duke abruptly enters to take possession of the room and of Bianca, just as the chess-piece duke takes possession of the pawn in the chess-game below. As a figure for the concerted power of wealth, art, and authority, with specifically Italianate reference, the scene would be difficult to parallel. The Duke exhibits simple (perhaps one can say inherited) authority: "I can command, / Think upon that" (2.2.362–63). But he shows also a readiness to construe the desired woman as *objet d'art:*

> ... thou seem'st to me
> A creature so composed of gentleness,
> And delicate meekness—such as bless the faces
> Of figures that are drawn for goddesses
> And makes art proud to look upon her work—
> I should be sorry the least force should lay
> An unkind touch upon thee.
>
> (2.2.339–45)

It needs no sophisticated commentary to show how these lines conflate and even confuse (as the stuttering syntax records) art, sexuality, and power. As a fictionalized account of the historical Francesco, the scene carries a good deal of conviction.

But Middleton's audiences would, one suspects, have picked up references nearer home. Much has been written, especially in recent years, about the Italianate art collections and connoisseurship of leading aristocratic figures at James's court, especially (in the years around 1620 and after) Arundel.[34] But James's favorite, Buckingham, also used the prominence conferred by the ownership of art as a means of achieving status. As Graham Parry puts it, "by about 1620 Buckingham already recognized that a great art collection and a profession of connoisseurship were indispensable to distinction at home and abroad."[35] James's earlier favorite, Somerset (Robert Carr), it has recently been shown, amassed a notable collection of works of art, not only before but for three decades after his fall. In A. R. Braunmuller's words, "as a collector of art works—jewels, tapestries, pictures, statues, metalwork—Carr responded to the dictates of both fashion and the artistic agents who more and more intensively competed in European art markets on behalf of James's courtiers."[36] If Zara Bruzzi is right in identifying allusion to Buckingham and Somerset in *Women Beware Women,* her case is strengthened by these associations. But, going beyond possible specific allusions, the general equation of art (including notably Florentine art) equals power (including sexual power) is one that would have struck home to a Jacobean audience alert to the social developments of their own cultural moment.

Middleton draws in, I would argue, an even more detailed parallelism between the social life of Florence and that of London as a way of exploring the social relationships of his play's characters. A good deal of attention is paid to the physical circumstances of his characters' lives, from the restricted space and furnishings of the Mother's house (Bianca frets at its limitations after her meeting with the duke) to the ample proportions of the duke's banqueting hall and masquing place.[37] More significant, I believe, since it represents the living space of those with power (the favorite and his companion), we have Livia's house, about which she boasts to the compliant (and socially ambitious) Leantio,

> You never saw the beauty of my house yet,
> Nor how abundantly fortune has blessed me
> In worldly treasure.
>
> (3.3.358–60)

Bianca, when she has "come here to court," sparks off in Leantio's mind envious feelings only assuaged by his own recent good fortune:

> These are her lodgings;
> She's simply now advanced. I took her out
> Of no such window, I remember, first:
> That was a great deal lower, and less carved.
>
> (4.1.42–45)

This consciousness of the physical space within which the characters conduct their lives may have been picked up in part from the play's sources. Malespini tells us, for example, that Francesco gave the historical Bianca a fine palazzo in the Via Maggiore (or Via Larga), a fact confirmed by more reliable historians, with the added information that the palazzo was designed by the festival designer, Buontalenti.[38] But the emphasis on architectural space in the play suggests that Middleton had more current (and not just historical) references in mind. There was something of a building boom in Florence under Francesco.[39] More immediately obvious to Middleton's audience, there was a surge of new and ostentatious building in London in the early seventeenth century, a matter that drew from James repeated orders and prohibitions, in keeping with his prejudice against living in London rather than the country.[40] The penchant of the Jacobean nobility for constructing prodigy houses on their country estates is well known but, as Linda Levy Peck remarks, "the Jacobean nobility built city palaces too, among them Northampton House, Buckingham's York House, and Arundel House. Robert Cecil built both Hatfield and the New Exchange ... the one, a great prodigy house, the other, part of the development of the Strand and the West End."[41] Peck interprets these architectural developments as representing a significant psychosociological process. "These houses," she writes, "suggest not only changing tastes but changing conceptions of the role of the nobility, from magnate to courtier and from courtier to virtuoso."[42] In *Women Beware Women* the noble figures are in this sense virtuosi, exercising their power through their privileged status as connoisseurs (as noted above) and owners of fine houses. The association in Middleton's mind and that of his audience with a Florentine nobility is perhaps not accidental. Hale remarks that under the Medici Florence experienced "the transformation of a republican patriciate into a courtier caste."[43]

Given the English reputation of Florence as a place of art and courtly living, it is not surprising that Middleton should create the Florence of his play in these terms.

I have referred to the seduction scene as one in which what we might call the Florentine equation of art and power makes itself most apparent. To give the point a little more resonance, it may be worth quoting James's address to the Lords and Commons (Whitehall, 1610), in which he uses the analogy of the chess game as a figure for the exercise of royal power. James tells his listeners,

> They [kings] make and unmake their subjects; they have power of raising and casting down, of life and of death. . . . They have power to exalt low things and abase high things, and make of their subjects like men at the chess: a pawn to take a bishop or a knight, and to cry up or down any of their subjects, as they do their money. And to the King is due both the affection of the soul and the service of the body of his subjects.[44]

If the accents of this speech sound very much like the duke's words to Bianca (quoted above), this does not of course suggest that Middleton is writing satirically of James. The words are the words of absolutism, untempered (as James's speech is not) by consideration of the rights of subjects. The duke of *Women Beware Women* is engaged in rape, imposing his sexual will on Bianca. James is talking of political control (though it would not require a mind as soaked in sexual punning as Middleton's to read James's "the service of the body of his subjects" in a sexual sense). *Women Beware Women* explores authoritarian power, financial as well as sexual, through its use of the Florentine setting. The near convergence of James's words and the duke's, confirmed by the common idiom of chess, perhaps specify something of that overlap between current political experience and the narrative of the play upon which Middleton depends for the social and political currency of his work.

5

Florentine cultural practice is most obvious in *Women Beware Women* in the disastrous nuptial masque (which we may call for convenience *The Masque of Juno*) that concludes the play. Masques are far from uncommon in Tudor and Stuart

drama—Sarah P. Sutherland counts more than one hundred[45]—
and a number of these draw directly on their Italian origins. But
the intercultural significance of *The Masque of Juno* for the
Florentine setting of *Women Beware Women* is especially
marked. Roy Strong claims that "the gradual emergence of the
Medici as a ruling dynasty owed much to a deliberate artistic
policy . . . [including] the public staging of stupendous fetes."[46]
While this may overstate, there can be little doubt that in the
Jacobean public mind the authority of the Florentine court was
directly associated with festival display. One aspect of this, the
costly nuptial masque, must have seemed particularly relevant
for audiences of *Women Beware Women.* Among marriages associated with the dramatis personae of the play, which enjoyed
spectacular public celebrations (and subsequent published accounts), were those of Francesco de' Medici and Joanna of Austria (1565), Francesco and Bianca (1579), Cesare d'Este and
Virginia de' Medici (Francesco's half-sister) (1586), Ferdinand de'
Medici (the cardinal) and Christine of Lorraine (1589), and Henri IV of France and Maria de' Medici (Francesco's daughter)
(1600). It would be idle to suppose that a Jacobean audience
would have been familiar with the details of these celebrations,
though it is worth recalling that a number of them (for example
those for Henri IV) were of particular interest at the court of
Prince Henry. What is more probable is that the practice of costly
wedding masques and entertainments as a way of certifying the
political import of marriage was directly associated with Florentine court practice—especially as that practice made itself apparent in England, through the work of Jonson, Jones, and others.

It is notable that the details of Middleton's masque approximate to those of parallel Florentine occasions. For example, in
the 1586 entertainment, the fifth intermezzo included a pageant
of Juno, Iris, and fourteen nymphs, with Juno sitting in a car
drawn by two peacocks and supported on a cloud, and in 1600
the opening theater piece staged a *contesa* between Minerva and
Juno, with Juno again seated in a chariot drawn by peacocks.[47]
There is no question of sources here (the figure of Juno and her
peacocks is an obvious one for marriage entertainments, and
much employed in Italy, England, and elsewhere), but rather of
a kind of authenticity. Middleton did not adopt in *The Masque
of Juno* the subject matter of the entertainment for the marriage
of the historical Francesco and Bianca. We do not know whether
he was aware of it. He *did* refer to its haste and cost (a vast sum
of three hundred thousand scudi was expended). Guardiano

mentions "the Duke's hasty nuptials" (4.2.164) and Livia explains that the marriage will take place "with all speed, suddenly, as fast as cost / Can be laid on with many thousand hands" (4.2.200–1). What is more significant is the "authenticity" associated with allusion (within the resources of the Jacobean public theater) to the occasion's spectacular presentation and to its transparent effrontery. In Florence, in the midst of all the cost and pomp, Bianca (who had been formally banished from Venice on her elopement) was proclaimed a "vera, & unica figliuola della loro Republica, e di San Marco," and her marriage celebrated as an instance of harmony and love.[48] In Middleton's *Masque of Juno* Bianca's scandalous liaison with Francesco is celebrated with equal ceremony and ostensibly sanctified by marriage and marriage masque. The Florentine pageantry, in both history and fiction, is shown as simultaneously the index of wealth and power and as specious fake.

The relationship between *The Masque of Juno* and Ben Jonson's and Inigo Jones's (Florentine) masque *Hymenaei* has been a good deal explored.[49] I want to focus here on a detail of the staging of both masques as a way of emphasizing the intertextual (and by extension intercultural) awareness of Middleton's audience, coming to terms with one definition of (Florence-derived) court culture. I shall refer also to staging details in Shakespeare's and Fletcher's *The Two Noble Kinsmen,* a text widely understood as making direct allusion to persons and affairs at James's court.[50]

Almost nothing has been written about the stage presentation of *The Masque of Juno.* We know very little about the extent to which the resources of the stage company (probably the King's Men) would have been strained to mimic the spectacular presentation of a court masque such as *Hymenaei.* The probability is that a much scaled-down form of presentation was employed, given budget constraints and the practicalities of staging an inserted masque in the fifth act of a tragedy. Yet stage directions and references in the text at least refer to the splendors of Florentine and Jacobean court practice (Juno's descent, peacocks, flaming gold). Moreover, it is quite possible that masquing costumes were used, perhaps even borrowed from court occasions (one possible instance is mentioned below). Whether a more direct form of visual allusion to specific masquing occasions was offered is again unknown, though it is intriguing to note that the puzzling reference to the Ward's masquing costume of "a foul fiend's head with a long contumelious tongue i' th' chaps on't" (5.1.19–22) may refer to Rumor in Campion's *Masque of Squires* (performed for the Howard/Carr marriage celebrations) wearing "a skin coate full of winged Tongues . . . on his head a Cap like a tongue, with a large paire of wings to it."[51] Again, the cupids who play a disastrous role in *The Masque of Juno* may have offered a visual reference to Middleton's own (now lost) *Masque of Cupid,* also written for the Howard/Carr marriage. However these may be, there seems an altogether more distinct possibility that Middleton's audience will have recognized a direct allusion in one property, the altar, that must have been prominent in staging *The Masque of Juno,* and which was center stage, practically and in significance, in Jonson's *Hymenaei.*

D. J. Gordon has explained that in *Hymenaei* "the altar that meets the curious eyes of the spectators becomes the nodal point on which the lines that connect the universe converge."[52] The universe he has in mind is that predicated by Jonson's lofty ambition in this masque "to relate present occasion [the marriage] to sublime and removed mysteries, to link Whitehall, the marriage of the Earl of Essex with Frances Howard, James and his cherished plan [an acknowledged union of the kingdoms] to the union of men, the universe and God."[53] All this heavy freight of meaning rests on the stage-property of the altar, with its learned and witty lettering: Ioni. Oimae. Mimae [Iunoni Optimae Maximae] Unioni Sacr., a punning tribute to Juno arising from the near-coincidence of her name with the Latin word for union. In Middleton's *Masque of Juno* the altar is that on which Isabella and the nymphs set their censer and tapers, and from which a poisoned smoke ascends to "try" Juno's "immortality" (5.2.102). We have no knowledge of the stage-property Middleton's company used. It would be the merest speculation to think that the property was lettered like Jonson's, or was even that property itself, retrieved from the royal store. Yet, given the clear reminiscences of *Hymenaei* elsewhere in *The Masque of Juno,* such speculation is not inherently absurd. It is altogether plausible that some among Middleton's theater company would recollect the stage settings for the very memorable 1606 masque, and some among his audience too. If so, and given the notably checkered, indeed notorious, history of the Howard/Essex marriage, this visual reinforcement of the play's ironies would become emphatic indeed. Not only would the inverted ritual of the poisoning of Juno underline the court's desanctification of marriage (a judgment prepared for in the cardinal's great speech in act 4) but the ripples would spread out to embrace a whole ethic (or counterethic) of court behavior (in the play and by extension in James's court) for which the play's Florence stands model.

It may be possible to extend this point by referring to another visual reference, or potential reference, in the staging of *The Masque of Juno*. D. J. Gordon's learned exposition of *Hymenaei* refers to an intriguingly related instance of staged Hymeneal ceremony in Shakespeare's and Fletcher's *The Two Noble Kinsmen,* a play performed at court in 1613 as part of a series of entertainments for the marriage of James's daughter Elizabeth with the elector Palatine. Other commentators, including Glynne Wickham and Eugene Waith, have developed the play's connections with James's court, and I have myself argued that it incorporates a subtly nuanced set of reflections on marriage as entertained by Elizabeth, James, and Anne. Zara Bruzzi has carried this discussion further by pointing out, here and elsewhere, that *Women Beware Women* appears to cite not only *Hymenaei* in the opening moments of *The Masque of Juno* but also *The Two Noble Kinsmen,* where details of staging and the central dilemma of the heroines are very similar.[54] What we may take this scholarship to mean is that, at least in the years immediately after 1613, *The Two Noble Kinsmen* will have carried for knowledgeable audiences and companies (the King's Men performed *The Two Noble Kinsmen* and are the probable company of *Women Beware Women*) an almost iconic status in relation to courtly marriage. The performance parallels with *The Masque of Juno* (to develop points made by Zara Bruzzi below) are striking. The Nymphs who enter in *The Two Noble Kinsmen* in act 1, scene 1 at least share that name with the masquing Nymphs of *Women Beware Women,* and Emilia's sacrifice to Diana (*TNK* 5.3.1ff) inversely parallels that of Isabella to Juno (*WBW,* 5.2.72–83). More obviously, the settings and costuming of the fifth act of *The Two Noble Kinsmen* recall those of Middleton's *Masque of Juno*. Again, the focal property is an altar around which the action is memorably, indeed spectacularly, staged, and at which the opposed knights express their devotion to Emilia in ways reminiscent of the "shepherds" expressing their devotion to Isabella in *The Masque of Juno*. The spoken text is remarkably similar. Emilia addresses Diana:

> *Emilia.*   Out of two, I should
>   Choose one and pray for his success, but I
>   Am guiltless of election . . .
>   Therefore, most modest queen,

He of the two pretenders that best loves me
And has the truest title, let him
Take off my wheaten garland.

(5.3.16–24)

In *Women Beware Women* a "Ditty" is sung, followed by Isabella's spoken words:

> *I love both, and both love me,*
> *Nor know I where to give rejection,*
> *My heart likes so equally,*
> *Till thou set'st right my peace of life,*
> *And with thy power conclude this strife.*
>
> · · · · · · · · · · · · · · ·

Isabella.   Thou sacred goddess,
And queen of nuptials, daughter to great Saturn,
Sister and wife to Jove, imperial Juno,
Pity this passionate conflict in my breast,
This tedious war 'twixt two affections;
Crown one with victory, and my heart's at peace.

(5.2.78–89)

Costume and stage properties are also remarkably similar. *The Two Noble Kinsmen* stage direction reads (in part), *"Enter Emilia in white, her hair about her shoulders, with a wheaten wreath; one in white holding up her train, her hair stuck with flowers"* (5.3.1–4). The *Women Beware Women* direction suggests a similar visual effect: *"Enter two dressed like Nymphs, bearing two tapers / lighted; then* ISABELLA *dressed with flowers and / garlands."* (5.2.72.1–3) The action and properties extend the costume parallels. *The Two Noble Kinsmen* stage direction goes on:

> *one before her carrying a silver hind in which is conveyed incense and sweet odours, which being set upon the altar, her maids standing apart, she sets fire to it.*

In *Women Beware Women,* Isabella enters *"bearing a censer with fire in it,"* after which she and her attendants *"set the censer and tapers on Juno's altar with much reverence."* In view of the language and visual parallels, it seems highly probable that an audience for *Women Beware Women* (or a knowledgeable proportion) would interpret what they were hearing and seeing as an implicit and inverse parallel to *The Two Noble Kinsmen* and the vision it offers of court marriage. This would be especially so in 1613–1614, and Bruzzi may be right in arguing that, as the topic of the Palatine marriage was again in the forefront of observers' minds in the late teens and early twenties, the later date for *Women Beware Women* would again make the allusions pertinent. (It is worth recalling in this connection that *The Two Noble Kinsmen* was revived at court in 1619.)[55]

What we are dealing with in these theatrical crossreferences is not I think merely allusion nor (or not only) factional comment, but rather an extension of dramatic vocabulary which permits the playwright, through calling on an audience's theatrical memory and intercultural awareness, to specify more fully and richly his analysis of the issues that were present to the minds of his audience. *The Masque of Juno* serves, that is, as a receptive source for associations and understandings that would reach out to embrace both specific occasions of court entertainment as well as standing for general patterns of (quasi-Florentine) self-fashioning on the part of James's court.

6

I have argued above for interpreting the Florentine setting of *Women Beware Women* more seriously as a cultural referent than is usual in Middleton commentary. The setting operates, I want to suggest, in elusive yet powerful ways as an element in the total theatrical vocabulary of the play, providing what Roland Barthes calls a "situation of writing" that allows Middleton to explore and specify meanings otherwise beyond expression.[56] The image or stereotype of Florence, I wish to urge, provides for Middleton an instance of cultural otherness that is also and simultaneously cultural identity. In tantalizing ways, Middleton's use of the Florentine stereotype recalls Barthes' use in *The Empire of Signs* of a self-constructed image of Japan, an image rooted in impressions and endlessly resourceful in generating glimpses of meaning, but of its essence fictional. Similarly, Middleton's Florence is not an historical Florence, but a construct mediated through literature, theatrical performance, and the practice of cultural mimicry. In the teens or early twenties of the seventeenth century, I want to say, *Women Beware Women* made its contribution to the circulation of cultural energy in

London through overt recollection and (re)construction of a recognizable but fictional image of Florence.

Notes

1. Leonard Tennenhouse, *Power on Display: The Politics of Shakespeare's Genres* (New York: Methuen, 1986), 13 and 186.

2. *Women Beware Women,* ed. J. R. Mulryne (London: Methuen, 1975) and J. R. Mulryne, *Thomas Middleton* (Harlow, Essex: Longman Group Ltd., 1979), 28-36.

3. For a discussion of the date of the play, *see Women Beware Women,* ed. Mulryne, xxxii–xxxviii. For discussion of additional evidence for an earlier date and Bruzzi's placing of the play in 1622, see pp. 302–20 below. Zara Bruzzi tells me that in a private communication, commenting on an early draft of her essay, Richard Dutton felt her findings pointed toward a date of around 1613–14.

4. *See* Kevin Sharpe and Peter Lake, introduction to *Culture and Politics in Early Stuart England,* eds. Sharpe and Lake (Basingstoke and London: Macmillan, 1994), Introduction, pp. 1–20.

5. Robert Ashton, *The City and the Court, 1603–1643* (Cambridge: Cambridge University Press, 1979).

6. Simon Adams, "Early Stuart Politics: Revisionism and After" in J. R. Mulryne and Margaret Shewring, eds., *Theatre and Government Under the Early Stuarts* (Cambridge: Cambridge University Press, 1993), 47.

7. Margot Heinemann, *Puritanism and Theatre: Thomas Middleton and Opposition Drama under the Early Stuarts* (Cambridge: Cambridge University Press, 1980).

8. *See* James Knowles, "The Spectacle of the Realm: Civic Consciousness, Rhetoric and Ritual in Early Modern London," in *Theatre and Government,* eds. Mulryne and Shewring, 157–189.

9. Malcolm Smuts, "Cultural Diversity and Cultural Change at the Court of James I," in *The Mental World of the Jacobean Court,* ed. Linda Levy Peck, (Cambridge: Cambridge University Press, 1991), 112.

10. Susan Wells, "Jacobean City Comedy and the Ideology of the City," *ELH* 48 (1981): 37–60.

11. Wells, "Jacobean City Comedy," 38. Mikhail Bakhtin, *Rabelais and His World,* trans. Helene Iswolsky (Cambridge: MIT Press, 1968), 155.

12. Wells, "Jacobean City Comedy," 38.

13. Gail Kern Paster, *The Idea of the City in the Age of Shakespeare* (Athens: University of Georgia Press, 1985), 125, 147.

14. Knowles, "The Spectacle of the Realm," 157.

15. Theodore B. Leinward, *The City Staged: Jacobean Comedy, 1603–1613* (Madison: The University of Wisconsin Press, 1986), 26.

16. *The Works of Thomas Middleton,* ed. A. H. Bullen (London: John C. Nimmo, 1885), vol. 7, p. 237.

17. Paster, *The Idea of the City,* 141.

18. For an example, *see* Jean Wilson, ed., *Entertainments for Elizabeth I* (Woodbridge, Suffolk: D. S. Brewer, Rowman and Littlefield, 1980), and *The Elvetham Entertainment,* 96–118.

19. Bullen, *The Works of Thomas Middleton,* vol. 7, p. 238.

20. *See* Roland Barthes, *Empire of Signs,* trans. Richard Howard (London: Jonathan Cape, 1982), 4.

21. *See* Zara Bruzzi, "A device to fit the times: Intertextual Allusion in Thomas Middleton's *Women Beware Women,*" 302–20.

22. *See* Sir Roy Strong, *Henry Prince of Wales and England's Lost Renaissance* (London: Thames and Hudson, 1986), especially pp. 138–40. De Servi's designs for Thomas Campion's *The Masque of Squires,* presented on 26 December 1613 for the wedding of Frances Howard and Robert Carr (Somerset) were late in arriving and widely criticized.

23. Jean Remple, *The Apotheosis of Venice in the Elizabethan Imagination* (Tromso: University of Tromso Press, 1995).

24. Roberta Mullini, "Streets, Squares and Courts: Venice as a Stage in Shakespeare and Ben Jonson," in *Shakespeare's Italy: Functions of Italian Locations in Renaissance Drama,* eds. Michele Marrapodi et al. (Manchester: Manchester University Press, 1993), 158, 164.

25. *See,* for example, J. R. Mulryne, "History and Myth in *The Merchant of Venice,*" in *Shakespeare's Italy,* 87–99.

26. Paster, *The Idea of the City,* 25, 26.

27. Donald Weinstein, "The Myth of Florence," in *Florentine Studies: Politics and Society in Renaissance Florence,* ed. Nicolai Rubinstein (London: Faber and Faber, 1968), 1–44.

28. Niccolò Machiavelli, *Florentine Histories,* trans. Laura F. Benfield and Harvey C. Mansfield Junior (Princeton: Princeton University Press, 1989), 105.

29. J. R. Hale, *Florence and the Medici: The Pattern of Control* (London: Thames and Hudson, 1977; 1986 ed.). Quotation p. 154.

30. Lawrence Stone, *The Crisis of the Aristocracy, 1558–1641* (Oxford: Oxford University Press, 1965) and "The Bourgeois Revolution of Seventeenth-Century England," *Past and Present* 109 (1985), 44–54.

31. Hale, *Florence and the Medici,* 146.

32. *See* Luciano Berti, *Il Principe dello Studiolo: Francesco de' Medici e la Fine del Rinascimento Fiorentino* (Florence: Edam, 1976).

33. Hale, *Florence and the Medici,* 146.

34. *See* D. Howarth, *Lord Arundel and his Circle* (New Haven: Yale University Press, 1985).

35. Graham Parry, *The Seventeenth Century: The Intellectual and Cultural Context of English Literature, 1603–1700* (London: Longman, 1989), 48.

36. A. R. Braunmuller, "Robert Carr, Earl of Somerset as Collector and Patron," in *The Mental World of the Jacobean Court,* 230.

37. *See Women Beware Women,* 3.1.1–81.

38. *See Women Beware Women,* ed. Mulryne, 173 for translation of the relevant passage from Celio Malespini, *Ducento Novelle* (Venice, 1609) 2, novelle 84, 85.

39. *See* Hale, *Florence and the Medici,* 162.

40. *See* Johann P. Somerville, ed., *King James VI and I: Political Writings* (Cambridge: Cambridge University Press, 1994), 226, 227.

41. Linda Levy Peck, Introduction to *The Mental World of the Jacobean Court,* 10, referring to an essay in the same volume by Pauline Croft, "Robert Cecil and the early Jacobean Court," 134–47. The entertainment for the opening of the New Exchange (Britain's Bourse) in 1609, now lost, was devised by Ben Jonson and Inigo Jones.

42. Peck, Introduction to *The Mental World of the Jacobean Court,* 10.

43. Hale, *Florence and the Medici,* 155.

44. David Wootton, ed., *Divine Right and Democracy* (Harmondsworth: Penguin Books, 1986), 107.

45. Sarah P. Sutherland, *Masques in Jacobean Tragedy* (New York: A.M.S. Press, 1983), ix.

46. Sir Roy Strong, *Art and Power: Renaissance Festivals, 1450–1650* (Woodbridge, Suffolk: The Boydell Press, 1984), 127.

47. *See* A. M. Nagler, *Theatre Festivals of the Medici 1539–1637* (New Haven: Yale University Press, 1964), 58–69, especially pp. 66–67.

48. Nagler, *Theatre Festivals,* 49. *See also* Leo Schrade, "Les Fêtes du Mariage de Francesco dei Medici et de Bianca Cappello," in Jean Jacquot, ed., *Les Fêtes de la Renaissance* I (Paris: Éditions du Centre National de la Recherche Scientifique, 1956), 107–132.

49. For some of the detailed parallels see *Women Beware Women,* ed. Mulryne, act 5, scene 2, and footnotes to lines 50.1, 97.1, and 117. 1–2.

50. *See,* for example, Glynne Wickham in *The Elizabethan Theatre,* ed. George Hibbard, 7 (1980), 167–96; Eugene Waith ed. *The Two Noble Kinsmen* (Oxford: Oxford University Press, 1994); and J. R. Mulryne, "'Here's Unfortunate Revels,' War and Chivalry in Plays and Shows at the time of Prince Henry Stuart," in *War, Literature and the Arts in Sixteenth-Century Europe,* eds. Mulryne and Margaret Shewring (Basingstoke and London: The Macmillan Press, 1989), 165–189.

51. Walter R. Davis, ed., *The Works of Thomas Campion* (New York: Doubleday, 1967), 271.

52. D. J. Gordon, *The Renaissance Imagination* (Berkeley: University of California Press, 1975), 174. The essay was originally published in the *Journal of the Warburg and Courtauld Institutes,* 8 (1945).

53. Gordon, *The Renaissance Imagination,* 174.

54. *See* the works cited in note 50 and Bruzzi and Bromham in *Shakespeare's Italy,* 259–62.

55. *See* Waith, Introduction to *The Two Noble Kinsmen,* 3.

56. *See* Barthes, *Empire of Signs,* especially pp. 3–8.

Italy Revisited: John Ford's Last Plays

Lisa Hopkins

In the early part of his career, the Caroline dramatist John Ford created a picture of Italy that was very little dissimilar from the violent, deceptive world of the earlier Jacobean playwrights such as Middleton and Ford's occasional collaborator, Webster.[1] In his 1606 poem "The Monarchs' Meeting," written to celebrate the visit of King Christian IV of Denmark to the court of his brother-in-law James VI and I, the young Ford claims, with rather more patriotism than poetry, that,

> We are not subtle French, to fawn and flatter;
> Nor Spaniards, hot in show, yet cold in matter;
> Trothless Italian; fleeting Irish wiles,
> Whose trust when most protesting most beguiles;
> We deem dishonour German policies;
> Or everchanging Indian fopperies
> We spurn.[2]

Twenty years later, when he comes to write his four major tragedies, his views of Italy seem to have changed little. Two of them, *Love's Sacrifice* and *'Tis Pity She's a Whore* (both first printed in 1633), are set in Italy, in Pavia and Parma respectively. The country they portray is a violent, unhappy one, where men and women are hopelessly trapped between passionate emotions their society cannot sanctify and a ruthless code of honor that leads to nothing but cruelty. The clergy, as so often in Jacobean depictions of Italian priests, are either corrupt—the Cardinal in *'Tis Pity She's a Whore* shelters his nephew from the law after he has committed murder and at the end of the play shows himself more concerned with appropriating property for the church than with fully investigating facts and dispensing justice—or ineffectual, like Father Bonaventura in *'Tis Pity,* unable to deter his protégé from incest, or the Abbot of Monaco in *Love's Sacrifice,* whose presence does nothing to save his niece, her husband, or her lover from their fates. Perhaps the attitude toward Italy that these plays seem to express is most tellingly encapsulated in Vasques's comment at the end of *'Tis Pity:* "'Tis well; this conquest is mine; and I rejoice that a Spaniard outwent an Italian in revenge."[3]

Although the precise order of composition of Ford's plays is unknown, it is often thought that both *'Tis Pity She's a Whore* and *Love's Sacrifice* show clear marks of sensationalism and of reworkings of Jacobean situations which seem more likely to precede than to follow the quieter, more reflective techniques of *The Lover's Melancholy* and *The Broken Heart.*[4] If, as seems likely, these two plays are indeed later works, they took him a considerable distance from Parma and Pavia, to the island of Cyprus and the austerity of ancient Sparta. For his two last plays, *The Fancies Chaste and Noble* (1638) and *The Lady's Trial* (1639), he returned to Italy. He did so, however, with a very different perspective on the country, one that was informed far more by factual knowledge about it than by traditional literary stereotypes and was profoundly colored, too, by the interest in Neoplatonic theory that emanated from the court of Queen Henrietta Maria. In these two plays, Jacobean views of Italy give place to Caroline ones.

Ford had, in fact, always been rather noticeably well informed about matters Italian. In *Love's Sacrifice* he had drawn much of his main plot from the life story of the Italian princeling and musician Duke Carlo Gesualdo, Prince of Venosa, who had murdered his first wife, Maria D'Avalos (the name of the secretary in Ford's play) after finding her with her lover, just as the duke in *Love's Sacrifice* murders Bianca after misunderstanding the Platonic nature of her involvement with Fernando.[5] The likeliest source for Ford's knowledge of the story seems to be Henry Peacham's retelling of it in *The Compleat Gentleman*— Peacham was tutor to the son of the earl of Arundel, and Ford had offered a dedication to Arundel at a very early stage of his career—but it is also possible that he might have come across it by other routes, and one of these might have involved a more direct contact with Italy. Gesualdo's maternal uncle was the famous San Carlo Borromeo, bishop of Milan, and Borromeo's confessor was a Welshman, Dr. Gruffydd Robert, author of a Welsh grammar. Ford too had Welsh connections.[6] One of his maternal great-grandmothers had been a Stradling of St. Donat's, in Glamorganshire, and he was thus allied to a family that was at the forefront of the advancement of Renaissance learning in Wales.

In 1726 Edward Gamage commented on the presence in St. Donat's library of books "in Italian, a language, with its books, much respected at St. Donats' [*sic*] Castle; for, in the principal schools of Italy, were the sons of this family brought up in learning, from very distant generations."[7] Sir Edward Stradling was the patron of the Welsh grammarian Sion Dafydd Rhys, and the family was also closely associated with Humphrey Llwyd, who on his trip to Italy in 1566 may perhaps have met Gruffydd Robert.[8] This may, therefore, have been a means by which Ford's family might have become acquainted with the story; and either the same family connections or an ongoing link with the earl of Arundel, whose interest in art collecting had led him both to undertake and to sponsor several visits to Italy, may have contributed to a similarly accurate reference in Ford's last play, *The Lady's Trial*. There, the heroine, Spinella, is subjected to a seduction attempt by Adurni, a nobleman of her own native town of Genoa. Genoa is an unusual setting for a Renaissance play, and it is perhaps still more unexpected that Ford should appear fairly knowledgeable about his setting: Adorno was in fact the name of a family of considerable prominence in the city, and one of its members, Giuliano Adorno, was a libertine very much in the style of Ford's Adurni until his marriage to the woman who was later to be canonized as St. Catherine of Genoa, much as the Adurni of the play has the seal set on his reformation by his marriage to Spinella's sister Castanna.[9]

As well as this tiny detail, however, *The Lady's Trial* and *The Fancies Chaste and Noble* both represent a genuine sensitivity to the distinctive facets of Italian culture of the early seventeenth century. *The Fancies Chaste and Noble,* as Juliet McMaster has shown,[10] is of far greater interest than Gifford implied when he magisterially dismissed it with his comment that

> Much cannot be said in favour of the plot of this drama, as Ford has conducted it . . . with his usual ill-fortune, he entangled himself at the outset with a worthless rabble of comic characters, and after debasing his plot to the utmost, is compelled, by their outrages on decorum, to terminate it prematurely.[11]

The comic subplot is provided by the intrigues of the newly married barber Secco, his rather aged wife Morosa, guardian of the so-called 'Fancies,' the page Nitido, and Spadone, a supposed eunuch who is first being suspected of being Morosa's lover before in a final speech surprise being revealed as the foster-brother of Troylo-Savelli, successful suitor of the heroine. (One hesitates to call him the hero, as might perhaps be expected, since the plot is too convoluted to admit of so straightforward a designation.) The subplot is certainly not a masterpiece of mirth, but it does provide a genuine counterpoint to the events of the main plot, since there, too, one of the leading characters, Octavio, the marquis of Siena, is generally termed impotent (whether this is in fact the case or not the play never actually appears to confirm).

The marquis's nephew and heir, Troylo-Savelli, explains to his best friend, Livio, that

> Our great uncle-marquis,
> Disabled from his cradle by an impotence
> In nature first, that impotence since seconded
> And render'd more infirm by a fatal breach
> Receiv'd in fight against the Turkish galleys,
> Is made uncapable of any faculty
> Of active manhood, more than what affections
> Proper unto his sex must else distinguish;
> So that no helps of art can warrant life,
> Should he transcend the bounds his weakness limits.
>
> (2.2. p. 254)

Despite this infirmity, Troylo-Savelli goes on to explain, Octavio still enjoys female company and has therefore surrounded himself with a bower of "Fancies," whom Livio's sister Castamela is to join. Much suggestive speculation is proffered about what the marquis actually does with this quasi-harem, and, as McMaster shows, we the audience have plenty of opportunity to demonstrate the lubriciousness of our own imaginations by the ways in which we choose to interpret the various hints dropped by the characters about the activities that take place in the bower of "Fancies." In fact, however, as is revealed at the end of the play, the three "Fancies" are none other than the Marquis's motherless nieces, whose education he has taken in hand, and Castamela has been invited to join them to prepare her to become the bride of Troylo-Savelli.

Such an explanation may seem to leave several crucial questions unanswered, such as whether or not the marquis is in fact impotent and why Troylo-Savelli could not simply have proposed in the normal way. It certainly did not satisfy Gifford, who remarked darkly that "the 'great marquess' must have imbibed strange notions of female elegance and delicacy, when he confided the education of his nieces to the vulgar and profligate set who conduct his boasted academy."[12] It is, however, eminently comprehensible when viewed in terms of Platonic love, a phenomenon of the most absolute innocence susceptible of the most absolute misconstruction. McMaster points out that Bembo in *Il Cortegiano* actually sees old men like Octavio as the most suitable of Platonic lovers[13] and also that Castamela invokes something very like the Platonic "ladder" when she tells her brother,

> Prithee, interrupt not
> The paradise of my becharming thoughts,
> Which mount my knowledge to the sphere I move in,
> Above this useless tattle.
>
> (4.1. p. 285)

If, as Sensabaugh suggested many years ago, Ford was considerably influenced by Queen Henrietta Maria's fostering of Neoplatonic love cults, this play certainly becomes more comprehensible than it otherwise appears: it can be read as a prolonged disquisition on love of all sorts, and not only physical.[14] Spiritual affection is manifested in the religious vocation of Fabricio, who becomes a monk from guilt at having sold his wife; selfless devotion in the person of Flavia, the wife, who continues to love Fabricio. Familial love is seen in the touching attachments between Troylo-Savelli and his uncle and cousins, between Livio and Castamela, and between Flavia and her brother Romanello. There is even a masque of lovers, to conclude the play.

Apart from this broader theme, however, there are also some small but convincing details in the play which cannot be so readily traced back to the court of Queen Henrietta Maria. The name of the marquis's nephew, Troylo-Savelli, was shared with the important Roman family of Savelli; in the late sixteenth century a Cardinal Jacopo Savelli had rendered a singular service to Elizabeth I's chief minister William Cecil, Lord Burghley, when the latter's grandson had undertaken, without leave, a journey to Rome.[15] A Catholic grandson would have been an appalling liability for the staunchly loyal and Protestant Burghley, but Savelli, instead of taking advantage of the youth, had looked after him and then returned him intact and unconverted, a courtesy that Burghley had gratefully acknowledged. This little incident had happened the year before Ford was born, and the cardinal had died very soon afterwards, but Ford might nevertheless have heard of it through his influential great-uncle, Lord Chief Justice Popham, who presided over the trials of Essex and Raleigh and was a very considerable figure in the last years of Elizabeth's government. At any rate, the choice of name is an interesting one, as is the choice of setting. Siena, like Genoa, is distinctly unusual, as is the care taken to convey the precise flavor of its political life, with its ultimate dependence not on its own marquis but on the duke of Florence—details perhaps reflecting the Stradling family's long association with the Welsh grammarian Sion Dafydd Rhys, who had lived some years in the city. If one compares this with, say, Shakespeare's cavalier bestowal of Italian names on the entire populace of Vienna or a seacoast on Bohemia, the attention to geographical and geopolitical detail is striking.

The duke of Florence is also the presiding political force of Ford's last play, *The Lady's Trial.* A duke of Florence had of course already featured prominently in Jacobean drama, in Middleton's *Women Beware Women,* where his rape of a married woman in a gallery passes a sophisticated comment on the corruption that Jacobeans were so ready to believe in beneath the decorative veneer of Italian civilization. *The Lady's Trial* seems to promise a virtual rerun of this scene in act 2, scene 3 where Spinella is decoyed away from the main body of her party, and her sister Castanna, concerned for her safety, is told by Futelli that she is

> Viewing the rooms,
> 'Tis like you'll meet her in the gallery:
> This house is full of curiosities
> Most fit for ladies' sights.
>
> (2.3. p. 40)

The audience may easily suspect that one of the "sights" Futelli means will be Adurni, who desires Spinella. Here, though, as in *The Fancies Chaste and Noble,* the apparent threat of Italian corruption is soon dissipated, for although Adurni did indeed harbor dishonorable designs, he, unlike Middleton's duke, takes no for an answer and does not proceed to violence. Nevertheless, the scene may well serve to reinforce our awareness of the duke of Florence's significance in this play, for, as well as fulfilling the plot function of acting as Auria's patron, he also serves the thematic purpose of reminding us of a very important feature of seventeenth-century Italy, which profoundly colors the creation of a sense of location for the play: its predominant subjection to foreign powers, amounting, in effect, to a form of colonialism.

That Ford lived and wrote in the immediate aftermath of the first wave of English colonialism is a fact invariably absent in accounts of his work, and yet in this play, at least, it seems of considerable significance. It was, after all, Ford's great-uncle, Lord Chief Justice Popham, who had presided over the trial of that archcolonizer Raleigh, and Ford's first published work was an elegy for Charles Blount, Lord Mountjoy, the man who had succeeded Essex and had successfully subdued Ireland. That colonialism may be an issue in *The Lady's Trial* seems clearly signaled when Guzman refers to

> Our cloak, whose cape is
> Larded with pearls, which the Indian cacique
> Presented to our countryman De Cortez
> For ransom of his life.
>
> (2.1. p. 28)

Cortez's efforts in the Americas may seem a long way from Italy, but at the time when Ford was writing the ducal family of Florence had so extensively intermarried with the Spanish invaders of Naples and Milan as to be effectively representative of a foreign power. The duke's mother, Maria Maddalena, was the sister of Emperor Ferdinand II; his great-aunt had been Joanna of Austria, and his great-grandmother Eleonora of Toledo. That the rulers of Spain were actually Habsburgs of Austrian origin— they had acquired their Spanish possessions via a Low Countries marriage—only added another layer to the confusion of cultural identities generated by this inter-European colonialism. This is something to which Guzman seems indeed to refer when he goes on to term the cloak

> the guerdon
> Of our achievement, when we rescued
> Th'infanta from the boar in single duel,
> Near to the Austrian forest.
>
> (2.1. p. 29)

It is, therefore, presumably no coincidence that the subplot of the play revolves around the courtship of the lisping Amoretta by two rivals who are, respectively, Spanish and Dutch, and who

twit each other at every turn with the national hostility bred by
the long history of Spanish struggle for full possession of the
Low Countries lands that Charles V had abandoned to the government of his aunt when he moved to Spain to take up his
rule there.[16] Moreover, Italy, despite its apparently anomalous
geographical position, did in fact represent the key to the Nether-
landish wars: with the land route between Spain and Holland
controlled by France, and the channel patrolled by English shipping (as Charles V's parents had found to their cost when, blown
ashore in England, they had been forced to make expensive trade
concessions to Henry VII), northern Italy represented the only
viable link between the Habsburgs' dispersed dominions, as was
demonstrated by their furious struggle for domination of Milan.
And to cap these multiple layers of national conflict, it is war
with the Turks which precipitates much of the plot of the play,
since it beggars and embitters Benatzi while enriching and en-
nobling Auria, who, fittingly, ends the play as none other than
colonial administrator, in his new role as Genoese governor of
Corsica.

Thus, this apparently simple play, with (unusually for Ford)
only one subplot and (equally unusually) a total avoidance of
any violence and indeed of much action in the plot, is set against
a highly complex background of national feuds, racial prejudices, and international struggles over land, power, and identity
that inform every aspect of it. Even during the seduction scene,
we are not allowed to forget the root source of Genoa's wealth.
As Adurni says to Spinella,

> Now could I read a lecture of my griefs,
> Unearth a mine of jewels at your foot,
> Command a golden shower to rain down,
> Impoverish every kingdom of the East
> Which traffics richest clothes and silks.

(2.4. p. 41)

Perhaps most subtly of all, this story of an aging military man
with a much younger wife whom a friend calumniates as unfaithful must surely be reminiscent of that ultimate Renaissance study of cultural difference, *Othello*. Whereas in that play
Iago is able to goad Othello with his ignorance of the sophisticated customs of Venice, in *The Lady's Trial* Auria draws on his
own experience of life, of female behavior, and of platonic love to
decide that, despite his profound awareness of traditional Italian

ideas of honor, it is possible for men and women to conduct themselves in a more civilized way:

> I tell you, sir, I in my younger growth
> Have by the stealth of privacy enjoy'd
> A lady's closet, where to have profan'd
> That shrine of chastity and innocence
> With one unhallow'd word would have exil'd
> The freedom of such favour into scorn.
>
> (3.3. p. 55)

Refusing blindly to believe the worst of his wife, he facilitates a reasoned solution to the crisis, which appeases all parties and leaves them with honor vindicated and enables the threatened tragedy to be resolved into the traditionally comic closure of marriage.

What Ford seems to be doing here is consciously reworking *Othello*—a play he had already drawn on extensively in *Love's Sacrifice,* whose triad of husband, husband's friend, and younger, impoverished wife offers, in turn, the same basic structure as *The Lady's Trial*. At the same time, though, he is also introducing significant variables, forcing a careful reappraisal of the messages to be drawn from Shakespeare's play. For Ford to use Shakespeare in this way is nothing new: *'Tis Pity She's a Whore* draws substantially on *Romeo and Juliet, The Lover's Melancholy* is heavily indebted to both *King Lear* and *Twelfth Night,* and *Perkin Warbeck* has clear affinities with the Shakespearean history plays, particularly *Richard II*.[17] However, whereas the greater part of Ford's career was marked by a distinct fascination with pathological and abnormal psychologies, he has, unusually for him, eschewed such a case study in *The Lady's Trial,* presenting us instead with a husband who, pointedly unlike Othello or Leontes or Ford's own Bassanes in *The Broken Heart,* responds rationally to the rumor of his wife's infidelity.[18] Doing what every reader or viewer of *Othello* must surely wish Shakespeare's hero would do—actually *talking* to his wife—he successfully avoids what recent psychiatrists have termed "the Othello syndrome" to become one of the most astonishingly well-balanced characters in the entire Ford canon.

What, then, is the significance of all these reversals? One immediate result is that by his own unaccustomed concentration rather on the normal than on the abnormal psychology, Ford rewrites Shakespeare's hero as definitively pathological in his reactions, offering him up as the foil to Auria's maturity and wisdom. Moreover, the extensive concentration on the cultural confusions of colonized Italy invites similar parallelisms. Auria's situation is in many ways precisely analogous to Othello's—elderly military husband of a younger wife from whom the need to fight the Turks calls him away, made governor of Corsica just as Othello is made governor of Cyprus—except that he is a white, indigenous Genoese whereas Othello was that anomalous creature, the Moor of Venice. One easily available reading would be that since their positions differ only in this variation of their racial and cultural position, it must be this that is responsible for their differing reactions to it. This would certainly derive support from the close similarities between the fantasy Venetian bedchamber scenario with which Iago inflames the imagination of Othello, taunting him with his cultural inability to decode its niceties, and the Italian-born Auria's own easy familiarity with the Genoese analogue which makes him so much less ready automatically to condemn all things carried on behind closed doors.

It might be worth bearing in mind, however, that Shakespeare's Leontes, as well as Ford's own Bassanes and Caraffa, all suggest that unjustified jealousy is not the preserve of the outsider alone. It is also worth noting that Auria's situation does have one other difference from Othello's: Auria is forced to leave Genoa not so much because of the urgency of the military situation as because of his own shortage of money. Introducing here a motif which hardly ever finds a place in Shakespearean tragedy, Ford points to a social factor that, temporarily at least, ostracizes Auria from his own city in a way which Othello's color never did, and that is also responsible for the desperation of Benatzi in the subplot. Ford does not stress the point—Auria's fortunes are, after all, miraculously restored through his military success, and the play is no tragedy—but we do not forget that, in the trade-oriented society of Genoa, money is at least as important as it was in Shakespeare's other Venetian play, *The Merchant of Venice*. Indeed, when Auria tells his wants to Aurelio just as Bassanio does to Antonio, the dark comedy of *The Merchant of Venice* may be seen to be briefly united with the tragedy of *Othello* in this most indeterminate of genres.

In his rewriting of Shakespeare, Ford powerfully suggests that cultural differences may be both more extensive and more subtly constituted than the obvious racial marker of Othello's blackness. This is, after all, a society where a Dutchman and a Spaniard playact their differences in a city under the influence of an Italian-Spanish duke whose dynastic allegiances are to an Austro-Dutch house ruling in Spain and with large possessions in both Italy and the New World. In such a world, nothing is as clear-cut as the black-white polarities of the Moor of Venice: Levidolche in the subplot is a clear instance of this, since she manages simultaneously to fulfill the seemingly impossible roles of cast-off lover to Adurni, in a way initially reminiscent of Hippolita in *'Tis Pity She's a Whore,* and devoted wife to Benatzi (whose reappearance in disguise is again reminiscent of the Hippolita-Richardetto subplot). Spinella, the younger wife, *is* extravagant—she loses heavily at cards—but, despite this apparent evidence of profligacy, is *not* unfaithful; the hero's friend, Aurelio, is not a villain, but is nevertheless mistaken; a nobleman may find his apparently splendid position undermined by pecuniary difficulties; and the very system of nobility itself comes under debate between Aurelio and Malfato, whose views verge on the leveling kind.[19] A woman and her husband who remarry each other in disguise, a Dutchman, and a Spaniard whose hostility is merely assumed, are apt symbols for a world structured by gradations rather than by antinomies; and it is only appropriate that for his creation of this society, Ford offers us an Italy made up not of the generalities and stereotypes of his predecessors and of his own earlier plays but of startling cultural specificity.

Notes

1. For their joint work on the lost play *Keep the Widow Waking,* see C. J. Sisson, *Lost Plays of Shakespeare's Age* (Cambridge: Cambridge University Press, 1936).

2. William Gifford and Alexander Dyce, eds., *The Works of John Ford,* 3 vols (London: James Toovey, 1869), 3: 377. Unless fleeting is (unusually) a transitive verb here, it looks rather as though this passage has been emended by Peter Quince. It would surely be better with the semicolon after "dishonour" than after "beguiles," making both "German policies" and "Indian fopperies" the objects of "we spurn."

3. *John Ford: Three Plays,* ed. Keith Sturgess (Harmondsworth: Penguin, 1970), 5.6.151–52.

4. For a good summary of the arguments that *'Tis Pity* and *Love's Sacrifice* preceded *The Lover's Melancholy* and *The Broken Heart,* see Derek Roper, ed., *'Tis Pity She's a Whore* (London: Methuen, 1975), xxiv.

5. *See* my note (published under my maiden name of Lisa Cronin), "A Source for John Ford's *Love's Sacrifice:* The Life of Carlo Gesualdo," *Notes and Queries,* new ser., 35 (March 1988): 66–67.

6. *See* my "John Ford: The Welsh Connection,'" in *Writing Region and*

Nation (a special number of *The Swansea Review*), ed. James A. Davies and Glyn Pursglove (Swansea, Wales: University College Swansea, 1994), 326–31.

7. Quoted in Graham C. G. Thomas, "The Stradling library at St. Donats [sic], Glamorgan," *National Library of Wales Journal*, vol. 24, no. 4 (winter, 1986): 402–19, 411.

8. *See* Ceri Davies, *Latin Writers of the Renaissance* (Cardiff: University of Wales Press, 1981), on Humphrey Llwyd and Gruffydd Robert.

9. St. Catherine of Genoa also had an elder sister named Bonaventura, the name Ford had chosen for the Friar in *'Tis Pity She's a Whore*.

10. *See* Juliet Sutton (later McMaster), "Platonic Love in Ford's *The Fancies Chaste and Noble*," *Studies in English Literature, 1500–1900* 7 (1967): 299–309, and Juliet McMaster, "Love, Lust and Sham: Structural Pattern in the Plays of John Ford," *Renaissance Drama,* new ser., 2 (1969): 157–66.

11. Gifford and Dyce, eds., *The Works of John Ford*, 2: 321. All quotations from *The Fancies Chaste and Noble* and from *The Lady's Trial* are taken from this edition.

12. Gifford-Dyce, *The Works of John Ford*, 2: 321.

13. Sutton, "Platonic love," 303.

14. G. F. Sensabaugh, *The Tragic Muse of John Ford* (Stanford: Stanford University Press, 1944).

15. *See* John Bossy, *Giordano Bruno and the Embassy Affair* (New Haven: Yale University Press, 1991): 70–71.

16. Interestingly, in 1625 Ford's cousin Sir John Stradling had prophetically written that "the growing sea-power of the Dutch is greatly to be feared; it may 'prove more prejudicial to us and our state than the Spaniard or any bordering nation'" (Glanmor Williams, "Sir John Stradling of St. Donat's [1563–1637]," *Glamorgan Historian* 9 [1973]: 11–28, 24).

17. *See* Donald K. Anderson, "*Richard II* and *Perkin Warbeck*," *Shakespeare Quarterly* 13 (1962): 260–63.

18. On Ford's customary interest in mental aberration, *see* for instance Lawrence Babb, "Abnormal Psychology in John Ford's *Perkin Warbeck*," *Modern Language Notes* 51 (1936): 234–37; Sutton, "Platonic Love," 308; and my own "John Ford's *'Tis Pity She's a Whore* and early diagnoses of *folie à deux*," *Notes and Queries,* new ser., 41 (March 1994): 71–74.

19. For discussions of rank in *The Lady's Trial, see* Katsuhiko Nogami, "A Critical, Modern-Spelling Edition of John Ford's *The Lady's Trial*" (Ph.D. thesis, Shakespeare Institute, University of Birmingham, 1989), 28–42.

Part Two
Intertextuality

Intertextualities: Some Questions

LOUISE GEORGE CLUBB

INTERTEXTUALITY is an interpretive key to any culture, especially one like the western European literary tradition. How enter, without it, the landscape where Petrarch wanders back toward Cicero and forward to us? How acquire the audience and the interlocutors constituting the scriptural cloud of witnesses to the invisible inner life?

Renaissance reading and writing were notably intertextual and probably more confidently so than in times when past texts are felt as a threatening burden and hostile "anxiety" flavors the intertextual relationship. Echoing others, I repeat myself, "to conceive and discourse intertextually, we know to be not only indivisible from the act of writing itself but also to have been the principal aim of literary composition recognized in Renaissance poetics."[1]

In investigations of Italian and English Renaissance intertextualities a few Italian texts are canonical—the ones that inevitably turn up on lists of Great Books. *Il libro del cortegiano,* for one, always looms large because it was so much read, translated, and imitated. But it is itself a more complex piece of functioning intertextuality than most relationships posited for it with succeeding texts. Into the enthusiastically rediscovered genre of the dialogue many quattrocento and cinquecento writers poured blends of Platonic and Ciceronian readings laced with the printed or otherwise circulated views of the contemporaries they presented as interlocutors. Some invoked the *Symposium,* though none assimilated, inhabited, and populated it as Castiglione would do. Erasmus's Christian banquet by comparison is a simpler encounter between Plato and the New Testament, juxtaposing two texts across time to communicate timeless values by anachronistically canonizing Socrates. The intertextuality of *Cortegiano,* a confluence of the *Symposium, De Oratore, Gli Asolani,* the *Decameron,* and diplomatic dispatches remem-

179

bered in tranquility is a complicated competition among texts for eminence in a new imperial text.

Among pre-texts in general the *Decameron* had extraordinary weight. Certainly no post-trecento European *novelliere* wrote without implicitly or explicitly inviting his readers' recollections of Boccaccio into play, for comparison, contrast or, at least, to vouch for the successor's respectable literary lineage. In Renaissance drama the *Decameron* enjoyed a unique authority. For the Italian spectator its tales and its language would be evoked continually by innumerable cinquecento comedies and various tragedies of Gismonda and Tancredi of Salerno. Having plot features from the Decameronian tradition was virtually requisite to the genre *commedia* from its formative time, even when the Plautine or Terentian models were conspicuously set forth. Witness Ariosto's *Negromante,* Bibbiena's *Calandria,* or Machiavelli's *Clizia,* in which the avant-garde dramatists display themselves as intermediaries between the "Old Classic" Latin texts and one of the trecento "New Classics." For the Elizabethan audience, not conditioned to respond to distinctions in Italian turn of phrase or regional character and with more limited familiarity with the stories "out of Boccace," a homogenized notion of the "world" of the *Decameron* was in place to receive and process indications of Italian setting. And remains so still. When Kenneth Branagh's cinematic *Much Ado about Nothing* was previewed at the 1993 congress of the Shakespeare Association of America, the audience of Renaissance scholars had many criticisms, but not of the setting. The Tuscan villa in the film, which at first blush seemed a ridiculous misconception of the appearance of late-thirteenth-century Messina where the play is set, on second thought took on an Elizabethan appropriateness and lost the incongruousness precisely because the hills, loggias, and cypresses looked as if they belonged in Boccaccio's Settignano itself or in any one of a hundred other Decameronian *loci amoeni* between Fiesole and Siena. Though the story of *Much Ado* comes from Bandello's *novella* of Timbreo di Cardona and Don Pedro d'Aragona and the setting is a Sicilian city, the utterly different kind of place in which Boccaccio's ten beautiful young people refresh themselves with tales, flirting, and song and dance was happily accepted by the English-speaking audience as "Italy," not a place but a text in which the "Italians," Hero, Claudio, Beatrice and Benedick, might live. Branagh's reasons for using the Tuscan scenery may have had more to do with economics than with intertextuality, but his choice inevitably brought the *Decameron* into the picture.

Granted the continuing vitality of the Great Books style of intertextuality and the surprises it can still produce, today there are more engaging kinds on offer. The very idea of intertextuality has proved invaluable for liberating us from the trammels of source studies and absolutist chronological definitions of contexts, although, admittedly, it can release us too far, loose us into weight-free space. Which intertextualities are most instrumental to historical discovery? Even simple continuation is a primitive kind of intertextuality. A more evolved relationship exists when a work is polarized with another on which it depends for contrast. Parody and travesty are by definition intertextual. Similar in structure, though weightier in substance, is the joint connecting a work with a pre-text whose values it aims to subvert.[2] How broadly can "text" be defined before the term loses its critical edge? In this volume admirably sharp-edged results are hewn with the help of conceptual tools such as those offered by Kristeva (mosaic of quotations, space for interaction of other texts), Montaigne (the self-fashioned "moi"), and Barthes (the "Je" as plurality of texts).

The question of intertextuality may be posed for drama as for nondramatic work. Like writers in other genres, playwrights can send messages of praise, blame, or advice, colonizing previous texts for their purposes; what Tasso did to Vergil and Ariosto, Guarini could do to Sophocles and Tasso. In the theater, as Keir Elam observes, intertextuality functions to the degree that the audience has dramatic competence.[3] A reassembling of the staged action with reference to the audience's social reality by means of clues from other theatrical events may be required. This is one of the operations required to arrive at political levels of tragedy, as Michele Marrapodi's essay reveals, similar to the operation expected of spectators qualified to receive the warning against the favorites of James I that Zara Bruzzi finds in Middleton's dramatization of Medicean scandals in cinquecento Florence, encoded in clusters of visual citations from contemporary masques. Sometimes the demands are simpler, like those made by Massinger's *Roman Actor* and *Virgin Martyr,* in which hagiographical accounts of the persecutions of early Christians become signals to the audience to apply both the history and the fiction to the contemporary condition of the Catholic minority in England.

Convergences between the text presented to spectators and

the texts they are expected to have in mind generate messages from the author that may or may not be essential to the reception of the play. In contrast, convergences between the text studied by scholars and the texts they investigate as its antecedents produce explanations that are by definition essential, in that they may clarify the nature or origin of the object's being. In this case intertextuality is an instrument of reading, a choice of scholarly method. The method can also be used in the opposite direction, as a forward projection of capacities; texts can be analyzed for their relationship to texts not yet existing, texts *in posse* to be known only by the gene pool and reproductive organs of a text already in existence.

Manfred Pfister concludes *Shakespeare's Italy*[4] with an invitation to the New Historicism (geared to content and specifics) to visit Elizabethan Italy. Intertextuality offers a locus for the visit, conducted by some unexpected pathways, as suggested by Juliet Dusinberre's and Bruzzi's essays in the present volume. The invitation can profitably be accepted also by what might for symmetry be called the New Structuralism (geared to form and abstractions), for which intertextuality is a method of reading, producing genre theory and semiotic analysis of structures. As the content/form continuum goes, of course, the structures ultimately *signify* by their capacity for a range of specific contents and their ability to shape, slant, flavor, or otherwise affect them.

The well-established intertextual format of *topos* history is given an irresistible new impetus by Keir Elam's essay on "the prospect—promise or threat, fear or hope—of castration" as central to the development of comedy from Terence to Jonson by way of Bibbiena's *Calandria* and Aretino's *Cortigiana, Marescalco,* and *Talanta.* Elam's hypotheses about the function and force this *topos* accumulates in its passage through multiple texts have a power that can be measured by re-viewing Festa Campanile's 1971 *La Calandria,* a fairly unfunny but instructive cinematic reiteration of Renaissance *contaminatio* of Decameronian narremes and *commedia* theatergrams, including only a few of Bibbiena's own. The threat made act that ends the film, turning the stud Lidio into a singing *castrato,* from a merely appalling *contrappasso,* becomes a fulfilling eruption of the submerged volcano of significance that Elam brings to light. It also cuts off the comic future of the *topos.*

At the 1996 meeting of the International Shakespeare Association, a collaborative research seminar on Shakespearean intertextualities undertook simultaneous application of different but compatible approaches to some causal precedent texts. Following up the results of his *Nel laboratorio di Shakespeare. Dalle fonti ai drammi*,[5] Alessandro Serpieri directs work on processes involved in the construction of Shakespeare's plays from narrative "sources," the passage from one genre to another inviting semiotic analysis.

The Serpieri school of intertextual analysis probes Shakespearean operations of making theater from narration, history plays and tragedy from histories and chronicles. Serpieri thus uses intertextuality as a critical instrument to move from telling to showing. This demonstration of the creative act can be accomplished only by rigorous intertextual inquiry. An audience ignorant of Plutarch's *Lives* as a text presumably could respond to *Julius Caesar* as a reenactment of generally known historical events, but could receive at most a dim perception of Shakespeare's art. As Leo Salingar's essay shows, a spectator may taste the flavor of *Much Ado* without knowing the pre-texts from which its plot is fashioned, but can see farther into it when enabled to measure Shakespeare's departures.

The means of playmaking is paramount in Serpieri's definition of his object as

> research on Shakespeare's sources aimed at investigating not *why* he imitated imitations of action [in Aristotelian terminology], but *how* he imitated them, and thence the means by which he expressed his extraordinary creativity in choosing, transforming and transcodifying the histories he transmitted. Entering the laboratory of the imitator of imitations of actions we have a privileged view of the genesis of his dramas and of their meaning.[6]

The other side of the Shakespearean intertextual seminar moved in the direction indicated by my interest in accumulation of migratory motifs and structures from all "sources" into a theater culture, a collectivity of recognitions, in which Shakespeare and his audience encountered each other. While Serpieri's aim is to understand a process—how did Shakespeare make tragic drama of historical narrative?—mine is to solve a problem: Why are many of Shakespeare's plays so like cinquecento theater, when the sources are on the whole demonstrably nondramatic and/or non-Italian? The demonstrated connection of *The Taming of the Shrew* with Ariosto's *Suppositi* by way of Gascoigne's *Supposes* or that of *Twelfth Night*'s with *Ingannati* are exceptional. Even the latter is indirect, though it seems to grow stronger every time it is reviewed.[7]

In the absence of specific textual contacts, the conduit carrying knowledge of the Italian theatrical system to Shakespeare remains unidentified. It is not enough to know that well-traveled courtiers and imported musicians carried rumors of fashionable Italian drama to Elizabeth's court even as early as 1565, years before the Gelosi company visited Paris and fanned the fame of the *commedia dell'arte,* nor even to remember that Shakespeare's colleague in the Lord Chamberlain's troupe, Will Kempe, went to Italy in 1601 and lived among the *comici.*

The instrument needed to confirm the European community of Renaissance drama is a concept of intertextuality extended to treat, in this case, the Shakespearean canon as a single text and the Italian drama as another. To reduce the latter heuristically as far as possible to the common denominator, its enormous variety must be fused into distinct tractable blocs, such as Polonius's framework of "comedy, tragedy, pastoral, history." Italy not only had a tradition of popular drama but had also consciously developed a surprising range of means, including forms challenging the theoretical "unities," especially in experimental hybrids and *commedia dell'arte* spectaculars.[8]

The features of the entity "Renaissance drama," in distinction to drama of other eras in cultural history, include a technology and playmaking system developed in Italy based on intertextuality, triumphantly shanghaing the ancients. The intertextuality was compounded as this theatrical practice produced performance models in different *genres* whose specifications as they emerged assumed the status of texts interacting with individual plots/*favole* on whatever *argomenti* were selected. The specifications included the use of a repertory of structures which, for want of a better term, I have called "theatergrams."[9]

Some of the potential of this kind of intertextuality is elegantly demonstrated by Robert Miola. His recent work contributes to our understanding of the text-from-text-to-text movement of Renaissance comedy and tragedy, from classical antiquity to cinquecento Italy to Tudor and Stuart England. Taken together, his "*The Merry Wives of Windsor*: Classical and Italian Intertexts" and "New Comedy in *All's Well That Ends Well*"[10] confirm a fact usually ignored in controversy over sources, that is, that the "raw" material—chosen for interest or prestige, from Plautus or Terence, Boccaccio, Bandello, or Ariosto—and the dramatist's direct recourse to it do not conflict with his adopting the configurations of a genre such as "Italian comedy." Whether to show *All's Well* as Shakespeare's most Terentian comedy or *Merry Wives* as his most Italian one, Miola navigates the multiple intertextualities of Roman New Comedy, *commedia erudita* and Shakespeare with a Darwinian eye for structural adaptation. In the present volume, approaching the original version of *Everyman in His Humour,* he shows Jonson too in early engagement with the repertory and procedures of Italian comic dramaturgy.

Treating genres or text matrices as one pole of a possible intertextual relationship has proved especially useful with regard to the theatrical pastoralism so pervasive in the Renaissance yet so dissimilar in its Italian and English manifestations. To represent inner states, for example, Shakespeare used within-the-act masquelike spectacle, a specific microstructure developed for use in Italian pastoral drama. He also uses other theatergrams belonging to it and invokes the idea of the genre for the significance inherent in the form itself, that is, its invitation to self-knowledge and interior change, its capacity to show love's revenge on the fancy-free, in a space and time removed from the quotidian city and court. In *favola* and in *argomento Aminta* and *Il pastor fido* have nothing in common with *Love's Labour's Lost,* but conceiving of a genre as a text we can discern an intertextual relationship between the English play and the fashionable Italian genre represented by the other two that offered the most cultivated segment of Shakespeare's audience an enhanced perception of innovativeness and of universality.

Robert Henke's hypothesis that "Italian and Shakespearean plays are similarly structured according to a tragical-pastoral-comical generic alignment, with pastoral negotiating tragic and comic claims" rests on this understanding that the genre constitutes a text, an ideal one without local habitation or name but which, with its shape and features entire, must make its presence felt at every point in the acting out of a specific script. This is so even though Henke defines pastoral as a mode rather than a genre, in order to reserve the latter term for tragedy, as he investigates the way the pastoral functions as model and negotiator in late Shakespeare and in Marston's *Malcontent* to revise a tragic pre-text, or *antefatto,* into tragicomedy.

The question of relating English drama to the flourishing Italian pastoral theater bedeviled generations of scholars frustrated by the paucity of one-on-one cases of translation, imitation, or other adaptation of individual plays like *Aminta* or *Pastor fido* (though both were printed in London in 1591), and by the obliviousness of most English dramatists to Italian treatises on dramatic theory, including Tasso's and Guarini's own. There could be no intertextuality without the telltale texts, it seemed. But with the substitution of the concept of the genre itself as a text disseminated by practice, its theatergrams employed in variations and recombinations and fused with those of other genres, the nature of the connection becomes clear and warrants the kind of interrogation that Henke gives it.

The *commedia dell'arte* too, when regarded as a genre, a set of expectations, rather than simply a group of types or a style, becomes an occasion of intertextuality. The characters in whom the actors invested identities not confined by the boundaries of any individual play were living texts; the *innamorate* and *innamorati,* Pantalone, Dottor Graziano, Arlecchino and the other *zanni,* the *capitano,* Franceschina, and the rest together constituted a fictional society with an open-ended life of its own, of which any given performance represented only a single instance or possibility. The characters themselves in their continuity and availability were unceasingly adding to an unwritten and nonuniform text, a sort of individually imagined mental backdrop before which each spectator beheld each play. The unrecorded corpus of the *comici*'s improvisations brings to mind Franz Liszt's Romantic theory that Hungarian gypsy music was one large oral epic, of which fragments were broken off for performance; he was mistaken, as he was again in not recognizing the contemporary composed melodies appropriated for this supposedly "folk" music, but the description that did not fit the gypsies' art could aptly be applied to the *commedia dell'arte,* incidentally also thought in the nineteenth century to be of folk origin.

Into the improvisations went *favole* and *beffe* from *novelle* and regular comedy, verbal and gestural *lazzi,* monologues and songs, descriptive poetry, prose *bravure* and *ragionamenti* fashioned from the dialogue tradition, pregnant dramatic structures (like patterns for dance steps) familiar to the audience as the textual format for certain kinds of content, debates on questions or combats of wit, and for certain kinds and combinations of characters, say, Beatrice and Benedick, or perhaps shadowing forth (as Juliet Dusinberre persuades us) Elizabeth and Harington. At the French court where a queen once stood godmother to the child of a fashionable *comico,* the intertextuality of the performances would surely have been augmented by the masquerade of intimacy between monarchs and players.

The living, endlessly expanding, megatext was created by

actors playing to the tastes of various audiences and maintained by their rapport. Here scholarly questions multiply themselves and beckon alluringly to intertextualists. How much can be learned about the modes of communication that fed the interplay and the "texts" they generated? Can the substance of the performing art be partly recovered by research into what the *comici* spoke and read and wrote and quoted?

And played and sang? Music as a text or as one of the essential communicative parts of *commedia dell'arte* performance has recently been studied with valuable results. This welcome development is overdue, for music was fundamental to the Italian theater before the establishment of the *commedia dell'arte* proper. Ruzante, for example, was known to be, among other things, a song-and-dance man. These elements of his art are preserved indirectly by his speeches, as in *L'Anconitana* (2.2): "Let's see if I can do any turns, those pirouettes they do in Padua . . . Tiron, tirondon, tirondon!";[11] and in the titles of songs he mentions here (2.4.80) and elsewhere. For some of them lyrics are extant.

Ruzante's music has usually been regarded as extrahistrionic accomplishment, an unessential ornament. Bringing the discourse of musicology to bear on the study of theatrical texts, however, reveals unsuspected intertextualities. Nancy Dersofi's analysis of *Anconitana*'s structure discovers a four-part harmony as a model of fit proportion and a pattern for action and the use of tonal relationships to represent personal and ethical relations. She is further able to draw parallels with the function of music in *Two Gentlemen of Verona* and *As You Like It,* illuminating alignments made possible only by recognizing the idea of Italian comedy and its musical dimension as an informing pre-text.

Musical settings (where extant), song lyrics, musical relationships (polyphonic and monophonic), and music theory are among the texts currently being juxtaposed with others to uncover a functioning layer of Italian drama not touched by literary excavations. The "text" of music promises to be especially useful in reconstructing the *commedia dell'arte.*

A unique codex from the late cinquecento has recently added to theater history a series of watercolors perhaps illustrating an acting troupe's repertory or the variety of shows presented on some famous occasion. It is organized by categories of entertainment, classifying the company's range, as well as other kinds of spectacle. The theatrical content of the codex is divisible into five major groups: scenes of hellfire, comedy, chivalric jousting, acrobatic and grotesque farce, and dancing and music (sung and played on a striking range of instruments).[12] The intertwining of musical and verbal texts in the *commedia dell'arte* is confirmed by the often cited description of Isabella Andreini performing at the wedding of Ferdinando de' Medici and Christine of Lorraine in 1589, which shows the actress's music as part of her mask, her celebrated mad scene performed in prose ravings, and bursts of plurilingual mimicry and song.[13] Against this background it becomes less surprising that an actress whose technical range had been developed to memorize play texts and "improvise" from scenarios could be called upon suddenly to sing in an opera, as happened in 1608 when Isabella's daughter-in-law Virginia Ramponi of the Fedeli company replaced an ailing singer to create the title role in Monteverdi's *Arianna*. Granted that "opera" was not yet the genre it would become, still its identity as a sung text was discernible. The occasion offers a dramatic demonstration that the relationships implicit in the technical capacities of such *commedia dell'arte* actors are intertextual ones.

Important questions about the Italian theater, inevitably important for the English as well, are being formulated in musicology, as Anne E. MacNeil's work suggests. She maintains, for example, that "music, poetry, and theater during the 16th and 17th centuries share fundamental similarities in their composition and performance and . . . many theoretical arguments concerning one or two of these fields may be extended to encompass all three."[14] In addition, she argues that a Platonic principle directing the use of music in comedy and tragedy also functions for pastoral drama, which Guarini theorized as identifiable in its motion toward or away from the ideal texts of two genres necessarily present to the spectator's mind; in short, an intertextuality in action.

With the foregoing handful of questions I bring no answers, only a final question, as I wonder whether the theatrical intertextualities most evident here, primarily exchanges between, within, or about, genres, are signs of a new attempt on the remaining uncharted spaces of the Renaissance faith in "kinds."

Notes

1. Louise George Clubb, *Italian Drama in Shakespeare's Time* (New Haven: Yale University Press, 1989), 279.

2. *See* David Quint, *Epic and Empire. Politics and Generic Form from Virgil to Milton* (Princeton: Princeton University Press, 1993) on the *Pharsalia* and the *Aeneid,* for example.

3. *The Semiotics of Theatre and Drama* (London: Methuen, 1980), 98–99.

4. *Shakespeare's Italy: Functions of Italian Locations in Renaissance Drama,* ed. Michele Marrapodi, A. J. Hoenselaars, Marcello Cappuzzo, and L. Falzon Santucci (Manchester: Manchester University Press, 1993), 301.

5. With Anna Bernini, Aldo Celli, Serena Cenni, Claudia Corti, Keir Elam, Giovanna Mochi, Susan Payne, Marcella Quadri. 4 vols. (Parma: Pratiche Editrice, 1988).

6. Ibid., 1:21.

7. *See* Louise George Clubb and Robert Black, *Romance and Aretine Humanism in Sienese Comedy* (Florence: La Nuova Italia, 1993), 169–76.

8. Such practice, though popular with audiences, was open to the charge of lowness and old-fashionedness, at least until it turned into high art, a case rather like that of the "Singspiel" genre before and after Mozart's *Magic Flute.*

9. *Italian Drama in Shakespeare's Time,* chapter 1 and passim.

10. *Comparative Drama* 27 (1993): 364–76, and *Renaissance Quarterly* vol. 46, no. 1 (spring 1993): 23–43, respectively.

11. "Laghème vêr s'a' saesse far di qui pieripuoli, de qui revelin che i fa a Pava . . . Tirò, tirondò, tirondò." Ruzante (Angelo Beolco), *L'Anconitana/The Woman from Ancona,* translated with an introduction and notes by Nancy Dersofi (Berkeley and Los Angeles: University of California Press, 1994).

12. Selected images appear in *The Oxford Illustrated History of Theatre,* ed. John Russell Brown (Oxford: Oxford University Press, 1995), facing 118.

13. The passage from Giuseppe Pavoni's *Diario* is given by Ferruccio Marotti in his edition of Flaminio Scala's *Teatro delle favole rappresentative* (Milan: Edizioni Il Polifilo, 1976), 1: lxxiii–lxxv.

14. "Music and the Life and Work of Isabella Andreini: Humanistic Attitudes toward Music, Poetry, and Theater during the Late Sixteenth and Early Seventeenth Centuries." 3 vols. (Ph.D. diss., University of Chicago, 1994), 1: 2.

Retaliation as an Italian Vice in English Renaissance Drama: Narrative and Theatrical Exchanges

MICHELE MARRAPODI

IMAGINING his wife to have foully responded to the loving entreaties of Messer Guardastagno, Boccaccio's Guglielmo of Rossiglione becomes so full of jealous hatred as to plot the murder of his friend. After inviting him to his castle, Rossiglione waits for his victim about a mile from his residence and, in an ambush, kills the incredulous knight. Not content with this bloody deed, Rossiglione opens his dead rival's breast and tears out his heart. Once at home, he has his cook serve it at the table of his innocent wife, only to add after supper: "Thou hast eaten the heart of Messer Guiglielmo Guardastagno, whose love was so deare and precious to thee, thou false, perfidious, and disloyall Lady: I pluckt it out of his vile body with mine owne hands, and made my Cooke to dresse it for thy diet."[1]

Although blending with the ludic, didactic, and spectacular mood of Boccaccio's narratives, this is only one example of many revenge motifs interspersed in the *novelle* which—either directly or indirectly, via Bandello's own stories or Painter's adaptations—are amongst the commonest sources of Jacobean and Caroline drama.[2] What is striking in Rossiglione's case is the fact that the protagonist, no matter whether he is really abused or not, practices a form of revenge that does not end with the victim's death: it must continue with the mutilation of the body, the extirpation of the heart, and even with a cannibalistic banquet prepared at the expense of the allegedly adulterous wife. There is, of course, much more than a cynical retribution in this, since retaliation takes the shape of a perverse punishment, the lover's heart being literally replaced in the adulteress's body.

Other instances of retaliation as a sadistic kind of counterrevenge for a secretly pursued erotic relation abound in Boccaccio's *novelle*. Highly similar is the case of Tancredi (4.1), in the story which, as indicated by a recent commentator, discloses "paternal possessiveness, with a dark, incestuous sub-text."[3] Boccaccio summarizes it as follows: "Tancrede, Prince of Salerne, caused the amorous friend of his daughter to bee slaine, and sent her his heart in a cup of Gold: which afterwards she steeped in an impoysoned water, and then drinking it, so dyed."[4] The heart metaphor, conjoined here with the motif of the golden cup, runs all through the final part, becoming a central issue of the *novella*'s symbolism. In the daughter's words, they suit well together, since "so worthy a heart as this is, should have [no] worser grave than gold" (153). Hence personification becomes a natural feature as she addresses the heart directly, holding it on her breast in the death scene,

> Then calling for the glasse of water, which she had readily prepared the day before, and powring it upon the heart lying in the Cup, couragiously advancing it to her mouth, she dranke it up every drop; which being done, she lay downe upon her bed, holding her Lovers heart fast in her hand, and laying it so neere to her owne as she could. (154)

Translated by Painter in his *Palace of Pleasure,* this story enjoyed great popularity in the Renaissance. It was the source of Antonio Cammelli's *Panfila* (1499), of Girolamo Razzi's *Gismonda* (1569), and of several other Italian plays. In England it was dramatized by Robert Wilmot and others in the academic work *Gismond of Salerne* (1568), and we also have an interesting adaptation of the two Boccaccian stories joined together in William Percy's *A Forrest Tragaedye in Vacunium* (1602).[5] The Elizabethans enjoyed their translations of Seneca for their representation of violence, but the pervasive way in which the heart symbolism operates in many instances of retaliation in such Stuart dramas as Beaumont and Fletcher's *The Maid's Tragedy* or Ford's *The Broken Heart* and *'Tis Pity She's a Whore* indicates a more intimate acquaintance with Boccaccio than has generally been assured.[6] This is probably due to the fact that Italianate drama of the English Renaissance also drew heavily from the Senecan-Boccaccian tradition of cinquecento Italian theater, and especially on the *Tragedia nova* theorized by Giraldi Cinthio. As Giraldi's own tragedy explains to its readers,

> Né mi dèi men pregiar perch'io sia nata
> Da cosa nova e non da istoria antica:

Che chi con occhio dritto il ver riguarda,
Vedrà che senza alcun biasimo lece
Che da nova materia e novi nomi
Nasca nova Tragedia.

                                              (3171–76)[7]

[Nor must you less esteem me because I am born
Of new material and not of ancient history:
For whosoever looks upon the truth with keen eye
Will see that without any blame from new material
And new names new tragedy may be born.]

With *Orbecche* (1541)—a dramatization of one of his own *novelle* (*Hecatommithi,* 2.2)—Giraldi sets up the new genre which, unlike that of Seneca, often displays all kinds of atrocity on stage (including messengers and choruslike insets to enhance the sense of horror), provides fresh material not borrowed from the classics, adopts the Terentian order of *prologue-protasis-epistasis* and *catastrophe,* and brings the device of the mocking of the victim to its highest spectacular level.[8] This last issue, only hinted at in Seneca, becomes the climactic event of the dramatic action. What progressively assumed the semantic construction of an "Italian vice" in the performance of revenge was to Elizabethan eyes precisely the rhetoric of excessive theatricality, that kind of sadistic mockery enjoyed by the evil-doers and fashioned with such macabre effects as to appear perversely appealing on the stage.

It is true that the actual influence of Seneca on Renaissance tragedy has long been debated. G. K. Hunter has warned against the danger of overemphasizing the impact of Seneca and undermining the native cultural tradition and origin of the English drama.[9] Interestingly, his critical assumptions have been disputed by Joost Daalder in his edition of *Thyestes.*[10] It is my belief that the mocking-revenge motif as treated by Cinthio and his imitators is indeed the most effective intertextual linkage recurring in Italian and English Renaissance revenge theater. What has been called "the poetics of horror" is in fact the main distinctive element of Giraldi's contribution to Italian tragedy as well as his most influential trait on the European stage.[11] For the Italian dramatist this approach is felt as a necessity for theorizing about a new form of tragedy differing from that of Aristotle, whose aesthetics of pathos is regarded as an inherent aspect of Cinthio's idea of catharsis, as stated in his *Discorso intorno al comporre delle commedie e delle tragedie* (1543):

[M]i son risoluto che la tragedia ha anco il suo diletto, e in quel pianto si scuopre un nascosto piacere che il fa dilettevole a chi l'ascolta e tragge gli animi alla attenzione e gli empie di maraviglia, la quale gli fa bramosi di apparare, col mezzo dell'orrore e della compassione, quello che non sanno, cioè di fuggire il vizio e di seguir la virtù, oltre che la conformità che ha l'essere umano col lagrimevole, gli induce a mirar voluntieri quello spettacolo, che ci dà indizio della natura nostra e fa che l'umanità che è in noi ci dà ampia materia di aver compassione alle miserie degli afflitti.[12]

[I am convinced that tragedy also has its pleasure, and in that weeping we discover a hidden pleasure that makes it pleasurable to the listener and arouses the attention of the mind and fills it with wonder which makes it desirous of parrying, by means of horror and compassion, that which they do not know, that is to flee vice and to follow virtue, besides which the feeling that men have for the pathetic makes them watch the play willingly. This gives us a sign of our nature and provides the humanity that is within us with ample occasion to have compassion for the misery of the wretched.]

Interpreting Aristotle's doctrine of tragic catharsis in moral terms, Cinthio uses it—like Castelvetro—as a means to cleanse the passions of the spectator's mind, inducing him to become a better man by the crude exposure of violence (*scelus*).[13] Giraldi Cinthio's ideology of horror outdoes Seneca's use of sensational carnage in portraying the awesome crimes of both his revenging villains and revenging victims. Hence the necessity of exasperated realism, more aggressive and violent than that of Seneca and the parallel rejection of the fabulous, unnaturalistic world of the classical theater, to reinforce the analogy between stage and life.[14] The horror effect upon the audience comes from the disproportion of the victim's punishment inflicted in a rhetorical game of studied spectacularity, melting together the *fictio* of the story with the *actio* itself of *scelus*. The moral didacticism implied in this theory of tragedy is mirrored on the English Renaissance stage, where instances of didactic effects similar to Cinthio's dramatic mockery can be observed in many revenge plays.

In *Orbecche* the heroine is given as a wedding present by her tyrant father three silver vessels containing the head and hands of her husband and the mutilated bodies of her children, following the perverse symbolism of Tancredi's *novella*.[15] Sulmone's decision to spare his daughter's life but to show the *spettacol crudele* of her kinsmen's mutilated bodies is explained as a kind of didactic form of catharsis intended to promote compassion and expiation through horror in the inner and outer audience alike:

> Se l'uccido, fia fine al suo dolore;
> ché la morte a chi è miser, non è pena,
> ma fine de la pena e de l'angoscia.
> Però se viva ne riman costei
> e co gli occhi ambe due i suoi figli vegga
> morti e 'l marito, tal sarà l'affanno,
> che n'avrà invidia a que', che son sotterra;
> che d'ogni morte è via più grave sempre
> una infelice e miserabil vita.
>
> (3.3.51–9)

> [If I kill her, it will be an end to her woe;
> For death to the unhappy is no suffering,
> But the end of suffering and anguish.
> However, if she remains alive and
> With her own eyes sees both her children
> And husband dead, such will be her torture
> That she will envy those who are below the ground
> Since an unhappy and wretched life
> Is always more painful than any death.]

A similar effect of arousing emotions is evident in Sulmone's mocking of Oronte in the episode of the tyrant's slaughter of his son-in-law and nephews:

> E venuto il re poi ne l'alta torre,
> co le sue proprie mani il prese e disse:
> "Ti voglio far mio successor del regno
> Oronte, in questo luoco." E questo detto,
> pigliar gli fe' le braccia a que' malvagi,
> ch'ivi l'avean condotto, e ambo le mani
> gli fe' por sopra un ceppo, e da le braccia
> levogliele il crudele in due gran colpi,
> con un grave coltello. E dopo, alquanto
> trattosi a dietro, prese in man le mani,
> le porse a Oronte, lui dicendo: "Questo
> è lo scettro che t'offro, a questo modo
> ti vo' far re. Come ne sei contento?
> Fa ch'io lo sappia."
>
> (IV.i.72–85)

> [And when the king came up to the high tower
> He held him with his own hands and said:

> "I want to make you my successor in the kingdom
> Oronte, in this place." And this said,
> He ordered his arms to be grasped by those servants,
> Who had brought him there, and had
> Both his hands placed upon a block.
> Then the villain chopped them from the arms
> In two great blows, with a heavy knife.
> And, stepping back a little, he took the hands
> In his hands and offered them to Oronte, saying to him:
> "This is the sceptre that I offer you, in this way
> I will make you king. How are you pleased with this?
> Let me know it."]

Here the *beffa* on Oronte is not simplistic evidence of sadism: it reveals a kind of instructive retribution, mocking the rite of coronation through the exaggerated theatricality of revenge. Sulmone insists on this form of retributive retaliation in his answer to the servant Allocche:

> Egli l'ingiuria
> mi fece allor che per lo più fedele
> l'avea de la mia corte: e io ho voluto
> che la fè istessa lo conduca a morte.
>
> (5.1.73–6)

> [He offended me
> When I considered him the most faithful
> In the court: and I wished that faith
> Itself should lead him to death.]

With the same attitude, Sulmone sets up the punishment of his daughter. The dreadful sight of the slaughter is offered as a wedding present with words of satisfaction:

> Quanto ciò è a te dolente, è tanto lieto
> e piacevole a me, figlia proterva,
> e quanto più doler ti veggio, tanto
> più me n'allegro, e più me n'gode il core.
>
> (5.3.59–62)

> [The more woeful this is to you, the happier
> And more pleasing it is to me, wicked daughter,
> And the more I see you suffer, the more
> Content I am, and the greater my heart rejoices.]

For Sulmone, royal authority is a godlike quality devoid of mercy. His cruelty is an expression of kingly power whose intent it is to destroy the defences of his victims through shocking effects such as deceit and surprise. But Orbecche's reaction is equally deceitful and spectacular. She pretends to be pleased at her father's joy and the moral perversion of his mocking jest and asks for capital punishment. Then, thinking he has obtained filial obedience, Sulmone forgives his daughter. But Orbecche's sudden repentance is only a mockery. She feigns to yield to her father, and even offers to punish herself, only to stab him to death. Then she chops off her father's head and hands and, addressing the mortal remains of her kinsmen, commits suicide.

Drawing on Senecan antecedents (especially *Thyestes*), as well as Boccaccian narrative variations, Giraldi's poetics of horror is aptly sustained by effective iterative and animal imagery: as when a perfect parallel is made in the throwing of Oronte's mutilated body to dogs and vultures with the same end as is decreed for the tyrant's trunk. The monstrous ferocity of Sulmone toward his own blood is compared to the voracity of the wolf, whereas Orbecche's fury to vindicate the massacre of her sons and husband is compared to a tiger's. Nor is all this unique. In Lodovico Dolce's masterpiece *Marianna* (1565), the eponymous heroine receives as a gift from her jealous husband a basin containing the head, heart, and severed hands of her presumed lover. The abundance of macabre effects dominates the scene in all cinquecento revenge drama, invariably portraying onstage lurid stories of deceit, slaughter, mutilation, and cannibalism where the *beffa* motif occupies a recurrent presence, becoming a literary construct of an "Italian vice."

On the other hand, what we might call the sadistic mockery of retaliation was not confined to the *novelle* or the cinquecento Italian theater alone. The history itself of contemporary Italy provided many telling examples which might have inspired Elizabethan dramatists. Guicciardini's *Storia d'Italia* is a case in point. Apart from the numerous episodes of political killings for the conquest and exercise of power, stories of jealousy and blood with frequent incestuous overtones are sometimes reported, which the author himself defines "more trivial than the burning ambition to rule."[16]

Guicciardini's work is particularly important since it forms an ideal bridge uniting passionate love and political intrigue and coloring the Italianate scene with another significant element. This mixture of political plotting and excessive sexuality characterizes the Elizabethan exploitation of Italy's Renaissance courts in many Jacobean plays. Moreover, the frequent misinterpretation of Machiavelli's prince as an atheistic, deceitful villain and plotter, as derived from the *Contre-Machiavel* by Gentillet, was responsible for the pejorative meaning that "policy," "politic," and derivatives carried on the Tudor and Stuart stages.[17] Finally, the Italophobic prejudice arising from contemporary travelers' reports and various defamatory writings completes the evil side of the Italian picture, providing a perfect setting for both comedy and tragedy and contributing to the semantic construction of the Italianate court as a crossroads of multiple vices.

Some interesting developments of this kind of Italianate revenge are adopted in Thomas Kyd's *The Spanish Tragedy*. The stage Machiavel, Lorenzo, hires Pedringano to murder Serberine. After the killing, Lorenzo makes the watch arrest Pedringano and lets him know that "his pardon is already sign'd, / And thereon bid him boldly be resolv'd" (3.4.63–64).[18] But instead of the pardon he sends him an empty box. As the messenger ironically says, realizing that he is carrying nothing at all,

> I cannot choose but smile to think how the villain will flout the gallows, scorn the audience, and descant on the hangman, and all presuming of his pardon from hence. Will't not be an odd jest, for me to stand and grace every jest he makes, pointing my finger at this box, as who would say, 'Mock on, here's thy warrant.' Is't not a scurvy jest that a man should jest himself to death? (3.5.10–16)

This same sort of ironic trick is reserved to Lorenzo by Hieronimo in the play-within-the-play by which he avenges the murder of his son. Hieronimo's retaliation possesses the same spectacular twists of the *Tragoedia cothurnata* that he is going to enact: surprise, theatricality, sadistic mockery. As in the episode of the *beffa* on Pedringano, Hieronimo's victims are unaware that they are constrained to take part in their own death. More sardonically still, they are made to perform their death roles in the tragedy of Soliman and Perseda, whereas the court acts as an inner audience, watching an Italianate spectacle that produces the actors' own end as well as that of the king's brother. It is no coincidence that Hamlet's own play-within-the-play, *The Murder of Gonzago,* relying upon Kyd's metatheatrical device, stresses that "the story is extant, and written in very choice Italian" (3.2.256–7).[19]

Shakespeare's *Titus Andronicus* is perhaps the first Renaissance tragedy to use with great effect the sadistic mockery of retaliation as a centrally recurring motif. The play, of course, is typically Senecan in construction and also shows some direct borrowings from Ovid, as in the banquet scene.[20] And yet the grotesque irony of the *beffa* on the victims provides a strong Italianate coloring which echoes that kind of didactic horror theorized by Cinthio. Act 3, scene 1 opens with Titus pleading with the emperor and senators to spare his sons, condemned to death under the false accusation of killing Lavinia's husband. Aaron informs Titus that the only ransom for their lives is to send his hand to the king. Titus rejoices at this and, dismissing his youngest son and brother who wanted to offer their hand, begs Aaron to chop off his hand. Titus's hopes to see his sons alive are "ill repaid" by Aaron, since a messenger is sent to deliver

> the heads of thy two noble sons,
> And here's thy hand, in scorn to thee sent back:
> Thy grief their sports, thy resolution mock'd;
> That woe is me to think upon thy woes,
> More than remembrance of my father's death.
>
> (3.1.236–40)[21]

Titus's own retaliation on Tamora and her sons is no less effective. Believing him mad, Tamora pretends to help Titus to accomplish his vendetta. She scorns him, appearing as Revenge, and disguising her two sons, Demetrius and Chiron, as Rape and Murder. But Titus realizes the game and feigns to be mad only to play his own turn upon his enemies:

> I knew them all, though they suppos'd me mad,
> And will o'erreach them in their own devices,
> A pair of cursed hell-hounds and their dame.
>
> (5.2.142–4)

The episode is similar to the ending of *Orbecche,* where the heroine feigns to be reconciled with her father only to execute vengeance upon him with extreme fury, continuing the tyrant's mocking jest. Interestingly, in both plays the remains of the villains' corpses are thrown to dogs and vultures. Although Seneca's theater and Ovid's *Metamorphoses* inform the symbolic construction and general design of *Titus Andronicus,* it is significant that the use of the *beffa,* especially in the retaliation scenes, proves to be typically Cinthian in method in its common dramatic features and high sense of theatricality and didacticism as a consequence of *scelus.*

A notorious case of farcical retribution constitutes of course the whole construction of *The Revenger's Tragedy,* where the emblematic hero, Vindice, pursues throughout the play his secret desire to retaliate against the abuse and poisoning of his beloved, Gloriana. The Italianate mark of court corruption is symbolically centered on the idea of transgressive eroticism, depicting a locale of illicit sexual relations where rape, adultery, and incest make up a world of "strange lust" (1.3.57), masked by Machiavellian dissimulation and from which revenge and counterrevenge originate.

> Oh hour of incest!
> Any kin now next to the rim o' the sister
> Is man's meat in these days, and in the morning,
> When they are up and dressed and their mask on,
> Who can perceive this, save that eternal eye
> That sees through flesh and all?
>
> (1.3.62–7)[22]

The great scene of Vindice's retaliation on the Duke epitomizes the revenge themes of the play and is carried out with the same ironic jests as the Italianate avenger, unifying retribution with dramatic mockery. Acting as a pander for the Duke who believes he is being guided to a love meeting, Vindice makes him kiss the poisoned chops of Gloriana's skull. To accentuate the *beffa* on the Duke, he takes off his disguise and reveals to the Duke the incest between the Duchess and her bastard son, Spurio. Then he forces the poisoned Duke to watch the actual love-making of the incestuous couple:

> Nay to afflict thee more,
> Here in this lodge they meet for damned clips:
> Those eyes shall see the incest of their lips.
>
> (3.5.177–9)

The dreadful sight of incest constitutes an important part in Vindice's retaliation, and to be sure the Duke sees the lustful couple, Vindice and his brother "tear up" the Duke's eyelids to make him see the actual crime and die in despair:

> Nail down his tongue, and mine shall keep possession
> About his heart; if he but gasp he dies,
> We dread not death to quittance injuries. Brother,
> If he but wink, not brooking the foul object

Let our two other hands tear up his lids
And make his eyes, like comets, shine through blood.

(3.5.192–7)

Rather than demand a distinct dramatic decorum of satiric drama—as Brian Gibbons indicates[23]—in adopting such a characteristic use of the *beffa* motif in the retaliation scenes, these plays seem to comply with the macabre didacticism of a new tragic form.

In John Webster's Italianate tragedies the scorn of the victims is so ingeniously carried on as to produce bizarre, almost laughable, effects. Revenge and counterrevenge in both *The White Devil* and *The Duchess of Malfi* appear thematically linked with the Italianate coloring of the stage court, naturally flowing from it and presented as a common practice of Renaissance Italy. Hence retaliation is depicted in terms of a cynical, sophisticated, spectacular technique capable of enhancing the sufferings of the victims and affecting the audience's imagination with a continual series of ironic shocks and *coups de théâtre*. Various aspects, elements, and features of typical revenge drama are defined as thoroughly "Italian" and the relevant foreign setting is equally emphasized: "Italian cut-works" (1.1.52), "Italian means" (2.1.161), "Italian coast" (2.1.361), "Italian sallet" (4.2.61), "Italian beggars" (4.3.82), "Italian churchmen" (5.5.138), to refer only to *The White Devil*.[24] The course of action is moreover interspersed with the notorious Machiavellian misuse of the terms "politic," "policy," "politician," and derivatives, whereas the theatergram of prophetic dreams and premonitions occurs in both tragedies, paralleling Italian antecedents, most notably Orbecche's dream of an eagle attacking two white doves and their brood.

In *The White Devil,* the *beffa* motif recurs in the episode of the killing of Bracciano. After poisoning his helmet, Lodovico and Gasparo return disguised as Capuchins to bring him "the extreme unction" (5.3.38). Apart from the sharp irony of their feigned religious rite, clearly associated with the poisonous "unction" sent from the Duke, their intention is to heighten Bracciano's anguish with the shocking revelation of their true identity. The scene provides a crescendo of mocking effects starting from the sardonic jest of their religious Latin service (5.3.135–46), to the revelation of their real names and the listing of poisonous ingredients, up to the Duke's "true-love knot" (5.3.174) of their final strangulation when Bracciano attempts a desperate reaction. The very process of Bracciano's agony is signaled by a kind of frenzy during which the victim bursts into horrid laughter, perceiving the end of his hope of salvation as well as that of Vittoria and her allied brother. Bracciano's inflicted torture is commented on as an Italian vice by Flamineo for the overflow of despair caused by the peculiar way the Duke of Florence commissioned his enemy's death:

> O the rare tricks of a Machivillian!
> He doth not come like a gross plodding slave
> And buffet you to death: no, my quaint knave,
> He tickles you to death; makes you die laughing;
> As if you had swallow'd down a pound of saffron—
> You see the feat,—'tis practis'd in a trice
> To teach court-honesty it jumps on ice.
>
> (5.3.193–99)

A few lines later, Francisco himself praises Lodovico for his cunning scorn toward the dying Bracciano:

> Excellent Lodovico!
> What! did you terrify him at the last gasp?
> (5.3.212–13)

This same ironic jest is applied by the hired assassins in the episode of the final retaliation to Flamineo and Vittoria. Again, they enter disguised as Capuchins, announcing that they are bringing a revel which turns out to be a death masque, a sword-dance during which they execute the commissioned murder. But before the killing, they throw off their disguises and reveal that the Moor pensioned by Bracciano was indeed the Duke of Florence himself. Once again the *beffa* motif acts as a fundamental component of the revenge action and is employed to satisfy the perverse sense of moral retribution of the evil-doer.

The Duchess of Malfi offers the most extraordinary linguistic and thematic affinities with Cinthio's *Orbecche*. Ferdinand, the duchess's tyrant brother, is clearly presented as sexually jealous of his sister, disclosing an incestuous passion similar to that of Sulmone for his daughter. Both plays adopt the same rhetoric of animal imagery related to the voracity of the wolf and to the desperate fury of the tiger. Moreover, after the killing of the duchess, Ferdinand's lycanthropy indicates, in his gradual metamorphosis into a corpse-devouring wolf, the incestuous erotic drive for his own flesh.[25] But it is in the great retaliation scenes of the duchess's ordeal that we find the most effective linguistic and thematic similarities between the two plays. The calvary of the duchess is attentively prepared by Ferdinand. Feigning to be reconciled with his sister, he first gives her in the dark a dead man's hand bearing a ring, which she kisses as a sign of reconciliation. More satirically still, both hand and ring are left as a "love-token" to the horrified lady. This macabre *beffa* becomes more outrageous when the duchess is made to see the "sad spectacle" of the artificial figures of her husband and children, "appearing as if they were dead."[26] Bosola's comments on the mocking scorn echo the perversely moral effects of Sulmone's *spettacol crudele*:

> Look you: here's the piece from which 'twas ta'en:
> He doth present you this sad spectacle
> That now you know directly they are dead
> Hereafter you may wisely cease to grieve
> For that which cannot be recovered.
>
> (4.1.56–60)

The systematic torture of the duchess is completed by the madmen's masque by which Ferdinand aims to cure his sister's faults by bringing her to therapeutic despair:

> Your brother hath intended you some sport:
> A great physician, when the Pope was sick
> Of a deep melancholy, presented him
> With several sorts of madmen, which wild object,
> Being full of change and sport, forc'd him to laugh,
> And so th'imposthume broke: the self-same cure
> The duke intends on you.
>
> (4.2.38–44)

At the end of the madmen's dance, a final jest anticipates the actual murder. Bosola, disguised as a bellman, offers her the deadly instruments sent from the "Arragonian brethren": a coffin, some cords and a bell carried by "Executioners":

> Here is a present from your princely brothers,
> And may it arrive welcome, for it brings
> Last benefit, last sorrow.
>
> (4.2.166–68)

Like the tyrant Sulmone, Ferdinand rejoices at his sister's suffering. The fact that "she's plagu'd in art" (4.1.111) reveals a secret passion for inflicting perverse punishment intended to scorn his victim's defences through shocking visual effects.

If we examine Webster's tragedies against the background of Cinthio's theory and practice, a connection which in the case of *Orbecche* may also have arisen from its narrative version, it is possible to assess better the dramatic significance of his tendency toward intense gnomic verse and visual imagery. In Webster's concern with a grand rhetoric of moral spectacle and dumb shows is conveyed the idea of learning through scorn and didactic horror, especially transmitted by theatrical instances of sensational effects, which the dramatist, notorious for his intertextual activity, may have borrowed from Cinthio's new tragic form.

After considering the analogies between cinquecento tragedy and English Renaissance drama, the greatest differences lie in the divergent moral attitudes adopted by the dramatists of both countries. For the humanist ideal pursued by Cinthio, portraying strong individual passions as a mirror to cleanse our conscience and promote goodness, is totally subverted in Jacobean tragedy by the role of society. Here individual evil is replaced by worldwide corruption, which thrives at court and spreads like a disease throughout the social environment represented. Cinthio's stage-world, moved by Counter-Reformation beliefs, depicts a divinely ordered universe where the piling up of horrors provides a providential design that offers the spectator shocking bloodshed with the benign exposure of the cruelest passions. In this philosophy man is at the center of the cosmos and the individual tyrant appears as a microcosmic reflection of the whole, absorbing and exorcising the evils of the universe. Only in this condition may he act as a model, albeit altogether negative, of humanity, and as such his tragedy of vice and passions serves as a powerfully didactic and moral exemplum.[27] By contrast, Jacobean tragedy centers not on individual faults but on the idea of widespread corruption that characterizes a "gloomy world," a "deep pit of darkness," where "Doth womanish and fearful mankind live!"[28] A wave of general misguidance invests all vices of society at all levels, so that in the tragedies of Coriolanus, Vittoria, Flamineo, and Bosola—as Jonathan Dollimore has put it—"we 'read' not the working of Fate or God, but a contemporary reality which both creates and destroys them."[29]

In *The Revenger's Tragedy*, though, the attempted seduction by the disguised Vindice of his own sister, Castiza, on behalf of the duke's son, is reminiscent of recurring patterns from Italian "radical" comedy, fusing the two dramatic traditions together. While the theatergram of the constant woman can be seen in Castiza—the embodiment of purity, and indeed the only character in the play to keep her honor constantly aloof from the general corruption—Vindice's mother, by agreeing to persuade Castiza to respond to the sexual call from the court, follows the same evil steps as Machiavelli's Sostrata in *La Mandragola*. It is no coincidence that two of the most subversive writers of Italian comedy, both banned by the Inquisition, Machiavelli and Aretino, were in fact already printed in London in 1588.[30] But wider social and political concerns may also be envisaged in Cinthio's tragedy. One of the longest scenes in *Orbecche* is the dispute between the tyrant and the counselor about the nature of kingship. This enables the dramatist to invite thought on the Renaissance debate about the ethics of power as it is portrayed in the dialectics between Sulmone and his counselor Malecche. On the one hand, Sulmone represents the medieval tyrant who believes that he must prove himself to be pitiless and devoid of all compassion in punishing those who have offended him, because his godlike authority is exalted by his absolute power to inflict punishment. As Carla Bella expresses it, "to be a *real* king means for him never to forgive."[31] On the other hand, Malecche holds the Renaissance, Counter-Reformation view based on mercy and humane understanding of the faults of others. The more capable the king is of forgiving, the more exalted his kingly state. This lengthy sequence discloses the presence of a "political" level, which also for its extension in the play has been rightly considered "the center of gravity of the representation, the very moment in which the court changes from the ideal place for courtly love . . . to a locale for a debate on power."[32] Despite the cultural differences between the two countries and the influence of Seneca and the Machiavellian hero,[33] this political perspective bridges the gap between the ideological contents of *Orbecche* and the character of "opposition drama" of most Jacobean plays in which the rubric of power, with its ancillary reflections on the topic of retaliation as an Italian vice, absorbs the Italian tragic tradition and the relevant humanist controversy about the rules of drama, particularly reflected in Giraldi's example of *tragedia nova*. We can find in *Orbecche*, as brilliantly suggested by Bruscagli, a subversive potential due to its particular dramaturgical technique, which founds its efficacy on the emotional impact that the horror scenes produce on the audience.[34] In so doing, Giraldi performs an operation of great theatrical awareness, and, at the same time, attemps to affect incisively the sociopolitical reality of his age, warning his spectators about the consequences of evil and the abuses of absolute power. It is certain that the heroine Orbecche is seen with sympathetic participation, which the play's strategy passes on to the audience. Giraldi brilliantly theorized this successful operation of emotional transfer in his discussion of the didactic character of *tragedia nova.*

Notes

1. Giovanni Boccaccio, *The Decameron,* translated into English (1620), ed. W. E. Henley, with an introduction by E. Hutton, 2 vols. (London: D. Nutt, 1909), IV, 9, 2: 225.

2. Cf. H. G. Wright, *Boccaccio in England from Chaucer to Tennyson* (London: The Athlone Press, 1957), 196–260.

3. Martin Wiggins, *Journeymen in Murder: The Assassin in English Renaissance Drama* (Oxford: Clarendon Press, 1991), 32.

4. *The Decameron,* 2: 141.

5. Cf. Wright, *Boccaccio in England,* 196–98. According to Wright, an anonymous and undated manuscript (contained in Add. MS. 34312 in the British Library), conventionally entitled *Ghismonda,* "shows clear traces of the translation of the *Decameron* that first appeared in 1620" (199). A copy of the play is also available in the Bodleian Library.

6. On the heart imagery in Ford's plays, *see* D. K. Anderson Jr., "The Heart and the Banquet: Imagery in Ford's *'Tis Pity* and *The Broken Heart,*" *Studies in English Literature,* 2 (spring 1962): 209–17.

7. Giovan Battista Giraldi, *Orbecche—La tragedia a chi legge,* in *Teatro del Cinquecento,* ed. R. Cremante (Milan and Naples: R. Ricciardi Editore, 1988). Translation is my own.

8. The form of the new tragedy was generally taken up in the subsequent drama. *See,* for instance, Pietro Aretino's *Orazia* (1546); Lodovico Dolce's *Didone* (1547), *Giocasta* (1549), and *Marianna* (1565); Girolamo Parabosco's *Progne* (1548); Girolamo Razzi's *Gismonda* (1569); Luigi Groto's *Dalida* (1572); Cesare Della Porta's *Delfa* (1587); and Muzio Manfredi's *Semiramis* (1593), to mention only the most famous. *See* Marvin T. Herrick, *Italian Tragedy in the Renaissance* (Urbana: University of Illinois Press, 1965); Louise G. Clubb, *Italian Drama in Shakespeare's Time* (New Haven: Yale University Press, 1989).

9. G. K. Hunter, "Seneca and the Elizabethans: a Case-study in 'Influence'" and "Seneca and English Tragedy," in his *Dramatic Identities and Cultural Tradition: Studies in Shakespeare and His Contemporaries* (Liverpool: Liverpool University Press, 1978), 159–73 and 174–213.

10. Seneca, *Thyestes,* translated by Jasper Heywood (1560), ed. J. Daalder, The New Mermaids (London: Ernest Benn, 1982), xx–xxxviii.

11. Marco Ariani, "Ragione e furore nella tragedia di G. B. Giraldi Cinthio," in *Tra Classicismo e Manierismo: il teatro tragico del Cinquecento* (Florence: Olschki, 1974), 115–78.

12. Giovan Battista Giraldi, "Discourse on the Composition of Comedies and

Tragedies," in *G. B. Giraldi Cinzio: Scritti critici,* ed. C. G. Crocetti (Milan: Marzorati, 1973), 223–24. Translation is my own.

13. *See* Madeleine Doran, *Endeavors of Art: A Study of Form in Elizabethan Drama* (Madison: University of Wisconsin Press, 1954), 89–90.

14. *See* Carmelo Musumarra, "La poetica del Rinascimento e la tragedia," in *La poesia tragica italiana nel Rinascimento* (Florence: Olschki, 1972), 1–48.

15. Important similarities between Cinthio's *Orbecche* and Boccaccio's narrative have been noted by P. R. Horne, *The Tragedies of Giambattista Cinthio Giraldi* (Oxford: Oxford University Press, 1962), 60–62.

16. Francesco Guicciardini, *The History of Italy,* trans., ed., with notes, and an Introduction by S. Alexander (London: Macmillan, 1969). Guicciardini refers to the Ferrarese story of Ippolito d'Este and his bastard brother Don Giulio:

> the Cardinal Ippolito d'Este was fervently enamored of a young maid, his kinswoman, who with no less fervour was loved by Don Giulio, bastard brother to Ippolito; when the girl confessed to the Cardinal Ippolito that what attracted her beyond all else and fanned her love to such heat was the beauty of Don Giulio's eyes, the infuriated Cardinal, having waited for a convenient moment when Giulio would be hunting outside the city, set about him in the field, and forcing him to dismount from his horse, ordered several of his pages to pluck out his brother's eyes as rivals of his love; and he had the heart to remain present during such a horrid act, which later resulted in the most serious troubles among the brothers. (188).

17. Cf. Mario Praz, "Machiavelli and the Elizabethans," *Proceedings of the British Academy,* 14 (1928): 49–97; "'The Politic Brain:' Machiavelli and the Elizabethans," in *The Flaming Heart: Essays on Crashaw, Machiavelli, and Other Studies in the Relations between Italian and English Literature from Chaucer to T. S. Eliot* (Gloucester, Mass., 1966), 90–145. But *see,* for a different perspective, Margaret Scott, "Machiavelli and the Machiavel." *Renaissance Drama,* n.s., 15 (1984): 147–74.

18. *The Spanish Tragedy,* ed. J. R. Mulryne (London: Ernest Benn Ltd., 1970).

19. *Hamlet,* ed. Harold Jenkins (London: Methuen, 1982).

20. Cf. Robert S. Miola, *Shakespeare and Classical Tragedy: The Influence of Seneca* (Oxford: Clarendon Press, 1992), 29–30.

21. *Titus Andronicus,* ed. J. C. Maxwell (London: Methuen, 1953).

22. *The Revenger's Tragedy,* ed. Brian Gibbons (London: Ernest Benn Ltd., 1967).

23. Gibbons, introduction to *The Revenger's Tragedy,* xi.

24. John Webster, *The White Devil,* ed. John Russell Brown (Manchester: Manchester University Press, 1977).

25. Robert Ornstein, *The Moral Vision of Jacobean Tragedy* (Westport, Conn.: Greenwood Press, 1977), 140.

26. John Webster, *The Duchess of Malfi,* ed. John Russell Brown (Manchester: Manchester University Press, 1976). 4.1.45ff.

27. *See* Carmelo Musumarra, "La 'riforma' giraldiana e l'*Orbecche*," in *La poesia tragica italiana nel Rinascimento,* 93–111.

28. *The Duchess of Malfi,* 5.5.100–2.

29. Jonathan Dollimore, *Radical Tragedy. Religion, Ideology and Power in the Drama of Shakespeare and his Contemporaries,* 2d ed. (New York: Harvester Wheatsheaf, 1989), xxxi.

30. *See* Clubb, *Italian Drama in Shakespeare's Time,* 50.

31. Carla Bella, "Giovan Battista Giraldi Cinzio," in *Eros e censura nella tragedia dal '500 al '700* (Firenze: Vallecchi Ed., 1981), 87.

32. Riccardo Bruscagli, "La corte in scena. Genesi politica della tragedia ferrarese," in his *Stagioni della civiltà estense* (Pisa: Nistri-Lischi, 1983), 142–43.

33. Cf. Antonio D'Andrea, "Giraldi Cinthio and the Birth of the Machiavellian Hero on the Elizabethan Stage," in *Il teatro italiano del Rinascimento,* ed. Maristella de Panizza Lorch (Milan: Edizioni di Comunità, 1980), 605–17.

34. Cf. Riccardo Bruscagli, "La corte in scena. Genesi politica della tragedia ferrarese," 127–59.

The Italian *Every Man in His Humour*

Robert S. Miola

THE Quarto version of *Every Man in His Humour (EMI)*, printed 1601, features a Florentine setting and characters with Italian names; the Folio version, printed 1616, features a London setting and English character names, along with many additions and deletions.[1] Editors and critics have been nearly unanimous in approving the revision. Jonson's early editor, Whalley, wrote that the changes effected "a more becoming and consistent aspect" to the play. Since English varieties of folly were on display, the English setting was clearly more appropriate. Cunningham quoted Charles Lamb: "How say you, reader? Do not Master Kitely, Mistress Kitely, Master Knowell, Brainworm, &c., read better than these Cisaplines?" Carter declared that Jonson's revision freed the play "from its false dress." In their monumental edition Herford and Simpson noted changes in externals, in language and style, and in structure, asserting that they marked "a very definite advance in technical and stylistic maturity." The playwright made some attempt at sustaining the conventional setting, "but Jonson knew too little of Italy for effective realism, even had this been his aim. The transfer to London liberated his vast fund of local knowledge." In the program/text for the 1986 Swan revival of the play, the director, John Caird, justified the choice of the Folio by appealing to "the obvious rightness of the English setting" and the inherent superiority of the Folio "in nearly every respect." (This superiority did not, however, prevent significant borrowings from the Quarto for the production.)[2] This paper attempts to discern reasons for Jonson's original choice of an Italian setting by examining the 1598 context of *EMI,* i.e., contemporary dramatic and nondramatic texts, particularly Jonson's early works, the plays of Chapman, Dekker, and Shakespeare, Elizabethan verse satires, Italian literature, and poetic theory.

In Jonson's day Italy was an enormously important, richly

208

polyvalent, and widely pervasive presence. Many volumes have outlined the story of English engagement with Italy: with Italian travel, cities, books, universities (Bologna, Padua, Pavia), expatriates (Florio, Ubaldini, Pallavicino, and various churchmen, artists, travelers, and merchants), political thought (Guicciardini and Machiavelli), biology, mathematics, science, philosophy (including the influential Neoplatonists), history (including the story of ancient Rome), religion, music, customs (dueling), crafts (glassblowing), *cortesia* (Guazzo and Castiglione), arts (painting, dancing, war), drama (both the *commedia erudita* and *dell'arte*), poetry (Dante and Petrarch), *novelle* (Boccaccio, Bandello, Giraldi Cinthio, Fiorentino), verse romance (Boiardo, Ariosto, Tasso), and poetic theory (Castelvetro, Scaliger, Robortello, Minturno).[3] In early modern England Italy was a *mundus significans* that supplied many and varied meanings to dramatists and other writers.

Among these dramatists was, of course, Ben Jonson, whose reputation as a provincial un-Italianate Londoner may have proceeded from Drummond's misleading comment that he "neither doeth understand French nor Italianne" (HS 1: 134).[4] As an accomplished Latinist Jonson could have deciphered simple Italian with minimal study. He probably owned books in Italian— Colonna's *La Hypnerotomachia,* Aretino's *La prima parte di Ragionamenti* with *Commento di Ser Agresto,* as well as a complete Petrarch (mostly Latin, some Italian);[5] he peppered his early plays with Italian names and phrases, including an extended bit of dialogue in *Cynthia's Revels.* Jonson criticized Petrarch, called Harington's Ariosto "the worst" of all translations, and apparently translated some verses from the Italian of Girolamo Parabosco (HS 1: 133–5). He numbered among his professional friends John Florio, who was a rich resource for Italian language, books, and information; Thomas Wright, the Jesuit who had studied at the English College in Rome and in Milan; and Alphonso Ferrabosco, with whom he collaborated on masques. Whatever the status of Jonson's Italian, he certainly knew Italian authors, books, and culture: Castiglione contributed to *Every Man out of His Humour (EMO),* Bruno (perhaps) to *The Alchemist,* Aretino to *Epicoene,* Boccaccio to *The Devil Is an Ass,* Conti, Cartari, Giraldi, and Ficino, as well as Italian entertainments and Ariosto to the masques, despite his scorn of those, like Daniel, who simply put "a few *Italian* herbs" into a "*sallade*" (HS 7: 209–10). Jonson discoursed in *Timber* on Machiavelli and Italian painters and scattered numerous references to Italian customs and theater (including *commedia dell'arte*) throughout his works. *Volpone,* the most complete evocation of an Italian setting in English Renaissance drama, shows a detailed knowledge of the topography, customs, vocabulary, and myths of Venice.

The selection of Italy, then, specifically Florence, for the setting of *EMI,* accorded with Jonson's own interests and those of the audience. It was not a youthful indiscretion but a characteristically deliberate and theatrically shrewd choice. Two specific literary phenomena, in fact, recommended Italy as the appropriate place for Jonson's first humors comedy: the rebirth of New Comedy on stage, and the current rage for verse satire. Moreover, the playwright skillfully uses the Italian language along with Italian theatrical traditions and poetic theory to construct the play and evocatively figure forth meanings for its audiences.

Composing *EMI,* Jonson must have had in mind *The Case is Altered,* written probably in 1597–8 and revised later, a comedy based on a *contaminatio* of Plautus's *Captivi* and *Aulularia,* set in an Italian city, Milan. Both plays adapt New Comedy while featuring satire on contemporary figures and fashions, an intricate plot, and an Italian locality that has some recognizably English characters (Jupiter and Onion clearly parallel Cob and Tib). Exploring the new fashion of humors comedy that Chapman had just initiated in *An Humorous Day's Mirth* (1597), Jonson modeled *EMI* on no particular classical comedy; instead he relied on generally classical configurations, characters, and devices: the father-son conflict between Lorenzo Sr. and Lorenzo Jr. (represented well by *Adelphoe,* which Jonson paraphrases directly in the revision (1.2.209–16)); the intriguing slave/parasite in Musco; the fraternal opposition between Giuliano and Prospero; the *miles gloriosus* in Bobadilla; the use of contrary settings (Cob's and Thorello's homes); the covert marriage; the use of letters and messengers; the culminating anagnorises and judgements.

In the sixteenth century Italy provided a choice locality for the staging of such New Comedic action. Plautus and Terence had found new life on Italian stages and in Italian pages, the *editiones principes* of Terence (1470) and Plautus (1472), and had enjoyed a considerable efflorescence in cinquecento learned and popular theater. Other English playwrights who adapted New Comedy often chose Italy as a setting: Gascoigne's *Supposes* (1566) began the trend; there followed *The Two Gentlemen of*

Verona (c. 1592), *The Taming of the Shrew* (c. 1592–4), *The Merchant of Venice* (1596) with its Rialto and eloping Lorenzo, *Much Ado about Nothing* (1598), Chapman's *All Fools* (1599), *May-Day* (c. 1601), and *The Gentleman Usher* (c. 1601). Like his fellow dramatists, Jonson placed Londoners in a fictionalized Italy created from Plautus and Terence to play out the configurations of New Comedy. (Similarly, in *Poetaster* he would anatomize their follies in a fictionalized Rome created from Juvenal, Horace, and Martial.) Setting the scene of *EMI* in a Florence replete with Anglicisms, Jonson gives witness both to the antiquity of the humors displayed and to their modernity. He evokes the polyvalent alterity of Italy while supplying all the familiar discomforts of home.

Contemporary verse satire—trenchant, controversial, topical—constitutes another specific and immediate context for Jonson's Italy. Beginning with Lodge's *A Fig for Momus* (1595), verse satires reached a peak in popularity between 1598 and 1601, the years of the Hall-Marston quarrel, the years of the writing and printing of *EMI* Q: there were Donne's verse satires, written though not printed by 1597, Hall's *Virgidemiarum* (1597), Marston's *The Metamorphosis of Pigmalions Image and Certaine Satyres* (1598) and *The Scourge of Villanie* (1598, 1599), Guilpin's *Skialethia* (1598), Rankins's *Seauen Satyres* (1598), T. M.'s *Micro-Cynicon* (1599), Weever's *Epigrams* (1599) and *Faunus and Melliflora* (1600), Davies' *Epigrams* (c. 1599), Rowlands's *The Letting of Humors Blood* (1600), the Whipper pamphlets (1601; Weever, Guilpin, Breton). These works adapted ancient methods to scornful ridicule of local gallants and would-be gallants, wits, jealous husbands, braggart soldiers, poetasters, and love-struck sonneteers. Significantly, these London gulls and fools often sport Italian or Italianized names.[6] The swaggering Bobadilla has obvious affinities with Marston's cowardly braggart Tubrio (*Certaine Satyres*, 69–71; cf. Capro *Scourge of Villanie*, 137) as well as Guilpin's Captain Tucca, also a swearer (*Skialethia*, 59–60; cf. Jonson's Captain Tucca, *Poetaster*, and Dekker's *Satiromastix*). Marston presents a cousin-german to Matheo (and also Stephano)—Inamorato Curio, the courtly, smitten poetaster (*SV*, 150ff.); similarly, Hall portrays Labeo, who filches "whole pages from honest *Petrarch*, clad in English weed" (*Virg.*, 94). Guilpin draws on the Italian literature of jealousy, particularly the *novelle* and Ariosto, to present another Thorello, Trebatio, the jealous man who haunts his wife and displays pathological suspicions (*Skialethia*, 78, 190–1). In his choice of setting and his portraits of contemporary humors Jonson was catering to audiences who regularly enjoyed verse representations of English/Italian folly.

Slight as it has seemed to later generations, Jonson's Italian setting in *EMI* gratified those many who exhibited continuous fascination with Italian arts, culture, and language. The market for Italian books was so good in London that John Wolfe faked Italian imprints to boost his sales. And according to John Lievsay, "Almost every cultivated Elizabethan had at least a smattering of Italian."[7] Florence is named eight times in act 1 (1.1.116, 125; 159, 162; 1.2.74, 79, 108; 1.4.11) and three times thereafter (3.2.73; 4.2.82; 5.3.148).[8] Cob calls Doctor Clement "the honestest old Trojan in all Italy" (3.5.18–19); Thorello concludes that he has "the faithful'st wife in Italy" (5.3.395). Padua and Venice get mentioned in the dialogue (3.2.51; 4.4.8), as well as the academies (1.1.13; "universities" in F), Saint Anthony's church (2.3.199; 3.2.85; "Coleman Street" in F), the Friary (4.3.56; "the Tower" in F), a Rialto (5.3.192), and the duke (4.2.53 "Her Majesty and the Lords" in F; 5.2.36; "Her Majesty" in F). Prospero identifies Doctor Clement as "the *gonfaloniere* of the state here" (3.2.44), i.e., the bearer of the gonfalon, a streaming banner or ensign, or a justice (emended to the colorless "a city magistrate" in F). We hear of Saint Peter (2.1.40–42), St. Mark (3.6.25), St. Mark's Day (2.3.94), the Pope and excommunication (3.4.86–7; deleted in F), and a tabernacle (3.4.93; also deleted in F; Jonson adds a joke at the expense of Roman Catholics in F, 3.2.89). Prospero significantly refers to Matheo and Bobadilla as "my two zanies" (2.3.49; "hang-bys" in F), the servants who act as clowns in the *commedia dell'arte*. Bobadilla extols tobacco as an antidote to even "the most poisonous simple in all Florence" (3.2.73; "all Italy" in F), thus employing the popular stereotype that enhances Thorello's mad fears of poisoning later (4.3.15ff.). Throughout, Jonson provides some flavor of the Italian language, ranging from the scurrilous (and entirely authentic) "*cazzo*" (1.2.108; deleted in F; cf. 2.1.18) and "*fico*" (2.1.5) to the pseudo-Italian "Rashero Baccono" (1.3.23; deleted in F) and "cavaliero" (1.4.129), to the mention of "Ghibelletto," an Italian form of Jebeil (2.3.97; "Strigonium" in F), to the frequent appellation "Signior." Jonson's play with the Italian language, though relatively restrained, held special pleasures for audiences around the turn of the century, who apparently delighted in the exhibition of foreign dialects on stage.[9]

Jonson uses his Italian to even greater, though largely unnoticed, advantage in the important matter of names. Anne Barton observes that Jonson was habitually careful with names, and that he tended to employ "speaking names" early in his career when presenting humorous characters who showed little or no capacity for change. The Italian names in Q, however, she judges to be largely neutral and inexpressive, unlike the English names in the revised version.[10] Yet, the Italian names speak also. *Lorenzo* recalls Lorenzo il Magnifico, the famous Florentine potentate and patron of the arts. The two principal families in the play—the Pazzi and Strozzi—were in fact well-known powerful Florentine families involved in civic discord, the Pazzi having conspired against Lorenzo and his family.[11] Moreover, *pazzi* is the plural form for *pazzo,* "foolish, fond, mad, rash, doting rauing, or simple. Also a foole, a gull" (W). "Is this Pazzi house" (1.1.110), asks the Servingman, after Stephano's display of foolish humors; "Yes, marry, is it, sir," replies Lorenzo Senior, more truly than he intends. *Strózzo* signifies also "the gullet, the Vzel, the throat, or wind-pipe of any creature" (V); *Próspero,* "prosperous, successful, thriuing, lucky, in good plight, that giueth or receiueth prosperitie" (W). Prospero Strozzi, then, is a vivid and apt appellation for a young man about town.

Other names are equally suggestive. *Clement* identifies a judge who finally shows mercy and goodwill to the various gulls and fools; *Biancha* (from *bianco*) "white, blank, pale" (W), a woman who, like her namesake in *Othello,* is innocent though falsely accused. *Matheo* suggestively echoes *matto,* "mad, fond, foolish, simple, a mad, foolish simple gull" (W). *Peto,* "goat-eied, roulingeyed" (W) or perhaps *petto,* "also vsed for a fart" (W), well describes one whose main role in the play is to pass out drunk offstage, get stripped, and reappear in armor. *Thorello,* the diminutive of *thoro,* "a bull" (W), indicates the fundamental bestiality of jealous rage. *Hesperida,* from *hespero,* "the eeuening star" (W), seems right for the romantic female lead, such as she is, who elopes with Lorenzo Jr., the swain who may or may not know that *hespera* is "an herbe smelling more in the night then in the day" (W).

A final significant use of Italian in this play is the fencing terms, appearing in slightly Anglicized forms in Q, mostly corrected in F.[12] These references evoke a contemporary and highly charged site of intersection between Italian and English cultures at the turn of the century. Londoners then were fascinated with the new art of Italian rapier fence, studying the technique from Giacomo Di Grassi's *True Arte of Defence* (1594), Vincentio Saviolo's *Practice* (1595), and from resident Italian masters like Rocco Bonetti, Ieronimo Saviolo, and his brother, Vincentio himself. Interest in the Italian style ran so high that George Silver, champion of the short sword, published a defense of traditional methods and an attack on the new Italian style, *Paradoxes of Defence* (1599). The drama around 1598 reflects the contemporary controversy: Morsberger well identifies and discusses relevant passages from Porter's *Two Angry Women of Abingdon* (1598), Shakespeare's *Romeo and Juliet* (1595), *The Merry Wives* (1597–8), *Twelfth Night* (1600), and *Hamlet* (1601), Jonson's *EMI* (1598) and *EMO* (1599). Nor was fencing merely a literary matter for the first audiences of *EMI* in the fall of 1598. On 9 February of that year, *An Acte for punyshment of Rogues Vagabondes and Sturdy Beggars* designated for censure "All Fencers . . . wandring abroade" (Chambers, *ES* 4, 324); on 11 July 1598, a Burgonian fencer who had challenged all English masters of fence was hanged (the play recalls the incident in the reference to the "fencing Burgullian," 3.5.15); on 22 September 1598 Jonson killed Gabriel Spenser by sword in a duel; on 6 June 1599 fellow playwright John Day stabbed fellow playwright Henry Porter with a rapier (Porter died the next day). The Italianate fencing terms, Stephano's buying of Portensio's fake Toledo rapier, Bobadilla's imposture as a master of fence—all evoked current controversies and reflected daily realities. Indeed, Morsberger (23ff.) even suggests that certain details of Bobadilla's career mirror interestingly those of the well-known Italian expatriate, Saviolo.

Just as the Italian language with all its associations constructs *EMI* Q, evocatively shaping its meanings, so do Italian theater, lyric traditions, and poetic theory. Gosson complained about the ransacking of Italian comedies to furnish London playhouses;[13] Chapman casually mentioned four Italian plays in the dedication to *The Widow's Tears* (c. 1605). Many distinguished comparativists have demonstrated the pervasive influence of cinquecento drama on Renaissance England. Bobadilla presents a distinctly Italianate version of the *miles gloriosus*—impecunious, boastful about his part in historical battles, pretending to gentility and to expertise in military arts, finally exposed as a coward in a duel, despite silly rationalizations. The play's action resembles that of the *commedia erudita,* with its cast of middle-class families, servants, soldiers, innkeepers, and courtesans, "joined in a series of encounters in the street, in doorways, and at windows," engaging in "farcical intrigue" with a romantic element, compli-

cated by "misunderstanding, disguise, and mistaken identity."
Some have argued for specific Italian antecedents of *EMI*: Herrick sees parallels with Bentivoglio's *Il Geloso,* featuring a jealous husband and a soldier who brags about his part in famous sieges; Cairns adduces Aretino's *Talanta,* with its scourging of vice, noninteractive plotting, mannerist reduplication of language, and humor characters, including the braggart Tinca. Hesperida, like Shakespeare's Anne Page and other heroines, fetches her being from Italian adaptations of the classical *virgo,* from their presentation of ever more active and complex women.[14] The identification of specific affiliation is less important here than the recognition of family resemblance. *EMI* Q bears important affinities in character and action to the learned Italian comedy of the Renaissance.

And to the *commedia dell'arte,* as Prospero's mention of *zani* suggests. Judging from the many other allusions to *commedia dell'arte* in Elizabethan drama, this improvisatory theatrical form, often set in Florence, was widely familiar to audiences in 1598.[15] Even without Prospero's allusion, recognizable types and situations from the *commedia dell'arte* are easily discernible in *EMI* Q: the clever Zanni (Musco), with his talent for disguise and invention, entertaining the audience with various *lazzi,* or comic bits, like clothing switches and door-knocking scenes; the dull Zanni (Peto), often a foil for the clever one; the Pantalone (Lorenzo Sr.), often a sententious father angry with his son for misbehavior, as in Scala's *The Alexandrian Carpets;* the boastful Capitano (Bobadilla), often not Italian himself; the lovers (Lorenzo Jr. and Hesperida), arranging their affairs in secret. Most important is the jealous husband (Thorello), often cuckolded in fact and in his own imagination, as in Scala's *The Jealous Old Man.* This figure also has numerous comic and tragic counterparts in the enormously popular *novelle* which supplied so many plots for European stages. In *EMI* as in the later *Volpone,* however, Jonson subverts the *commedia dell'arte* stereotypes: he subordinates the *commedia dell'arte* action to the display of humors, deemphasizes the love affair, keeps Biancha conspicuously chaste, mirrors the jealousy in Cob and Tib, provides for Thorello's limited recognition of his folly. Yet, *commedia dell'arte* scenarios shape the action of the play; and this shaping was probably more evident to original audiences, since Will Kemp and other members of the cast knew well this Italian art form and easily could have integrated its distinctive style and improvisatory mannerisms into performances.[16]

The Italian lyric tradition, very widely imitated in England, also constructs the play and contributes to its harmonies. Petrarch's descendants, the sonneteers, flourished in the Elizabethan era, their most intense period of activity being the late 1590s. Eight sonnet sequences appeared between 1582 and 1593; eleven, between 1594 and 1599; only five thereafter till 1619.[17] An Italianate Englishman, Samuel Daniel, who imitated Petrarch loosely in *Delia,* is an extremely appropriate and well-chosen figure of fun in *EMI.* His sonnet sequence appeared in the 1590s more frequently than any other and he first combined his sequence with a narrative poem, thus beginning a popular trend. Judging from the number of editions and references to him by contemporaries, Daniel was the hottest sonneteer of the late 1590s.[18] Moreover, he clearly considered himself as practicing an Italian art. The editions of *Delia* from 1594 on contain a sonnet, "At the Authors going into Italie"; and in all editions the poet explicitly compares his love to Laura and himself to Petrarch, "I loue as well, though he could better shew it" (Sonnet 35, line 8). Depicting Matheo as plagiarizing the first sonnet of Daniel's sequence, Jonson pokes fun at witless copycat poetasters who follow fashion and also at the entire amatory tradition, with its plaintive register, abject pose, and Italian origins. Jonson wrote only five sonnets himself ("quite undistinguished," HS 1: 155), "cursed Petrarch for redacting Verses to Sonnets" (HS 1: 133), excused himself from the current amatory fashions ("Why I write not of love," HS 8: 93), and composed "A Celebration of Charis," which ends in a frank expression of female desire, and which, according to Roche, kills off "the sonnet sequence by bringing in a voice and the light of common day."[19] By the time of the Folio the vogue had passed and so had the fine edge of Jonson's satire: there Jonson drops the explicit reference to Daniel, truncates the quotation while presenting it as Matheo's own, and explains the joke with the exclamation: "A parody! A parody! With a kind of miraculous gift to make it absurder than it was" (5.1.221–22).

Italian dramatic and poetic theory also informs the play, both its deep structure and its debate on the art of poetry. Jonson's original version of *EMI* contributes to the ongoing and animated Elizabethan conversation about the nature and purpose of poetry; it is specifically contemporary with the 1598 prefaces to Chapman's *Seaven Bookes of the Iliades* and *Achilles Shield,* both of which Jonson owned, and with Francis Meres's *Palladis Tamia* (1598), which featured comparison of English, Greek,

Latin, and Italian poets. Jonson's Italian setting gains point and power from the historical fact that Italians originated the discussion and established for the Elizabethans its central issues and key terms. Spingarn observed long ago that the entire theory of comedy in the Elizabethan era derived from "the body of rules and observations which the Italians, aided by a few hints from Aristotle, had deduced from the practice of Plautus and Terence." Herrick agreed, specifically linking Jonson's views on comedy as corrective and cathartic with Italian scholars like Castelvetro and Trissino.[20] In an extremely influential treatise, *De Poeta,* important to Puttenham and Sidney, Minturno observed the corrective agencies of Old Comedy and New, particularly the censuring of specific vices and the exhortation to specific virtues.[21] This conception of comedy implied a specific theory of characterization, one that urged the presentation of recognizable types with propriety and consistency. Jonson's practice of humors characterization (outlined clearly in *EMO,* Induction, 88–114) derives quite naturally from such doctrines. Moreover, Italian theorists established quite detailed guidelines for comedic characterization, according to categories such as gender, age, profession, and disposition. Spingarn, in fact, located a specific antecedent of Jonson's humors in Salviati's *Del Trattato della Poetica,* which defines a humor as "a peculiar quality of nature according to which every one is inclined to some special thing more than to any other."

Influential Italian theories of comedy and characterization, then, find entirely appropriate local habitation and names in Jonson's Italy. Moreover, the Italian discourse on poetics directly or indirectly underlies the play's overt concern with the proper imitation of models and the notion of "invention." In lines deleted from the Folio, Prospero urges Lorenzo Jr. to "invent some famous memorable lie" for his father; "thou hast been father of a thousand in thy days, thou couldst be no poet else" (1.1.151–53). In the climactic scene of the play, Clement asks if some recited verses are Matheo's "own invention"; Matheo replies that they are not, that he "translated" them from *Delia.* In response to the repeated request for "your own," Matheo hands him the "beginning of a sonnet I made to my mistress." Clement reads the first line and then asks sarcastically if he "translated" this too. Prospero says, "No, this is invention; he found it in a ballad" (5.3.272ff.). Here Matheo summarily reduces to mere parroting the complicated Renaissance notions of *imitatio, translatio,* and *inventio,* subjects of serious and sustained discussion throughout the cinquecento, particularly in the voluminous commentaries on Aristotle and Horace. The Folio version cuts the quoted line, drastically reduces the exchange, and deletes reference to translation and invention.

Moreover, Italian discourse, particularly the defense of poesy against the perceived attacks of Plato, informs the debate on the value of poetry that frames *EMI* Q. Weinberg well analyzes this controversy in Italy, noting the charges against poetry as vain and immoral by polemicists like Grasso, Gambara, Panicarola, and Possevino.[22] Gambara, for example, representing a particularly vehement, Christianizing strain, argues that the lying fables of poetry make men "revolt against reason and develop the habit of sin" (Weinberg, *History,* 1: 306). The Puritans in England continued the attack with renewed vigor, leading it in two new directions, according to Smith: "against the playhouse and its associations, and against the foreign, especially the Italian, influences in society."[23] In these contexts, Lorenzo Sr.'s concerns about his son's attachment to poetry, often a source of critical puzzlement, become intelligible and significant. Lorenzo Sr. objects to the "vain course of study" his son affects, "idle poetry" (1.1.9 and 18). To this folly he opposes his own experience, wherein "reason" taught him "to comprehend / The sovereign use of study" (20–1), that is, the pursuit of the good, we presume, through philosophy or theology. Lorenzo repeats his objection later, when he plans to "reduce" his son from "affected will / To reason's manage" and expatiates on reason's sovereignty (2.2.4ff.; the key terms are dropped in F). To Lorenzo Sr., as to generations of continental and English theorists, the study of poesy offered vain pleasures, seduced the soul from rational activity, and instigated moral turpitude.

Lorenzo Jr.'s defense of poetry, correspondingly, follows the conventional lines established in the cinquecento and developed by English apologists like Puttenham and Sidney. A cardinal precept of the Italian defense was the assertion that poetry was itself the first philosophy, historically and educationally, first in the development of humanity and first in the development of children; early on, Mancinelli (*De poetica virtute,* c. 1490) made the point that would recur innumerable times in the following century:

Antiqui vero poeticam primam philosophiam quandam esse perhibent: quae ab ineunte nos aetate ad uiuendi rationes adducit: que mores: que affectiones edoceat: quae res gerendas cum iucunditate precipiat.

[The ancients, in fact, say that poetry is a kind of first philosophy, which brings us from youth to the art of living, which teaches the mores and the passions, which in a pleasant way teaches us our duty.] (Weinberg, *History,* 1: 254–55)

The linking of poetry and philosophy became in English hands a standard weapon of defense against Puritan attacks, as maintained by Puttenham (*Of Poets and Poesy,* Ch. 4) and Sidney *(Apology).*[24] In keeping with these traditions, Lorenzo Jr. extols poetry, "Attired in the majesty of art, / Set high in spirit with the precious taste / Of sweet philosophy" (5.3.307–9). Some Italians also asserted that poetry was divine, a notion deriving from the divine furor of Plato's *Phaedrus* and *Ion.* The idea became a commonplace in English defenses, echoed by Lodge (1579), Webbe (1586), Puttenham (1589), Sidney (1595), and Chapman (1598). Prospero evokes the doctrine and the debate when ridiculing the "tame poetical fury" (3.4.111) of Matheo. More respectfully, Menechini apostrophized divine poetry:

Ò santa Poesia, ò ben somma inspiration diuina; poiche purgandoci da ogni macchia, rendendone casti, & semplici, rilucer fai l'anima col proprio splendore.

[Oh holy Poetry! oh highest of divine inspirations! for by purging us of every stain, making us pure and simple, you make our soul shine with its own splendor.] (Weinberg, *History,* 1: 299)

So Lorenzo Jr. in a similarly rhapsodic vein, praises "The state of poesy, such as it is, / Blessed, eternal, and most true divine"; and so he admires her "soul / That hates to have her dignity profan'd / With any relish of an earthly thought" (5.3.298–99, 310–12).

In this emphasis on poetics and on the value of poetry the Quarto is entirely distinct from the Folio. For Lorenzo Jr.'s defense of poesy, often considered an irrelevant set piece, the Folio substitutes Clement's comparatively lame comment: "There goes more to the making of a good poet than a sheriff, Master Kitely" (5.2.33–4). Throughout, however, the Italian version of the play more emphasizes the debate on poetry. The rankling letter from Prospero teases Lorenzo Jr. several times about being a poet, one of Apollo's own (1.1.139 and 163ff.). The culminating scene of Matheo's exposure (5.3) features more of Clement's parodic verses (258–60), longer plagiarism from *Delia,* the beginning of a sonnet made to Matheo's mistress, in turn exposed as a line stolen from a ballad (279–81). Lorenzo Jr.'s defense answers Lorenzo Sr.'s original objections and culminates the running satire on false poets and poetry.

Moreover, this defense evokes Clement's response, largely unnoticed but centrally important to the play:

> Ay, Lorenzo; but election is now govern'd altogether by the influence of humour; which, instead of those holy flames that should direct and light the soul to eternity, hurls forth nothing but smoke and congested vapours, that stifle her up and bereave of all sight and motion. But she must have a store of hellebore given her to purge these gross obstructions. (326–31)

Here the *gonfaloniere* contrasts "election" (in the sense of discriminating literary judgment) and misperception, those lapses in judgment caused by the noxious influence of humors (cf. 1.4.36; 2.2.68). But "election" also has theological resonance, signifying admittance into the elect, the saved; this meaning, combined with the image of holy flames that should light the soul to eternity, suggests the contrast between the moral agency and redemptive power of true poesy and the stifling smoke and vapor of humors. Thus, Clement draws into coherent relation the two principal concerns of the play, poesy and humors, while asserting that the purging of humors restores moral vision and frees the soul for progress to heaven. The Folio omits this passage entirely and moves to the punishments—the skipping of supper and fasting in the courtyard without Clement's door. Insisting more on the moral dimensions of humorous behavior, the Quarto assigns stricter penalties—Matheo and Bobadilla will be bound, costumed, carried to market cross where they will mourn all day and sing a ballad of repentence "very piteously" (5.3.346).

The point here is simply that the Italian setting was entirely appropriate and richly resonant for turn-of-the-century audiences. And moreover, that the play, as originally written and performed, is a successful artistic whole in its own right, not merely a first draft or a preliminary sketch for the comical satire or London city comedy that it became in its next life.

Notes

1. For references to the Quarto and Folio versions, I have used J. W. Lever's parallel-text edition, *Every Man in His Humour* (Lincoln: University of Ne-

braska Press, 1971). Other citations from Jonson are to *Ben Jonson,* ed. C. H. Herford, Percy and Evelyn M. Simpson, 11 vols. (Oxford: Clarendon, 1925–52; hereafter HS). The date of revision is uncertain with scholars favoring 1604–5, 1607–8, and 1612–13. *See* HS 1: 332–5; 9: 334–6; Gabriele Bernhard Jackson's detailed analysis in her edition of the play (New Haven: Yale University Press, 1969), 221–39; Lever, *Every Man In His Humour,* xi–xii.

2. *Works,* ed. Peter Whalley, 7 vols. (London, 1756), 1: ix–x; F. Cunningham, ed., *Works,* 9 vols. (London: Bickers and Son, 1875) 1: 177; Henry Holland Carter, ed., *Every Man in His Humour* (New Haven: Yale University Press, 1921), xxxiiiff.; HS 1: 358–70, 331, 359; Simon Trussler, *Every Man In His Humour* (London: Methuen, 1986), 6.

3. *See* Lewis Einstein, *The Italian Renaissance in England* (New York: Macmillan, 1902); Mary Augusta Scott, *Elizabethan Translations from the Italian* (Boston: Houghton Mifflin, 1916), who provides a useful chronological index of translations in a variety of genres; Mario Praz, *The Flaming Heart* (Garden City, N.Y.: Doubleday, 1958); John L. Lievsay, *The Elizabethan Image of Italy* (Ithaca: Cornell University Press, 1964); Miranda Johnson-Haddad, *The Elizabethan View of Italy* (Folger Shakespeare Library, 1993) [exhibition booklet]. Queen Elizabeth's skill in dancing earned her the nickname "the Florentine" (*see De Maisse: A Journal,* ed. G. B. Harrison and R. A. Jones [London: Nonesuch, 1931], 95). There was a congregation of Italian Protestants in London who attended services in Italian (Einstein, *The Italian Renaissance,* 212–14).

4. Praz, for example, found Jonson's Italy insignificant before *Volpone,* and the images in that play derived largely from Florio (*The Flaming Heart,* 168–85). Providing a substantive and detailed review of the question is Brian Parker, "Jonson's Venice," in *Theatre of the English and Italian Renaissance,* eds. J. R. Mulryne and M. Shewring (Houndmills, Basingstoke: Macmillan, 1991), 95–112. For additional information, *see* the individual entries under Italian names in D. Heyward Brock's, *A Ben Jonson Companion* (Bloomington: Indiana University Press, 1983). On masques, *see* also John Peacock, "Ben Jonson's Masques and Italian Culture," in *Theatre of the English and Italian Renaissance,* 73–94.

5. *See* David McPherson, "Ben Jonson's Library and Marginalia: An Annotated Catalogue," *Studies in Philology* 71 (1974); Parker, "Jonson's Venice," 95, 111 n.2; Christopher Martin, "Retrieving Jonson's Petrarch," *Shakespeare Quarterly* 45 (1994): 89–92.

6. Below I refer to *The Poems of John Marston,* ed. Arnold Davenport (Liverpool: Liverpool University Press, 1961); Everard Guilpin, *Skialethia,* ed. D. Allen Carroll (Chapel Hill: University of North Carolina Press, 1974); *The Poems of Joseph Hall,* ed. Arnold Davenport (1949; Liverpool: Liverpool University Press, 1969).

7. Lievsay, *The Elizabethan Image of Italy,* 9; on Wolfe *see* Harry Sellers, "Italian Books Printed in England before 1640," *The Library,* 4th ser., 5 (1925), 105–28.

8. Florence, Ortelius says, "quae flos videatur Italiae," (*Epitome Theatri Orteliani,* Antwerp, 1595, 77ᵛ). Edward H. Sugden observes its reputation for the courtesy and manners of its citizens, for its pure and expressive Italian, for being the birthplace of Dante and Machiavelli, in *A Topographical Dictionary to the Works of Shakespeare and his Fellow Dramatists* (Manchester: Manchester University Press, 1925), 196–98. Also associated with the city were its stormy political past, artistic achievements, and expertise in trading and bank-

ing. *See* John W. Drapér, "Shakespeare and Florence and the Florentines," *Italica* 23 (1946): 287–93; Murray J. Levith, *Shakespeare's Italian Settings and Plays* (New York: St. Martin's, 1989), 34–5, 71 and 77. Beyond minor details and general correspondences—Lorenzo Jr. and Prospero are well-mannered Florentine youths (cf. Shakespeare's Claudio and Cassio), and Thorello, a merchant (cf. Fryskiball in *Thomas Lord Cromwell*), the city of Florence has no particular cachet here.

9. *Cynthia's Revels* (1600) has swatches of Italian and French, *The Merry Wives of Windsor* (1597–98) has the Latin lesson, *Henry V* (1599), the French lesson. There is Dutch in *The Shoemaker's Holiday* (1599), French in *Jack Drum's Entertainment* (1600) and *Sir Giles Goosecap* (c. 1602); a mixture of French, Dutch, and English in *Englishmen for my Money* (1598); *see* A. J. Hoenselaars, *Images of Englishmen and Foreigners in the Drama of Shakespeare and His Contemporaries* (London: Associated University Presses, 1992), index, *s.vv.* "Language"; *see also* his "'Under the dent of the English pen": The language of Italy in Renaissance Drama," in *Shakespeare's Italy,* eds. Michele Marrapodi, et al., (Manchester: Manchester University Press, 1993), 272–91.

10. Anne Barton, *The Names of Comedy* (Toronto: University of Toronto Press, 1990), 70–85. Alan C. Dessen observes that locale is often marked by people whose costumes or accessories establish place; "The logic of 'place' and locale," in *Elizabethan Stage Conventions and Modern Interpreters* (Cambridge: Cambridge University Press, 1984), 84–104. Italy then is the place where Italians like the Pazzi or Strozzi live.

11. Jonson could have heard of them in Machiavelli, *The Florentine Historie* (London, 1595), passim, especially chapters 2, 3, 8; or in Thomas *The Historie of Italie,* 138r, 154v. Castiglione mentions the Strozzi in *The Courtier* (1561; reprint, London: D. Nutt, 1900), 175, which Jonson used for his next play, *EMO. See also* Sir Robert Dallington, *A Survey of the Great Dvkes State of Tuscany in the Yeare of our Lord 1596* (London, 1605), 9; Fynes Moryson, *An Itinerary* (London, 1617), 150. Abbreviations for Florio's works are W for *A Worlde of Wordes* (London, 1598), Q for *Queen Anna's New World of Words* (London, 1611), and V for *Vocabolario Italiano & Inglese: A Dictionary* (London, 1659).

12. *Stoccado,* 1.3.177 and 210; *passado,* 202; *hay,* 4.2.11; *punto, reverso, stoccato, imbroccato, passado, montanto,* 4.2.64ff.; *passados, montantos,* 4.2.119; *retricato, assalto,* 4.4.11–12. (The last two are not technically fencing terms but part of the general play with the language.) The inconsistent forms could be merely errors or Jonson's deliberate attempt to show Bobadilla's incompetence. Below I draw on Robert E. Morsberger, *Swordplay and the Elizabethan and Jacobean Stage* (Salzburg: Institut für Englische Sprache und Literatur, 1974). Joan Ozark Holmer, "'Draw, if you be men': Saviolo's Significance for *Romeo and Juliet*," *Shakespeare Quarterly* 45 (1994): 163–89. Cf. Marston's exactly contemporary portrait of Martius, replete with Italian fencing terms, and references to "*Vincentio,* and the *Burgonians* ward," *The Scourge of Villainie,* 168–69.

13. Stephen Gosson, *Playes Confuted in Five Actions* (1582), ed. Arthur Freeman (New York, 1972), sig. D5ᵛ.

14. On Italianate soldiers, *see* Daniel C. Boughner, *The Braggart in Renaissance Comedy* (Minneapolis: University of Minnesota Press, 1954), 70–99; on the *commedia erudita, see* Louise George Clubb, *Italian Drama in Shake-*

speare's Time (New Haven: Yale University Press, 1989), 52–53. Marvin T. Herrick, *Italian Comedy in the Renaissance* (Urbana: University of Illinois Press, 1960), 116–20; Christopher Cairns, "Aretino's Comedies and the Italian 'Erasmian' Connection in Shakespeare and Jonson," in *Theatre of the English and Italian Renaissance,* eds. Mulryne and Shewring, 113–37; on the presentation of Italian heroines, *see* Robert C. Melzi, "From Lelia to Viola," *Renaissance Drama* 9 (1966), 67–81; and Clubb, *Italian Drama,* 65–89.

15. *See* K. M. Lea, *Italian Popular Comedy,* 2 vols. (1934; reprint, New York: Russell and Russell, 1962); Allardyce Nicoll, *The World of Harlequin: A Critical Study of the Commedia dell'Arte* (Cambridge: Cambridge University Press, 1963); Domenico Pietropaolo, *The Science of Buffoonery: Theory and History of the Commedia dell'Arte* (Ottawa: Dovehouse Editions, 1989); Thomas Heck, *Commedia dell'Arte: A Guide to the Primary and Secondary Literature* (New York: Garland, 1988); for Scala below, *see* Flaminio Scala, *Scenarios of the Commedia dell'Arte,* trans. Henry F. Salerno (New York: New York University Press, 1967), 184–92, and 47–54.

16. *See* Andrew Grewar, "Shakespeare and the actors of the *commedia dell'arte,*" *Studies in the Commedia dell'Arte,* ed. David J. George and Christopher J. Gossip (Cardiff: University of Wales Press, 1993), 13–47. According to Grewar, the other members of the cast with this experience included Richard Burbage, Thomas Pope, John Duke, Augustine Phillips, William Slye, and perhaps, William Shakespeare.

17. The figures, slightly adjusted, come from J. William Hebel, et al., eds., *The Works of Michael Drayton,* 5 vols. (Oxford: Basil Blackwell, 1961), vol. 5, 13, 137. In 1594–99 are Drayton's *Idea's Mirrour* (1594; with nineteen sonnets added in 1599); Percy's *Coelia* (1594); *Zepheria* (1594), framed by Italian tags and nominating each poem *canzon;* Spenser's *Amoretti* (1595), whose title proclaims the Italian origins, evident in sources, themes, imagery, and form; Barnfield's *Cynthia* (1595); E. C.'s *Emaricdulfe* (1595); Griffin's *Fidessa* (1596); Smith's *Chloris* (1596); Lynche's *Diella* (1596); Tofte's *Laura* (1597), which evokes Petrarch's lady in the title and names the Italian cities where individual sonnets were composed; and *The Passionate Pilgrim* (1599), Jaggard's collection. Meres's 1598 reference to Shakespeare's sugared sonnets circulating privately among friends is well known (*Palladis Tamia,* 1598, sigs. Oo^v-Oo2).

18. Some of his sonnets appeared in Newman's pirated edition (1591), and then as *Delia,* 1592 (two editions), 1594, 1595, 1598, 1601, and 1602. *See Poems and A Defence of Ryme,* ed. Arthur Colby Sprague (1930; reprint, Chicago: University of Chicago Press, 1965), 170. Samuel A. Tannenbaum lists contemporary allusions to Daniel, a large number of which cluster around the turn of the century, including references by Barnfield, Sir J. Davies, Drayton, Guilpin, Marston, Meres, the authors of *The Return from Parnassus,* Vaughn, and Weever, *Samuel Daniel: A Concise Bibliography* (New York: George Banta, 1942), 17–18. References to *Delia* below are on 187–88, and 28.

19. Thomas P. Roche, *Petrarch and the English Sonnet Sequences* (New York: AMS, 1989), 477.

20. J. E. Spingarn, *A History of Literary Criticism in the Renaissance,* 2nd ed., (1908; reprint Westport, Conn.: Greenwood Press, 1976), 287; Marvin T. Herrick, *Comic Theory in the Sixteenth Century* (Urbana: University of Illinois Press, 1950), 53–56.

21. Antonio Sebastiano Minturno, *De Poeta (1559)* (Munich: Wilhelm Fink Verlag, 1970), 277–78.

22. Bernard Weinberg, *A History of Literary Criticism in the Italian Renaissance,* 2 vols. (Chicago: University of Chicago Press, 1961), 1: 250–348.

23. G. Gregory Smith, ed. *Elizabethan Critical Essays,* 2 vols. (1904; reprint Oxford: Clarendon, 1971) 1: xvi.

24. *See* also Sidney's discussion of the poet as "right Popular Philosopher," in G. Gregory Smith, 1: 150–52, and 167.

Borachio's Indiscretion: Some Noting about *Much Ado*

Leo Salingar

In the sixteenth-century stories preceding that of Claudio and Hero in *Much Ado about Nothing* the crucial episode of the deception practiced on the lover is presented directly and forcibly. In Ariosto's tale of Ariodante and Genevra the handmaid Dalinda, who corresponds by role to Shakespeare's Margaret, relates in anguish how she had been manipulated by Ariodante's rival, the "false Duke," into acting unawares as a decoy, how she had shown herself at a window wearing the princess's hair net of "beaten gold" and her white gown "richly set / With aglets, pearle, and lace of golde wel garnished," how she embraced her treacherous wooer when he climbed a ladder to the window, and how Ariodante, planted to watch this charade from a distance, "straight resolves to die" at the sight and is only with difficulty restrained by his brother.[1] In *The Faerie Queene* (2.4) Phedon tells of his own similarly engineered despair. And in Bandello's *novella* about Timbreo and Fenicia, which was Shakespeare's principal narrative source (with some variations from Ariosto), the nocturnal deception of Sir Timbreo outside a window in Fenicia's house is recounted in circumstantial detail. The reader of these stories sees the outward event with the same eyes, if not the same duped understanding, as the lover and can identify with his pain. Similarly, in Giambattista Della Porta's play, *Gli duoi fratelli rivali,* also founded on Bandello, the spectator witnesses Don Ignazio's agonized deception directly.

Shakespeare was to bring a partly comparable scene into *Troilus and Cressida* (5.2), where Troilus spies on Cressida flirting with Diomedes, all three overseen by both Ulysses and Thersites. But *Much Ado* avoids such a direct presentation. We do not see Claudio watching Borachio's faked wooing at Hero's window (nor do we ever learn what Margaret thinks about her share in the business). Instead, after having shown the preparation of the

225

fraud, Shakespeare relegates the execution of it to a secondary plane, in Borachio's tipsy boasting confided to his friend Conrade, in nineteen lines of hasty, disorganized, and colorless prose (3.3.139–58).[2] "I will, like a true drunkard utter all to thee," the conspirator declares; but "I tell this tale vilely," he admits when he comes to the point; and meanwhile he has spent more time on a rambling, obscure digression about "fashion," which he calls a "deformed thief," than he devotes to the tale itself. Although the Watch overhear and arrest him, they have not really known what he is talking about.

In the logic of the stories Shakespeare is rehandling there has been no need for a tool-villain to give the game away like this, still less for him to tell his tale so clumsily. And Borachio has appeared quite sober before this, the fourth of his six scenes in the play. However, Shakespeare has taken care to state his name (from the Spanish *borracho,* drunkard) as soon as he comes on stage in act 1, thus preparing for his unregulated volubility here. Moreover, the dramatist muffles the pathetic impact of the main event still further by sandwiching the drunkard's boastful indiscretion between two passages given over to the comic nonsense of the Watch, the first of them being longer than Borachio's whole dialogue with Conrade, and embroidered with topical jesting. (Dogberry's preliminary instructions to his constables and the recital of likely nocturnal misdemeanors (3.3.1–93) form a parody, but not an utter travesty, of the real thing: for instance, the Mayor of Chester's address to his Watch for Christmas 1584 consisted of similar injunctions to look out for "any lewd Roges or vacabonds or other disordred persons in robbinge of shopps" or the like, for any drunken or disorderly behavior, and especially for "any mans children or servants" who "use themselves wantonly or otherways not as they ought"; for a sidelight on the "desartless" talent of Dogberry's men, Oatcake and Seacoal, it is recorded that that Mayor of Chester "could nether write nor read".)[3] With the extraneous additions provided by the Watch, the crucial episode in the love story is thus enveloped in several layers of mostly comic distortion. The person most affected by the masquerade had been Hero—who had been absent and unaware. The central figure had been Margaret, wrongly identified by Claudio and Don Pedro and unconscious of her actual role. Borachio's report to Conrade is not a transparent record of the event but a fuddled divagation. The watchmen presume that the word "deformed," which they overhear, must be the name of a confidence trickster; while Borachio and Conrade imagine that the watchmen's voices are nothing more than the sound of the wind; and the Watch arrest the two secret-sharers for the wrong reasons, charging them among other things with collusion with "one Deformed"—whom one of them now professes to know, adducing that "a wears a lock" (3.3.163). This blunder, which Dogberry solemnly repeats later on (5.1.301–7), very likely enfolds another topical joke; (in May 1600 the Cambridge University authorities punished a graduate named Pepper for having taken part in a "disordered meeting beholdinge certayne playes" at the Bear Inn, "without the habite of his degree and havinge *deformed longe lockes of hayre* and unsemely syde and great breaches undecent for a graduate or scholler of orderly carriage" [emphasis added]).[4] However this may be, Shakespeare has set up a whole spiral of falsifications, from the imposition of a lie upon Hero to the invention of an imaginary malefactor by the Watch. Why, one may ask, has he treated the crucial episode in this way?

Some theatrical reasons suggest themselves, such as the production of variations of tone and the management of suspense. Dogberry and the Watch, a fresh, unanticipated, and incongruous group of actors, have been brought on stage immediately after Don John's treacherous disclosure about Hero to Claudio and Don Pedro, so that Don John's exultant closing exclamation, "O plague right well prevented! So will you say when you have seen the sequel," is followed at once, with unconscious irony, by Dogberry's first words, "Are you good men and true?" Then the arrest of Borachio and Conrade seems to promise a happy ending, only for Dogberry's farcical bumbling to reintroduce suspense just before the church scene. On the other hand the impact of the betrayal itself has been reduced because of the way we hear of it through Borachio, so that when we come to the tragicomic climax in the church we can observe Claudio's vehement indignation with some detachment and can thus enter more fully into the reactions of the new stage witnesses of the crisis, first the Friar and then Beatrice and Benedick. This also gives dramatic space to the "merry war" between these two lovers, which is, of course, Shakespeare's invented counterpart to his borrowed plot concerning Claudio and Hero. And this enlargement of the focus of the action has been part of Shakespeare's scheme from the beginning.[5]

Every version of his borrowed story turns upon slander and masquerade: false appearances, false communications. Shakespeare seizes the theme of communications within society from the outset: in the first line of the play Leonato is speaking to a messenger and has just been reading a letter. Incidents of news, gossip, reporting follow thick and fast, including incidents of eavesdropping accompanied with misinterpretation. Social transmission becomes a medium of distortion. Shakespeare probably took hints from the Renaissance schoolmasters' favorite comedy, Terence's *Andria,* but he carries the process of planted observation and misleading inference further. There are the variant reports from Antonio's servant (1.2) and from Borachio (1.3) about Don Pedro's intentions toward Hero. And in the scene (2.1) of the masked dance—a visual emblem of sociability coinciding with disguise—come successive moments of falsification or attempted falsification of identity: Antonio pretending to his partner, ineffectively, to "counterfeit" himself (2.1.106); Benedick pretending to Beatrice that he does not know who Benedick is (115–24); Don John pretending to mistake Claudio for Benedick, and Claudio accepting the misidentification (148–50); and not only Don John (145–46) but Benedick also (175–9) misreading Don Pedro's attentions to Hero in the dance. None of these early mistakes or misattributions produces a lasting result; they are much ado about nothing. But they form a prelude and a social setting for the main intrigues that are to follow, based upon planted eavesdropping and provoked misconception: much ado about *noting.* The scene of Borachio's indiscretion is both a turning point and a climactic instance in this process of socialized distortion; a would-be confidence conveyed in the garbled words of a drunkard is made public through the blunder of eavesdroppers who, as Dogberry says, are appointed "to present the Prince's own person." The constables, after all, are specifically observers, whose particular office it is to watch.

Along one main line, the exploitation of "wit," *Much Ado* follows on from *Love's Labour's Lost.* And many details recall *Romeo and Juliet:* the placing of a crucial episode at the heroine's window, for example; the scene of masked dancing; the arranged marriage and the role of an angry father; the false reports, which recall the miscarried messages in *Romeo;* the talk of dueling, with sarcasm at the expense of the duelists' bravado; the character of Benedick, who resembles Mercutio—as well as Berowne in *Love's Labour's Lost;* and notably the role of the Friar, together with the heroine's supposed death. But behind *Romeo* lay the influence of Bandello, as Shakespeare must have been aware, since his direct source there, Arthur Brooke's poem, had been advertised as "written first in Italian by Bandell." And Bandello's story of Timbreo and Fenicia was important for *Much Ado,* not only by providing material details, such as the setting in Messina, the names of Pedro and Leonato, and the broad outlines of the Claudio-Hero plot, but also by providing suggestions for the comparatively realistic urban atmosphere that pervades Shakespeare's comedy. However, Shakespeare's treatment could be said to controvert rather than follow his original, and in this respect it is exceptional. In the main, Elizabethan derivations from Italian literature tended toward idealization, whether copying Petrarch or Tasso or Guarini, or (admittedly, a more debatable case) utilizing caricatures of Machiavelli's doctrines in order to condemn him. But Shakespeare's treatment of Bandello's material, far from idealizing, is critical and skeptical.

Bandello's *novella* is a blend of cool realism with a chivalric high-mindedness which the dramatist pointedly deflates. The Italian story begins with a historical reference to the notorious Sicilian Vespers of 1285 and the subsequent Aragonese conquest of the island following a great naval battle "with cruel slaughter of many men" ("con uccisione di molti crudele").[6] Sir Timbreo has distinguished himself in the war. Shakespeare makes Claudio distinguish himself likewise, and he does not forget this military background, but he omits the history and diminishes the battle. After falling in love with Fenicia but failing to seduce her, Timbreo decides to seek her hand honorably in marriage, although he considers he will be lowering himself because her father, Lionato, though of ancient stock, is much poorer than he is—whereas Shakespeare makes Leonato the governor of the city and makes Claudio seek his daughter's hand with diffidence and with the help of a conventional go-between, though not without a thought about her possible inheritance (1.1.274–75). Once Timbreo has sent his matchmaker to Fenicia's family he behaves with consistent magnanimity. When he hears the slanderous message contrived by his covert rival, his friend Girondo, he checks himself "for a long time" before giving vent to what seems to him his "just anger" against Fenicia and agreeing to spy on her. When, as he thinks, he sees another man enter her room by night he contains the furious impulse to kill him, "remembering that he had given his word."[7] He sends a message of rejection to Fenicia's father with lofty diplomacy. But when he learns that Fenicia has (apparently) died of shame, he reviews his own judgment with stern self-criticism; and when Girondo, overcome by remorse, leads him to the chapel containing the tomb for Fenicia and confesses the truth, addressing him as

"Magnanimous and noble knight" ("Magnanimo e gentil cavaliero") and begging him to avenge himself like "the true and
loyal knight" he has "always been," Timbreo weeps bitterly but
replies in sorrow rather than anger. In a spirit that the hero of
The Two Gentlemen of Verona might have envied, he even tells
Girondo that he would have done better to reveal his own desire
for Fenicia at the start:

> For then I should have relinquished my amorous enterprise to you
> before asking her father for her hand, and, as magnanimous and
> generous spirits are accustomed to do [come sogliono fare i
> magnanimi e generosi spiriti], in overcoming myself I should have
> preferred our friendship to my desire; or maybe you, hearing my
> arguments, would have desisted from your enterprise, and the ca-
> lamity which has followed would not have occurred.[8]

In the same spirit he humbly begs pardon from Fenicia's parents
and places himself unconditionally at her father's command.

On his side, the father has stoutly refused to believe in Fenicia's promiscuity, calmly observing that "It is indeed true that
all things are possible, but I know how my daughter has been
reared and what her habits are" ("Gli è ben vero che ogni cosa
fattibile può essere, ma io so come mia figliuola è stata allevata
e quali sono i suoi costumi").[9] There is no Friar on hand in
Bandello's story, but the father himself thinks of the plan, after
she swoons, to make it believed that she has really died and
meanwhile to hide her away in his brother's villa. When Timbreo
and Girondo come together to beg his forgiveness, he responds
without rancor but with equal magnanimity.

The tone of high romance in Bandello's story is intensified by
swoonings and many outbursts of tears. Timbreo almost swoons
when he sees the villain at Fenicia's window, and Fenicia swoons
in earnest when she has been humiliatingly rejected.[10] The ladies of Messina weep at her bedside and the public weep at her
funeral; Girondo weeps when he confesses to Timbreo and Timbreo weeps when he has heard him; when the two knights beg
forgiveness from Lionato the old man embraces them, "weeping
with joy and tenderness" ("di tenerezza e di gioia piangendo");
there is general weeping in the reconciliation at the wedding;
and at the end, the queen weeps when she has been told the
lovers' story.[11] At the same time, the characters behave realisti-
cally and rationally, as for instance in Lionato's dismissal of the
charge against his daughter. This is particularly noticeable in
the passage after Fenicia's funeral, when public opinion is en-

tirely on her side and Timbreo begins "to feel great sorrow and heartstirring such as he would never have thought possible." He reconsiders his impressions on the fatal night, and—"reason lending him new vision" ("la ragione aprendoli occhi")—he begins to think he could have been wrong. The man he had seen (actually, one of Girondo's servants) might not have been entering the window for an assignation with Fenicia, and in any case, the room belonged to an unoccupied part of a large house, which Fenicia, who slept with her sisters, could not have reached without difficulty. Timbreo is restlessly blaming himself, even before Girondo brings his penitent confession.[12] Possibly this passage furnished the base for the confident expectation by Shakespeare's Friar that Hero would be "lamented, pitied, and excus'd / Of every hearer" upon the news of her supposed instant death in the church, while her accuser himself would be inwardly converted (4.1.210–33). But nothing quite like this happens to Claudio.

Public opinion gives a social context to Timbreo's thoughts in Bandello. There is general satisfaction when the news of his betrothal to Fenicia spreads through Messina, and when she has been rejected the rumor of her sickness brings "many gentle ladies, relatives and friends" to console and to weep for her; there is general mourning at her funeral, while "people spoke freely everywhere" about the cause of her supposed death, discussing it often and all maintaining her innocence. The desire to reaffirm her good name is uppermost in Timbreo's mind after his renewed change of heart; and the story ends in a lavish celebration by the king for the two married couples (Girondo having wedded Fenicia's sister), "with the singular approval of the Sicilians and of all who heard of it."[13] Shakespeare's Messina is not the same city. But the consciousness of social surroundings, social approval, and social pressure repeatedly affects his people.

The leading characters in Shakespeare's Messina are witty and sociable, but more complicated than Bandello's people, more apt to be touchy, aggressive, and self-centered. The "merry war" between Beatrice and Benedick is a social game, but an ambiguous game, charged with indefinite personal animus. In this society Benedick jumps to the mistaken inference that Don Pedro has abused his trust as a wooer on Claudio's behalf and cynically blames Claudio for naivety (2.1.198–215). Unlike the slanderers in Bandello and other previous versions of the story, Don John is motivated by malice, not jealousy. Claudio reacts to the slander much more readily and drastically than Timbreo; and in the church scene Leonato sides indignantly with Hero's accusers, while his immediate thought is for himself—"Hath no man's dagger here a point for me?" (4.1.109).

Shakespeare limits the potential pathos at the core of his borrowed story by stressing Claudio's anger rather than his anguish and by shifting attention, in the church scene, from Hero to her father and the other onlookers. And the pathos is offset by the prevailing surface tone of sociable gaiety. To be more precise, the theme of the mixed, paradoxical nature of feelings, of the unexpected relations between pathos and gaiety, and outward expression and inward emotion, runs through the whole play.[14] In his opening dialogue with the messenger, for instance, Leonato asserts that "there are no faces truer" than those "washed" by affectionate tears: "How much better is it to weep at joy than to joy at weeping!" (1.1.25–7). The remark seems dramatically gratuitous: it sounds like an echo from the father in Bandello, "weeping with joy and tenderness." But these sententious crossed antitheses foreshadow apparent contradictions in the emotions of the main characters and problems about sincerity. Don John, the self-declared "plain-dealing villain," is to set his plot in motion precisely in order to enjoy the unhappiness of others. But Leonato's paradox also touches on the "merry war" between Beatrice and Benedick.

Neither of this witty pair upholds a convincing, consistent surface during their early scenes. They both seem more mature than Claudio and Hero, but less secure in their status; and both use their barbed wit to affirm and defend their independence. Emotionally, that independence has been shaken in the past, however, as Beatrice hints in her riddling account to the prince of how "once before" Benedick had won her heart "with false dice" (2.1.261–64). While she proclaims her happy freedom from love in the present, she sighs, or pretends to sigh, when Hero is about to be married—"I may sit in a corner and cry 'Heigh-ho for a husband!'" (2.1.300). And clearly, she and Benedick are still actively interested in each other, keen to wound one another in words. Moreover, in their friends' view at least, this aggressiveness is rooted in their characters. After Benedick has complained to Don Pedro that Beatrice "speaks poniards, and every word stabs" (2.1.231), Leonato informs the prince that

> There's little of the melancholy element in her, my lord; she is never sad but when she sleeps, and not ever sad then; for I have heard my

daughter say she hath often dreamt of unhappiness and waked herself with laughing. (2.1.321)

Beatrice, then, is an unexpected example of those who can joy
at weeping. But this self-assurance is also her weakness, as is
shown in her eavesdropping scene (3.1), where Hero's charges
of "Disdain and scorn" and remorseless "wit," intended for Beatrice to overhear, break through her defenses and trick her
into love.

Benedick likewise, in his eavesdropping scene, has been
tricked into a change of heart by overhearing that if he were to
be told how Beatrice loved him he would simply "make but a
sport of it and torment the poor lady worse" (2.3.153). He has
been posing as the invulnerable bachelor who has "challenged
Cupid" (1.1.35); "it is certain," he informs Beatrice in their first
stage "skirmish of wit," "I am loved of all ladies, only you excepted"—but "truly I love none" (1.1.114). When in private talk
Claudio invites praise of Hero from him, Benedick replies,

> Do you question me as an honest man should do, for my simple
> true judgement, or would you have me speak after my custom, as
> being a professed tyrant to their sex? .... Come, in what key shall
> a man take you to go in the song? (1.1.154, and 172)

Claudio is soon to retort that his friend "never could maintain
his part, but in the force of his will" (1.1.219). But Benedick has
persuaded himself that his own attitude is typical. In the soliloquy before his eavesdropping scene he wonders how Claudio
can have

> become the argument of his own scorn by falling in love. ... He was
> wont to speak plain and to the purpose, like an honest man and a
> soldier, and now is he turned orthography—his words are a very
> fantastical banquet, just so many strange dishes. (2.3.10, and 18)

Love, especially the language of love, is a "shallow [folly]," an
affectation. This repeats the satire in *Love's Labour's Lost*. But
Benedick goes further. Plain speaking belongs to soldiers, and
in his present company "a simple true judgement" is hardly to
be expected. When at the end of the scene he resolves to marry,
after all, he takes it for granted that he will be made the target
of "quips and sentences and these paper bullets of the brain"
(2.3.231).

The song he is obliged to hear in the orchard (2.3.62ff.) implies a retort to Benedick for any former double dealing of his toward Beatrice: "*Sigh no more, ladies, sigh no more, / Men were deceivers ever.*" It also counsels women to suppress their sighs and be "*blithe*," not merely in spite of men's inconstancy but because of it—"*Converting all your sounds of woe / Into Hey nonny, nonny.*" This obliquely foreshadows the general movement of the action, giving another twist to Leonato's theme of "joy at weeping."

In this courtly Messina there is no thought of magnanimity; and sincerity, the "honest" straightforward expression of feeling, becomes complicated or obscured. Don Pedro will "fashion" a match between Benedick and Beatrice, as if he does not believe it can happen spontaneously. And Leonato—"no hypocrite," according to the prince (1.1.140)—becomes entangled himself in the paradox he had pronounced on at the beginning. When it is a matter of entrapping the listening Benedick he pretends to wonder at the contrast between Beatrice's secret feelings and her "outward behaviours;" conceding, however, with affected compassion, that "wisdom and blood combating in so tender a body, we have ten proofs to one that blood hath the victory" (2.3.96, and 160). And when Benedick complains of toothache (perhaps genuinely)[15] in order to explain his change of tone, Leonato joins Pedro and Claudio in mocking him for giving way to what is no more than "a humour or a worm" (prompting the sufferer to reply that "every one can master a grief but he that has it" [3.2.25]). But his failure to extract a warning from Dogberry's bumbling report before the church scene is partly due to his own "haste" (3.5.47). And when the crisis comes, he reacts at once in a passion of self-pity and wounded pride, without considering Hero or pausing to reflect (4.1). Even after he has submitted to the Friar's remedial plan Leonato's rage continues, though now it is directed away from his daughter and against Claudio and Don Pedro—as if, however, he has ignored or else forgotten Benedick's suggestion (4.1.186–9) that Don John was really the man to blame. When his brother tries to moderate his anger, he petulantly retorts, with a lofty self-contradiction,

> I pray thee peace, I will be flesh and blood;
> For there was never yet philosopher
> That could endure the toothache patiently,
> However they have writ the style of gods,
> And made a push at chance and sufferance.

(5.1.34)

And when it comes to challenging Claudio he forgets that he is only pretending that Hero is dead, and, in any case, that he himself had accepted the "slander" in the first place (5.1.62–71). This is passion all right, but not exactly sincerity. Leonato is sometimes considered a pathetic figure here, a character belonging to tragicomedy.[16] But he is working up a pretended grief because his pride, his social personality, has been injured. He is almost the polar opposite of the father in Bandello.

Leonato and his friends all have to contend with the factor of convention or pretense in social intercourse. The two intrigues in the play, malicious and benevolent, both turn on manipulating someone's reputation, their social persona; and only two significant characters—the exceptions that prove the rule—resist the pressure of adapting to social appearances. Don John implicitly challenges Leonato's maxim about the virtue of showing joy by weeping. "I cannot hide what I am," he says. "I must be sad when I have cause, and smile at no man's jests; . . . laugh when I am merry, and claw no man in his humour" (1.3.12–17); and he declares that he would rather "be disdained of all than . . . fashion a carriage to rob love of any" (26). "Disdain" and "fashion" are two key words in the play. The other egotist is Dogberry, who is as blind to the opinion of others as Don John is hostile. According to Coleridge, the creation of Dogberry and his comrades exemplifies Shakespeare's interest in character as distinct from plot, since for the purposes of the plot "any other less ingeniously absurd watchmen and night-constables would have answered."[17] It seems rather that the characters are shaped to fit each other in a complex pattern. Dogberry contributes to suspense in the plot by obfuscating his vital report to Leonato. But it is appropriate that Don John's antisocial intrigue should be foiled in the end by the incompetent Watch, under Dogberry's self-satisfied command.

Dogberry fits into the pattern of the comedy also through his strenuous misapplication of words. *Much Ado,* like *Love's Labour's Lost,* is largely a play about courtly wit. It could be taken to illustrate George Puttenham's contention, in *The Arte of English Poesie,* that figures of speech such as metaphor, irony, hyperbole, the indispensable ornaments of polished and courtly language, are unavoidably "trespasses in speach, because they passe the ordinary limits of common utterance, and be occupied of purpose to deceive the eare and also the minde, drawing it from plainnesse and simplicitie to a certaine doublenesse."[18] The sophisticated speakers in *Much Ado* are engaged with wit as a mark of *savoir vivre* and a social game, where the players repeatedly and competitively outgo plain statement. In the opening dialogue, for instance, the messenger cannot reach high enough for words to praise Claudio's feats in the war; while Hero needs to explain to the others whom Beatrice means by the name "Signior Mountanto." As soon as Benedick comes on he quibbles with Leonato but has to face a verbal assault from Beatrice wherein each derides the other's style of talk. And Claudio's confidence to him about Hero runs into the hazard of distinguishing seriousness from "sport." For his part, Claudio, when alone with the prince, broaches the theme of his love with such diffident formality, moving now from prose to verse, that the latter cuts him short with "What need the bridge much broader than the flood?" (1.1.296). The actors in this long opening scene prefer stylishness to plain statement.

The characters repeatedly scrutinize each other's speech. Beatrice holds that it would be "an excellent man" who came "midway" between Don John's taciturnity and Benedick's "tattling" (2.1.6–9); while Benedick "cannot endure my Lady Tongue" (2.1.257). But after the crisis, skirmishes of wit give place to challenges, and there is scorn for merely verbal display. When Benedick hesitates to undertake to "Kill Claudio!" Beatrice protests that "manhood is melted into curtsies, . . . and men are only turned into tongue, and trim ones too" (4.1.318); conversely, in the old men's challenge scene, Antonio sneers at "fashion-monging boys" who dare no more than "speak off half a dozen dang'rous words" (5.1.94–99). However, these militant outbursts would seem to cancel each other.

What speakers actually mean is frequently brought into question. "Counterfeit" is seconded by misunderstanding. Benedick, eavesdropping, helps to deceive himself ("I should think this a gull, but that the white-bearded fellow speaks it" (2.3.118)); and, once persuaded that Beatrice secretly loves him, he twists the sense of her scornful invitation to dinner: "Ha! 'Against my will I am sent to bid you come in to dinner'—there's a double meaning in that" (2.3.248). Wishful thinking joins the causes of misapprehension.

Dogberry, the unwitting agent of plot clarification, makes hay of semantics. During Borachio's tipsy revelation, Conrade is puzzled over his meaning, and the Watch downright mistaken. When Beatrice shows symptoms of having fallen in love, Margaret teases her with a wit-display of her own, pirouetting around the meaning of "meaning" (3.4.74–81). On another level, the truth of "exterior shows" becomes the crucial question about Hero; her silent blushes in the church are interpreted in opposing ways by Leonato and the Friar. And later, a gesture by Claudio is liable to misinterpretation: "In faith, my hand meant nothing to my sword" (5.1.57).

The denouement leads to a revaluation of wit as well as a resolution of the intrigue. Just after Claudio and Don Pedro have been priding themselves on retaining a cool "wit," unlike Benedick (5.1.196–99), and Claudio has congratulated the prince upon finding "one meaning well suited" to Dogberry's rigmarole about his prisoners (5.1.220), the two wits find themselves hearing Borachio tell them, in front of the Watch, that "what your wisdoms could not discover, these shallow fools have brought to light" (5.1.227). On the other side, Benedick gives yet another turn to Leonato's initial paradox about sincerity when he tells Beatrice, "Thou and I are too wise to woo peaceably" (5.2.67). But the quirks of uncertainty persist to the end. When Benedick asks formally for Beatrice's hand in marriage and hears Leonato hark back to the eavesdropping scene, he observes that his answer has been "enigmatical" (5.4.27). And even after the decisive revelation of "Another Hero!"—"Nothing certainer" (5.4.62), the gleeful production by the others of undelivered love letters penned by Benedick and Beatrice leads Benedick to admit that "Here's our own hands against our hearts" (5.4.91). He only reaffirms himself by declaring, still in defiance of consistency, that "man is a giddy thing, and this is my conclusion" (5.4.107).

Bandello's story had celebrated the triumph of magnanimity over falsehood. Shakespeare has changed it into a bittersweet comedy revolving around the ambiguities of social intercourse.

Notes

1. *See* Charles T. Prouty, *The Sources of "Much Ado about Nothing"* (New Haven: Yale University Press, 1950). Geoffrey Bullough, ed., *Narrative and Dramatic Sources of Shakespeare,* 8 vols. (London and New York: Routledge and Kegan Paul, 1957–75), 2: 61–134, gives the relevant sections from *Orlando Furioso* (trans. Harington, 1591) and *The Faerie Queene,* and translates Bandello, *Novelle* I, xxii [Lucca, 1554]. *See also* Giambattista Della Porta, *Gli duoi fratelli rivali* [Venice, 1601], ed. and trans. Louise George Clubb (Berkeley and Los Angeles: University of California Press, 1980).

2. *Much Ado about Nothing,* ed. A. R. Humphreys, New Arden Edition (London: Methuen, 1981).

3. *Records of Early English Drama: Chester,* ed. Lawrence M. Clopper (Manchester: Manchester University Press, 1979), 142–43.

4. Alan H. Nelson, *Early Cambridge Theatres* (Cambridge: Cambridge University Press, 1994), 97–98.

5. *See* Juliet Dusinberre's article in the present volume, which suggests the speculation that Sir John Harington may have been in some measure the original for Benedick and that the pairing of Benedick with Claudio may have been prompted by Harington's comments on Ariosto.

6. Bullough, *Narrative,* 112; cf. Gioachino Brognoligo, ed., *Matteo Bandello, Le Novelle,* 2 vols. (Bari: Laterza, 1910), 1: 284.

7. Bullough, *Narrative,* 115, 117; Brognoligo, *Matteo Bandello,* 288, 290.

8. Bullough, *Narrative,* 125; Brognoligo, *Matteo Bandello,* 300.

9. Bullough, *Narrative,* 118; Brognoligo, *Matteo Bandello,* 292.

10. Bullough, *Narrative,* 117, 119–120.

11. Bullough, *Narrative,* 119, 122, 123–24, 126 (cf. Brognoligo, *Matteo Bandello,* 301), 129, 132.

12. Bullough, *Narrative,* 122; Brognoligo, *Matteo Bandello,* 297.

13. Bullough, *Narrative,* 114, 119, 122, 125, 133.

14. *See* A. P. Rossiter on *Much Ado* in *"Angel with Horns" and Other Shakespeare Lectures,* ed. Graham Storey (London: Longmans, 1961); Graham Storey, "The Success of *Much Ado about Nothing,*" in *More Talking of Shakespeare,* ed. John Garrett (London: Longmans, 1959); and cf. E. A. J. Honigmann, "Shakespeare's Mingled Yarn and *Measure for Measure*" [1981] in *British Academy Shakespeare Lectures 1980–89,* ed. E. A. J. Honigmann (Oxford: Oxford University Press, 1993). I have discussed this aspect of the play in a paper on "*Much Ado about Nothing:* Shakespeare et la *commedia grave* italienne" for a conference in Paris organized by the C.N.R.S., May 1994.

15. *See* Barbara Everett, "*Much Ado about Nothing:* The Unsociable Comedy," in *English Comedy,* ed. Michael Cordner, Peter Holland, and John Kerrigan (Cambridge: Cambridge University Press, 1994), 83.

16. *See* Philip Edwards, "Shakespeare and the Healing Power of Deceit," *Shakespeare Survey* 31 (1978): 123–25.

17. *Coleridge, Shakespearean Criticism,* ed. Thomas Middleton Raysor, 2 vols., Everyman's Library (London: J. M. Dent & Sons, 1960), 1: 200.

18. George Puttenham, *The Arte of English Poesie* [1589], ed. Gladys Doidge Willcock and Alice Walker (Cambridge: Cambridge University Press, 1936), book 3, chapter 7, p. 154.

Much Ado about Lying: Shakespeare and Sir John Harington in Dialogue with *Orlando Furioso*

Juliet Dusinberre

In *Much Ado about Nothing* Benedick is both a writer and a reader. He is a writer of halting love poetry, which is produced against him when he claims reluctance even at the altar to marry Beatrice. He cries, "A miracle, here's our own hands against our hearts: come, I will have thee, but by this light I take thee for pity."[1] He is also a reader of his own heart as well as of other people's hands. When Claudio questions him about Hero's virtues, enquiring, "Is she not a modest young lady?," Benedick replies,

> Do you question me as an honest man should do, for my simple true judgement? Or would you have me speak after my custom, as being a professed tyrant to their sex? (1.1.121–24)[2]

Benedick reads the text of his own discourse: "professed tyrant" or "honest man." He might have learned this mode of reading from another writer. In the orchard he sends the boy to fetch his book. What is he reading? I suggest that he is reading Sir John Harington's translation of the fifth canto of Ariosto's *Orlando Furioso,* which tells the story of Genevra and Ariodante, used by Shakespeare for the Hero-and-Claudio plot of the play.

To consider the figure of Sir John Harington as reader, writer, courtier, playgoer, as part of the cultural hinterland from which *Much Ado about Nothing* emerges, is to highlight the play's involvement, both in politics and in its treatment of women, in the world in which it was first performed. Harington constantly staged his life through his writings. Benedick occupies a stage space in Shakespeare's play comparable to that occupied by Harington in Elizabeth's court. Beatrice has often been seen as a prototype for the queen herself in her wit, acerbity, and scorn

239

of the male world.[3] In the summer of 1599, when *Much Ado* was probably performed in imminent expectation of Essex's disgraced return from Ireland, the discourses of politics and gender were intricately interwoven.[4] The play takes some of its color from Essex's Irish enterprise in which Harington—the queen's godson—played a part more dangerous than that of unofficial court jester. Claudio and Benedick are back from the war in the company of a noble prince, Don Pedro—a name Harington used for one of his contemporaries in his epigrams, also written some time in the 1590s. Both in the timing of its appearance during the summer of 1599 and in its literary connections, *Much Ado about Nothing* is a drama whose disclaiming title acquires irony within the context of its own times.

Harington's translation of Ariosto's *Orlando Furioso*—one of the play's main sources—demonstrates a subtle textual interplay between the translator and his original. As he reads and translates the text of Ariosto's *Orlando Furioso,* Harington constructs his own personal dialogue with it, just as Benedick in Shakespeare's play comments on the play in which he is an actor. Benedick performs a dramatic function in *Much Ado* which corresponds structurally and formally to Harington's function as translator of the Ariosto poem. Like the Harington of the commentary, he always speaks prose. The play's texture depends on a movement from written story to acted drama, from a text read to a text enacted. Benedick connects these different forms, a man brought to the altar to marry because his hand is proved against his heart.

Benedick as commentator on the roles available to men and women in his own world purveys to the audience values at odds with the main Claudio-and-Hero plot of the play. This is equally true of Harington's role as translator of Ariosto's poem. Harington perceived a discrepancy between his way of life as a devoted family man in an age where that seems an unlikely role and as sophisticated and merry courtier. That discrepancy struck him as he translated Ariosto; his anxiety about the reaction of the woman reader ensconced in his Somerset home—his wife—was as acute as his apprehensions about that other woman reader, his royal godmother, Elizabeth I. He scandalized the queen by giving the offending canto 28 to her ladies, an act for which she dispatched him to the country (albeit with the ambivalent order to translate the rest of the poem).[5] It opens with an apology to women:

> Turne ou'r the leafe, and let this tale alone,
> If any thinke the sex by this disgraced.[6]

The protest is Ariosto's, but Harington was conscious that the Italian poet often required the hand of his Elizabethan translator to trace on the page the tyrannies of men toward women. Harington was determined, both through his modifications of the translation and through his prose annotations, to construct for readers—and primarily for women readers—the man he wanted to be thought to be. His reputation with the queen depended on his wit and on his poetry, but perhaps more than anything else it depended on her observation of his honesty in the private sphere of his marriage as well as in the public sphere of the court. If one is to trust his record of it.

It would be naive to set Harington's private papers—the eighteenth-century collection of letters and notes entitled the *Nugae Antiquae*—as the true record of the heart, even if one can pose such a formulation in the first place in this age of complex political pressures and censorship, both inner and outer.[7] Contradictions abound in everything Harington wrote: whether in his judgments of the Countess of Pembroke's translation of the Psalms, in his views on the marriage of priests, or in his ideas about folly and wisdom, jesting and seriousness. Harington appeared to realize, like Montaigne, that he was himself the site on which contradictory discourses play. He enjoyed playing with them, as much as he enjoyed being "an humble presenter and assistant" at the plays of Elizabeth's court.[8]

Harington had some sense of his own translating of Ariosto's romance as an act of the feminine gender. Florio in his dedication to Montaigne's essays describes translation as a female form. Prose as the medium of letters, diaries, prayers, and sermons is hospitable to women in this period. Harington thought of himself as a writer for women, aiming the *Orlando* at the queen's ladies to make them laugh and using the vernacular in order to widen his readership, as Ariosto also had done.[9] Harington's final note to the *Orlando* addresses itself explicitly to court ladies, on the subject of ambition in marriage: "Onely one note I may not omit, yea though I were sure to be chidden by some of you (faire Ladies) for my labor, namely, the strong ambition of your sex which we call weake" (*Orlando*, 556). He never believed in the weakness of women, being one of the few Elizabethan men who had the courage to recognize that the figure of Elizabeth said something about women and strength, as did also the characters of the other women in his life: his mother—whose memory he lauded in a note to canto 29 of the *Orlando*—his mother-in-law, and his wife. In the "Apologie" for *The Metamorphosis of Ajax* (1596)—his tract on his invention of the water closet—Harington urged that the book should be shown to "all maner of ladies, of the Court, of the country, of the City, great Ladies, lesser Ladies, learned, ignorant, wise simple, fowle welfavoured, (painted unpainted) so they be Ladies, you may boldly prefer it to them."[10] Harington wanted to be thought of as a "ladies' man," ending a letter to his friend Sir Hugh Portman with the words, "Commend me to your Ladie and all other ladies that ever heard of me" (*Nugae Antiquae*, 1: 319). Benedick boasts to Beatrice of a similar role as "ladies' man": "It is certain I am loved of all ladies, only you excepted" (1.1.92–93). The approval of women mattered to Harington even more than the approval of men and if Donne has been, and is, persistently construed as a man's writer, Harington is a woman's writer.[11]

Harington was far more than what we would consider to be a translator. He not only tampered with the Italian text of the *Orlando Furioso,* abridging and expanding as he saw fit; he peppered each page with marginal notes, often reflecting his personal views on what he read and ending each canto with meditations on its content. Benedick's role in *Much Ado* as commentator on the action as much as participator in it re-creates Harington's stance in relation to the *Orlando Furioso,* a text that, in its translator's hands, ceases to be a master text and is forced to become a partner in a dialogue, just as the Hero-and-Claudio plot dances in partnership with the so-called subplot of the romance between Beatrice and Benedick.

Benedick and Beatrice speak prose to Claudio and Hero's blank verse, just as Harington glosses Ariosto's verse in his own "homely" prose. In *Much Ado* prose is privileged as the witness of truth over poetry, as it is, by implication, in Harington's commentary. Benedick, trying to warble a love song, concludes that he can't sing at all:

> But in loving—Leander the good swimmer, Troilus the first employer of panders, and a whole book full of these quondam carpet-mongers, whose names yet run smoothly in the even road of a blank verse, why they were never so truly turned over and over as my poor self in love: marry, I cannot show it in rhyme, I have tried. (5.2.22–28)

The written poetic record of Benedick's inept verse belies the heart; but Benedick implies that the accomplished written record of the true poet does not necessarily represent a true heart. In the final scene the audience believes that the halting sonnet bears witness to the heart, largely because it is halting. The rotten writer, like the inept performer, seems by definition to be the honest man. But there are extreme pitfalls in this argument. Education in rhetoric created anxiety about spontaneity, but that anxiety is contained within the forms and conventions of rhetoric itself. "'Foole,' said my Muse to me, 'Look in thy heart and write.'"[12]

In *Much Ado* the answer to the question put to the Watch—"Are you good men and true?" (3.3.1)—might be, within the play's economy, "Yea, an ye speak prose." In the notes to canto 32 of the *Orlando Furioso* Harington declares that he has always found it easier to write prose: "Prose is like a faire greene way wherein a man may travell a great journey and not be wearie, but verse is a mirie lane in which a mans horse pulls out one leg after another with much adoe" (*Orlando,* 368). "Honest prose" was for Harington *The Metamorphosis of Ajax,* which scandalized the court with its plain speaking on bodily matters and its free speaking about courts and courtiers. It was also, of course, the language of clowns, which in Shakespeare's play links Benedick with Dogberry, just as some of Harington's contemporaries linked him with Tarlton.[13] The contrasts between the irreverent Rabelaisian prose tract, with its "damned honesty," and the high culture Italian epic romance, with its smooth fictions—were they lies?[14]—is also a contrast between a domestic man who hates stinking houses and a courtier, between a private man and a public one, except that Harington's privacy is on display, as Benedick's also is in *Much Ado about Nothing.*[15]

Shakespeare—like Jonson—perhaps did not think much of Harington as a poet. The jokes in *Much Ado* against Benedick as a hopeless versifier easily transpose into the medium of a parallel text, Harington's translation of Ariosto into "English Heroical Verse"—*ottava rima*—which rhymes doggedly throughout. The manuscript studied by Kathleen M. Lea in the Bodleian Library shows how carefully Harington worked at his versification.[16] Parallels between Harington as versifier and Benedick as reluctant poet can be multiplied from a comparison between the text not only of *Much Ado* and the *Orlando,* but between Shakespeare's play and Harington's Epigrams, which were circulated among his friends in the 1590s and are likely to have been seen by Shakespeare.[17] More than one of Harington's epigrams resonate on Benedick's problems with masculine rhyme where he laments rhyming "lady" with "baby" (5.2.28), as Harington does in the closing couplet of an epigram entitled "The Author to his wife, of partition":

> For where this is my Lords, and that my Ladies,
> there some perhaps think likewise of their babies.[18]

The sly cuckoldry joke is there in Harington's couplet as it is also in Benedick's "foolish" (and, of course, feminine) rhyme. Harington's epigram on "The horne Cinque-apace" jingles on Beatrice's claim that "Repentance" follows "wedding" and "with his bad legs falls into the cinquepace faster and faster, till he sink into his grave" (2.1.55–56). In this poem Harington rhymes "horn and scorn," as Benedick also laments having to do. The husband in Harington's piece counts up five horns.[19] Benedick has other plans:

> That a woman conceived me, I thank her: that she brought me up, I likewise give her most humble thanks: but that I will have a reacheat winded in my forehead, or hang my bugle in an invisible baldrick, all women shall pardon me. . . . In time the savage bull may bear the yoke, but if ever the sensible Benedick bear it, pluck off the bull's horns. . . . Let them signify under my sign, 'Here you may see Benedick the married man.' (1.1.176–80, and 194–99)

This is an image that leads naturally into Harington's translation of the story of Ariodante and Ginevra in the *Orlando Furioso*.

The savage bull makes his entrance in the first stanza of Ariosto's canto 5, in which the poet talks about male and female living in concord according to the laws of nature: "The savage Lions, Beares, and Buls most wyld / Unto their females shew them selves most myld" (*Orlando*, 58). "Looke more at large in the end of the booke of this morall," admonishes the translator's prose note in the margin. That "Morall" is an extended disquisition on marital harmony: "If the male and female in beasts and foule for the most part live in concord and agreement, what a foule and worse then beastly thing is it for man and wife to be ever bralling and snarling" (*Orlando,* 68). Harington plays, at this point in his prose narrative, the part of the married man, who has nothing whatever to do with the savage bull, except in bearing the yoke with as much gentleness as Ariosto apparently claims for that creature. The prose commentary in praise of matrimony obliquely criticizes the poetic narrative of court infidelity. In *Much Ado* sympathetic laughter at a man who has trouble rhyming is prompted in part by acquiescence in Benedick's belief that the medium of an honest man is not poetry but prose.

I don't wish to argue an empirical case for a Benedick molded on Sir John Harington, but rather to suggest the subtle interplay between the theatrical text and the text of Harington's own writings, for if anyone deserved to be described as a set of competing texts, Harington is surely that person. He performed his own life for the benefit of his contemporaries, writing *himself,* while evading, as skillfully as Montaigne had evaded, any sense of stable personality fixed by the act of writing.[20] The consciousness of performance evident both in Harington's writings and in accounts of contemporary events, both his and other people's, illuminates the performative in *Much Ado about Nothing* at many different levels. David Wiles describes Benedick as a man "intruding upon the clown's functions," just as Harington intruded his fooling on the flatteries and hypocrisies of the court.[21] How honest was the man who took up his pen to declare his dissociation from the words Ariosto had written? Was his honesty just another role that he played? And, by analogy, how may one understand Benedick, who in *Much Ado* occupies the ground of honest man amidst the slanders and deceptions of those around him?

The story of Ariodante and Ginevra—a version of the Claudio and Hero story—in cantos 4 and 5 of *Orlando Furioso*—is a standard tale of alleged female infidelity and male jealousy. Harington's commentary on his translation of these cantos offers no easy insights into the correlation between the honest married man's heart and hand. Renaldo in this episode from *Orlando Furioso* is free thinking. The two kinds of lying, fornication and fiction, practiced in Shakespeare's play by Borachio, aided and abetted by Conrade and Don John, are equally trivial in the eyes of Ariosto's protagonist. He doesn't care whether Ginevra actually lay with her lover or not. But he thinks the law that condemns her to death is barbarous, because it enshrines a double standard for men and women:

> To graunt the men more scope, the women lesse,
> Is law for which no reason we can render:
> Men using many never are ashamed,
> But women using one or two are blamed.

> (*Orlando,* 55)

Harington's marginal note remarks that "Wise men should count it a greater notwithstanding good Renaldos opinion" (*Orlando,* 55). In the next stanza Renaldo claims that the law that punishes women so severely wrongs them and ought to be revoked. Harington adds another marginal thought of his own: "In this point I thinke many are of that religion." He apparently reneges on his own disapproval of canto 53 and under the cover of the general "many" acquiesces in the repudiation of the law which condemns women more than men.[22] In the prose "Morall" appended to the canto, Harington refers against to Renaldo's speech:

> As we may with him justly mislike such partialitie in lawes, so we may note the maner and phrase of speech of young gentlemen (as *Renaldo* was) that make so light of their sweet sinne of lecherie, as they call it, not regarding how sower heavie punishment hangs over it and what a foule reproch it is to both sexes.
>
> (*Orlando,* 56)

Here, the translator represents his own heart as one of exemplary fairness, condemning lechery in men and women alike.

However, Harington's even-handedness in repudiating Renaldo's frivolity about different kinds of lying, rather than expressing the translator's heart, expresses instead his sense of his readers. When he dedicated the work to Elizabeth he declared that if she approved it no one would dare to disapprove it. His "Morall" proclaims, under the thinnest of disguises, for the benefit of the royal reader, that he is not a young gentleman who makes light of the sweet sin of lechery. He has not been lying abroad: he has been translating fictions at home for his royal godmother's delectation. But as he worked, his wife no doubt looked over his shoulder; when he went to court she complained and wanted him to come home; his mother-in-law reproved him for enjoying the marriage bed too much. All three women readers, the queen, Lady Mary, and Lady Jane her mother, might have remarked with satisfaction the "merry blade's" declaration that his heart was in the right place. He was not, like Renaldo, a poetic hero who equivocated about the realities of men and women's lying together.

But other readers must wonder about this impeccable performance and enquire where Harington's heart lies in this matter. His writings on fornication are as inconsistent as the two marginal notes on Renaldo seem to be. In 1607 he wrote a letter about the marriage of priests to Bishop Joseph Hall, in which he declared bluntly, "If there be degres of sine I thinke that simple fornicatione is one of the lest." This to a man who had just been appointed one of Prince Henry's chaplains. When Christ wrote in the sand about the woman taken in adultery, argues Harington, he meant "to abate much of the vigor of moses law for women taken in adultere."[23] He recalls that "therfor I wright long since pleasantly to a Lady that was as austere as I was carlese," that she was mistaken in thinking that the worst sin was adultery. The unlikely recipient of this meditation, couched in the form of an epigram, was his own mother-in-law, Lady Jane Rogers. In the letter to Hall, Harington claims that he was specifically thinking of *women* taken in adultery and urging leniency toward them. But this represents a later gloss on the original epigram, which is contained in the collection sent to his mother-in-law in 1600, in which the saucy son-in-law is not thinking of women at all, but of the sophistry with which it is possible to argue the case for lying abroad:

> Now letchery (as showes the common sentence)
> begins with loue, and endeth with repentance,
> besides all those that take delight therein
> finde it a lively, not a deadly sin.
>
> ("Epigrams 1600")

This merry playing with words bespeaks the Lincoln's Inn man as used to manipulating language as the young men who evade their oaths in *Love's Labour's Lost*. Yet in his report to Hall, Harington represents himself as the champion of oppressed women, the wretched Ginevras of the world, rather than, as in the earlier version, one of those who might be doing the oppressing. However, as soon as he has quoted the poem in his letter to Hall, Harington continues: "But to leave sporting and handle this mater more seriouslye" which is followed in his manuscript by a blank half page. The blank page looks like a Tristam Shandyish joke, that where the serious man writes his true feelings, nothing is written at all. Perhaps Harington hoped for seriousness hereafter, but forgot to record it.

Like most jesters, he had trouble finding the serious man behind the harlequin's mask. He wrote in one epigram that his muse was "like king Edwards Concubine" who went to church when she wasn't otherwise engaged.[24] When he sent James I his translations of *Aeneid VI* for Prince Henry in 1605, he compared poetry to a concubine, but denied that it need necessarily corrupt the reader:

> The same pen oft tymes wrytes holly himns that wrate wanton sonnets, and the same pensyll draws the pictures of Chryste and owr lady that drew venus and Cupid. and neyther do amorows verses corrupt all reeders nor lascyvyows pictures provoke all beholders.[25]

He might have had the precept of his friend John Donne in mind, but it was equally true of himself, for while he wrote risqué epigrams he also translated the Penitential Psalms, probably his last gift of verse to James I.[26] Is the pen in this case true to the inconsistencies of the heart, or do the contradictions of the pen give the lie to the true heart? Harington might perhaps have replied with Montaigne in the essay "Des Boyteux" [Of Cripples]:

> La verité et le mensonge ont leurs visages conformes, le port, le goust et les alleures pareilles; nous les regardons de mesme oeil"

> [Truth and lies are faced alike; their port, taste, and proceedings are the same, and we look upon them with the same eye].[27]

Is language itself the real liar, and silence or the blank page the only true witnesses of truth? On the blank page of Hero's silent suffering in the shaming scene in *Much Ado about Nothing* the Friar reads her innocence.

Harington as writer perfected many different techniques for dissociating himself from what he had written. In the Ariosto translation he claims that what he is obliged to write as translator of another's text is sometimes flat against the dictates of his heart. He refers particularly to canto 27, stanza 99, in which he omitted two stanzas of Rodomonte's invective against women's fickleness. Ariosto apologizes for Rodomonte in a rather backhanded manner, claiming that although he himself believes in the possibility of a faithful woman, not a single one has crossed his path. Harington offers instead only four lines:

> I tremble to set downe in my poore verse
> The blasphemie that he to speake presumes,
> And writing this I do, know this that I
> Full oft in heart do give my pen the lye.[28]

Rodomonte, like Iachimo in *Cymbeline,* challenges his companions to declare their opinions of their wives' faithfulness. Harington at this point adds a stanza praising women:

> Straight all of them made answere they had wives,
> And, but mine host, all praisd the happie state
> And said they were the comforts of their lives
> That draw a happie yoke without debate,
> A playfellow that farre of all grief drives,
> A steward early that provides and late,
> Both faithfull, chast and sober, mild and trustie,
> Nurse to weake age and pleasure to the lustie.[29]

In the "Apologie" for *The Metamorphosis of Ajax,* Harington discovers for his readers, in a marginal note to this passage, his own policy in translating it:

> Where my autor very sparingly had praised some wives, I added of mine own (   ) so much as more I thinke was never said for them, which I will here set downe *ad perpetuam rei memoriam,* and that all posteritie may know how good a husband I would be thought.[30]

The marginal note on the blank in the brackets suggests two ways of filling the blank: "Mine owne *subauditur* verse or wife which you will." Did he add a verse? Or did he add praise of his own wife? He did, apparently, both, praising wives but transparently addressing himself to that sharp-eyed reader, Lady Mary Rogers, whom in one epigram he describes as a "Lyoness."[31] As he wrote he performed his role of good husband for an audience of three: himself, his wife, and the queen.[32] His techniques of dissociation allowed him maximum freedom to jest and satirize but also to conciliate and harmonize. He also perfected his liberty to be lewd without being offensive. Most of the time.

In both his epigrams and the Ariosto translation Harington often concealed an obscene word by leaving a blank space, using this device to juggle with authorial responsibility. The idea of the master text makes no sense in relation to his writings as he alters spelling and text incessantly. The scribal manuscript collection which Harington presented to his mother-in-law in 1600 together with *Orlando Furioso* contains an epigram entitled "The author to his wife of a womans' Eloquence." In this poem Harington describes his wife's using all her arts of persuasion and concludes,

> But shall I tell what most thy sute advaunces
> Thy fair smooth words, no no, thy fayr smooth (   ).

In this manuscript, intended for Lady Rogers, and probably also for her daughter, his wife Mall, the scribe stops writing after "no, no." The repeated words in the second half of the line, "Thy fayr smooth," have been written in by Harington; and empty brackets follow, as if he dare not write the word "hawnches," at least for these particular readers. For in the manuscript copy in the British Library the word "hawnches" (probably scribal) is firmly in place, as it is also in the printed version.[33] Harington apparently baulked at writing the word "hawnches" when he knew his readers would be his wife and his mother-in-law. He was both unwilling to be seen to have written the word himself, or to have allowed his scribe to write it. When he thought of the royal male readers, the prince and his father, James I, he was less squeamish. But Harington knew as well as any that the blank space functioned to draw attention to the absent risqué word whose presence was felt more powerfully by omission.

At the end of *Much Ado* Benedick challenges the tyranny of the writer: "I tell thee what, prince: a college of witcrackers cannot flout me out of my humour: dost thou think I care for a satire or an epigram?" (5.4.98–100). June 1 1599 marked the calling-in of all epigrams and satires to be burnt.[34] In all his works Shakespeare uses the word "epigram" only once, at this point in Benedick's speech in *Much Ado about Nothing*.[35] The play was "staid" in the Stationer's Register in a special note for 4 August—year unspecified, though assumed by Arber to be 1600—a fate usually reserved for seditious material.[36] Leishman claims that the effect of the ban on the printing of satires and epigrams was to channel satire into comedy.[37] But equally, the theater provided an arena for voicing the sidelong criticism of the ban offered by Benedick in the final act of *Much Ado*.

Much Ado about Nothing ends declaring roundly, as *The Metamorphosis of Ajax* has also done, for freedom of speech. In doing so, it allies itself once again with the volatile translator of *Orlando Furioso*. Harington wrote to his wife in 1602, when the old queen was approaching death, of her "liking for my free speech" (*Nugae Antiquae* 2.77). In an age of egregious flattery, Harington boasted some freedom of spirit:

> My writings oft displease you: what's the matter?
> You love not to heare truth, nor I to flatter.

(I.59).

His epigrams are often sharply critical of social abuses, yet equally they are texts skilled in the evasion of authorial responsibility for their satire.[38]

Harington claimed that in his epigrams he was not a "maker" but a recorder of truths: what he thinks he writes.[39] Drummond reports Ben Jonson's scorn of this attitude.[40] Harington retorted in the epigram "That Poetrie shall be no fictions but meere truths":

> But read to carpe, as still hath been thine vse:
> Fret out thine heart to search, seeke, sift and pry,
> Thy heart shall hardly giue my pen the ly.
>
> (1.1)[41]

Benedick's scorn of being mortified by the epigram made against him embraces both the carping writer and the oversensitive hearer. In defending the epigram, the player also defends the play.

Plays in 1599 were classed with satires as dreaded weapons of insult by a man who had most cause to fear them. On 20 May 1599, less than two weeks before satires and epigrams were censored, Essex wrote to Elizabeth of the slanders that her treatment of him had unleashed: "The tavern-haunter speaks of me what he lists. Already they print me and make me speak to the world; and shortly they will play me in what forms they list upon the stage. The least of these is a thousand times worse than death."[42] *Much Ado about Nothing* attacks that fear of the stage play by offering an indictment of the suspicious, dangerous, and repressive court that watched it.

The atmosphere of that court can be gauged by some of the letters in the *Nugae Antiquae,* which refer constantly to the fear of interception, of the hand being used against the heart. Mistrust accompanied the Irish expedition from its inception, if the evidence of a letter to Harington from his cousin Robert Markham is to be credited. Markham wrote to Harington soon after the latter was commissioned under Essex for the Irish expedition, urging him to keep a secret journal, and admonishing him against too much plain dealing, concluding: "The hart of man liethe close hid oft time; men do not carrye it in their hand, nor should they do so that wish to thrive in these times and in these places." Do not carry your heart in your hand. The hand against the heart. The extraordinary statement about the relation between the heart and the hand puts a gloss on the lighthearted world of *Much Ado,* which, with its overhearing, suspicion, mis-interpretation, and the producing of letters to belie the heart, must have touched nerves exceptionally raw even before the final Irish debacle of August 1599.

In a letter to the Catholic Sir Anthony Standen, a man employed for spying who, like Harington and most of his contemporaries, would eventually spend some time in the Fleet, Harington records that on his return from Ireland in the summer of 1599 the queen threatened him with imprisonment there: "I answered (poetically) that comminge so late from the land service I hoped that I shuld not be prest to serve in her Maj[esty']s Fleet in fleet street. after iij daies every man wondrad to see me at libertye."[43] Harington mused privately: "I had nearly been wracked on the *Essex coaste* in my laste venture, as I tolde the Queene, had it not been for the sweete calme of her specyal forgiveness" (*Nugae Antiquae,* 1: 178–79). In the masqued dance scene in *Much Ado* (1.2), Beatrice and Benedick move into center stage, and Beatrice laments the apparent absence of Benedick: "I am sure he is in the Fleet, I would he had boarded me" (2.1.96–107). In the 1600 Quarto, and in the Folio, "fleet" begins with a capital "F" but in modern editions this has fallen out, thus removing the pun.[44] The Irish accent adopted by Mark Rylance as Benedick in the London production of *Much Ado* at the Queen's Theatre in 1993 had its own weird appropriateness for a drama that animadverts on the Irish expedition as daringly and lightly as Harington jested his way out of trouble to a dangerous audience. The queen sent him an angry message when she heard of his knighthood from Essex in July 1599: "'Go tell that witty fellow, my godson, to get home; it is no season now to foole it here.' I liked this as little as she dothe my knighthood, so tooke to my bootes and returned to the plow in bad weather."[45] The one jest that he was a very dull fool sticks with Benedick: "She told me, not thinking I had been myself, that I was the prince's jester, that I was duller than a great thaw, huddling jest upon jest, with such impossible conveyance upon me, that I stood like a man at a mark, with a whole army shooting at me" (2.1.181–85). The fountain modeled on Ariosto, the water closet, and the shooting target were the three elements that Harington felt made his country house at Kelston remarkable. His jesting saved him from the mark, but it also rusticated him.

The narrowness of his escape remained vivid within Harington's consciousness. Stick to your books and be careful with your jokes had indeed been sound counsel; he felt that his book had

saved his reputation with Elizabeth. It had also served the purpose of conveying a covert, if unheeded, warning to the Irish
rebel, the earl of Tyrone. Harington's mercurial nature demonstrated itself not only in a real love of Ireland but even in a wish
to save the Irish rebel from imminent disaster: "I turn'd (as it
had been by chance) to the beginning of the 45th canto."[46] Only
Harington could have been so naive and yet so disingenuous,
for the canto deals with the slipperiness of fortune and the fall
of the great. The warning might have been more appropriate for
the English commander, an earl whose fortunes were indeed on
a dangerous decline. When Harington performed canto 45 of the
Orlando—in that oblique form, the translation—to the audience
of the Irish rebel and his sons, turning to it as if by accident,
his voice reading from the words his own hand had written
perhaps gave a truer testimony of his heart than his hearers
realized.

At the end of canto 45 Harington recalls in his prose notes
another victim of fortune, held prisoner at Woodstock, whom
his own parents had served in captivity in the Tower, a royal
writer who had flaunted with her hand the inability of her cap-
tors to read her heart:

> *Much suspected by me,* }
> *Nothing proved can be.* }   quoth *Elizabeth* prisoner
> (Orlando, 541)

Much ado about *nothing.* The atmosphere of 1599 was for
Harington a reliving of the times when his father and mother
had proved their loyalty: his father imprisoned in the Tower for
carrying a letter to the princess.[47] The dangers of the hand's
being allowed to witness against the heart were in his blood
from birth, as the queen, who rewarded his parents by standing
godmother to their first son, knew only too well.

Much Ado about Nothing returns the reader to Harington's
translation of Ariosto with a wish not to concentrate on Ariosto's
verse, but rather on the prose commentary that creates a dialogue with it. The poetic text interlaced with prose commentary
becomes itself a kind of play, in which the translator marks out
his own stage. Harington, as Virginia Woolf said of Dorothy Osborne, another inspired letter writer, might have been a novelist
had he been born a century later, writing in a form that addressed itself particularly to women readers. Harington wrote
to please many women. Above all, he played his competing parts

of honest man and professed tyrant to the sex, as Benedick also plays them, for a woman who was both a Beatrice of blessed memory and my Lady Tongue, the royal godmother whom he loved and feared as a reader of hearts as well as of hands, a dangerous watcher of men's plays.

Much Ado about Nothing celebrates the human capacity to turn and turn again. But strangely, in that celebration it convinces the audience that the turncoat Benedick, a man who will wear his faith but as the fashion of his hat, is nevertheless an honest man. This seems to have been the contemporary view of Sir John Harington, in a world of fashion mongers and time servers. He believed it of himself, and thought it was the reason for his lack of advancement at court, which he both regretted and yet, in a way, was proud of. Harington's changes of heart, his jesting, equivocation, and refusal to retain any position that he has taken up beguile the reader with a sense of the real thing, the heart itself, which manipulates discourse without itself being subject to those manipulations. If this is a final illusion, it is an illusion perpetuated in *Much Ado about Nothing*, a work shadowed by the translator of the Ariosto source. Benedick and Beatrice, trapped into loving by lying, promise steadfastness from a base of fickleness, which convinces the audience of constancy. Somewhere in the space between heart and hand lurks the true man, refusing to be confined within what he has written: "For man is a giddy thing, and this is my conclusion."

Notes

1. *Much Ado about Nothing,* ed. F. H. Mares, The New Cambridge Shakespeare (Cambridge: Cambridge University Press, 1988): 5.4.91. All quotations from the play are from this edition.

2. *Much Adoe about Nothing; A New Variorum,* ed. Horace Howard Furness, 27 vols. (Philadelphia: J. R. Lippincott, 1899), 12:24, notes Benedick's consciousness of playing a role.

3. Leah Marcus, *Puzzling Shakespeare: Local Reading and its Discontents* (Berkeley: University of California Press, 1988), 99.

4. James Nielson, "William Kemp at the Globe," *Shakespeare Quarterly* 42 (autumn 1991): 467–68, argues that Kemp may have been acting at the Globe as late as 1600; cf. David Wiles, *Shakespeare's Clown* (Cambridge: Cambridge University Press, 1987): 35–36.

5. Sir John Harington, *An Apologie* [for *The Metamorphosis of Ajax,* printed simultaneously with it] in *Sir John Harington's A New Discourse of a Stale Subject, called The Metamorphosis of Ajax,* ed. Elizabeth Story Donno (London: Routledge and Kegan Paul, 1927), 256. *The Metamorphosis of Ajax* is also quoted from this edition.

6. Ludovico Ariosto's *Orlando Furioso, translated into English Heroical Verse by Sir John Harington* (1591), ed. Robert McNulty (Oxford: Clarendon Press, 1972), 313. All references to Harington's translation and commentary on *Orlando Furioso* are to this edition. This will be referred to hereafter as *Orlando*.

7. Annabel M. Patterson, *Censorship and Interpretation: The Conditions of Writing and Reading in Early Modern England* (Madison: University of Wisconsin Press, 1984); Jonathan Goldberg, *James I and the Politics of Literature* (Baltimore: Johns Hopkins University Press, 1983); Richard Dutton, *Mastering the Revels: The Regulation and Censorship of English Renaissance Drama* (London: Macmillan, 1991); Janet Clare, "'Greater Themes for Insurrection's Arguing': Political Censorship of the Elizabethan and Jacobean Stage," *Review of English Studies,* n.s., 38 (May 1987): 169–83.

8. Letter to Mr Secretary Barlow, *Nugae Antiquae,* ed. Thomas Park, 2 vols. (London: Vernor and Hood, 1804): 1: 252.

9. Harington, "The Life of Ariosto," *Orlando,* 571.

10. Harington, *An Apologie,* 219.

11. *See* Stanley Fish, "Masculine Persuasive Force: Donne and Verbal Power," in *Soliciting Interpretation,* eds. Elizabeth D. Harvey and Katharine Eisaman Maus (Chicago: University of Chicago Press, 1990): 223–52.

12. Sir Philip Sidney, *Astrophel and Stella,* sonnet 1, in *Elizabethan Sonnets,* ed. Maurice Evans (London: Dent, 1977), 2.

13. Wiles, *Shakespeare's Clown,* 100–1; *Ulysses upon Ajax, written by Misodiaboles to his friend Philaretes* (Printed at London, for Thomas Gubbins, 1596), sig. E9.

14. Harington's "Apologie for Poetrie," prefaced to *Orlando Furioso,* denies, as strenuously as his model, Sidney, denies in his *Apology,* that fiction and lying are the same thing.

15. Goldberg, *James I and the Politics of Literature,* 147–52; Katharine Eisaman Maus, "Proof and Consequences: Inwardness and Its Exposure in the English Renaissance," *Representations* 34 (spring 1991): 47.

16. Kathleen M. Lea, "Harington's *Folly,*" in *Elizabethan and Jacobean Studies Presented to Frank Percy Wilson* (Oxford: Clarendon Press, 1959): 50.

17. See my "As Who Liked It?," *Shakespeare Survey* 46 (1994): 14–15.

18. "Epigrams" in a scribal hand with letter and holograph signature, addressed to Lady Mary Harington and Lady Jane Rogers, bound in to the 1600 edition *Orlando Furioso* in English Heroical Verse by John Harington Esquire (imprinted at London by Richard Field, 1591). These will be referred to hereafter as "Epigrams 1600."

19. Sir John Harington, *Epigrams 1618,* 4: 25.

20. Stephen Greenblatt, *Renaissance Self-Fashioning: From More to Shakespeare* (Chicago: University of Chicago Press, 1980), 168–69.

21. *Shakespeare's Clown,* 76.

22. *See* Pamela Joseph Benson, *The Invention of Renaissance Woman* (University Park: Penn State University Press, 1992), 90–101.

23. M. H. M. MacKinnon, "Sir John Harington and Bishop Hall," *Philological Quarterly* 37 (January 1958): 84–85, from BL Add. MS. 27632, ff. 35–40.

24. "Misacmos of his Muse," final epigram in "Epigrams 1600."

25. "Of Reeding Poetry," in *The Sixth Book of Virgil's Aeneid VI, translated by Sir John Harington* (1604), ed. Simon Cauchi (Oxford: Clarendon Press),

96; Townsend Rich, *Harington & Ariosto* (New Haven: Yale University Press, 1940), 78.

26. BL Add. MS. 27632, f. 30, contains an autograph note: "Walter Brisco came for the Kings verses 10th day of April 1610."

27. Michel de Montaigne, *Essais,* 3 vols. (Paris: GF Flammarion, 1979), 3: 239, quoting Cicero, "Ita finitima sunt falsa veris, ut in praecipitem locum non debeat se spaiens committere" (*Academics,* 2: 21); the translation is from *Essays of Montaigne,* trans. Charles Cotton, ed. William Carew Hazlitt, 5 vols. (London: printed for the Navarre Society, 1923), 5: 192; Florio's less elegant version reads: "Truth and falsehood have both alike countenances, their port, their taste and their proceedings semblable: Wee behold them with one same eyes" (*The Essayes of Michael Lord of Montaigne,* introduced by Desmond MacCarthy, 3 vols. (London: J. M. Dent, 1928): 3: 279. The French was added by Montaigne to the second edition; the Cicero original to the third.

28. *Orlando,* 310; *see* Harington, *An Apologie,* 256.

29. *Orlando,* 311. These lines, and an undated entry in Harington's Commonplace book, BL Add. MS. 27632, 34: "mariage. quasi mery age," echo Henry Smith, *A Preparative to Marriage* (London: Thomas Orwin for Thomas Man, 1591), 66: "Mariage doth signifie merriage, because a playfellow is come to make our age merrie."

30. Harington, *An Apologie,* 256–57. Rich, *Harington & Ariosto,* 120–22.

31. "To his wife for stryking her Dogge," "Epigrams 1600," reprinted in *Epigrams 1618,* 1: 71.

32. According to Harington his good marriage met with royal approval:

> The Queene did once aske my wife in merrie sorte, 'how she kepte my goode wyll and love, which I did alwayes mayntaine to be trulie goode towardes her and my children?' My Mall in wise and discreete manner, tolde her Highnesse, 'she had confidence in her husbandes understandinge and courage, well founded on her own stedfastness not to offend or thwart, but to cherishe and obey; hereby did she persuade her husbande of her own affectione, and in so doinge did commande him.'—'Go to, go to, mistresse, saithe the Queene, you are wisely bente I finde: after such sorte do I keepe the good wyll of all my husbandes, my good people; for if they did not reste assurede of some specyal love towarde them, they would not readilie yeilde me such goode obedience.'—This deservethe notinge, as beinge both wise and pleasaunte. (*Nugae Antiquae,* 1: 177–78)

33. BL Add. MS. 12049. R. H. Miller, "Unpublished Poems by Sir John Harington," *English Literary Renaissance* 14 (spring 1984): 149, considers this copy to be an early version of the presentation copy for Prince Henry, now in the Folger Library; by the same author, "Sir John Harington's Manuscripts in Italic," *Studies in Bibliography* 40 (1987): 106.

34. Philip J. Finkelpearl, "The Comedian's Liberty: Censorship of the Jacobean Stage Reconsidered," *English Literary Renaissance* 16 (winter 1986): 136.

35. I dealt with this in a version of this essay delivered to the biennial conference of the Shakespeare Association of Australia and New Zealand at the University of Western Australia. I am extremely grateful for the comments and criticisms offered by members of the conference, as well as for criticisms on earlier drafts made by members of graduate seminars at the Universities of Kent, Sussex, and Cambridge.

36. The other plays "staid" with *Much Ado* were *Henry V, As You Like It,* and *Every Man in His Humour. Henry V,* like *Much Ado,* was probably performed

between March and September of 1599. Annabel Patterson, "'The Very Age and Body of the Time His Form and Pressure': Rehistoricizing Shakespeare's Theater," *New Literary History* 20 (autumn 1988): 98, argues the significance of the Bishops Order for the censorship of Shakespeare's histories. The "bad" first Quarto of *Henry V* was printed in summer 1600 with the fifth Chorus's reference to Essex excised.

37. J. B. Leishman, *The Three Parnassus Plays (1598–1604)* (London: Ivor Nicholson & Watson Ltd., 1949): 44–45.

38. *See,* for example, *Epigrams 1618,* 2: 7.

39. *Epigrams 1618,* 1: 44.

40. Conversations with William Drummond of Hawthornden, in *Ben Jonson,* ed. by C. H. Herford and Percy Simpson, 11 vols. (Oxford: Clarendon Press, 1966), 1: 133, and 153 n. 38.

41. Ibid., 1.1. In BL Add. MS. 12049, this epigram is the second to be printed, whereas in *Epigrams 1618* it begins the first of the four books of Harington epigrams.

42. *Memoirs of the Reign of Elizabeth,* ed. Thomas Birch, 2 vols. (London: A. Millar, 1754): 2: 445.

43. Letter to Sir Anthony Standen, 20 February 1599 [1600], BL Add. MS 46369, f. 8; reproduced (with modernized spelling) in Park, *Nugae Antiquae,* 1: 309.

44. Furness, in *Much Adoe about Nothing,* 72–73, doubts that the double meaning could be present in Shakespeare's text, but the grounds of his argument are unconvincing. The only other use in Shakespeare of "Fleet" with the initial capital is at the end of *Henry V:* "Carry Sir John Falstaffe to the Fleet." If Harington could make the pun, there is no reason to suppose that Shakespeare was incapable of it. The Riverside, New Cambridge, and Arden editions all print "fleet" without the initial capital.

45. Letter to Sir Hugh Portman [Kelston, 9 October 1601], *Nugae Antiquae,* 1: 317–18.

46. "Report of a Journey into the North of Ireland," written to Justice Carey by Sir John Harington, 1599, *Nugae Antiquae,* 1:247–52. This report is reprinted by Park from the autograph text in BL Add. MS. 46369.

47. Sir John Harington to Prince Henry, 1606, *Nugae Antiquae,* 1: 364.

"Bridegroom uncarnate": Comedy and Castration from *The Eunuch* to *Epicoene*

Keir Elam

1. *Eunuchus:* The Performance of the Castrate

Among the debts English comedy owes to the Italian Renaissance *commedia* was the crucial role the latter played in "recycling," i.e., rediscovering and rehistoricizing the great *topoi* of classical comedy. This chapter examines the transmission from classical to English drama, via the mediating agency of the *commedia,* of a *topos* that, I argue, is central to the development of comedy as a dramatic genre, namely the prospect—promise or threat, fear or hope—of castration.

The fullest classical treatment of the castration topic occurs in what might be considered as the New Comedy prototype of all cross-dressing drama, namely Terence's *Eunuchus.* Terence's comedy was revered by both Italian and English dramatists as formal and thematic model and was in varying degrees imitated in countless Renaissance plays, from Ariosto's *I suppositi* to the Intronati Academy's *Gl'Ingannati,* and from Udall's *Ralph Roister Doister* to Jonson's *Epicoene.* The main plot of *Eunuchus* hinges on the brilliant ploy of a young lover, Chaerea, who, in order to gain access to his beloved, the slave girl Pamphila, pretends to be a eunuch servant. Terence makes great play of the paradox whereby in order to fulfil his uncontrollable desire, the protagonist has to feign to be desire*less*. Chaerea presents himself as his own opposite, as a minus sign standing for what is in fact an emphatic plus, as he goes on to demonstrate when he finally gains access to Pamphila's bed and thus to her sleeping body.

The external social context of Terence's "eunuch" was one of religious ritual. The comedy was first performed in 161 B.C.E. during the Megalensian Games in honor of the "Great Mother" Cybele.[1] The cult of the Asiatic goddess Cybele had been introduced into Rome by Elagabalus in 204 B.C.E., and was strictly bound up with castration rituals. Attis, the vegetarian god associated with the cult, died and was resurrected after castrating himself; Cybele's priests were in consequence traditionally eunuchs, while Elagabalus himself was notorious for having his friends' bodies symbolically shaved and his own testicles tied up when celebrating the rites of Cybele and Attis. In this context the fruits of castration are direct: unmanning is synonymous with self-transcendence and "rebirth" in the guise of regression to an infantile state:

> "The act of castration," observes Aline Rousselle, "has two meanings [in antiquity]: the return to childhood, which makes the castrated male the perfect victim for Saturn, and the adult whose *pneuma* can be purely psychic, since there can be no further loss of the vital seed. The practices described in the life of Elagabalus mark the return to a pre-pubertal condition: he had his friends' bodies shaved of 'the positive signs of puberty.'"[2]

A play centered on the figure of a eunuch is thus an appropriate homage to Cybele, although the kinds of transcendence celebrated in Terence's comedy have less to do with religious rebirth than with role playing and the representation or realization of masculine desire. The extraordinary influence of Terence's play seems to lie largely in the vertiginous reversal at the center of the plot, whereby what looks like the neutralizing of male sexuality turns out instead to be a triumphant assertion of virility. It is only by transcending his male identity through self-"castration" that Chaerea is able to realize his desire for the slave girl. In narrating his offstage triumph, Chaerea relishes the ironical contrast between his assumed role and his actual performance (I quote from Richard Bernard's 1598 translation[3]):

> *Chaerea.* I boult the door.
>
> *Antipho.* What then?
>
> *Chaerea.* Should I let go such opportunitie and occasion offered me, hauing so short a time to doe it in, so greatly desired, so sudden, and nothing looked for? then was I hee indeede, whom I did counterfait.

Admitted into Pamphila's bedroom as eunuch-guard, Chaerea "boults the door" ("pessulum ostium obdo"), a metonymy for the act that he is employed not to (be able to) perform.

What Chaerea's account enthusiastically underlines is the irresistible theatrical competence of his performance. His fictitious sexlessness becomes an allegory for the professional self-
transcendence of the actor in performing his part, his ability to
become a man without qualities who conquers helpless, and
perhaps—like Pamphila—sleepy audiences by sacrificing his
personal and physical attributes. It is doubtless this histrionic
force of the eunuch device—neutered sign of an "empty" signifier (compare Viola's "blank" in Shakespeare's *Twelfth Night*),
namely the actor and his body—that contributed to its longevity
as theatrical *topos*. Like Aristophanes' Mnesilochus, Chaerea has
to be "trained," by his servant Parmeno, to adopt the disguise:
in his case not a cross-dressing but a self-un-dressing. Parmeno
emphasizes his master's natural disposition for the role, with
a hint at androgyny that suggests the young actor's necessary
ability—again in an all-male performance—to move readily
across all three genders (male, female, and neuter):

> *Parmeno.* Thou maist take [the eunuch's] clothes.
>
> *Chaerea.* His clothes! and what must I doe then afterwards?
>
> *Parmeno.* Marrie I will carrie in thee in stead of him to Thais.
>
> *Chaerea.* I heare you, tell on.
>
> *Parmeno.* And I will tell them that you are he.
>
> *Chaerea.* I perceiue well your meaning.
>
> *Parmeno.* . . . Besides your countenance, and also your age it selfe
> is such, that you may easily make them beleeue that you are the
> Eunuch.
>
> *Chaerea.* Its well spoken. I neuer knew better counsell giuen: there-
> fore goe to, let us goe in: and now doe on me the Eunuches apparrell,
> carrie me away, and bring me thither as soone as you can.
>
> (135)

Once he is disguised and engaged in his new part as Pamphila's
guard, Chaerea's performance takes on further theatrical implications, regarding the role of the audience as witness to all this.
His main activity as eunuch, namely that of guarding or ogling
his beloved in her toilette, becomes an unflattering icon of the
"male gaze,"[4] and thus of the masculine spectator as pornophi-
liac voyeur:

> *Chaerea.* One of the wenches came and said, Hoe thou Dorus, take
> this fanne, and make thus a little winde for this maide, whilest we

are washing . . . In the mean season, the maide falleth asleep. I looke a squint thus privily with the fanne, and I prie about to see to other things also, whether they were sure or no: I seeing this to be so, I boult the door.

(151)

As Paul Veyne notes, voyeurism is the social condition not only of the eunuch slave but of the slave *tout court* in ancient Rome: "with nothing else to guide them, slaves shared the values of their master, admired him, and served him jealously. Like voyeurs they watched him live his life with a mixture of admiration and scorn."[5] There is a more than a suggestion here that Terence's audience is complicit in a scopophiliac "enslavement" to vicarious sexual pleasure, ogling in turn the antics of Chaerea. And that the business of watching others "performing" (or at least representing) rape is potentially contagious. Chaerea himself is encouraged to take possession of the defenseless Pamphila when he beholds the visual representation of another and more authoritative act of sexual violence, Jove's rape of Danae:

Chaerea. . . . beholding a certaine table that was painted, whereupon this picture was, how Iupiter on a time (so men say) let fall into the lappe of Danae a golden showre, I my selfe also began to looke on it: and because now long agoe, hee had plaide the like pranke, I was much more glad, that God had changed himselfe into the shape of a man, and to haue come priuily through the tiles of other mens houses by a showre of raine to delude a woman.

(151)

Here the theatrical and the social coincide in holding a mirror or "table" up to the Roman community. In offering the spectacle of a Jovianly potent castrate, moreover, Terence seems to be dramatizing, and perhaps burlesquing, the Roman cult of self-mutilation as the supreme or "divine" form of sexual self-realization. "Self-denial," as Carlin Barton observes with reference to Roman culture,

becomes the culmination of the spiral of desire . . . Emasculation is, then, the ultimate price a man pays for lust, and he pays it voluntarily. . . . As a result, self-castration, what we would think of as an extreme act of asceticism or self-sacrifice, is often categorized as a form of self-indulgence by the Romans, and the castrated as extreme libertines.[6]

The paradox of the lascivious castrate—expressed in Quintilian's proverb "Libidinosior es quam ullus spado" ("You are more libidinous than any eunuch")[7]—is the expression of a society in a phase of political and moral decadence. Terence's rapist eunuch satirizes such decadence, and seems to preannounce the phenomenon that Keith Thompson defines as "political eunuchism," whereby eunuchs were to become paradoxically potent, and increasingly hated, as bureaucrats within the central administration of republican Rome, so much so as to lead eventually to the banning of castration as a source of social unrest.[8]

Thus, Terence's fake eunuch is a figure for social as well as sexual and theatrical intercourse, the more so since he knowingly exploits a particular form of symbolic interchange (prominent also in *Twelfth Night*), namely the giving of presents. In offering himself as a devirilized body, Chaerea becomes a literal exchange object within the master-slave economy that governed second-century republican Rome and that regulates the somewhat sordid world of the play. In an act of precipitous social self-relegation or -castration, Chaerea, at the suggestion of his own servant Parmeno, takes the place of the eunuch slave Dorus who has been given as a present to the courtesan Thais, owner of his beloved Pamphila (whom Thais has likewise received as a gift). Chaerea, doubly depersonalized as eunuch and slave, offers himself as one in a whole series of presents—jewels, money, as well as other servants—that the *bona meretrix* Thais, prototype of the kind-hearted whore,[9] receives in exchange for her desired favors:

> *Parmeno.* . . . a gift he [Thraso] on the other side hath brought to match this notwithstanding.
>
> *Chaerea.* What is it, I pray thee tell me truly.
>
> *Parmeno.* An eunuch.
>
> *Chaerea.* What I pray thee that foule ill fauoured wisened and effeminate fellow, which he bought yesterday.
>
> *Parmeno.* The same is he.
>
> *Chaerea.* . . . O the good fortune that this Eunuch hath, thats sent for a gift to be in this house! . . . he shall alwaies behold his fellow maide seruant that is of most excellent beautie, he shall talke with her, he shall be togither with her in one house, sometime he shall dine or suppe with her, and sometime he shall sleepe by her side.
>
> *Parmeno.* What would you say Cherea, if so be that you your selfe shoulde be made thus fortunate?
>
> *Chaerea.* How canst that be Parmeno? answer me.

Parmeno. Thou maist take his clothes. . . . Thus may you enjoy those commodities, which you said erewhile that he should haue: you may eate and drinke togither, you may be by her, you may touch her, you may dallie with her, you may sleepe by her side: because neuer one of them euer knew you, or can tell who you are.

(142)

Gift exchange becomes the play's central economic and semiotic paradigm. The governing social framework here would seem to be the one outlined in Marcel Mauss's classic 1925 essay on the gift, in which the French anthropologist states "that the spirit of gift-exchange is characteristic of societies that have passed the [archaic] phase of 'total prestation' but have not yet reached the stage of pure individual contract, the money market." In such postarchaic societies, the gift is the primary symbolic token of a reciprocal system that includes the exchange of "courtesies, banquets, rites, military performances, women, children, dances, feasts, fairs, of which economic negotiation is but one moment."[10]

Here lies the dazzling success of Chaerea's self-election to the status of gift. In a "natural" exchange economy suspended between archaic rites and modern market negotiation, an economy that levels the distinction between subjects, physical objects, and symbolic objects, Chaerea the gift item is able to exploit his zero subjectivity, his invisibility as *persona,* in order to fool the courtesan and her court. Terence figures the brutality of this economy in the very violence of Chaerea's return to malehood, as he possesses the sleeping Pamphila, herself deprived of rights, of personality, and of volition:

Pithyas. O what stirre hath the Eunuch made which thou gauest us! he hath deflowered the damsell which the Captaine bestowed on my mistres.

Phaedria. Thou art out of thy witts. How could an Eunuch doe this thing?

Pithyas. I know not who he was, this which he hath done, the thing it selfe will shewe.

(156)

The implications of the castration trope do not end with Chaerea, however. Cynthia Dessen observes, in her excellent article on Terence's play,[11] that the identity of the "eunuch" in *The Eunuch* is less univocal than it appears. Apart from the doubling or splitting of the castrate figure into the "real" eunuch Dorus

and his "fictional" other Chaerea, there are rival candidates for
the titular role: the *miles gloriosus* Thraso, presented as the
reverse of Chaerea, a sexual braggart lacking in actual sexuality
(*"Thraso.* [The king] befriends few men. *Gnatho.* None, I'd say,
if he befriends you"); the somewhat androgynous parasite Gnatho; the raped Pamphila, "castrated" of her freedom, her subjectivity, and her virginity; even the whore Thais, deprived of
citizenship and of political rights. Eunuchhood, as Dessen suggests, becomes the play's "controlling metaphor,"[12] whereby the
condition of sexual mutilation comes to stand for quite different
forms of social and psychological dispossession. The castration
topic thus becomes a kind of internal contagion or *contaminatio,* spreading out from the play's neutered center. As the
Pseudo-Servius observed in the ninth century, "This one as a
eunuch who deflowered the virgin is the principal subject-
matter in this comedy. If other persons are brought in, they are
subordinated to the eunuch, and all parts of the fable in some
way have reference to the eunuch."[13]

Terence's eunuch, therefore, is in all senses at the middle,
albeit a surgically mutilated middle, of a paradoxical system of
signification through opposition—minus for plus, loss for gain—
and establishes himself, or itself, as a successful dramatic *topos*
precisely because it is already a disfigured figure for social and
theatrical exchange as such, a metasemiotic vehicle that can be
resemanticized and rehistoricized in later contexts. This dia-
chronic transmission of the *topos* from Roman New Comedy
through to Elizabethan comedy, via—as we will see—the Italian
commedia, is itself a passing on of a *model* of exchange that is
progressively modified within the different historical and theatrical conditions to which it is subjected. But at the same time,
each recontextualization of the *topos* will bear the indelible
traces of the eunuch's own stage history.

2. Missing parts: Castration in the *Commedia*

As a result of his versatility and indeterminacy, Terence's fictional castrate turns out to be not only unexpectedly virile but
also hyperbolically fertile, disseminating late in life an almost
interminable series of sixteenth- and seventeenth-century prog-
eny. Indeed, it is fair to say that comedy as dramatic genre is
"reborn" in early modern Europe through the good offices of
castration. When reworked within the Italian Renaissance

commedia, however, the eunuch *topos* is drastically modified, or in Freudian terms, further castrated, in that Terence's disguised male is more often than not transformed into a cross-dressed female, the mimesis of the unmanned into the mimesis of a (non-)man. This change is in part due to altered theatrical circumstances, since in certain performances of the erudite comedy in the Italian courts and academies female roles were performed by actresses rather than boy actors. But it is also a measure of a radically changed social context: the exchange system within which the disguise operates is no longer the master-slave economy of republican Rome but the mercantile economy of early modern Italy, with its burgeoning individualism, its power struggles between rival city states, and its new codification of civility and courtesy.

The Renaissance legacy of Terence's *Eunuchus* is twofold. It serves as a model for any number of disguise plots from which the "real" and/or "feigned" eunuch as such have disappeared. But at the same time, the *eunuchus* survives as a powerful verbal and stage trope within disguise comedy itself. This double legacy corresponds to Louise Clubb's definition of Renaissance dramatic *contaminatio:* "Constant as a principle from the time of Ariosto on was construction by contamination, the mediated and usually explicit combination of pre-texts. But in addition to the mere fusion of borrowed plots, this demanded the interchange and transformation of units, figures, relationships, actions, *topoi,* and framing patterns."[14]

As Clubb suggests, Ariosto is the first Italian dramatist to use *contaminatio* both in the form of "borrowed plots" and in the form of "figures" and *"topoi."* The prologue to *I suppositi* (1509)—which, together with the same author's *La cassaria* (1508), is the first example of "regular" vernacular comedy— proudly declares its debt to the Terentian model ("From Terence's *Eunuch* . . . the author has drawn part of the argument"), although it is mainly the secondary Thraso plot that Ariosto borrows and adapts. The castration *topos* is itself "disguised" and displaced to other parts of the play, notably Filogono's story of being robbed during his sea voyage from Catania to Ferrara. Here is George Gascoigne's 1566 version of Filogono's maritime mishap:

Philogano. Jesus! How often they untrussed my male, and ransacked a little capcase that I had, tossed and turned all that was within it, searched my bosom, yea, my breeches, that I assure you I thought

they would have flayed me to search between the fell and the flesh
for farthings.[15]

Filogono's untrussed male and little ransacked capcase figure
the robbery as a mode of rape ("searched . . . my breeches") but
also as a form of physical disfigurement ("flayed me alive"),
which suggests the main metaphorical force that castration will
take on in Italian comedy, namely material deprivation. Just as
they suggest a significant shift in the primary object of "castration" itself in Renaissance comedy: no longer the surgically removed testicles of the ancient eunuch slave but the absent or
truncated phallus of modern psychosexual fantasy.

A key text in the transmission of the castration topic in its
"phallic" guise, and indeed in the development of Renaissance
comedy in general, is the first modern cross-dressing play, Bibbiena's *La Calandria*. First performed at Urbino in February
1513 during the city festivities, the comedy is intimately connected with the development of a humanistic culture of courtesy. Indeed its author, Cardinal Bernardo Dovizi da Bibbiena, is
one of the speakers in Castiglione's *Il Cortegiano*, set in the
Urbino ducal palace where *La Calandria* probably had its first
performance. Castiglione is also credited with writing the prologue to the comedy.[16]

The "Urbino" connection between the new Renaissance *civiltà*
and the new Renaissance *commedia* is quite explicit. In the
second book of *Il Cortegiano*, Bibbiena makes a long speech on
the subject of laughter, which he defends as the distinctive feature of human nature, and of which theatrical performance is
a legitimate source: "this laughing is perceived only in a man . . .
For which cause we see men have invented manie matters as
sportes, games and pastimes, and so many sundrie sortes of
open shewes . . . great Theaters, and other publicke buildinges,
and there to shew new devices of pastimes."[17] Bibbiena goes on
to establish the proper modes and limits of laughter for the
courtier, a decorum of jokes. Bibbiena's speech makes explicit
what Wayne A. Rebhorn describes as "the theater metaphors
structuring Castiglione's view of the world and of his ideal courtier," who "produces an endless series of brilliant performances,
pausing only long enough to exchange one mask for another."[18]
The relationship between court and theater is thus bilateral: if
the ideal courtier is a performer, the performance of comedy can
likewise embody courtly ideals.

In practice, despite "Castiglione"'s defense of the play in the prologue, *La Calandria* seems far removed from the courtly refinement of the Urbino palace, and its own central joke is anything but decorously polite. Derived from a *contaminatio* of Terence, Plautus (*Menaechmi*) and Boccaccio, the comedy's plot centers on different-sex twins and on two-way transvestism. The twins, Lidio and Santilla, separated at birth, grow up apart, and while Lidio spends his time searching for his sister, the latter, by way of self-defense, disguises herself as her brother, whom she believes dead. Cross-dressing here combines with cross-desire: Lidio falls in love with Fulvia, wife of the foolish Calandro, and in order to gain entry into Fulvia('s house) dresses as a woman. Here lies Bibbiena's most immediate debt to *Eunuchus*. Calandro, meanwhile, falls in love with the cross-dressed Lidio. Fulvia likewise cross-dresses in order to go to Lidio. Inevitably, Santilla is mistaken for her transvestite twin, and is taken to the appointment with Fulvia. Thus, a transvestite woman has an amorous encounter with another woman whom she takes to be the cross-dressed man who, at the same time, is the object of her husband's desire.

It is Fulvia's erotic (dis)appointment with Santilla that brings the castration theme to the surface. Stunned at her discovery of Lidio's missing link, Fulvia blames the go-between necromancer Ruffo:

> *Fulvia.* Alas! you have transformed my Lidio from male to female. I've handled and touched everything; but cannot find any of the usual things except his external appearance [*presenzia*]. And I don't weep so much for the privation of my pleasure as for the damage done to him, who, for me, finds himself without that which one most desires. . . . But if you give me back my Lidio whole, my money and goods are yours.
>
> *Ruffo.* . . . to avoid misunderstandings, say exactly what you want.
>
> *Fulvia.* The first thing, that you restore to him the knife of my sheath, you understand?
>
> *Ruffo.* Perfectly.[19]

Fulvia registers the shock of the absent phallus, thereby perceiving female sexuality, in classic Freudian terms, as a lack (her being dressed as a boy underlines the point.)[20] Herein lies the comedy's own link with *Il Cortegiano*. The play dramatizes relations not only between the sexes, but between genders, and defines the female primarily in terms of missing or lost masculinity. At the same time it offers opposing models of female behavior in relation to this lack. The cross-dressed Fulvia's frenetic search for the phallus is a perfect anticipation of Pallavicino's thesis regarding women's erotic overcompensation for their "imperfection." Santilla, on the contrary, expresses her femininity through the self-abnegation that will be championed by Castiglione's Gonzaga, using her masculine disguise as a mode of self-protection and as a reinvocation of her lost brother.

Between the two genders lies an indeterminate middle ground, that of the eunuch (Santilla as unmanned Lidio) or alternatively of the hermaphrodite. Santilla's servant Fannio leads the necromancer Ruffo to believe his mistress is double-sexed, able to adopt whichever organ proves appropriate to the occasion:

> *Fannio.* You should know that my master Lidio is a hermaphrodite. [*ermafrodito*]
>
> *Ruffo.* And what does this flowering shit [*merdafiorito*] mean?
>
> *Fannio.* Hermaphrodite, I say. . . . Hermaphrodites are those that have both sexes . . . with Fulvia he will use only the female sex for that which, she having requested in form of a woman, and finding him a woman, will give such faith to the spirit that she will adore you.
>
> (69)

So, in a sense, it turns out: the revirilized Lidio takes the place of Santilla in Fulvia's bed, but when they are caught *in flagrante* by Calandro, Santilla saves her brother by resubstituting (re-"castrating") him. Like Aristophanes' split hermaphroditic halves, the twins finally come together and recognize each other.

The threat or promise of castration is disseminated throughout the play. The gulling of Calandro is figured in the vivid verbal and stage image of a trunk (*forziero:* Gascoigne's "male") in which he is to hide in order, so he believes, to be conducted to his beloved Lidio-Santilla. In a surreal apocalyptic fantasy, Calandro's servant Fessenio warns him that to get a man to fit in a trunk, certain bodily parts have to be amputated, as happens with stowaways on ships:

> *Fessenio.* They don't fit if you don't cut off their hands, arms and legs according to need. . . . Then once you get into the port, anyone who wants to takes back his member and screws it back on, it often happens that inadvertently or maliciously, someone takes another's member and puts it where he likes best; and sometimes it doesn't work out because he takes a member which is bigger than his own."
>
> (44)

Fessenio's sadistic surgical delirium imagines cuckoldry as evi-ration: Calandro's amputated organ will be replaced by "a mem-ber which is bigger than his own." The servant underlines the point later when he takes his master to an appointment with a prostitute:

> *Fessenio.* I'll go and unite the castrated sheep [*castron* = fool] with the sow [*troia* = whore].
>
> (52)

And the gull himself is later forced to admit "Oh what a simple-ton/castrated sheep [*castron*] am I!" (73).

La Calandria is a comedy of the disappearing member. And while it might seem surprising that a cardinal and leading court-ier should engage with such dubious material, it is clear that the play's variations on the missing phallus serve Bibbiena pri-marily as a source of discursive energy and wit. The sexual in-trigues are conducted with the same *sprezzatura* and witty lightness of touch that characterizes the discourse on laughter attributed to Bibbiena by Castiglione. Indeed, the back-and-forth vicissitudes of the hidden, absent, or amputated organ coincide with the to-and-fro of verbal interchange itself, so much so that "castration" may be said to empower speech in the play. Here again, therefore, the *castrato topos* becomes synonymous with social exchange, the means whereby the court stages its own "sweete conversation" ("never so tasted in other place" than in Castiglione's and Bibbiena's Urbino) as the ideal expression of modern civilization. And the means whereby drama itself, espe-cially comic drama, negotiates its rights to representation within this civilization.

The *Calandria* story, with its separated twins (and the pre-sumed death of the male twin), cross-dressed heroines, and erotic confusions, "contains" Shakespeare's *Twelfth Night,* just as it contains the plots of the majority of Renaissance disguise and transvestite comedies, including Machiavelli's *Clizia* (1525) with its substitution of a cross-dressed servant for the heroine in the bed of the lecherous old Nicomaco, and including likewise what appears at first sight an "anti-Bibbienian" burlesque, Pietro Aretino's *La Cortigiana* (also 1525). Aretino presents a corrupt and whore-ridden Rome in which the ingenuous Venetian Maco arrives, determined to become a courtier and cardinal *à la* Bib-biena. He falls prey to the painter Andrea, who promises to in-struct him in the arts of the court. Andrea's lesson on the

qualities of *Il Cortegiano* satirizes the "civilizing" process of the
court, presenting it as a disguise for moral decadence and sexual depravity:

> *Andrea.* The main thing the courtier has to know is how to swear,
> how to play cards, how to be envious, how to be a whoremonger
> (*puttaniere*), a heretic, an adulator, a gossip, an ingrate, an ignora-
> mus, an ass, how to lie, how to be effeminate (*far la ninfa*—literally,
> play the nymph) and how to be active and passive (*agente e paziente*).
>
> *Maco.* Slow down. What does active and passive mean? I don't under-
> stand this lingo.
>
> *Andrea.* It means wife and husband.
>
> *Maco.* I think I get it.[21]

Andrea's depiction of courtly gentility as a "feminizing" mode of
androgyny and bisexuality (active and passive, wife and husband) is the thematic key to the play's double plot, which on
the one hand has Maco "courting" Camilla Pisana, a true
cortigiana, and on the other the vain Parabolano pursuing another lady, Laura. Maco is punished for his absurd aspiration by
a "Spaniard"—Andrea in disguise—who abuses him physically,
allowing him ironically to achieve the supposed "wife and husband" status of the courtier. Expecting to become the active
"husband" of Camilla he becomes instead the passive "wife," being ritually sodomized and cut by the fake Spaniard's sword:

> *Maco.* I'm dead. Escape, escape, the Spaniards have made a hole in
> my behind with their sword: where shall I go? where shall I flee?
> where shall I hide? . . . The Spaniards have cut me to pieces.[22]

Parabolano's Laura, meantime, is substituted by a whore, Togna:
Aretino plays here on the two related meanings of *cortigiana*
already present in early-sixteenth-century Italy, namely the *cortigiana onesta,* or lady of the court, and the plain *cortigiana* or
whore.[23] But in this plot too the "wife and husband" trope is
dominant. In order to escape the wrath of her violently jealous
husband Arcolano, Togna runs off in his clothes, leaving him no
choice but to put on Togna's attire, and thus forcing him in turn
to become the "wife" and to be ridiculed in public.

The comedy appears to be a ferocious attack on the "wife and
husband" values of the court and of the church (the accusation
of clerical sodomy is blatant in an exchange between a pedantic
sexton and an unlatinate fisherman who interprets 'homo' as

a self-description by the priest: "SEXTON Et homo factus est. FISHERMAN Oh, sodomites!"). But it might equally be viewed as a confirmation of the civility of the "real" court and of the "real" *cortigiana,* since neither Camilla nor Laura ever appear on stage, and only their vain would-be courtiers, or their substitute courtesans, are punished. The "sodomizing" and "castrating" of Maco is in this sense a means of purging aristocratic *cortiziania* of contaminating alien elements.

Aretino's later comedy *Il Marescalco* [The stablemaster] (1533) is set instead in a "real" court, the ducal court of Mantua, and involves "real" (male) *cortigiani.* The duke himself sets in motion a plot—contaminated from Terence's *Eunuchus,* Plautus's *Casina,* and Machiavelli's *Clizia*—in which his misogynistic and misogamistic (and probably pederastic) stablemaster is punished by being "married" to a cross-dressed boy.[24] The play is thus on one level an aristocratic entertainment at the expense of a lower-class figure, and an assertion of the duke's absolute power as both director and principal spectator of the practical joke, forcing the stablemaster to make a public spectacle of his "deviant" private life. At the same time, however, the *beffa* against the stablemaster expresses anxieties concerning female sexuality and the assimilation of women within what is presented as a primarily homosocial community. The only women present, apart from a single "Lady" (*Gentildonna*) spectator, are the stablemaster's nurse and other servants. The all-male "marriage" parodies, within the court, the relationship between the cavalier and his catamite page, and, within Mantua at large, a society depicted—if only by the Pedant—as a new Sodom:

> *Pedant.* These temerarious adolescents, these effeminate Ganymedes[25] are degrading *istam urbem clarissimam* (this illustrious town); the treasures of Virgilian letters are succumbing to these shameless criminals and brazen sodomites. . . . *Me taedet,* it grieves me that the renowned city of Mantua *me genuit, id est Vergilius Maro,* is full of hermaphrodites.[26]

The Pedant's complaint is in a sense confirmed, and turned against him, when the "little catamite" page "sodomizes" him by tying fireworks to his back and setting light to them. The duke's practical joke acts out an analogous assault; the disguised Carlo is encouraged by the single "Lady" to "penetrate" the reluctant stablemaster with a French kiss:

Lady. Remember to stick your tongue in his mouth, for that's what the Duke desires.

Carlo. I shan't forget.

(103)

He does not forget:

Count. (to stablemaster) Come on, kiss her.

Giannicco. A hit.

Stablemaster. A French kiss [*la lingua*], eh? I'm dressed up for a feast. May God make her a martyr, because neither God nor his mother can make her a virgin. Oh horns, I couldn't escape your sad company. Too bad.

(110)

Carlo's natural disposition to play this part—as androgynous youth, presumably one of the "hermaphrodites" loathed by the Pedant—clearly recalls Chaerea's physical and actorial readiness for his eunuch role, just as his delight at his change of gender reworks Chaerea's glee at his performance as castrate:

Carlo. I'm a miracle-worker, and from male I've become female. Ha, ha! The stablemaster has to give me the ring! Ha, ha, ha!

Matron. Good heavens, everyone would believe that you really were a girl, judging by your airs, your language, and the way you walk. Ha, ha!

Lady. By the holy cross, you're right! I can assure you that his cheeks didn't need any make-up.

(102)

As in *Eunuchus,* moreover, the category of the "castrate" is mobile. If it is Carlo who is called upon to surrender his masculinity through the "miracle" of his performance, this loss of manhood then "infects" (by means of the French kiss?) the stablemaster himself who, in a desperate last attempt to avoid marriage, claims to be physically incapable of sex, and thus unsuited to matrimony:

Stablemaster. Don't upset me, I'll tell you why I can't take her.

Count. Why?

Stablemaster. I'm all open [*sono aperto*].

Cavalier. Close yourself if you're open, ha ha! . . .

Pedant. Spectabili viro domino Marescalco placet vobis does it please you to take for your bride, wife, woman and companion—

Stablemaster. Didn't I tell you I can't, because I'm open.

Giannicco. Nonsense, he's completely closed up [*chiusissimo*].

(110)

The stablemaster's "open" is itself semantically open or ambiguous: he seems to be claiming to have an open hernia or rupture that has rendered him impotent and so unfit for marriage, but his "confession" might be read as an admission of sodomy (he has been "opened," *aperto*). And when he discovers the duke's trick, he is prompted to a further public confession, namely of being a castrate or gull:

Stablemaster. Oh what a gelding [*castrone*], what an ox, what a buffalo, what a fool am I, it's Carlo the page, ha ha!

(110)

The stablemaster's sense of relief and release at discovering he is a *castrone,* and not a husband, underlines the fact that, unlike *Eunuchus,* the play's dominant force is not desire but its specular image, namely revulsion. In this homosocial context, women are perceived as a repugnant Other, heterosexual relations as perilous and marriage as a perverse mode of self-punishment. The stablemaster, the most virile character in the play because uneffeminized by contact with the opposite sex, represents matrimony as a form of financial as well as sexual loss, and women as repulsive leaky vessels (their sexual organs good only for devouring and urinating):

Stablemaster. Wives are merchandise [*mercanzie*] on which you lose one hundred percent.

Count. Yours isn't the kind of woman who pierces her ears. She is not one of those.

Stablemaster. If she pisses [*piscia*] like the others, she must be one of those.[27]

(96)

The metonymic chain here linking piercing with pissing with the female sex organ with loss of money reproduces the stablemaster's circular nightmare of the phallus-castrating woman as bankrupting commodity. But his friend Ambrogio, sent to persuade him to marry, presents an even more catastrophic ac-

count, figuring wedlock as rape, robbery, and destruction/
penetration:

> *Ambrogio*. The devastation of Rome and Florence was mild com-
> pared with the way they demolish, flatten, and plunge into [*profon-*
> *dano*] their wretched trusting husbands.

(61)

The duke's plot puts these misogynistic visions into double effect, forcing the stablemaster to admit a humiliating loss of
"manhood" and subjecting him to the devastating assault of a
penetrative "woman."

Il Marescalco offers two social variations on the castration
topos: heterosexual bonding is represented as material deprivation and as political and military rape. While the stablemaster
fears the total erosion of his money, identified with his phallus,
Ambrogio's comparison of marriage with "the devastation of
Rome and Florence" reminds the audience of the most violent
events in recent Italian political history: the sack of Rome (1527)
and the siege of Florence (1530), both perpetrated by the "penetrative" troops of Emperor Charles V. The sack of Rome, in particular, in which German soldiers besieged the Papal stronghold
of Castel Sant'Angelo before being forced to withdraw due to the
plague, was perhaps the most traumatic event in early modern
Italian history, and is described by Aretino himself in the *Sei
giornate* (1534) precisely as the mass rape of nuns by the invad-
ing soldiers, caused by the Pope's sodomistic predilections. As
James Grantham Turner has commented,

> The "public" realm of the Sack and the 'private' realm of sexuality
> invade one another. The violated woman became a figure for the
> devastation of the city, while the Sack itself was conceived in sexual
> terms; before and after the event, Rome was represented as a new
> Sodom destroyed on account of the pope's affairs with men.[28]

3. Just impediment: Jonson's *Epicoene*

However one reads *Il Marescalco*—whether as a satirical "exorcising" of pederasty or as an exercise in misogyny—Aretino's
transformation of the castration *topos* can only be understood
in terms of a crucial structural characteristic of early Renaissance Italy: the new dominance of a monetary economy. We are

no longer in the realm of Mauss's postarchaic "natural" economy of gift exchange, but in that of a predominantly modern economy of mercantile transaction.[29] Renaissance Italy is a society of *mercatores* in which the circulation and accumulation of money gives rise to a social mobility unparalleled in the rest of Europe.[30] As Richard Goldthwaite comments, "Italian society was subject to a dynamic of change unlike that of any other in Europe. Elsewhere, wealth was predominantly in land and therefore less subject to instability, it was largely in the hands of a closed caste that experienced less mobility."[31] "Elsewhere" means above all England, a society not of Italian *mercatores* but of English *possessores,* a rigidly hierarchical order, dominated by landowners, with consequently less circulation of wealth and less mobility.[32]

This difference in the socioeconomic order is reflected in what is probably the most direct descendant of *Eunuchus* in English, Jonson's *Epicoene* (1609), a revisitation of Terence's comedy, contaminated with *Casina, Clizia,* and above all Aretino's *Marescalco. Epicoene,* first performed by the Children of Her Majesty's Revels at Whitefriars, reworks the duke of Mantua's prank against his stablemaster in the form of the marrying-a-boy trick played by Dauphine on his uncle Morose, although Dauphine's motives are not aristocratic *divertimento* but economic self-interest, namely the saving of his inheritance. What is at stake in the context of Jonson's Jacobean England is not loss of face or even loss of liquid capital but loss of land. Morose's will decrees his nephew's eviration through permanent dispossession, and Dauphine's revenge takes the appropriate form of the unmanning of Morose's will, in all its Jacobean senses.

Jonson also varies the stablemaster's obsessive misogyny in Morose's pathological aversion to noise. Which, however, turns out to be the same thing since "noise" is identified primarily with female verbal incontinence. From Terence, via Aretino, Jonson inherits the trope of castration as social epidemic: not the political corruption of Rome or the universal sodomy of Mantua[33] but the generalized gender reversal that afflicts contemporary London, peopled by effeminized men like Otter (the otter being a indeterminate *"animal amphibium,"* neither flesh nor fish) and virilized women such as the domineering Mistress Otter or Madame Centaure (an equally emblematic hybrid [male] creature with rapist proclivities) and her virile coterie of collegiate ladies.

The play's transvestite plot, presided over by the ominously named Cutbeard, who finds Morose a silent "wife," enacts such reversals through the exchange of the play's floating signifier, the phallus. Morose is obliged, in order to avoid a loquacious wife, to make a public confession before the phallic ladies of his congenital (or perhaps nongenital) lack of attributes:[34]

> *Morose.* Ladies, I must crave all your pardons—. . . For a wrong I have done to your whole sex, in marrying this fair and virtuous gentlewoman—. . . Being guilty of an infirmity, which, before I conferred with these learned men, I thought I might have concealed— . . . I am no man ladies.
>
> *All.* How! . . .
>
> *Morose.* Utterly unabled in nature, by reason of frigidity, to perform the duties, or any the least office of a husband.
>
> *Mavis.* Now out upon him, prodigious creature!
>
> *Centaure.* Bridegroom uncarnate!
>
> *Haughty.* And would you offer it, to a young gentlewoman?
>
> *Mrs. Otter.* A lady of her longings?
>
> (5.4.31–48)[35]

Morose's confession of his "uncarnate" state coincides with the relinquishing of his financial means, as he is contemporarily obliged to restore Dauphine's inheritance and pay him an allowance. The floating phallus passes, meanwhile, to the other side of the gender divide, when Morose's "wife" is discovered to be in possession of the very attributes he claims to be missing.

With respect to his sources, Jonson elaborates the theme of impotence with sadistic or masochistic rhetorical gusto in the fake doctors' pseudo-legal cataloging of all the male sexual pathologies that can lead to the annulling of marriage, from excessive development (elephantiasis) to childlike underdevelopment (with a probable glance at the prepubescent actors of Her Majesty's Revels) to various kinds of organic dysfunction:

> *Cutbeard.* [*Disguised as a canon lawyer*]. The twelfth and last is *si forte coire nequibus* [if it chances that you are unable to copulate].
>
> *Otter.* [*Disguised as a divine*]. Ay, that is *impedimentum gravissimum*. It doth utterly annul and annihilate, that. If you have a *manifestam frigiditatem*, you are well, sir.
>
> *Truewit.* Why, there is comfort come at length, sir. Confess yourself but a man unable, and she will sue to be divorced first.
>
> *Otter.* Ay, or if there be *morbus perpetuus et insanabilis*; as *paralysis, elephantiasis,* or so—

Dauphin. O, but *frigiditas* is the fairer way, gentlemen.

Otter. You say troth, sir, and as it is in the canon, master doctor. . . . That 'a boy, or child, under years, is not fit for marriage, because he cannot *reddere debitum*' [render what is required]. So your *omnipotentes—*

Truewit. [*Aside to* Otter]. Your *impotentes,* you whoreson lobster!

Otter. Your *impotentes,* I should say, are *minime apti ad contra-henda matrimonium* [least suited to contracting marriages].

(5.3.163–79)

The overall sociosexual panorama that emerges, with its rich typology of real or false male *impotentes* and castrating female *omnipotentes,* is less than reassuring for male members (in various senses) of the audience. Indeed, as Laura Levine has observed, Jonson, like the Puritan antitheatricalists, seems to associate theatrical performance itself with eviration, and specifically eviration of the spectator. Thus, Truewit's insistent adoption of castration threats toward Daw and La Foole—"Well, I'll try if he will be appeased with a leg or an arm. . . . Why, if he will be satisfied with a thumb or a little finger, all's one to me" (4.5.112–16)—within a secondary gulling plot that Truewit himself presents explicitly as a theatrical display ("here will I act such a tragicomedy" [4.5.27]) bodes ill for the audience. As Levine comments, "theatre per se is being identified with this impulse toward dismemberment, this very real capacity to diminish the spectator."[36] The dismemberment threat is in a sense fulfilled in the play's denouement, since Jonson, unlike Terence and Aretino, has kept his spectators in the dark regarding Dauphine's trick until the very end, thereby leaving them as disarmed as Morose himself. Ay, that is *impedimentum gravissimum.*

Notes

A differently focused, and substantially longer, treatment of this topic appears in my article "The Fertile Eunuch: *Twelfth Night,* Early Modern Intercourse, and the Fruits of Castration," *Shakespeare Quarterly* 47 (Spring 1996): 1–36.

1. *See* Douglass Parker, introduction to *The Eunuch,* in *Terence: The Comedies,* Palmer Bovie, ed. (Baltimore: Johns Hopkins University Press, 1974), 147–53, 153.

2. Aline Rousselle, *Porneia: On Desire and the Body in Antiquity* (Oxford: Blackwell, 1984), 122. Martial (*Epigrams,* Book 9, page 7) claims that "The boy, mutilated by the grasping slave-dealer's art, does not lament the loss of

his ravished manhood," but also describes (9, 20) how Cybele's priests drown the chosen infant's cries with their clashing weapons (trans. Walter C. A. Ker, Loeb Classical Library [Cambridge: Harvard University Press, 1961]).

3. Richard Bernard, *Terence in English: Fabulae comici facetissimi et elegantissimi poetae Terentii* (Cambridge, 1598), 151–52.

4. On the "male gaze," *see* Laura Mulvey's classic essay, "Visual Pleasure and Narrative Cinema," *Screen,* vol. 16, no. 3 (1975): 6–18, and Barbara Freedman's excellent discussion of the "Lacanian" gaze in relation to theater and feminism in "Frame-up: Feminism, Psychoanalysis, Theatre," *Theatre Journal,* vol. 40, no. 3 (1988): 375–97 (now in *Staging the Gaze: Psychoanalysis and Shakespearean Comedy* [Ithaca: Cornell University Press, 1991]).

5. Paul Veyne, "Slavery," in *From Pagan Rome to Byzantium,* ed. Paul Veyne, vol. 1 of *A History of Private Life,* eds. Phillippe Ariès and Georges Duby, trans. Arthur Goldhammer (Cambridge: Harvard University Press, 1987), 63.

6. Carlin A. Barton, *The Sorrows of the Ancient Romans: The Gladiator and the Monster* (Princeton: Princeton University Press, 1993), 72–73.

7. Barton, *Sorrows of the Ancient Romans,* 72. The proverb is from Quintilian, *Institutiones oratoriae,* 6.3.64. Compare the denunciations of Juvenal in *Satire 8:* "You will find [the legate] lying cheek by jowl beside an assassin, enjoying the company of sailors, thieves and runaway slaves . . . on his left the silent drums of a sprawling eunuch priest *[et resupinati cessantia tympana galli].* Here is liberty Hall," *The Satires,* trans. Niall Rudd (Oxford: Clarendon Press, 1991), 173. Basil of Ancyra in the fourth-century *De virginitate* warns virgins not to trust eunuchs—those castrated in adulthood "burn with greater and less restrained desire for sexual union, and . . . not only do they feel this ardour, but they think they can defile any woman they meet without risk," quoted by Rousselle, *Porneia,* 123.

8. Keith Thompson, *Conquerors and Slaves: Sociological Studies in Roman History* (Cambridge: Cambridge University Press, 1978), 175–97.

9. The stereotype of the whore with a heart of gold is largely a Terentian invention. *See* Giulia Dwora, "The Concept of the Bona Meretrix: A Study of Terence's Courtesans," *Rivista di Filologia e di Istruzione Classica* 108 (1980): 142–65. Bernard translates Terence's meretrix as "a light huswife."

10. Marcel Mauss, *The Gift: Forms and Functions of Exchange in Archaic Societies,* trans. Ian Cunnison (New York: W.W. Norton, 1967), 45 and 160–63. In a stimulating recent essay, Mark Thornton Burnett applies Mauss's exchange model directly to Elizabethan society and to Shakespeare's *Love's Labour's Lost* ["Giving and Receiving: *Love's Labour's Lost* and the Politics of Exchange," *English Literary Renaissance* 23 (1993): 287–313.] However, whether Mauss's model is directly applicable to early modern England is questionable. As Patricia Fumerton suggests, Elizabethan England "constituted itself not as something akin to septs in 'primitive culture,' but as precisely the 'civilized' state that suppresses the merely 'primitive' . . . system of total prestation" ("Exchanging Gifts: The Elizabethan Currency of Children and Poetry," *ELH* 53 [1986], 241–79; 246). On Mauss's theory, *see also* Peter M. Blau, *Exchange and Power in Social Life* (New York: Wiley, 1964); Pierre Bourdieu, *Outline of a Theory of Practice,* trans. Richard Nice (Cambridge: Cambridge University Press, 1977); Jean-Christophe Agnew, *Worlds Apart: The Market and the Theatre in Anglo-American Thought, 1550–1750* (Cambridge: Cambridge University Press, 1986).

11. Cynthia Dessen, "The Figure of the Eunuch in Terence's *Eunuchus,*"

Helios (forthcoming). I am very grateful to Professor Dessen for the opportunity to read her important article in typescript and to exchange ideas with her about the play and its heritage.

12. Ibid.

13. *Terentius cum quinque comentis,* quoted in T.W. Baldwin, *Shakespeare's Five-Act Structure* (Urbana: University of Illinois Press, 1947), 80.

14. Louise George Clubb, *Italian Drama in Shakespeare's Time* (New Haven: Yale University Press, 1989), 6. *See also* Leo Salingar, *Shakespeare and the Traditions of Comedy* (Cambridge: Cambridge University Press, 1974).

15. George Gascoigne, *Supposes* (1566), in *Five Pre-Shakespearean Comedies,* ed. Frederick S. Boas (London: Oxford University Press, 1934), 313. In his first prose version, Ariosto has "quante volte aperto m'hanno il forziero che ho meco in barca, e quella valigia, e rouersciato, e uoltimi sottosopra cio ch'ho dentro, nella tasca me hanno uoluto uedere, e cercare nel seno, io dubitai qualche uolta non mi scorticassero per uedere se tra carne e pelle hauero robba da datio." (*Comedia di Lodovico Ariosto intitolato Gli soppositi,* Venice, 1525, xxxiii^r). The ambiguous theme words here are *"forziero"* (coffer), *"valigia"* (case), *"cio ch'ho dentro"* (what I have inside), and *"tasca"* (pocket). The verb *"scorticare,"* literally "to skin (an animal)"—Gascoigne's "flayed me"—has the extended meaning "to cut." In his second version, in verse, Ariosto adds the modifier *"piccolo"—"un forzier piccolo,"* Gascoigne's "little capcase"—to underline the ambiguous referentiality of the narrative (*I suppositi comedia di M. Lodovico Ariosto. da lui medesimo riformata, e ridotta in versi*). Gascoigne hammers the point home with his pun on "male" (bag or masculinity, the former being the sign of the latter). On the theme of castration in George Gascoigne's own poetry, with reference to his career as courtier poet, *see* Richard McCoy, "Gascoigne's 'Poëmata castrata': The Wages of Courtly Success," *Criticism* 27 (1985): 29–55.

16. Giorgio Padoan has suggested that "Castiglione"'s prologue is really by Bibbiena himself. *See* Louise George Clubb, "Castiglione's Humanistic Art and Renaissance Drama," in *Castiglione: The Ideal and the Real in Renaissance Culture,* eds. Robert W. Hanning and David Rosand (New Haven: Yale University Press, 1983), 191–208.

17. Castiglione, 137.

18. Wayne A. Rebhorn, "Spectacles in a Courtly Theater," in *Courtly Performances: Masking and Festivity in Castiglione's* Book of the Courtier (Detroit: Wayne State University Press, 1978), 23–52, 25; on drama and performance in *Il Cortegiano, see also* Louise George Clubb, "Castiglione's Humanistic Art and Renaissance Drama."

19. Bibbiena (Bernardo Dovizi), *La Calandria,* ed. Paolo Fossati (Turin: Einaudi, 1967), 76–77; my translation.

20. *See* Freud's account of the little boy who discovers his mother's or sister's missing phallus: "It is self-evident to a male child that a genital like his own is to be attributed to everyone he knows, and he cannot make its absence tally with his picture of other people" (*Three Essays on Sexuality: II. Infantile Sexuality,* Translated and newly edited by James Strachey [New York: Basic Books, 1979]), 60.

21. Pietro Aretino, *Tutte le commedie,* ed. G.B. De Sanctis, Milan: Mursia [1968], 214; my translation.

22. On the loss of the phallus as punishment in the comedy, *see* Giudeo's curse "May your prick get cancer (*Cancaro a la falla*)," *Tutte le commedie,* 284.

23. On the distinction between "honest" courtesans and prostitutes, *see* Paul Larivaille, *La vie quotidienne des courtisanes en Italie au temps de la Renaissance: Rome et Venise, XVᵉ et XVIᵉ siècles* (Paris: Hachette, 1975), 32–35.

24. Aretino's closest adaptation of *Eunuchus* is *La Talanta* (1537), in which the courtesan Talanta—directly modeled on Terence's Thais—is courted by three *innamorati*: the earnest young Orfinio (the Phaedria role), the *miles gloriosus* Captain Tinca (Thraso), and the old Venetian miser Vergolo (Aretino's addition). In a hectic reworking of Terence's present-giving rites, Talanta receives a gift from each suitor—from Orfinio a necklace, from Tinca a slave girl, who in reality is the cross-dressed Antino, and from Vergolo a Turkish male slave who in reality is the cross-dressed Lucilla, Antino's sister. The extraordinarily complex plot of interwoven desires, both heterosexual and homosexual (for example Armileo's love for Antino), is further complicated when another cross-dressed girl, Oretta—who turns out to be sister of the other two "slaves"—is mistaken for Antino. Aretino here reduces the transvestism device *ad absurdum,* producing a grotesque excess of gender exchanges that leads the comedy to a kind of entropic implosion. As Giulio Ferroni affirms, "Aretino works in the direction of a multiplication that does not aim explicitly and consciously to contest the [Terentian] model·. . . but in the end the thickening of the plot translates into disintegration, into a position of negativity" (*Le voci dell'istrione: Pietro Aretino e la dissoluzione del teatro,* Naples: Liguori [1977], 221) The eunuch topic is lexicalized in the comedy in association with Talanta's profession—in the opening scene she hypothesizes unemployment due to male impotence: "if the hammer didn't work, we could shut up shop." (Pietro Aretino, *Tutte le commedie,* ed. G.B. De Sanctis, Milan: Mursia [1968], 345; my translation)—and with the age of her suitor Vergolo: as Orfinio's companion Pizio observes to her, "Old men are eunuchs [*eunuchi*] due to time," 363. The play's derivation and departures from Terence are raised explicitly by Orfinio's disclaimer to Talanta: "I who am not Thais's Phaedria," 365.

25. *See* Rosalynd's choice of "Ganymede" as male pseudonym in *As You Like It,* Arden edition, ed. Agnes Latham (London: Methuen, 1975): 1.3.121; and Stephen Orgel's comments on the name as Renaissance synonym of "homosexual" in "Nobody's Perfect: Or Why did the English Take Boys for Women?," *South Atlantic Quarterly* 88 (1989): 7–29.

26. Pietro Aretino, *Tutte le commedie,* 67; my translation.

27. Compare Malvolio's "unconscious" reduction of Olivia's sexual organ to the act of urinating in *Twelfth Night:* "these be her very C's, her U's, and her T's, and thus she makes her great P's," 2.5.87–89.

28. James Grantham Turner, "Introduction: A History of Sexuality," in *Sexuality and Gender in Early Modern Europe: Institutions, Texts, Images,* ed. James Grantham Turner (Cambridge: Cambridge University Press, 1993), 1–9, and 2.

29. The classic—if controversial—study of the transition from the medieval and feudal "natural" economy to the Renaissance protocapitalist "mercantile" economy is Henri Pirenne's *Histoire économique de l'Occident mediéval* (Bruges: Brouwer, 1961) (*Economic and social history of medieval Europe,* tr. I. E. Clegg, London: Routledge and Kegan Paul, 1972). *See also* C. H. Wilson's comments on the transition "from barter to money" in *The Economy of Expanding Europe in the Sixteenth and Seventeenth Centuries,* vol. 4 of *The Cambridge Economic History of Europe,* eds. E.E. Rich and C. H. Wilson (Cambridge: Cambridge University Press, 1967), 513.

30. *See* Philip Jones, "Economia e società nell'Italia medievale: la leggenda della borghesia," in *Storia d'Italia, Annali I: Dal feudalesimo al capitalismo,* eds. Ruggiero Romano and Corrado Vivanti (Turin: Einaudi, 1978), 187–364, especially the section on "Sviluppo e sottosviluppo: *mercatores e possessores,*" 200–29.

31. Richard A. Goldthwaite, "The Renaissance Economy: The Preconditions for Luxury Consumption," in his *Aspetti della vita economica medievale* (Florence: Università di Firenze, Istituto di Storia Economica, 1985), 671.

32. *See* Jones, "Economia e società nell'Italia medievale," 200–29.

33. Jonson associates castration with homosexuality in *Bartholomew Fair,* in Edgeworth's description of "One Val Cutting," a "circling boy" or thief's decoy, "with whom your Numps is so taken that you may strip him of his clothes, if you will. I'll undertake to geld him for you, if you had but a surgeon, ready, to sear him" (4.3.106–10).

34. The conceit of physical deprivation survives, with variations, into Restoration comedy. *See* the libidinous Horner in William Wycherley's *The Country Wife,* who publicizes his supposed "castration" due to the clap as a means of gaining entry, in all senses, to the company of polite ladies.

35. Ben Jonson, *Epicoene, or the Silent Woman,* ed. R.V. Holdsworth (London : A. & C. Black, 1979 [New Mermaids]).

36. Laura Levine, *Men in Women's Clothing: Anti-theatricality and Effeminization, 1579–1642* (Cambridge: Cambridge University Press, 1994), 76–77. *Bartholomew Fair* (1614) also identifies performance with the absent phallus, in the puppet's revelation of his lack of genitals by way of a confutation of Busy's puritanical attack on theatrical transvestism (5.5). In this case, argues Levine, the puppet's "nothing" is equivalent to the nonreferentiality of the performance: "in the world the puppet presents to Busy, there is no relationship between sign and thing because there is no 'thing' under the sign, no genital under the costume for the sign to refer to" (101). At the same time, however, the puppet's "nothing" emblematizes the actor's paradoxical and dangerous eroticism—that so disturbs Busy—in the very sacrificing of his "thing." Chaerea docet.

Pastoral as Tragicomedic in Italian and Shakespearean Drama

Robert Henke

One of the best examples of generic intertextuality in Renaissance drama is provided by pastoral tragicomedy, which assumed several different guises in Italy and England. The two most prestigious Italian examples of the form, both well known to Shakespeare and his English contemporaries, were Torquato Tasso's *Aminta* and Battista Guarini's *Il pastor fido*.[1] *Il pastor fido* sparked a series of vitriolic exchanges between Guarini and a displaced Cyrian nobleman and professor of moral philosophy at Padua named Giason Denores, in which the former defended both tragicomedic and pastoral drama and elaborated one of the most detailed and suggestive dramaturgical theories of the Renaissance.[2] As Louise George Clubb has amply demonstrated, however, the plays of Tasso and Guarini represent only a small sample of late cinquecento pastoral tragicomedy—known variously as *favola boschereccia, favola pastorale, tragicomedia pastorale,* and *tragicomedia boschereccia*—which was widely performed in Italian courts and academies in the latter part of the century.[3] In fact, Tasso and Guarini inherit a tradition of pastoral drama dating from the late quattrocento, a drama always inherently tragicomedic at least in respect to social register, though until the 1540s indifferent to generic codification and neo-Aristotelian dramaturgy. And spanning the careers of both Guarini and Shakespeare, a *commedia dell'arte* version of pastoral tragicomedy was both performed by actors and scripted by actor-writers. As Ferdinando Neri argued in 1913, several *commedia dell'arte* pastoral scenarios dated between 1618 and 1622, but they surely represented a form of theater long in place, strikingly replicating the characters, plot, and notorious neoclassical unities of *The Tempest*.[4] In both amateur and professional Italian Renaissance theater, pastoral was often tragicomedic and generically liminal.

English responses to the avant-garde Italian hybrid took various forms. As G. K. Hunter has shown, John Marston's *The Malcontent,* entered in the Stationer's Register in 1604 as "Tragiecomedia," closely echoes passages from the first English translation of *Il pastor fido* (1602). It seems to be a programmatic attempt to transplant Guarinian tragicomedy, if not pastoral, to English soil.[5] The first avowed English imitation of Guarini's pastoral tragicomedy was Samuel Daniel's *Queenes Arcadia,* performed in 1605 for Queen Anne at Oxford University and published the following year. John Fletcher tested pastoral tragicomedy on the commercial stage with *The Faithful Shepherdess,* performed at the Blackfriars theater in 1609 by the Children of the Queen's Revels—a company with which Daniel had been affiliated, and which had first performed *The Malcontent.* The play was not successful. Fletcher's arch note "To the Reader," introducing the 1609–10 edition, flaunts Guarini's theory of tragicomedy and castigates the unsophisticated tastes of the Blackfriars audience. Like Guarini, Fletcher rejects popular, traditional pastoral, with its "whitsun ales, creame, wassel and morris-dances."[6] The play's failure would seem to indicate that Fletcher misjudged the cultural tastes of the Blackfriars theatergoers, an audience more socially heterogeneous that he had calculated.

Understanding pastoral not as a genre with fixed external characteristics but as a capacious and flexible mode admitting both learned and popular strains, Shakespeare is the English dramatist who most fully explores pastoral drama and the ways in which it might function in the genre of tragicomedy.[7] The court-based *Malcontent* all but abandons pastoral, unless one considers that in the person of Malevole Marston replaces the shepherd as pastoral protagonist with the satyr or the "satyrist"—as that felicitous Renaissance etymological confusion construed it.[8] Daniel repeated his experiment only one more time with *Hymen's Triumph* (1615), which again limited pastoral to its familiar external appurtenances. Embittered with the failure of *The Faithful Shepherdess,* Fletcher only returned to pastoral in a schematic fashion. In *Philaster,* for example, pastoral is not developed as an extended world or *topos* as it is in Shakespeare's late plays, but mainly serves as a site for extraordinary action.

Cymbeline, The Winter's Tale, and *The Tempest* were performed at the Blackfriars theater as well as at the Globe and at court, and were likely to have been viewed by some of the same theatergoers who had seen the experiments of Marston and Fletcher. In these plays, Shakespeare pursues the invitation to pastoral in a more sustained and flexible manner than other English playwrights. The plays are not only "pastoral" in that they involve an escape to the wild or "green" world, as does *A Midsummer Night's Dream,* but because there is an examination of both realistic and idyllic experience in the pastoral locus. Although only *The Winter's Tale* has actual shepherds, who celebrate the kind of festive pastoral disdained by Fletcher, the Wales scenes of *Cymbeline* provide a fine example of "hard pastoral": a difficult life in a forbidding natural environment consciously differentiated from the ease and corruption of the court.[9] Especially if one considers that Italian pastoral was sometimes extended to maritime locales, *The Tempest* suggests itself as pastoral drama by various indexes, including Gonzalo's golden age revery, the play's implicit debate between nature and civilization, and the familiar pastoral opposition between the innocent nymph and the libidinous satyr. Like *The Winter's Tale, The Tempest* includes popular strains: the knockabout farce of Stephano, Trinculo, and Caliban strikingly resembles the shenanigans outlined in the *commedia dell'arte* scenarios mentioned above.

The late nineteenth-century term "romance" has tended to obscure the generic multiplicity of Shakespeare's late plays. Despite their romance plots and motifs such as the displaced and suffering protagonist of "exemplary romance," they are products of generic and modal "polyglossia."[10] *The Winter's Tale,* for example, separates Robert Greene's romance *Pandosto* into a tripartite, tragical-pastoral-comical scheme, which follows the genre system of the Italian *genus mistum.* Shakespeare's late plays are tragicomedic in a very different sense than the problem comedies *Measure for Measure* and *All's Well that Ends Well.* Either in narrated *antefatti* or in their initial scenes, they establish a tragically coded action, which is transformed toward a comedic *telos* in a pastoral arena. As befits pastoral, tragic fear and pity modulate into a pathetic, elegiac register. Not unlike the Mirtillo-Amarilli alliance of the theocratic *Il pastor fido,* the final, pastoral-royal marriages of Shakespeare's late plays carry more crucial and explicit political importance than in the comedies, reestablishing bonds broken by prior tragic discord.

It is the striking similarity in the tragical-pastoral-comical genre systems of the Italian and Shakespearean hybrids that encourages intertexual investigations beyond the province of positivistic studies. "In generic resemblance," argues Alastair Fowler, "the direct line of descent is not so dominant that genre theory can be identified with source criticism."[11] In plays in which pastoral bridges tragedy and comedy, certain theatrical structures and dramaturgical strategies may independently repeat themselves, irrespective of direct influence: a recapitulation and revision of tragedic action, a stylistic and tonal diminution of tragic intensity, nuanced registers of pathos and sentiment, and a tendency to marginalize the most extreme, buffoonish elements of comedy. Although most Renaissance tragicomedy is not pastoral, both Italian pastoral tragicomedy and Shakespeare's late plays demonstrate that the conjunction of pastoral and tragicomedy is more than accidental. In both Italian and Shakespearean drama, the generic ambivalence of pastoral allows it to include both tragedic and comedic elements. Furthermore, the middle ranges of pastoral style, its nuanced emotional registers, the generically capacious range of its decor from the pleasance of the meadow to the roughness of the forest, cave, or mountain, and the indeterminate social status of its protagonists all allow pastoral to function as a bridge between tragedy and comedy.

In plays based on similar genre systems similar "theatergrams" arise, independently of direct and conscious influence.[12] In the case of tragicomedy mediated by pastoral, generic liminality characterizes these theatrical moving parts: dreams of diminished terror (*Il pastor fido, Cymbeline, The Winter's Tale*); the calmed deluge or storm of *Il pastor fido* (1.4), Guidubaldo Bonarelli's *Filli di Sciro,* the Bohemian seacoast scene of *The Winter's Tale,* and the beginning of *The Tempest;*[13] generically flexible deities such as Hercules (*Il pastor fido*) and Proserpine (*The Winter's Tale*); gnomic but ultimately benign oracles or prognostications (*Il pastor fido, Cymbeline, The Winter's Tale);* the figure of the satyr—either in its traditional guise in Italian drama, briefly staged in the "dance of the twelve satyrs" of *The Winter's Tale,* or blended with the literary wild man and the American native (Caliban in *The Tempest*); and the tragicomic bear common to Italian pastoral drama, *Mucedorus,* and *The Winter's Tale.*[14]

Marzia Pieri has provided a detailed account of Italian pastoral drama from the late quattrocento to the early seicento, giving due attention to its popular, folkloric, and anticlassical strains.[15] Pieri demonstrates that Poliziano's *Orfeo,* too often seen as an isolated example, was part of a large body of late quattrocento

pastorals, often performed as aristocratic nuptial entertainments, that mixed high mythological and low rustic strains.
Much early pastoral drama, argues Pieri, departed from Theocri-
tean and Vergilian pastoral in being structured by a "double
linguistic and social code," normally represented by the elegiac,
Petrarchan *pastore* and the coarse, realistic *villano*.[16] This binary alignment, which might also inform the dance and musical
styles integrated into the drama, existed without concern for
dramaturgical regularization according to neoclassical or any
other standards. Not yet, claims Pieri, did the "tragicomic . . .
become a problem to be resolved along Aristotelian lines."[17] And
in later rustic pastoral drama such as Ruzante's *La pastoral*
(1518), the salient point is the incongruous juxtaposition of two
antithetical character groups: the Petrarchan, amorous shepherds and the realistic, Paduan-speaking peasants. But after
1525 both mythological and rustic pastoral drama begin to seem
old-fashioned compared with the increasingly classicized and
developed forms of tragedy and comedy.

With *Egle* (1545–50), and its theoretical companion *Lettera
sovra il comporre le satire atte alla scena,* the Ferraran playwright and theorist Giovanni Battista Giraldi Cinzio aimed to
raise the generic status of pastoral or "satyric" drama and integrate it into the triadic, neoclassical system of genres adum-
brated by Horace in the *Art of Poetry.* Although Giraldi
preferred the term *satira* to Guarini's term *tragicomedia* his
version of the third genre was intrinsically tragicomedic and was
an important model for later Ferraran experiments in tragicomedy. It is difficult to know, says Giraldi in the *Lettera,* whether
the ancient satyr play preceded or postdated comedy and tragedy,
but it is certainly the case that each kind historically evolved
toward more and more developed states.[18] This evolutionary theory of kind, shared by Guarini in opposition to Denores's static,
Platonic theory of genres, justifies Giraldi's project of informing
the pastoral drama with state of the art dramatic theory.

Pieri emphasizes the repressive and homogenizing effects of
the cinquecento theoretical revolution on pastoral drama. Certainly the neoclassical claims of decorum could suppress the
plebeian strains that, in an earlier playwright like Ruzante, do
not sublimate themselves into the higher elegance of the
pastore but parody and critique courtly discourse. (Shakespeare, it may be observed, has it both ways, both offsetting
plebeian and courtly "shepherds" in *As You Like It* and *The
Winter's Tale* and sublimating the only apparently rustic Perdita

into a pastoral-aristocratic synthesis in *The Winter's Tale.*) But Giraldi and, later, Guarini demonstrate the fact that neo-Aristotelian theory was not only a force for conservatism but could be invoked to foster innovation and experimentation. Cinquecento poet-theorists interpreted Aristotle in widely varying fashions and often attributed principles to the *Poetics* not justifiable by the treatise itself, but very useful in defending poetic experiments scarcely imaginable by "il maestro."[19] Although the dearth of extant satyr plays (taken by many as the classical precedent for pastoral drama) and apposite theory might frustrate the classicizing poet-theorists, it also allowed a certain experimental latitude. If Francisco Robortello could extrapolate a theory of comedy from the *Poetics,* Giraldi and Guarini could do the same thing with pastoral and be even less constrained by classical and Renaissance exemplars.

Giraldi's *Lettera sovra il comporre le satire* provides the first theoretical soldering of pastoral drama and the tragicomedic. Giraldi's neo-Aristotelian definition of the satyric play is notable for its careful calibration of tragic and comic registers, therein anticipating Guarini. According to Giraldi,

> La satira è imitazione di azione perfetta di dicevole grandezza, composta al giocoso ed al grave con parlar soave ... rappresentata a commovere gli animi a riso, ed a convenevole terrore e compassione.

> [The satyric play is an imitation of a complete action of suitable grandeur, mixing the light and the serious with sweet diction, performed in order to move the soul to laughter and to appropriate levels of terror and pity.][20]

A "complete action" aligns the Giraldian plot with the teleological and syllogistic plot outlined in the *Poetics.* A "suitable grandeur" distinguishes the satyric play from minor forms like the epigram and elegy (with which Denores wanted to group pastoral poetry), and raises its generic status above that of the pastoral eclogues written by Andrea Calmo and others. The "sweet diction" of pastoral provides the right tragicomic blend of style. Finally, the satyric play elicits a careful meld of tragic and comic emotions: laughter, pity, and "appropriate" terror. Just as Guarini modulates the terror admissible in tragicomedy, Giraldi carefully circumscribes it within the decorum of the new genre. At the same time, although the prologue suggests Giraldi's pastoral experiment as a leisured retreat from the court and tragedy,

Egle actually has several appurtenances of tragedy (as does, in fact, the Greek satyr play): verse, a linear and suspenseful plot, an alternation of chorus and action, and an unhappy ending (the satyrs' anguished loss of the nymphs to their Ovidian transformation into trees and fountains).

Unlike his Ferraran successors Tasso and Guarini, but like Euripides and, arguably, Shakespeare, Giraldi places the satyr at the heart of his pastoral play. Like Shakespeare's Caliban, the satyrs of *Egle* elicit tragicomic tonalities, evoking in the internal and external audiences the conflicting responses of farcical laughter, elegiac pathos, and fear. The satyr's bestiality and relentless pursuit of the pleasure principle might place him at the lower end of the chain of being except for, as Giraldi puts it, "quella parte di divinità che portano i satiri con esso loro, secondo la superstizione di quegli antichi" (that aspect of divinity that comprises their being, according to the superstitions of the ancients).[21] The ancient fiction of semidivinity becomes immensely useful in dramaturgical terms because it allows Giraldi to grant a higher style, more momentous action, and more serious emotions to the satyrs than could be given to the typical denizens of pastoral. As natural man vouchsafed occult knowledge, Giraldi's satyr correctly reads a tragically-coded omen (3.3). And he is also something of a poet. Whereas earlier in the play the satyr rejected the courtly poetry of pastoral pathos in favor of aggressive action, in the final half of the play he commits, along with Pan, the pathetic fallacy, reading in the landscape signs of his own amatory woes. We might observe the same pattern in Caliban, whose aggressive pursuit of Miranda bespeaks his inability to perform the courtly love poetry of Miranda's successful lover Ferdinand, but who, later in the play, "crie[s] to dream again" the riches of music and poetry (*The Tempest*, 3.2.133–41).

Despite the large range of cinquecento pastoral drama, *Aminta* and *Il pastor fido* do merit special consideration in regard to Shakespeare's late plays. They were known by English playwrights as early as 1591, when John Wolfe's Italian edition of the two plays was printed in London. Many late cinquecento pastorals transplant comedic plotting and character typology to Arcadia.[22] But *Aminta* and *Il pastor fido* are the most *tragedic* of Italian pastoral tragicomedies, concentrating most explicitly on raising the generic status of pastoral. In this regard the famous Italian plays resemble the pastoral of Shakespeare's late plays, which carry more tragic strains than the *Queenes Arcadia* and *The Faithful Shepherdess.* Guarini's sophisticated and detailed dramaturgy of tragicomedy, which in the *Verati* includes a discussion of the bridging function played by pastoral, can illuminate the "unwritten poetics" of Shakespeare's final hybrids, in which the unities of *The Tempest* and the deference toward the unities by Time in *The Winter's Tale* are only the most obvious examples of dramaturgical awareness.[23] Following their Ferraran predecessor Giraldi, Tasso and especially Guarini most fully explore the generic calibration of tragicomedic dramaturgy, in regard to action, scenic semiotics, style, and audience response. And although the social tensions of pastoral are largely mystified or elided in the canonical Italian playwrights, the *Verati* supply an interesting theory of the social negotiations possible in both pastoral and tragicomedy.[24]

Although Tasso, in *Delle differenze poetiche,* argues against the mixing of genres, his *Aminta* is important for the way it accommodates higher generic registers than those normally allowed by pastoral and thus anticipates Guarini's tragical-pastoral-comical experiment.[25] Tasso actually would have rejected the label of "tragicomedy" for *Aminta,* but his project of heightening the generic status of pastoral prepares the way for Guarini, who took Tasso's play as a prototype. In the person of Tirsi, Tasso describes how, after having worked on *Gerusalemme Liberata,* he intends to graft epic elements onto a pastoral tree:

> né già suona
> la mia sampogna umil come soleva:
> ma di voce più altera e più sonora
> emula de le trombe, empie le selve
>
> $$(1.2.633\text{–}43)^{26}$$

[my pipe does not sing humbly as before, but with a higher and more sonorous voice; it emulates the trumpets, filling the woods.]

Tasso proposes an alloy of pastoral and epic, which will engage higher subjects, more socially elevated characters, and a higher style and diction than appropriate to the decorums of rustic pastoral. Instead of setting off the *villano* against the *pastore* as in Ruzante, Tasso aims to transform the *villano* into the refined *pastore*—in effect, supplanting the supernatural Ovidian metamorphosis typical of much cinquecento pastoral with a kind of social sleight of hand. The courtier disguised as a shepherd might imply, in Empson's words, "a beautiful relationship between rich and poor."[27] Amore boasts in the prologue, "Spirerò nobil sensi a' rozzi petti, / raddolcirò de le lor lingue il suono" ("I will inspire noble sensibilities in rustic hearts, I will sweeten their speech") (Prologo, 80–81). The theme of the entire play is metamorphosis on various levels: social metamorphosis, generic transformation, and internal change. But for .Tasso as for Guarini, love does not only function as the agent of social sublimation. It is also capable of generating potentially tragic experience of harsher registers than those of Petrarchan poetics, productive of suicidal falls that only in perspective turn out to be fortunate. In addition to the typical local deities of pastoral (Pan, Pomona, Pale, Priapus), the lovers of *Aminta* and *Il pastor fido* call upon hellish powers reminiscent of Senecan tragedy. Tasso's Aminta invokes "Ecate notturna" ("nocturnal Hecate") (*Aminta,* 4.4.1686), and Guarini's Mirtillo calls upon the "lagrimosi spirti d'Averno" ("mournful spirits of Avernus") (*Il pastor fido,* 3.6).[28]

Guarini goes beyond Tasso in raising the generic level of pastoral drama by superimposing an extensive tragedic apparatus on the pastoral stage. Mostly excised from Guarini's *Compendio* (and, of course, the abridged English translations of the *Compendio* on which Anglo-American critics have relied) is an argument in the *Verati* for the generic capaciousness of pastoral, which, Guarini would argue, is a mode and not a genre.[29] As a mode (expressed adjectivally) pastoral is generically protean, capable of serving as an arena for tragedy as well as comedy. In humanist fashion, Guarini locates classical precedents in Theocritus and Vergil for an extended concept of pastoral that accommodates tragedic form and experience: "Le pastorali sono capaci della grandezza Tragedica, e che d'loro soggetti si possano formare buone Tragedie" ("Pastorals are capable of tragic grandeur, and good tragedies can be made out of pastoral subjects") (*Verato,* 2: 291). Even the paradigmatic tragedy *Oedipus the King* contains significant pastoral elements: Oedipus is raised by a shepherd who, in the denouement of the play, clinches Oedipus's self-recognition. In fact, if recognition becomes a standard element of neo-Aristotelian tragedy, pastoral stories can easily produce the requisite device because shepherds often travel from one country to another (*Verato* 2: 288). And shepherds, Guarini continues, can themselves be tragic protagonists, not merely ancillary to an Oedipus: "La nobiltà, e i casi orribili de' pastori non sono cose abborrenti dal verisimile del poeta" ("The nobility of shepherds and the horrifying events that befall them do not violate poetic verisimilitude") (*Verato secondo* 3: 252). In pointing out that tragedic atrocities such as blindness and hanging have befallen literary shepherds, Guarini's scheme in its widest interpretation would allow for blind Gloucester on the heath.

Cinquecento innovators like Giraldi and Guarini place great emphasis on the cognitive, ethical, and especially emotional responses elicited by their experimental genres on the theater audience. In large part, they define new genres by the new responses hypothetically elicited in their audiences. Guarinian tragicomedy explores nuanced, calibrated registers of audience response between the horror elicited by the atrocities of Senecan tragedy and the laughter of low comedy. Guarini's hybrid does not eradicate tragic terror, but modulates it into tragicomic registers by the following means: the interjection of fictional distance, the enactment of dangerous but not mortal events, the diminished terror of dreams, the deployment of tragedic rhetoric (as opposed to tragedic action), and the aestheticizing of tragedy. One only has to consider how many of these techniques Prospero employs to gain a sense of their centrality in *The Tempest*, and to see how Guarini's theory may illuminate the implicit poetics of Shakespeare's late plays.

The mode of pastoral, it may be observed, provides intermediate emotional registers highly appropriate for tragicomedy. The sweet style of pastoral, argues Guarini, tempers tragic intensity (*Verato* 2: 274). Normally, pastoral protagonists do not heroically defy their fates but rather passively endure suffering, experiencing what might be called pathos: a plaintive, elegiac register of grief. Compared with the tonalities of farce which neoclassical humanists like Guarini and clerical antitheatricalists believed to denigrate the ancient art of comedy, pathos bespoke a certain dignity and prestige. It was the major key played by leading actresses of the *commedia dell'arte* such as Isabella Andreini, who often performed pastoral roles with her husband Francesco and even wrote a pastoral play herself, entitled *La Mirtilla* (1588). In Shakespeare's late plays, the pathos of Imogen in the Wales wilderness, Hermione in the trial scene, and Gonzalo in Prospero's cell as described by the feminine Ariel (5.1.7–20) are given sharp focus. The pastoral speakers of *Cymbeline* nicely express a nuanced, tragicomic blend of contrapuntal emotions in their account of the androgynous Fidele, who blends "smiling with a sigh" and "grief and patience" (*Cymbeline* 4.2.52–58). Shakespeare certainly does not reject the pleasures of coarse laughter in his late plays—featured especially in the "Armin" line of Cloten, Autolycus, and Caliban, but the relatively genteel and sophisticated audience of the Blackfriars playhouse seems to tip the hand slightly in favor of pathos.[30] As the shepherds of *The Winter's Tale* are raised to gentlemanly status, they also seem elevated to new emotional registers: "and so we wept; and there was the first gentleman-like tears that ever we shed" (5.2.144–45). Autolycus, who before has provided much of the theatrical pleasure with his *commedia dell'arte*-like *lazzi,* is notably subdued and overshadowed in his encounter with the newly gentled shepherds, who are socially sublimated in the manner of Tasso's "rozzi petti."

The capacity of pastoral to assimilate a tragedic apparatus is tested in *Il pastor fido.* Guarini reprises the general contours of Tasso's Aminta-Silvia plot in the tragedic *antefatto* of the play, the story of Aminta and Lucrina narrated by Ergasto in act 1, scene 2, but in Guarini's case the "danger not the death" is turned into actual suicide. Like Tasso's Silvia, Lucrina spurns Aminta's love, but since the rejected lover is a priest of Diana's temple, the results are more public and more grave than in the earlier play. Aminta beseeches Diana to revenge his broken faith, and she answers by imposing a Sophoclean blight on the country of Arcadia—turning, in effect, the pastoral landscape into a tragedic one. Only the sacrifice of Lucrina or a substitute will abate Diana's fury, and so Lucrina "fu con pompa solenne al sacro altare / vittima lagrimevole condotta" ("was led in solemn pomp to the sacred altar, a pitiful victim") (I.2). Seemingly about to perform the tragedic act of vengeance, apparently incensed with tragic fury, Aminta suddenly turns the sword onto himself, "vittima e sacerdote in un" ("at once victim and priest"), whereupon Lucrina follows suit. Not even this double suicide, however, removes the blight, which is not lifted until a long recognition scene, based on the ending of *Oedipus the King,* sanctions the natural erotic link between Amarilli and Mirtillo. Like Shakespeare's late plays, *Il pastor fido* recollects prior tragedy in order to revise it.

Even the scenic decor of pastoral suggested tragicomedic possibilities. Sebastiano Serlio codified the comedic scene in an urban locale, the tragedic scene in a courtly place, and the *scena satirica* in a sylvan setting.[31] The pastoral set afforded the greatest opportunities for imaginative experimentation and was generically ambivalent, sometimes incorporating elements of tragedic and comedic decors. In addition to the pleasance, the *scena satirica* could include mountains, rocks, deserts, and terrifying, labyrinthine mazes, providing a fit stage for tragicomic experience. For the benefit of the internal and external audiences of *Aminta,* the *nuncio* evokes a rugged place "ov'è scosceso il colle, / e giú per balzi e per dirupi incolti . . . cala un precipizio in una valle" ("where the hill is precipitous, and below, in cliffs and wild crags ... the precipice tumbles into a valley") (4.2.1687–89), as the site of the apparently tragedic but ultimately therapeutic narrative told to Silvia.

As Guarini argues in the *Verati,* the temples and statues that normally adorn the courtly tragedic decor might be incorporated by the pastoral set (*Verato secondo,* 3: 270). The pastoral temple, for Guarini, transforms the opulence of the tragedic palace into a more humble, religious decorum. In the theocratic *Il pastor fido,* the action converges on the temple, a place of both tragedic conflict and tragicomic resolution. The solemn temple and religious ceremony of the "isle of Delphos" as described by Cleomenes and Dion in *The Winter's Tale* (3.1) should then be seen as an enabling pastoral code, prefiguring the play's pastoral deliverance from the claustrophobic tragedy of Leontes' court.

Like Shakespeare's late plays, *Aminta* and *Il pastor fido* counterpose soft and hard versions of pastoral, the latter capable of accommodating tragedic conventions and experience. Representations of the pastoral pleasance, mythologized as the golden age and fantasized as escape from the court or city, are proposed only to be tested against the harsher realities of nature or the intrusion of court and city into the pastoral space. If the mode of pastoral must, by definition, bound itself by moral contrast and physical distance from the court or city, those boundaries are soon revealed as porous. Aminta's childhood friendship with Silvia—"conforme era l'etate, / ma 'l pensier più conforme" ("they were equal in age, but even more in thought") (*Aminta* 1.2.416–17)—bears comparison with that between Polixenes and Leontes ("twinn'd lambs that did frisk i' th' sun" [*The Winter's Tale,* 1.2.67]) for a pastoral idyllism suddenly unable to accommodate the "stronger blood" of sexuality, that, in both cases, nearly generates tragedy. In *Il pastor fido,* the idyllic pastoral fantasized by Amarilli ("*Felice pastorella*" [2.5]) with its corresponding vision of altogether benign and nonviolent love, is not Guarini's pastoral, which admits within its borders city sharpers like Corisca, beasts even more dangerous than the wolf typical of pastoral, and love in its tragicomic, even violent dimensions.

To a much greater degree than *The Faithful Shepherdess* and the *Queenes Arcadia,* pastoral in the last phase of Shakespeare's career accommodates tragic experience. Recent criticism of *Cymbeline, The Winter's Tale,* and *The Tempest* has emphasized the tragic conflicts and irresolutions of the last plays, specifically in their political dimensions. Although English tragicomedy of the "public," "private," and court stage produced in the center of a nation referred much more directly to political issues than did the court-based Italian tragicomedy produced in an age of Counter-Reformation absolutism, the Italian hybrids of Tasso and Guarini provide a model for the counterpointing or fusion of tragedy and pastoral that could take a more political and more unstable form on English soil. *Cymbeline, The Winter's Tale,* and *The Tempest* initially posit a version of soft pastoral, only to extend the mode's range by moving to the mountainous, hard life of Belarius and his sons, traveling to the strange Bohemian "sea-coast" plagued by violent storms and terrifying bears, and admitting the Antonios and Sebastians not taken into account by Gonzalo's idyllic republic. In the late plays, pastoral reprises and reforms tragic action, constructs a generically pivotal space for the bridging of tragedy and comedy, tempers the pitiable and fearful extremity of tragic response, and performs generically coded social negotiations. The late plays, then, employ techniques very similar to those of Giraldian and Guarinian dramaturgy.

The first explicit version of pastoral in *Cymbeline* is static, escapist, and soft, recalling Henry VI's vision of timeless pastoral otium (*King Henry VI, Part 3:* 2.5.21–54). Beset by the oppressive court, Imogen fantasizes a pastoral retreat in which she and Posthumus would innocently play at being shepherds:

> Would I were
> A neat-herd's daughter, and my Leonatus
> Our neighbour-shepherd's son!
>
> (1.2.79–81)

Such pastoral defines itself in absolute opposition to court and city. It is a pure, enclosed kind, such as pastoral was understood by Denores, not capable of interacting with other genres. Tonally, it is aligned with the ideal and organic account of Posthumus given by the First Gentleman (1.1.16–25 and 45–46), a characterization soon to be belied by the tragic events of the play.

The version of pastoral actually enacted by the play is tougher and more porous than that fantasized by Imogen. *Cymbeline*'s pastoral set, featuring a cave and mountains, extracts the roughest aspects of the *scena satirica,* with the rough weather of which the boys complain practically removing any traces of the pleasance. As in *Il pastor fido,* the pastoral cave provides a site of apparently tragedic action when Imogen mistakes Cloten's body for that of Posthumus. At first, the salient point of Belarius's pastoral space is precisely its utter isolation from the rest of the world, as the boys complain (2.3.29–35). The boundaries of Wales, however, turn out to be much more malleable than those of soft pastoral or of Belarius's moral vision. Belarius recognizes that the arrival and killing of Cloten spells the beginning of the end of his protected, pastoral theater and initiates the move back into history. Cloten initiates the kind of historical engagement that the boys have only rehearsed, like actors, in the pastoral space (3.3.79–97). The killing of Cloten initiates a more active interplay between pastoral and tragedic history than occurs in the cave stories narrated by Belarius and enacted by his foster sons. Violence inappropriate to the pastoral decorum invades its boundaries—although the displacement of the violence offstage does adjust tragic horror in a Guarinian manner. As a tragical-pastoral-historical play, *Cymbeline* aims to join the "lopp'd branches" back to the "old stock" of the "stately cedar": to graft the pastoral denizens Guiderius and Belarius back onto the British dynastic tree (5.4.140–43).

Like *Cymbeline, The Winter's Tale* dramatizes a pastoral much more capable of dialogy with tragedy than the soft pastoral nostalgically remembered in Polixenes' "twinn'd lambs" speech (*The Winter's Tale,* 1.2.62–65 and 67–75). The innocent pastoral friendship between Polixenes and Leontes cannot withstand the onslaught of sexual and tragic awareness. With the harshness of its desert shore, a savage bear, and tempests, the maritime pastoral of act 3, scene 3 resembles the hard pastoral of Wales in *Cymbeline:* it is a generically pivotal place of "things dying" and of "things new born." Placed in the middle of the play, it negotiates, as soft pastoral cannot do, the turn from tragic conflict to comedic denouement. Whereas Leontes as "twinned lamb" suddenly become adult is unequipped to recognize sexuality in terms other than guilt and illegitimacy, the old shepherd is not shocked at the sight of what he takes to be illicit sexuality (3.3.68–78). Autolycus's frank and accepting attitude toward sexuality, establishing a context for the sexual play between Perdita and Florizel, further differentiates the enacted pastoral of *The Winter's Tale* from the presexual, soft pastoral vision. The greensward outside the shepherd's cottage incorporates the pastoral pleasance, but the old shepherd's admonishment to Perdita that she must labor as his late wife did complicates the pleasance with a hint of georgic (4.4.55–70). For her part, Perdita does check the idyllism and fantasy of Florizel, for whom pastoral serves quite literally as escape. She questions the capacity of the courtier to become a shepherd, and expresses her fears in language closer to tragedic dichotomy than pastoral lyricism ("the difference forges dread . . . O the Fates! . . . How should I behold the sternness of his presence? . . . you must change this purpose, / or I my life" [4.4.17–24, 39–40]). Realizing Perdita's fears, Polixenes does transgress the pastoral boundaries and becomes the new tyrant, reprising aspects of Leontes' earlier actions, threatening to hang the shepherd, deface Perdita, and bar Florizel from succession. But despite Florizel's heroic bluster (4.4.477–80), he submits as a "faithful shepherd" to the providential plan imagined by Camillo, and the pastoral scene does not have tragedic issue. In general, the pastoral episode proves sufficiently capacious to address important issues of the tragedic section of the play: sexuality and tyranny. Somewhat like the London theater itself, the pastoral place of *The Winter's Tale* is marginally positioned in relation to the tragedic court, neither one with it nor absolutely isolated from it in the manner of soft pastoral. It is a place of measured liberty and license for the Bohemian courtiers, both Autolycus, who formerly served Prince Florizel, and the prince himself. The pastoral is also marginally positioned in relation to the Sicilian court, as the place consigned to Perdita by Leontes. The pastoral locus becomes a "theater" capable of playing with problems that had had catastrophic issue in the first part of the play.[32]

The pastoral landscape in *The Tempest* is a function of imaginative projection, a "landscape of the mind."[33] Soft pastoral is critically invoked both in Gonzalo's visionary discourse and, to a lesser extent, in the wedding masque. If soft pastoral is often formed as an escapist reaction to the court, the court party in act 2 scene 1 dramatizes both the formation of the utopian vision and the critique of the vision by the cynical court realists Sebastian and Antonio. Whereas Gonzalo and Adrian see the pleasance ("How lush and lusty the grass looks! how green!" [2.1.51]), Sebastian and Antonio see tawny ground. From the reports of the court party and Caliban, the actual landscape of *The Tempest* is much rougher than Gonzalo and Adrian imply, if not as bleak as the satirists' account. Gonzalo himself later complains that the island is not as idyllic as it originally appeared: "a maze trod, indeed, / Through forth-rights and meanders!" (3.3.1–3). Here, indeed, is the Dantesque, labyrinthian maze common to Italian pastoral.[34]

The famous Montaigne passage describing the new world that is lifted for Gonzalo's speech resonates with literary pastoral, and its "Golden Age" tag links the speech with the well-known choruses from Tasso and Guarini's pastoral tragicomedies. Gonzalo's ideal society allows no *negotium* or financial exchange, no political or social hierarchy, no labor, no violence, and no impure sexuality ("all men idle, all; / And women too, but innocent and pure" [2.1.150–51]). The slave Caliban's labor on which Prospero depends and the love-trial task of log bearing that Ferdinand undergoes introduce not only the georgic element present in the actualized pastoral of the two other plays but the socioeconomic differentiation that belies Gonzalo's egalitarianism. Prospero's violence and the nearly violent actions of Caliban and the two groups of conspirators sharply contrast Gonzalo's pacifism. The libido of the satyr Caliban and Prospero's obsession with sexuality (an element, in fact, found in the *mago* of the *commedia* scenarios) all contrast the now familiar *topos* of presexual soft pastoral.

Unlike Gonzalo's golden age vision the pastoral of Prospero's masque recognizes the civilizing need for both labor (e.g., "pollclipt vineyard" [4.1.68]) and sexual repression. As Stephen Orgel has argued, the masque recapitulates issues central to the play: the fear of rape and the power of virginity, as well as the conjunction of marriage and royal power.[35] But like Gonzalo's pastoral, the masque leaves no place for eros outside of marriage, with its "cold nymphs," "dismissed batchelor," and banishment and unsexing of Venus and Cupid. Although Shakespearean pastoral, from *As You Like It* on, does elide winter and rough weather, Ceres wishes to the royal couple the very elision of winter, that "Spring come to you at the farthest, / In the very end of harvest" (4.1.114–15). A world from which violence, lust, mortality, and time have been removed, as Orgel argues, is fragile and delicate, and it is not surprising that the mere recollection of the buffoons' conspiracy interrupts it.

The pastoral of *The Tempest* itself, however, is much more capacious than the pastoral of Gonzalo and Prospero; it is a place where tragedy is remembered and replayed in the manner of Guarinian tragicomedy. If *Il pastor fido* recollects past literary tragedy in the form of *Oedipus the King, The Tempest* both reprises past Shakespearean tragedy (the introspective ruler, violent sibling rivalry, physical and symbolic tempests) and begins with Prospero remembering his own tragedic past, as Belarius does in *Cymbeline*. From Vergil to Sannazaro, pastoral is a site of memory where one remembers painful events of the past such as political usurpation and amatory loss. Prospero also jogs and reshapes the memories of Miranda, Caliban, Ariel, and especially his Italian enemies. In a pastoral arena, he stages a kind of theater of memory in order to remind Antonio and Alonso of their earlier tragedic actions and to move them toward repentance. Prospero even readjusts and tempers, in a Guarinian manner, the tragically coded responses elicited by his spectacles: the pity, wonder, and amazement felt by Miranda in response to the shipwreck; and the passion felt by Ferdinand in response to the tragicomic illusion of his father's death.

In these late plays, Shakespeare follows the idea, if not the external form, of Guarinian tragicomedy in creating a variegated, capacious pastoral arena capable of incorporating tragic modalities. To be sure, Shakespeare departs from Guarini and most other Renaissance playwrights of tragicomedy in allowing the death as well as the danger, and in developing the political and existential claims of tragedy much more than the Italian playwrights. And whereas the full spectrum of late cinquecento pastoral tragicomedy contains a wide range of social and cultural registers, from the *commedia dell'arte* to Guarini, Shakespeare incorporates both "high" and "low" strains in each of the late plays. Still, a knowledge of Italian theory and practice can tell us much about the unwritten poetics of Shakespearean tragicomedy, especially when pastoral mediates tragedy and comedy.

Notes

1. Tasso's play was written in 1572, probably first performed in 1573, and published in Venice in 1583. Guarini wrote *Il pastor fido* between 1580 and 1585, publishing it in 1590 and then, in a definitive edition, in 1602. Both of these editions were published in Venice.

2. In 1586 Giason Denores presented his theories of genre and criticized tragicomedy and pastoral, without explicitly naming Guarini, in his *Discorso di Iason DeNores intorno à que' principii, cause, et accrescimenti, che la comedia, la tragedia, et il poema eroico ricevono dalla philosophia morale, e civile, e da' governatori delle repubbliche* (Padua, 1586). Guarini responded, anonymously, in his *Il verato ovvero difesa di quanto ha scritto M. Giason Denores contra le tragicomedie, et le pastorali, in un suo discorso di poesia* (Ferrara, 1588). Denores sallied back in his *Apologia contra l'auttor del Verato*

di Iason De Nores di quanto ha egli detto in un suo discorso delle tragico-medie, e delle pastorali (Padua, 1590). Guarini countered again with *Il verato secondo ovvero replica dell'attizzato accademico ferrarese in difesa del pastor fido* (Florence, 1593). Finally, in 1601 Guarini published a work incorporating the major points of his two earlier treatises, the *Compendio della poesia tragicomica, tratto dai duo Verati, per opera dell'autore del pastor fido, colla giunta di molte cose spettanti all'arte* (Venice, 1601). The five exchanges of the quarrel, treatises relevant to the quarrel by Angelo Ingegneri, Faustino Summo, Giovani Pietro Malacreta, Paolo Beni, and Giovanni Savio, and Guarini's principal literary works are collected together in an eighteenth-century edition: *Delle opere del cavalier Battista Guarini*, ed. Giovanni Alberto Tumermani, 4 vols. (Verona, 1738). All of my citations of Guarini and Denores include the volume number of the eighteenth-century edition as well as an abbreviated title of the treatise. *Verato secondo* 3: 100, then, refers to page 100 of the second *Verato*, found in the third volume of the Tumermani edition. *Verato* simply refers to the first *Verato*.

3. *See* Louise George Clubb, *Italian Drama in Shakespeare's Time* (New Haven: Yale University Press, 1989), 93–187. "Tragicomedia" and "boscherec-cia" have variant spellings in Renaissance Italian texts.

4. *Scenari delle maschere in Arcadia* (Città di Castello: S. Lapi, 1913).

5. For the argument that Marston adapted Guarinian tragicomedy to an English context, *see* Hunter's introduction to his edition of *The Malcontent* (London: Methuen, 1975), lxi–lxiv.

6. Citation refers to *The Dramatic Works in the Beaumont and Fletcher Canon*, ed. Fredson Bowers, 8 vols. (Cambridge: Cambridge University Press, 1976), 3: 497.

7. Like satire, pastoral is a mode and not a genre because it has principally been defined by characteristics—such as emotional register, attitude, subject—that may be termed "modal" because they are unfixed to any particular external structure. Some conservative Renaissance critics, such as Denores, wished to tie pastoral to certain generic features; one of Guarini's theoretical innovations is to untether pastoral from generic constraints. The famous title page to Ben Jonson's 1616 works suggests that the pastoral and satiric modes are aligned with the genre tragicomedy. For the distinction between mode and genre, *see* Alastair Fowler, *Kinds of Literature: An Introduction to the Theory of Genres and Modes* (Cambridge: Harvard University Press, 1982), 106–11. Here, I use "tragicomedic" to indicate "that which pertains to the genre tragicomedy" and "tragicomic" to refer to modal characteristics such as emotional register and tone. I distinguish "tragedic" from "tragic," and "comedic" from "comic" in the same manner.

8. *See* Eugene M. Waith, *The Pattern of Tragicomedy in Beaumont and Fletcher* (New Haven: Yale University Press, 1952), 50–53.

9. For a discussion of *Cymbeline* as "hard pastoral," *see* Michael Taylor, "The Pastoral Reckoning in *Cymbeline*," *Shakespeare Survey* 36 (1983): 97–106.

10. "Polyglossia" is M. M. Bakhtin's term for the proliferation of generic and speech discourses that, as he sees it, began in Shakespeare's time. *See The Dialogic Imagination: Four Essays*, ed. Michael Holquist, trans. Caryl Emerson and Michael Holquist (Austin: University of Texas Press, 1981), 12. For an excellent discussion of romance elements in Shakespeare's late plays, *see* Leo

Salingar, *Shakespeare and the Traditions of Comedy* (Cambridge: Cambridge University Press, 1972), 28–75.

11. Fowler, *Kinds of Literature*, 43.

12. The term, of course, is that of Clubb. *See* especially *Italian Drama*, 1–26.

13. Bonarelli's play, first published in 1607, may be found in a modern edition: *Filli di Sciro, discorsi, e appendice*, ed. Giovanni Gambarin (Bari: Laterza, 1941).

14. Clubb explores the generic resonance of animals in *The Winter's Tale* and Italian pastoral drama, and in particular the tragicomic nature of the bear, in *Italian Drama*, 140–52.

15. *See* her *La scena boschereccia nel rinascimento italiano* (Padua: Liviana Editrice, 1983).

16. Pieri, *La scena boschereccia*, 44.

17. Ibid., 47.

18. Giraldi's treatise may be found in a modern edition: Giovanni Battista Giraldi Cinzio, *Egle e Lettere sovra il comporre le satire atte alle scene*, ed. Carla Molinari (Bologna: Commissione per i testi di lingua, 1985). For Giraldi's discussion of the evolution of the classical genres, *see* pp. 144–53.

19. For the argument that cinquecento theory was potentially innovative, *see* Daniel Javitch, "Pioneer Genre Theory and the Opening of the Humanist Canon," *Common Knowledge* 3 (1994): 54–66.

20. Molinari, *Egle*, 153.

21. Ibid., 160.

22. *See* Clubb, *Italian Drama*, 93–123.

23. For the notion of "unwritten poetics" and the creative function of genre in the Renaissance, *see* Claudio Guillén, *Literature as System: Essays Toward the Theory of Literary History* (Princeton: Princeton University Press, 1971), 107–34.

24. *See Verato secondo* 3: 243–47.

25. *See* the discussion of Tasso's *Delle differenze poetiche* in Bernard Weinberg, *A History of Literary Criticism in the Italian Renaissance*, 2 vols. (Chicago: Chicago University Press, 1961), 2: 1077.

26. Tasso had begun working on *Gerusalemme Liberata* in the 1560s. I quote from Torquato Tasso, *Aminta*, ed. Giorgio Bàrberi Squarotti (Padua: R.A.D.A.R., 1968). Line references are consecutive. My translation.

27. William Empson, *Some Versions of Pastoral* (1935; reprint, New York: New Directions, 1974), 11.

28. Against Denores, who argues that tragedy is an exclusively political genre that treats the fall of tyrants, Guarini points to the many domestic tragedies in the ancient Greek canon that concern love (*Verato* 2: 242).

29. *Verato secondo* 3: 265. The standard version of Guarini's theoretical writings that many critics use is that anthologized by Allan H. Gilbert, in *Literary Criticism: Plato to Dryden* (1940; reprint, Detroit: Wayne State University Press, 1962), 504–33.

30. For the Shakespearean roles played by Robert Armin, *see* David Wiles, *Shakespeare's Clown: Actor and Text in the Elizabethan Playhouse* (Cambridge: Cambridge University Press, 1987), 136–63. All citations refer to the Arden Shakespeare editions.

31. Serlio discusses the three theatrical sets in the 1551 *Il secondo libro di perspettiva*. A useful reprint of Serlio's works is *Tutte l'opere d'architettura*

et prospettiva (1619; Ridgewood, N.J.: The Gregg Press, 1964), in which the discussion of the three scenic decors may be found on pp. 45–47.

32. *See* my "The Winter's Tale and Guarinian Dramaturgy," *Comparative Drama* 27 (1993): 197–217.

33. The term supplies the title of a comparative treatment of Italian and Shakespearean pastoral by Richard Cody: *The Landscape of the Mind: Pastoralism and Platonic Theory in Tasso's Aminta and Shakespeare's Early Comedies* (Oxford: Clarendon Press, 1969).

34. For a discussion of the maze, *see* Clubb, *Italian Drama,* 112–13.

35. *See The Tempest,* ed. Stephen Orgel (Oxford: Oxford University Press, 1987), 44.

A Device to Fit the Times: Intertextual Allusion in Thomas Middleton's *Women Beware Women*

Zara Bruzzi

This essay proposes that the masque of *Women Beware Women* is a mosaic of citations, verbal and visual, of English and Italian court texts. These, read in conjunction with the play's narrative, seem to accord with the principal features observed even in rather differing analyses, by Richard Dutton and Annabel Patterson for example, of writing under conditions of censorship: the distancing of a text from an obvious political reading by situating the plot in the past or in a foreign setting, combined with some kind of textual indication of the presence of topical matter (defined by Patterson as an entry code). The intertextuality considered here is thus of two kinds: citation, the insertion into a text of significant pre-texts as entry code to a political reading; and the more speculative intertextuality of an audience's construction of a topical reading from the historical analogue offered.[1] If these criteria are applied to *Women Beware Women,* it is possible to read into the story of Francesco de' Medici and Bianca Cappello a concealed commentary on the court of King James I, especially upon the influence of favorites.

As very little is known about the date of writing or the conditions of performance of *Women Beware Women,* any political reading must remain speculative. It is difficult to know how much of the unstated Italian material considered here would have been known by an audience, and could have been brought to bear on a political reading of the play (although the topic of favorites can be assumed to be of general interest). It seems likely that only a coterie group was expected to follow the intricacies of possible analogies between Medicean and Stuart courts.[2] On the other hand, to those familiar with Stuart court culture, the choice of grand ducal Florence as an analogue of

Jacobean England could be considered an apposite one from very different perspectives. The style of royal panegyric at James's court, particularly that of court masques, was deeply indebted to Medicean taste and spectacle; and if Medicean culture is closely associated with King James, it is also associated with his wife, Queen Anne, and with his son, Prince Henry, whose passionate interest in the arts and architecture of high Renaissance Florence, shared by a group of courtiers who were fellow connoisseurs, is well documented. Thus there was clearly the possibility of access to fairly detailed information about contemporary and near-contemporary Florence in courtly circles, given personal visits by and correspondence from aristocratic travelers (and such influential members of their retinue as Inigo Jones), and the employment in London of a Florentine architect who had actually worked for Francesco, Constantino de' Servi. Roy Strong has established Prince Henry's particular interest in the design of Francesco de' Medici's strange and marvelous garden at Pratolino, and that Middleton's patron, the third earl of Pembroke, belonged to the prince's circle of collectors and cognoscenti.[3]

However, English attitudes to Medicean culture and influence were ambivalent; for Florence had, under the renewed Medici supremacy, moved from democracy to oligarchy to virtual absolutism, and Sir Robert Dallington's critical survey of grand ducal rule, which provides a detailed analysis of the hardship caused to the common people by royal taxes and monopolies, concludes with an account of the strong but secret discontent of the people under the rule of the Medici, "having fresh in their mindes their former libertie."[4] Moreover, religious difference made it possible for militant Calvinists to present Medicean influence as sinister and unpatriotic.[5] Francesco de' Medici, regent and subsequently grand duke of Tuscany, and the duke represented in *Women Beware Women,* was, and is, a figure of mixed reputation. To scholars and art historians he is a patron and inventor of unusual fantasy: he was a learned man who gave public lectures on topics he was expert in, such as chemistry, alchemy, and Neoplatonism; he created extraordinary artefacts from melted rock crystal and metals; he restructured the Uffizi as a museum for the Medici collection; he manufactured porcelain, fireworks, a flying bomb, poisons. But despite his achievements he seems to have been an unpopular ruler. English reactions to Francesco's rule were colored by murders alleged to have been committed by close relatives, including that of his sister, Isabella, duchess of Bracciano, by his brother-in-law (an event known to London audiences through Webster's dramatization of it in *The White Devil*). Francesco's major Italian biographers, on the other hand, Riguccio Galluzzi in the eighteenth century and Luciano Berti in the twentieth, have difficulty in explaining the evil reputation that they document. Both impute much of Francesco's unpopularity to his relationship with Bianca Cappello. He became Bianca's lover in 1564, less than a year after her elopement with a Florentine clerk and his accession to the regency. He maintained his relationship with her after his marriage to the Habsburg grand duchess Joanna of Austria in 1566 and married her almost immediately after Joanna's death in childbirth in 1578.[6] Joanna was as beloved by the common people as Bianca was loathed. Malespini records the account of a friend who passed Bianca's door early one morning and found it adorned with animals' horns and heaps of rubbish. Bianca was alleged to control Francesco's affections by magic, and obscene ballads and graffiti celebrated her unpopularity as a whore and her reputation as a witch: "La Bianca Capella / Puttana, strega, maliarda e fella." She successfully feigned pregnancy and tricked Francesco into accepting a changeling as his own son. (It was alleged that she subsequently had her servant and accomplice murdered to silence her.) Moreover, Francesco's prolonged absences at Pratolino gave rise to rumors of the couple's wild orgies, and his experiments with chemicals and poisons were alleged to be for Bianca's use.[7]

There were more rational reasons for Bianca's unpopularity with disaffected aristocrats and citizens. For her position as the ruler's favorite, which she exploited as dispenser of all favors, led to corruption at court and in government, which was exacerbated by the promotion of her own relatives and cronies to positions of power and influence, particularly her all-powerful brother, Vittorio, who was later dismissed back to Venice as a result of his flagrant dishonesty and unpopularity.[8] The only overtly outspoken opponent of Bianca was Francesco's brother, Cardinal Ferdinando, and it is thus unsurprising that, when Francesco and Bianca died unexpectedly while entertaining Ferdinando, rumor attributed their deaths to poisoning by the cardinal. Another tradition, however, was followed by Middleton. In this story Bianca, in attempting to murder her enemy with a poisoned tart, accidentally poisoned the duke and immediately committed suicide by eating the rest herself.[9] The symmetry of these conflicting accounts illustrates the existence of fierce factional rivalry between Bianca and Ferdinando, and suggests how that enmity was mythologized.

A similar rivalry existed between the two principal factions at James's court: the pro-Spanish group, led by the Howards, and the more loosely knit militant (or radical) Protestant group, to which belonged the earl of Pembroke and George Abbot, archbishop of Canterbury.[10] There are other features of Francesco's court that might also call to mind events at James's court during the latter half of his reign: favorites, corruption, witchcraft, murder. The most resounding court scandal had been that of the divorce of Frances Howard from her first husband, the earl of Essex, in 1613, and her remarriage in the same year to the king's then favorite and alleged lover, Robert Carr, created earl of Somerset for the occasion. The divorce had already encountered opposition. The marriage aroused more profound hostility, as it altered Somerset's position from factional independence into alliance with the Howard group. The later revelation that Somerset's former confidant and advisor, Sir Thomas Overbury, who vehemently opposed the match, had been murdered in the Tower to silence him, resulted in the conviction of the Somersets for murder, for which they were subsequently pardoned, Frances almost immediately, and Somerset, who had insisted on pleading innocent, in 1624. Frances Howard's reputation (carefully fostered by her enemies) for involvement with witchcraft, drugs, and poisons—first to incapacitate her husband sexually and to attract Somerset, and then to eliminate Overbury—created a sinister atmosphere which overhung the rest of the reign.[11]

There are some resemblances between the careers of Frances Howard and Bianca Cappello. They were both young women attempting to escape unhappy marriages; and both were demonized as whores, witches, and murderers. It is not surprising, therefore, that there are references to texts connected with Frances Howard in the masque of *Women Beware Women*. The descent of Juno Pronuba, the marriage goddess, has long been recognized as having been inspired by a similar spectacle in Ben Jonson's *Hymenaei,* performed in 1606 to celebrate Frances Howard's (first) marriage to the earl of Essex.[12] I have argued elsewhere that the opening moments of the play masque also seem to echo Jonson's: the initial altar on the stage, the attendants with tapers, the two garlanded women, and the hymns addressed to Juno are all hints of an allusion that the appearance of Juno from the heavens would confirm. I have also argued that the significance of the double wounding by Cupid's arrows to

ensure marital fidelity, as revealed by Juno in the course of the
masque, repeats the (apposite) central motif of Eros and Anteros
in Ben Jonson's *A Challenge at Tilt,* performed during the festivities for Frances Howard's (second) marriage to the earl of Somerset.[13] The Slander episode of the play masque, described in
the plot outline presented to Francesco but never reached in
performance, is also reminiscent of texts concerned with the
marriage of Frances Howard to Somerset, such as Thomas Campion's *The Masque of Squires,* written for the wedding (and
designed by Constantino de' Servi), and George Chapman's *Andromeda Liberata,* which both set out to refute as malicious
slander the gossip and scandal surrounding the couple. Perhaps
significantly, both of these texts echo one of the principal plots
of the *sbarra* celebrating the marriage of Francesco and Bianca,
in which a knight errant is held prisoner by an evil enchantress,
and guarded by a five-headed dragon, until released and restored
to his wife by Bianca herself.[14] *The Masque of Squires* depicts
knights impeded from arriving to celebrate the marriage by en-
chanters and enchantresses, emblematic representations of Error, Rumor, Curiosity, and Credulity, until released by the queen.
Andromeda Liberata depicts Somerset as a beauteous Perseus
rescuing his Andromeda/Frances from the monster of public
slander and rumor.

However, citations from at least the Somerset marriage
masques in *Women Beware Women* could serve as an entry
code to allusions to Somerset himself as well as to his wife.[15]
If Bianca's matrimonial career has some parallels with Frances
Howard's, her career as a ruler's favorite has features in common with Somerset's in relation to James. James had had favorites before, but he had never given them the political
prominence that he did to Somerset, who became a member of
the Privy Council in 1612, and, after the death of the king's
chief minister, the earl of Salisbury, acted as James's assistant
when the monarch decided to run the government personally.
In 1613 he became lord treasurer of Scotland, as well as earl of
Somerset, and in 1614, lord chamberlain.[16] Bianca's rapid social
and financial promotion as the ruler's favorite is stressed in the
confrontation between Leantio and Bianca in act 4; indeed the
scene draws particular attention to the topic of "court-saints,"
or favorites, as Leantio, too, is a courtier's favorite. It is, of
course, the elimination of Leantio as impediment to a second
marriage which provides the strongest parallel with the murder
of Sir Thomas Overbury, and suggests the sinister events sur-

rounding the Somerset marriage. Moreover, there are also hints that King James might be, in part, associated with the duke. The duke is a rather strangely contradictory figure, and clearly not a portrait of King James; but the reiteration of the word "peace" throughout the play might well encode reference to the king, as it does in Jonson's masques, especially "a good king that keeps all in peace" (1.3.48).

Interpretation of the relationship between Bianca and Francesco as suggestive of that between Somerset and James as well as of the Howard circle might well account for a further, different, textual citation in the masque of *Women Beware Women*. The central emotional impasse outlined in the masque, the inability to choose between two suitors, and the surrender of the power of choice to a goddess are strongly reminiscent of Emilia's dilemma and the resolution of it, in *The Two Noble Kinsmen*. In act 5 Emilia enters, *"her hair stuck with flowers; one before her carrying a silver hind in which is conveyed incense and sweet odours, which being set upon the altar, her maids standing apart, she sets fire to it."*[17] If the altar and tapers and invocation to Juno of the masque in *Women Beware Women* recall the opening of *Hymenaei,* the altar, the censer with the fire in it, and the "precious incense" which Isabella offers to Juno/Livia are also reminiscent of Emilia's entry in act 5, and her prayer to Diana for a sign of her destiny. Glynne Wickham has suggested that *The Two Noble Kinsmen* touches on the death of Henry, Prince of Wales and the marriage of Princess Elizabeth to the elector Palatine.[18] If this interpretation is accepted, then we have Howard texts laid against a text associated with the figureheads of militant Protestantism. The juxtaposition suggests one of the principal reasons for opposition to Somerset: his support of a Spanish marriage. As Kevin Sharpe has observed, Somerset was brought down by a cabal of the old nobility led by the earls of Pembroke and Southampton, who were both opposed to the pro-Spanish policy supported by the Howards.[19]

There has been considerable debate over the dating of *Women Beware Women*. The current consensus is that it was written around 1621.[20] It will have been noted, however, that all the texts alluded to in the play's masque belong to 1613, which was the year of the Essex/Howard divorce and the Howard/Somerset marriage (with which *Hymenaei, The Challenge at Tilt,* and *The Masque of Squires* are all associated), and the year of Princess Elizabeth's marriage to the elector Palatine (with which *The Two*

Noble Kinsmen is associated). Moreover, it has been noted that *Women Beware Women* echoes other texts Middleton wrote around the years 1613–1616, and which have been associated with the Somersets, *The Triumphs of Truth* and *The Witch.* Are we then to ascribe the date of the text to 1613, as Jackson Cope proposed, or perhaps slightly later, somewhere between 1614 and 1616?[21] There are strong arguments for accepting an earlier date for the play.

On the other hand, there would seem to be reasons for ascribing the play to a later date and for thinking that it may be concerned with the marquis of Buckingham as well as with the earl of Somerset. One is the tantalizing reference to the age of the duke as fifty-five (James's fifty-fifth birthday was on 19 June 1621). Middleton chooses to dramatize the story of Francesco and Bianca as that of an older widower and a young woman (Queen Anne had died in 1619, and Buckingham was a youth when the aging king became his lover). Another is the savagely comic nature of the masque itself, which seems to have some savor of the later Howard scandals of 1618–19 as well as the Somerset affair. For there is a self-destructive element to the successive disasters of the Howard faction, which would be comical if the events concerned were not so serious. The machinations of the earls of Northampton and Suffolk over Frances's divorce and remarriage resulted in the political death of the favorite they sought an alliance with as well as the death of the opponent they attempted to silence. Lady Suffolk's ill-fated attempts to supplant Buckingham as favorite with her own protégé resulted in Suffolk's dismissal as Lord Treasurer in 1618 for bribery and corruption (on the initiative of Buckingham), which in turn led to the dismissal of his sons from court and of his son-in-law, Viscount Wallingford, from the position of Master of the Wards. Sir Thomas Lake, the secretary of state in charge of negotiations for the Spanish marriage, was dismissed in 1619 as the result of his wife's slanderous accusations of incest and attempted poisoning among members of their family.[22] Thenceforth, Buckingham was the unchallenged power at court. These events might be perceived to find echoes in the destruction of Livia and her family: incest, poison, internecine squabbles, and malicious accusations (perhaps even the surprise exit of the Master of the Wards?)

Hints that the topical allusions in *Women Beware Women* might extend to include Buckingham's years of ascendancy as favorite might, I suggest, be found in yet another citation in the play. The only textual indication that an audience is invited to compare Francesco's regime in Florence with events in England is an apparent allusion to a completely different text, an account of a Medicean event involving both Francesco and Bianca directly, the tale of a merry jest played by Francesco on his courtiers. In 1578 Francesco organized a dress rehearsal of a "happening" commissioned by Bianca to entertain her brother on his return to Florence. Unsuspecting courtiers were sat in a magic circle in the garden that concealed a deep hole, covered by planks and grass that could be opened suddenly by pulling on a chain. Within the circle were two braziers filled with burning coals, and a jar of chemicals for producing smoke: sulphur, pitch, and asafetida. As the presiding necromancer conjured up devils, an over-enthusiastic volunteer put too many chemicals on the coals, so that some of the participants were nearly killed by asphyxiation. Amid explosive noises and devils' howls, and in the eerie light of underground fires, the trap door was opened, and the group of courtiers, including Francesco, were precipitated into the pit. Many of them were terrified, unsure whether they were alive or dead. The "entertainment" finished much more serenely, with bejeweled, almost naked girls coming to greet the participants with angelic song, leading them out through an underground passage to a lavish banquet of sugar fruits in a gilded tent. The experience thus offered to participants was to pass through hell and to reach paradise, a Dantesque or Mozartian voyage of mystical initiation. Several did not complete the journey, however. Overcome by the smoke and injured by the fall, they had to be carried to bed and attended by doctors. None of this pain and damage dampened Francesco's enthusiasm for the event, which he had every intention of performing for Bianca's brother; but during the preparations news suddenly reached him of his wife's death, and the joke was never repeated.

The account of this extraordinary event is given in Malespini's *Ducento Novelle*, Middleton's probable source for the main plot.[23] Elements of the masque in *Women Beware Women* echo Malespini's narrative: Isabella bearing "a censer with fire in it," her offering of "this precious incense" and Livia overcome by the poisonous fumes. The ward's reference to his costume with "a foul fiend's head," as well as his interest in the mechanics of the trick, would seem to link the trap-door plot with Bianca's. The most deliberate (if indirect) reference to Francesco's and

Bianca's entertainment seems to occur, however, in Livia's initial description of the masque her family is to perform:

Livia.   This gentleman and I had once a purpose
          To have honoured the first marriage of the Duke
          With an invention of his own; 'twas ready,
          The pains well past, most of the charge bestowed on't,
          Then came the death of your good mother, niece,
          And turned the glory of it all to black.

                                                    (4.2.202–207)

Livia's account of the history of the play masque both gives a garbled version of events in Florence and confirms the masque's links with them: Francesco did write "an invention" for his first marriage, *Il Trionfo de' Sogni,* but he also contributed the later episode of the paradisal banquet to the entertainment in Bianca's garden. Livia says the performance was canceled because of the death of Isabella's mother; the performance of Bianca and Francesco's entertainment for Vittorio Cappello was canceled because of the death of Francesco's wife. Once again, there are too many coincidences to be accidental, and allusion to Malespini would seem to be deliberate.

Indeed, once hints of the presence of the tale have been observed, it is possible to see that the structure of the play may be based on it, or rather a reversal of it. For the shock descent into hell comes at the close of the play, and emphasis is put on the fact that the intended conclusion of the masque will not be, and is not, reached. It is Bianca's version that is performed at the close of *Women Beware Women,* whereas the duke's banquet is performed earlier, in the third act. Francesco's paradisal banquet of sugared or marzipan fruits is echoed in the play by the reiterated wordplay on delicate morsels, "sweetmeats," "marchpane," and Leantio's description of the rich who "Grow fat with ease, banquet and toy and play" (1.3.33). The context of metaphors of food in *Women Beware Women* is that of "Cupid's feast" (2.2.402), reducing all sexual relations to coarseness or confusion of appetite. The play presents a ruling class that cannot differentiate between the taste of sin and virtue, wormwood and nectar, or for that matter between offering worldly advancement and the fruit of damnation:

          She that is fortunate in a duke's favou'r
          Lights on a tree that bears all women's wishes;
          If your own mother saw you pluck fruit there

> She would commend your wit, and praise the time
> Of your nativity. Take hold of glory.
>
> (2.2.370–74)

Malespini seems to have regarded his tale of the Medicean "garden-party" as an instance of aristocratic wit and good taste; but it is transposed by Middleton into a different garden event, into an analogue of the tale of Eden. Beyond any topical significance lies a somber moral theme closely associated with Middleton's Calvinism and accessible to all members of an audience.

However, it would seem that the references to Francesco and Bianca's entertainment, positioned as they are among the hints of other texts alluded to, indicate that Malespini's text should be included in the network of topical allusions in the play. If we return to Livia's speech, which prepares us for the multiple citations in the masque, it will be recalled that she stresses the performance will be a *revival*. True, her words prepare us for the "revival" of the Howard masques; but they could be saying more than that. They could be intimating that the entertainment, although relevant to or referring to events from the past (the duke's first marriage), is also applicable to the present (the duke's second marriage): a device to fit "these times so well *too*." Thus the play might present us, on a political level, with a composite view of James's reign since 1606, dominated by two principal favorites, with references to Somerset implying that Buckingham's ascendancy over the king was proving equally disastrous.

Buckingham's replacement of Somerset was initially regarded with optimism, for he had been (successfully) promoted by opponents of the Howards as a rival for the king's favor. His rise was even more meteoric than Somerset's: in 1615 he became a knight, Groom of the Bedchamber, and, according to Roger Lockyer, James's lover. In 1616 he became Master of the Horse, a member of the Order of the Garter, and Viscount Villiers, in 1617 the earl of Buckingham and a member of the Privy Council (five years before the heir to the throne, Prince Charles), in 1618 the marquis of Buckingham. His position also led to great wealth: Roger Lockyer has documented the gifts of land, property, and money that, in addition to the income which his virtual monopoly of patronage brought him, made him one of the richest men in the land in a few short years.[24] By 1621, however, it might well have seemed that the regime he presided over was a revival of the years of Howard dominance and their ills. His original backers were profoundly disappointed by his support for the king's pro-Spanish policy, and by the corruption he practiced and encouraged. His extortionate fortune hunting for himself and for his relatives, his sale of peerages, his responsibility for increasingly absurd but lucrative monopolies had alienated many members of both Lords and Commons, as well as the city. It has been argued that he sacrificed his client, Sir Francis Bacon, who was impeached for corruption in the Parliament of 1621, in order to save himself.[25]

Conrad Russell has remarked that "almost inevitably, a history of James's reign becomes a history of sexual politics."[26] The career and reputation of Bianca Cappello seem particularly apt as an analogue of the two principal favorites of James's reign, her association with necromancy, poison, and murder giving the flavor of events during Somerset's supremacy, and her reputation for promoting her relatives and corrupting the processes of government giving the flavor of Buckingham's years of influence. For if one looks at Bianca's career, there are similarities with Buckingham's. He shared Bianca's distinctive combination of extraordinary charm and beauty, intelligence, and ruthless ambition (and contemporary accounts describe his almost feminine allure). Both rose from impoverished gentility to supreme power and riches as the consequence of being the lover of their head of state. If Buckingham could not marry James, James frequently addressed him as "wife"; and David Bergeron cites a letter from Buckingham to James acknowledging "more affection than between lovers in the best kind man and wife."[27] If Bianca poisoned Francesco, Buckingham was accused of poisoning James.[28]

Consideration of the portrayal of Bianca in *Women Beware Women* reveals possible traces of Buckingham's career as well as that of Somerset. Bianca is virtually prostituted to the duke by conniving courtiers once she has caught his eye; Abbot and his allies behaved in a similar manner with Buckingham when attempting to supplant Somerset.[29] Moreover, allusion to Buckingham may account for the alteration in the tale of the duke's death; for the substitution of a cup of wine for a poisoned tart may be a reminder of Buckingham's first court position, that of the king's cupbearer. There might also be an allusion to Buckingham in the play's central banquet scene: for there was an extraordinary banquet thrown by Buckingham in 1618, known as "the friends' feast" as it was designed to reconcile the conflicts of Prince Charles with the favorite and the king. James took the opportunity to pledge his devotion to the entire Villiers family, virtually ordering his son and heir "to advance that house above all others whatever." Whether the impropriety of the duke's exaggerated public praise of Bianca as his mistress in act 3 reflects this occasion, or hints more generally at James's indiscreet public pronouncements on his devotion to Buckingham—in 1617 he announced to the Privy Council that "Christ had His John and I have my George"—there could certainly be an element of topicality in the scene.[30]

The possibility that *Women Beware Women* is concerned with James's relationship with Buckingham as well as with Somerset may be confirmed in the very last lines of the play, spoken by the Cardinal:

> Two kings on one throne cannot sit together,
> But one must needs down, for his title's wrong;
> So where lust reigns, that prince cannot reign long.
>
> (5.2.223–25)

The allusion is to Ovid's account of Jove's self-transformation into a bull to carry off Europa in book 2 of the *Metamorphoses:* "Non bene conveniunt, nec in una sede morantur, / maiestas et amor." ("Majesty and love go ill together, nor can they long share one abode.") (Arthur Golding translates *"sede"* as "state," an ambiguous word that might well signify "chair of state"; Middleton clearly thinks of it as chair or throne.)[31] Ovid's tale is one of the degradation of divine kingship: "Abandoning the dignity of his sceptre, the father and ruler of the gods, whose hand wields the flaming three-forked bolt, whose nod shakes the universe, adopted the guise of a bull."[32] The tale was a traditional one in treatments of kings and their favorites. It is used, for instance, by Samuel Daniel in his *Complaint of Rosamond* when describing the grief of King Henry after Eleanor of Acquitaine has murdered his mistress, Rosamond.[33] The allusion recurs in Marlowe's *Edward II.* Moelwyn Merchant, in the New Mermaids edition of the play, first pointed out the visual impact of the royal entry to the New Temple in act 1, scene 5: Edward seats his lover, Gaveston, in his queen consort's throne, thus forcing the peers of the realm to do obeisance to the upstart favorite while doing so to the king. An indignant Mortimer Senior protests: "What man of noble birth can brook this sight? / *Quam male conveniunt.*"[34] Middleton's politicization of Ovid, "two kings," "reign," seems a deliberate echo of another moment in *Edward II,* however, that in act 5 when Edward removes his crown and surrenders to Mortimer: "Two kings in England cannot reign at once" (5.1.58).

It does seem possible that allusion to the story of Edward II was an established one in commentary upon the amours of King James. It has recently been suggested that Marlowe took the relationship between James and his favorites as the inspiration for his *Edward II*.[35] The comparison between Somerset and Gaveston was made in 1616, by Richard Niccols in *Sir Thomas Overburies Vision:* "Thy foes decline, proud *Gaveston* is down, / No wanton *Edward* weares our Englands crowne."[36] In April 1621 a similar allusion had been made, sensationally, in a speech to the House of Lords by Sir Henry Yelverton, the former attorney general, as part of a maneuver to topple Buckingham. Parliament, in investigating the abuse of monopolies, had turned to investigate the patent of gold and silver thread owned by Buckingham's brothers, Sir Edward and Kit Villiers. This patent was particularly unpopular in the city, as it was considered to infringe the rights of the company of goldsmiths. Yelverton defended himself by saying he had allowed unlicensed manufacturers to be imprisoned only because threatened with dismissal by Buckingham: "I dare say if my Lord of Buckingham had but read the articles exhibited in this place against Hugh Spencer, and had known the danger of placing and displacing officers about a King, he would not have pursued me with such bitterness." Hugh Spencer was the hated successor to Gaveston in Edward II's favor. The allusion was not missed by Prince Charles, who was present at the debate and who leaped to his feet demanding that Yelverton be stopped, "as he could not permit his father's government to be 'paralleled and scandalised' with the reign of Edward II."[37] Opponents of Buckingham in the Lords tried to limit the damage by maintaining that only the favorite had been offended, not the king. But James's interpretation was different: "If [Buckingham] Spencer, I Edward II [. . .] To reckon me with such a prince is to esteem me a weak man, and I had rather be no king than such a one as King Edward II."[38] It would thus seem that the final lines of *Women Beware Women* confirm that the play is concerned with the king's relationships with favorites; and if Middleton's allusion to Ovid does incorporate an allusion to Marlowe's *Edward II,* then the reference would be highly relevant to controversy over Buckingham during the first session of Parliament in 1621.

The argument that *Women Beware Women* is concerned with Buckingham as well as Somerset is also strengthened by consid eration of his role in the release of the Somersets from the Tower in January 1622. In 1621 he was negotiating the purchase of Viscount Wallingford's London residence; and Wallingford's condition for selling was the release of his sister-in-law, Frances Howard. In the event, both husband and wife were released into Wallingford's custody; and Lockyer regards Buckingham's action as "marking the final stage of the reconciliation between Buckingham and the Howards."[39] There would thus be good reason for allusion to Howard texts and reevocation of earlier scandals surrounding the Somersets around January 1622, which I believe to be the approximate date of the play. In the crucial act 4, scene 2, where Livia provides the clues to intertextual references to come in the masque, she hands Hippolito the duke's pardon for the death of Leantio. Francesco did nothing to punish the killers of Bianca's husband. Likewise, James allowed the Somersets to evade the consequences of their conviction for the murder of Overbury (although, as already noted, he did not pardon the earl officially until 1624).

A dating of the play around 1621–22 would also make more sense of an allusion to *The Two Noble Kinsmen*. The expulsion of King James's daughter and son-in-law from Bohemia and the Palatinates, and their exile in The Hague, had polarized antagonism between those who favored peace with Spain, ratified by a marriage treaty, and those who supported war on behalf of international Protestantism. Members of the audience who knew the play (and it had been revived at court in 1619) might have recalled that it opens with an intended marriage, that of Theseus and Hippolyta, which is interrupted by the entrance of three grieving queens, whose plight could have suggested that of Elizabeth of Bohemia:

> *First Queen.* ... of thy boundless goodness take some note
> That for our crowned heads we have no roof.
> (1.1.51–52)

The debate between the queens and Theseus on the possible options of war or marriage in this scene, taken together with the insistent interrogation of the value of peace which is a recurring motif in *Women Beware Women,* might hint at concern in the play over the defence of Protestantism and the Spanish marriage.

For members of an audience sufficiently familiar with Italian history to perceive unuttered political analogies, within the fatal love story of an Italian duke and his mistress the potential for the construction of another text is contained, one concerned the corruption of the English monarch and his surrender of the control of public affairs to his favorites, just as Francesco's authority and reputation had been destroyed by his liaison with Bianca Cappello. We are dealing with political mythologies here, and the way in which a hostile stance modifies official propaganda by modifying the texts that construct official representations of power. In *Women Beware Women* Middleton deconstructs the myth of Jamesean authority through the implicit contrast in the play masque between *Hymenaei* and Francesco's diabolic "garden party." *Hymenaei* shows an emblem of the house of Stuart at the height of its prestige, a spectacle of divine right and just rule, personated by Juno in all the magnificence a court masque could bestow upon her, aloft in the heavens, second only to a vigilant Jove. Malespini's account of Francesco and Bianca's practical joke, on the other hand, which recounts the descent of a ruler and his courtiers into hell, provides Middleton with an alternative emblem for James's court toward the end of his reign. In the play masque, Juno collapses to earth, and if the duke initially seems set above and apart from his doomed courtiers, the play action suggests he joins them in his dying moments.[40] For those unfamiliar with Malespini, the cardinal's metaphors of conflagration seem to offer a similar spectacle:

> The sparkles fly through cities—here one takes,
> Another catches there, and in short time
> Waste all to cinders. But remember still
> What burnt the valleys first came from the hill
> . . . .
>   If men of good lives,
> Who by their virtuous actions stir up others
> To noble and religious imitation,
> Receive the greater glory after death—
> As sin must needs confess—what may they feel
> In height of torments, and in weight of vengeance,
> Not only they themselves not doing well,
> But sets a light up to show men to hell?
>   (4.1.211–14, 20–27)

The picture is one of a whole nation being precipitated into damnation. If *Women Beware Women* was written around the beginning of 1622, Middleton is not alone in perceiving the times with great pessimism, linking the failure to defend Protestantism with the morally ruinous conduct of the ruling class. The theme runs through other oppositional texts of the time, such as George Wither's *Wither's Motto* (1621) and Thomas Scot's *The Belgicke Pismire* (1622). Livia's description of the masque holds true for the play as a whole: "'Tis a device would fit these times so well too."

Notes

I am deeply indebted to colleagues and friends for their comments on drafts of this paper, especially to Professor Richard Dutton, to Dr. Sandra Clark, and to Dr. A. A. Bromham.

1. The transaction has been described by Patterson as "the institutionally unspeakable mak[ing] itself heard inferentially, in the space between what is written or acted, and the audience, *knowing what they know,* might expect to read and see." *See* Annabel Patterson, *Censorship and Interpretation: The Conditions of Writing and Reading in Early Modern England* (Madison: University of Wisconsin Press, 1984), 63. *See also* Richard Dutton, *Mastering the Revels: The Regulation of Censorship of English Renaissance Drama* (London: Macmillan, 1991). Dutton observes that too literal and exact an allegory would invite objections. The analogue should suggest points of comparison rather than establish exact parallels (*see* 205).

2. A political reading is not the only, or necessarily the most important, one of *Women Beware Women. See* Zara Bruzzi and A. A. Bromham, "'The soil alters; Y'are in another country': Multiple Perspectives and Political Resonances in *Women Beware Women*," in *Shakespeare's Italy: Functions of Italian Locations in Renaissance Drama,* ed. Michele Marrapodi et al. (Manchester: Manchester University Press, 1993), 251–71.

3. For a detailed account of Medicean influence on Stuart court culture, *see* Roy Strong, *Henry, Prince of Wales and England's Lost Renaissance* (London: Thames and Hudson, 1986). G. P. V. Akrigg also has a useful chapter on "The Whitehall Connoisseurs," in *Jacobean Pageant: The Court of King James I* (Cambridge: Harvard University Press, 1963). For correspondence from Italy and manuscript travel diaries, *see* David Howarth, *Lord Arundel and His Circle* (New Haven: Yale University Press, 1985).

4. Sir Robert Dallington, *A Survey of the Great Dukes State of Tuscany In the yeare of our Lord 1596* (London, 1605), especially 37–39 and 66. J. R. Hale outlines the changes in the Florentine constitution under Grand Ducal rule in *Florence and the Medici: The Pattern of Control* (London: Thames and Hudson, 1977). It is interesting to notice that Jacopo Riguccio Galluzzi, in his *Istoria del Granducato di Toscana sotto il Governo della casa Medici,* 5 vols. (Firenze, 1781), still the most comprehensive study, is convinced that Dallington associated with oppositional factions to have written of Ferdinando as he did.

5. When the earl of Arundel, a Howard and a Catholic, spent a prolonged period of study in Tuscany while on a connoisseur's tour of Italy and France, accompanied by Inigo Jones, "in London there was talk of how Arundel was not merely eccentric but fundamentally unsound and possibly even treason-

able." He was later cross-questioned by George Abbot, archbishop of Canterbury, about his activities in Italy. *See* Howarth, *Lord Arundel*, 43 and 51.

6. This account is based principally on Galluzzi, Hale, and Luciano Berti, *Il Principe dello Studiolo: Francesco de' Medici e la fine del Rinascimento fiorentino* (Firenze: Edam, 1976).

7. Janet Steegman, *Bianca Cappello* (London: Constable, 1913), 100–101, 148–54, 164–66 and 217–18. The rhyme about Bianca is cited from Marcello Vannucci, *I Medici: Una famiglia al potere* (Roma: Newton Compton, 1987), 329.

8. Galluzzi, book 4, 2: 179–80 and 222–25.

9. For a discussion of sources of *Women Beware Women, see* J. R. Mulryne's edition for The Revels Plays (Manchester: Manchester University Press, 1975). All citations from the play are from this edition.

10. For shifts in English foreign policy in this period *see* S. L. Adams, "Spain or the Netherlands? The Dilemmas of Early Stuart Policy," in *Before the Civil War: Essays on Early Stuart Politics and Government,* ed. H. Tomlinson (London: Macmillan, 1983).

11. This account is taken principally from William McElwee, *The Murder of Sir Thomas Overbury* (London: Faber and Faber, 1952). David Lindley's recent *The Trials of Frances Howard: Fact and Fiction at the Court of King James* (London and New York: Routledge, 1993) offers a fascinating deconstruction of the myth, whereas my argument is concerned with its construction.

12. *See* Mulryne's edition, 145, 159–62.

13. *Shakespeare's Italy,* 259–60.

14. *See* Raffaello Gualterotti, *Feste Nelle Nozze Del Serenissimo Don Francesco Gran Duca di Toscana Et della Sereniss. Sua Consorte la Sig. Bianca Cappello* (Firenze, 1579).

15. A. A. Bromham, "Thomas Middleton's *The Triumphs of Truth:* City Politics in 1613," in *The Seventeenth Century* 10 (spring 1995) 1–25.

16. *See* David Harris Willson, *King James VI and I* (London: Jonathan Cape, 1956), and David Bergeron, *Royal Family, Royal Lovers: King James of England and Scotland* (Columbia and London: University of Missouri Press, 1991).

17. Opening stage directions to act 5, scene 3, in *William Shakespeare: The Complete Works,* ed. Stanley Wells and Gary Taylor (Oxford: Clarendon Press, 1988). All citations from the play are from this edition.

18. Glynne Wickham, *"Two Noble Kinsmen* or *A Midsummer Night's Dream, Part II?,"* in *The Elizabethan Theatre,* ed. G. R. Hibbard (London: Macmillan, 1980), vol. 7, pp. 167–96, cited in the Oxford Shakespeare edition of *The Two Noble Kinsmen,* ed. Eugene M. Waith (Oxford: Oxford University Press, 1989). Waith gives a very useful account of the affinity of the play with the taste of Prince Henry, and with entertainments for the marriage of Princess Elizabeth.

19. Kevin Sharpe, "The Earl of Arundel, His Circle, and the Opposition to the Duke of Buckingham, 1618–1628," in *Faction & Parliament: Essays on Early Stuart History,* ed. Kevin Sharpe (London: Methuen, 1978), 211.

20. *Women Beware Women* was published only in 1657, and there have been widely differing views about the date of writing ranging from 1613 to 1627. Margot Heinemann favors a late date, hearing "the authentic ring of the late-Jacobean court" and echoes of Buckingham in "the Duke's mixture of

naked power, bribery and over-sweet romantic rhetoric." See *Puritanism and Theatre: Middleton and Opposition Drama under the Early Stuarts* (Cambridge: Cambridge University Press, 1980), 193. Mulryne, after summarizing various theories, himself settles for 1621 as the date of composition or performance (xxxvii–xxxviii). Recently, there has been a general consensus of a date of circa 1621: Brian Loughrey and Neil Taylor, for example, in their Penguin edition of *Five Plays: Thomas Middleton* (London, 1988), xix; R.V. Holdsworth in *Three Jacobean Revenge Tragedies* (London: Macmillan, 1990), 276; Martin White, *Middleton and Tourneur* (Basingstoke and London: Macmillan, 1992), 174.

21. Jackson I. Cope, "The Date of Middleton's *Women Beware Women*," *Modern Language Notes* 76 (1961): 65–78.

22. Akrigg, *Jacobean Pageant* 210–14; Samuel Rawson Gardiner, *History of England from the Accession of King James to the Outbreak of Civil War 1603–1642,* 10 vols (London: Longmans, Green & Co., 1885), vol. 2, chapter 27.

23. Celio Malespini, *Ducento Novelle* (Venezia, 1609), Part 2, *novella* 24, pp. 80–86.

24. Roger Lockyer, *Buckingham: The Life and Political Career of George Villiers, First Duke of Buckingham, 1592–1628* (London: Longman, 1981).

25. This account is based on Lockyer, *Buckingham;* Conrad Russell, *Parliaments and English Politics, 1621–1629* (Oxford: Clarendon Press, 1979); and Robert Zaller, *The Parliament of 1621: A Study in Constitutional Conflict* (Berkeley: University of California Press, 1971).

26. Conrad Russell, *The Reign of King James* (London: Methuen, 1973), 38.

27. Bergeron, *Royal Family,* 124.

28. Linda Levy Peck, *Court Patronage and Corruption* (London: Routledge, 1991), 178. Peck also mentions the rhetoric of sorcery associated with corruption.

29. Lockyer, *Buckingham,* 16–20.

30. Lockyer, *Buckingham,* 34, and Bergeron, *Royal Family,* 168.

31. Ovid, *Metamorphoses,* book 2, lines 846–47; trans. Mary M. Innes (Harmondsworth: Penguin, 1955), 73; *Shakespeare's Ovid: Being Arthur Golding's Translation of the Metamorphoses,* ed. W. H. D. Rouse (London: Centaur Press, 1961), 61.

32. Ovid, *Metamorphoses:* 72.

33. "The Complaint of Rosamond," in *Motives of Woe: Shakespeare and "Female Complaint"—A Critical Anthology,* ed. John Kerrigan (Oxford: Clarendon Press, 1991), 188, lines 696–700:

> He doth represse what grief would els bewray,
> Least that too much his passions might discouer:
> And yet respect scarce bridles such a Louer.
> So farre transported that he knowes not whether,
> For loue and Maiestie dwell ill together.

34. Christopher Marlowe, *Edward II,* ed. W. Moelwyn Merchant, New Mermaids Series (London: Ernest Benn, 1967), 1.4.12–13. All citations are from this edition.

35. *Edward II,* ed. Richard Rowland, in *The Complete Works of Christopher Marlowe,* 4 vols. (Oxford: Clarendon Press, 1994) 3: xxi—xxxiii, where Rowland also comments on Jacobean applications of Edward's story to James's relationships with Somerset and, especially, Buckingham.

36. The point is made in Peck, *Court Patronage and Corruption,* 177.

37. Zaller, *The Parliament of 1621,* 120.

38. A fuller version of the affair may be found in Lockyer, *Buckingham,* 100–103, from which this account is taken.

39. Ibid., 119.

40. *See* R. V. Holdsworth, "*Women Beware Women* and *The Changeling* on the Stage," in *Three Jacobean Revenge Tragedies,* 258.

Bibliography

This is a bibliography of secondary literature. Primary sources and editions of plays may be located through the endnotes and the index. Although this bibliography specifically refers to the intertextual relevance of Anglo-Italian drama of the Renaissance, important entries of some theoretical works in adjacent fields are also listed.

Agnew, J.-C. *Worlds Apart: The Market and the Theater in Anglo-American Thought, 1550–1750*. Cambridge: Cambridge University Press, 1986.

Akrigg, G. P. V. *Jacobean Pageant: The Court of King James I*. Cambridge: Harvard University Press, 1962.

Alonge, R. *Struttura e ideologia nel teatro italiano fra '500 e '900*. Turin: Edizioni Stampatori, 1978.

Altman, C. F. "Intratextual Rewriting: Textuality as Language Formation." In *The Sign in Music and Literature,* edited by Wendy Steiner, 39–51. Austin: University of Texas Press, 1981.

Altman, Joel B. *The Tudor Play of Mind*. Berkeley: University of California Press, 1978.

Anderson, D. K., Jr. "The Heart and the Banquet: Imagery in Ford's *'Tis a Pity* and *The Broken Heart*." *Studies in English Literature* 2 (spring, 1962): 209–17.

Anderson, G. *Ancient Fictions: The Novel in the Graeco-Roman World*. London: Croom Helm, 1984.

Andrews, J. F., ed. *William Shakespeare: His World, His Work, His Influence*. 3 vols. New York: Charles Scribner's Sons, 1985.

Andrews, R. "*Gl'Ingannati* as a Text for Performance." *Italian Studies* 37 (1982): 26–48.

———. *Scripts and Scenarios: The Performance of Comedy in Renaissance Italy*. Cambridge: Cambridge University Press, 1993.

Angenot, M. "Intertextualité, interdiscursivité, discours social." *Texte* 2 (1983): 101–12.

Apollonio, M. *Storia del teatro italiano*. 2 vols. Florence: Sansoni, 1981.

Ariani, M. "L'*Orbecche* di G. B. Giraldi e la poetica dell'orrore." *Rassegna della letteratura italiana* 75 (1971): 432–50.

———. "La trasgressione e l'ordine. L'*Orbecche* di G. B. Giraldi Cinthio e la fondazione del linguaggio tragico cinquecentesco." *Rassegna della letteratura italiana* 83, nos. 1–3 (1979): 117–80.

———. *Tra Classicismo e Manierismo. Il teatro tragico del Cinquecento*. Florence: Olschki, 1974.

321

Armato, R. P. "The Play is the Thing: A Study of Giraldi's *Orbecche* and Its Senecan Antecedents." In *Medieval Epic to the "Epic Theatre" of Brecht: Essays in Comparative Literature,* edited by R. P. Armato and J. M. Spalek, 57–83. Berkeley and Los Angeles: University of California Press, 1968.

Armstrong, W. A. "The Influence of Seneca and Machiavelli on the Elizabethan Tyrant." *Review of English Studies* 24, no. 93 (1948): 19–35.

Arnott, W. G. *Menander, Plautus, Terence.* Oxford: Clarendon Press, 1975.

Arthos, J. "Shakespeare's Transformation of Plautus." *Comparative Drama* 1 (1967–68): 239–53.

Ascoli A. R. *Ariosto's Bitter Harmony.* Princeton: Princeton University Press, 1987.

Ascoli, A. R., and V. Kahn, eds. *Machiavelli and the Discourse of Literature.* Ithaca: Cornell University Press, 1993.

Astington, J. "Malvolio and the Eunuchs: Text and Revels in *Twelfth Night.*" *Shakespeare Survey* 46 (1994): 23–34.

Attolini, G. *Teatro e spettacolo nel Rinascimento.* Bari: Laterza, 1988.

Bakhtin, M. M. *Rabelais and His World.* Translated by Helene Iswolsky. Cambridge: MIT Press, 1968.

———. *Estetica e romanzo.* Turin: Einaudi, 1979.

———. *The Dialogic Imagination: Four Essays.* Translated by Caryl Emerson, edited by Michael Holquist. Austin: University of Texas Press, 1981.

———. *The Bakhtin Reader: Selected Writings of Bakhtin.* London: Edward Arnold, 1994.

Baldi, G. "Le commedie di Sforza Oddi e l'ideologia della Controriforma." *Lettere italiane* 23 (1971): 43–62.

Baldwin, T. W. *William Shakespeare's Small Latine and Lesse Greeke.* 2 vols. Urbana: University of Illinois Press, 1944.

———. *Shakespeare's Five-Act Structure.* Urbana: University of Illinois Press, 1947.

———. *On the Literary Genetics of Shakespeare's Plays, 1592–1594.* Urbana: University of Illinois Press, 1959.

———. *On the Compositional Genetics of "The Comedy of Errors."* Urbana: University of Illinois Press, 1965.

Balk, A. "Revolting against the Legend: Anti-Shakespearean Elements in Jules Laforgue's *Hamlet.*" In *Reclamations of Shakespeare,* edited by A. J. Hoenselaars, 151–58. Amsterdam: Rodopi, 1994.

Ball, R. H. "Cinthio's *Epitia* and *Measure for Measure.*" In *Elizabethan Studies and Other Essays in Honor of George F. Reynolds,* edited by E. J. West, 132–46. Boulder: University of Colorado Studies, 1945.

Barasch, F. K. "The Bayeux Painting and Shakespearean Improvisation." *Shakespeare Bulletin* 11, no. 3 (1993): 33–36.

Baratto, M. *La commedia del Cinquecento.* Vicenza: Neri Pozza, 1977.

Barber, C. L. *Shakespeare Festive Comedy.* Princeton: Princeton University Press, 1959.

Bàrberi Squarotti, G. *Machiavelli o la scelta della letteratura.* Rome: Bulzoni Editore, 1987.

Barish, J. "Shakespearean Violence: A Preliminary Survey." In *Violence in*

Drama, edited by James Redmond, 101–21. Cambridge: Cambridge University Press, 1991.

Barkan, L. *The Gods Made Flesh.* New Haven: Yale University Press, 1986.

Barker, F., and P. Hulme, "Nymphs and Reapers Heavily Vanish: The Discursive Con-texts of *The Tempest.*" In *Alternative Shakespeares,* edited by John Drakasis, 191–205. London: Methuen, 1985.

Baron, H. *The Crisis of the Early Italian Renaissance.* Princeton: Princeton University Press, 1966.

Barthes, R. *S/Z.* Paris: Seuil, 1970. Translated by by Richard Miller. London: Cape, 1975.

———. *Le Plaisir du Texte.* Paris: Seuil, 1973. Translated by Richard Miller as *The Pleasure of the Text.* London: Cape, 1976.

———. *Empire of Signs.* Translated by Richard Howard. London: Cape, 1982.

Bartlett, K. R. "The Strangeness of Strangers: English Impressions of Italy in the Sixteenth Century." *Quaderni d'italianistica* 1 (1980): 46–93.

Barton, A. *Ben Jonson, Dramatist.* Cambridge: Cambridge University Press, 1984.

———. "Livy, Machiavelli and Shakespeare's *Coriolanus.*" *Shakespeare Survey* 38 (1985): 115–29. Reprinted in A. Barton, *Essays Mainly Shakespearean,* 91–160. Cambridge: Cambridge University Press, 1994.

———. "Falstaff and the Comic Community." In *Shakespeare's 'Rough Magic:' Essays in Memory of C. L. Barber,* edited by Peter Erickson and Coppélia Kahn, 131–48. Newark: University of Delaware Press, 1985. Reprinted in A. Barton, *Essays Mainly Shakespearean,* 70–90. Cambridge: Cambridge University Press, 1994.

Barton, C. A. *The Sorrows of Ancient Romans: The Gladiators and the Monster.* Princeton: Princeton University Press, 1993.

Bate, J. "Ovid and the Mature Tragedies." *Shakespeare Survey* 41 (1989): 133–44.

———. "Ovid and the Sonnets; or, did Shakespeare Feel the Anxiety of Influence?" *Shakespeare Survey* 42 (1990): 65–76.

———. *Shakespeare and Ovid.* Oxford: Clarendon Press, 1993.

Bates, C. "Weaving and Writing in *Othello.*" *Shakespeare Survey* 46 (1994): 51–60.

Bawcutt, "Machiavelli and Marlowe's *The Jew of Malta.*" *Renaissance Drama,* n. s., 3 (1970): 3–49.

Beacham, R. C. "Violence on the Street: Playing Rough in Plautus." In *Violence in Drama,* edited by James Redmond, 47–68. Cambridge: Cambridge University Press, 1991.

Beck, E. "Terence Improved: The Paradigm of the Prodigal Son in English Renaissance Comedy." *Renaissance Drama,* n. s., 6 (1973): 107–22.

Beecher, D., and M. Ciavolella, eds. *Comparative Critical Approaches to Renaissance Comedy.* Ottawa: Dovehouse Edition, 1986.

Beiner, G. "The Libido as Pharmakos, or The Triumph of Love: *The Merry Wives of Windsor* in the Context of Comedy." *Orbis Litterarum* 43 (1988): 195–216.

Bella, C. *Eros e censura nella tragedia dal '500 al '700.* Florence: Vallecchi Editore, 1981.

Belsey, C. "Senecan Vacillation and Elizabethan Deliberation: Influence or Confluence?" *Renaissance Drama,* n. s. 6 (1973): 65–88.

———. *The Subject of Tragedy. Identity and Difference in Renaissance Drama.* London: Routledge, 1985.

Bennet, M. L. "Shakespeare's *Much Ado* and Its Possible Italian Sources." *Studies in English* no. 17 (1937): 52–74.

Bennett, K. C. "Reconstructing *The Winter's Tale.*" *Shakespeare Survey* 46 (1994): 81–90.

Bergel, L. "The Rise of Cinquecento Tragedy." *Renaissance Drama* 7 (1965): 197–217.

———. "Imitation and Originality in Cinquecento Tragedy." In *Proceedings of the Fourth Congress of the International Comparative Literature Association,* edited by F. Jost, 764–73. Fribourg, 1964; The Hague, 1966.

———. "Semiramis in the Italian and Spanish Baroque." *Forum Italicum* 7 (1973): 227–49.

Berger, H., Jr. "On the Continuity of the *Henriad:* A Critique of Some Literary and Theatrical Approaches." In *Shakespeare Left and Right,* edited by Ivo Kamps, 225–40. London: Routledge, 1991.

Berrigan, J. R. "Latin Tragedy in the Quattrocento." *Humanistica Lovaniensia* 23 (1973): 2–19.

Berry, H. "Italian Definitions of Tragedy and Comedy Arrive in England." *Studies in English Literature* 14 (spring, 1974): 179–87.

Berti, L. *Il Principe dello Studiolo: Francesco de' Medici e la fine del Rinascimento fiorentino.* Florence: Edam, 1976.

Berveiller, M. "Influencias italianas en las comedias de Ben Jonson." *Filosofía y letras* 3 (1942): 51–71.

Bevington, D. *From 'Mankind' to Marlowe: Growth of Structure in the Popular Drama of Tudor England.* Cambridge: Harvard University Press, 1962.

———. *Tudor Drama and Politics: A Critical Approach to Topical Meaning.* Cambridge: Harvard University Press, 1968.

———. *Action is Eloquence: Shakespeare's Language of Gesture.* Cambridge: Harvard University Press, 1984.

Bloom, H. *The Anxiety of Influence. A Theory of Poetry.* Oxford: Oxford University Press, 1973.

———. *Agon: Towards a Theory of Revisionism.* Oxford: Oxford University Press, 1982.

Bloomfield, M. W. "Quoting and Alluding: Shakespeare in the English Language." In *Shakespeare: Aspects of Influence,* edited by G. B. Evans, 1–20. Cambridge: Harvard University Press, 1976.

Bluestone, M. *From Story to Stage. The Dramatic Adoption of Prose Fiction in the Period of Shakespeare and His Contemporaries.* The Hague, 1974.

Boas, F. S. *University Drama in the Tudor Age.* Oxford: Clarendon Press, 1914.

———. *Ovid and the Elizabethans.* London: Morrison and Gibb, 1947.

Boitani, P. *The Tragic and the Sublime in Medieval Literature.* Cambridge: Cambridge University Press, 1989.

———. "Anagnorisis and Reasoning: Electra and Hamlet." *REAL: Yearbook of Research in English and American Literature* 7 (1990): 99–136.

————, ed. *The European Myth of Troilus*. Oxford: Clarendon Press, 1989.

Bolgar, R. R. *The Classical Heritage and its Beneficiaries*. London: Cambridge University Press, 1954.

Bono, J. B. *Literary Transvaluation: From Vergilian Epic to Shakespearian Tragicomedy*. Berkeley, 1984.

Boose, L. E. "The Father and the Bride in Shakespeare." *PMLA* 97 (1982): 325–47.

Borsellino, N., and R. Mercuri. *Il teatro del Cinquecento*. Bari: Laterza, 1973.

Borsellino, N. *Rozzi e intronati: esperienze e forme di teatro dal 'Decameron' al 'Candelaio.'* 2d edition. Rome: Bulzoni Editore, 1976.

Bossy, J. *Giordano Bruno and the Embassy Affair*. New Haven: Yale University Press, 1991.

Boughner, D. C. *The Braggart in Renaissance Comedy*. Minneapolis: Minnesota University Press, 1954.

————. "*Sejanus* and Machiavelli." *Studies in English Literature* 1 (spring, 1961): 81–100.

————. *The Devil's Disciple: Ben Jonson's Debt to Machiavelli*. New York: Philosophical Library, 1968.

Bowers, F. *Elizabethan Revenge Tragedy, 1587–1642*. Princeton: Princeton University Press, 1940.

Bradbrook, M. C. *Themes and Conventions of Elizabethan Tragedy*. Cambridge: Cambridge University Press, 1935.

————. *The Growth and Structure of Elizabethan Comedy*. London: Chatto & Windus, 1955.

————. "Courtier and Courtesy: Castiglione, Lyly and Shakespeare's *Two Gentlemen of Verona*." In *Theatre of the English and Italian Renaissance*. edited by J. R. Mulryne and M. Shewring, 161–78. Basingstoke: Macmillan, 1991.

Braden, G. *Renaissance Tragedy and the Senecan Tradition*. New Haven: Yale University Press, 1985.

Bradner, L. "A Check-list of Original Neo-Latin Dramas by Continental Writers Printed before 1650." *PMLA* 58 (1943): 621–33.

————. "The Latin Drama of the Renaissance (1340–1640)." *Studies in the Renaissance* 4 (1957): 31–70.

Branca, V., and C. Ossola, eds. *Cultura e società nel Rinascimento tra Riforme e Manierismi*. Florence: Olschki, 1984.

Brand, P. "Disguise, Deception and Concealment of Identity in Ariosto's Theatre." In *Renaissance and Other Studies: Essays Presented to Peter M. Brown,* edited by Eileen A. Millar, 129–43. Glasgow: University of Glasgow, 1988.

Braunmuller, A. R., and J. C. Bulman, eds. *Comedy from Shakespeare to Sheridan: Change and Continuity in the English and European Dramatic Tradition. Essays in Honor of Eugene M. Waith*. Newark: University of Delaware Press, 1986.

Briggs, J. *This Stage-Play World. English Literature and Its Background, 1580–1625*. Oxford: Oxford University Press, 1983.

Brockbank, P. *Urban Mysteries of the Renaissance: Shakespeare and Carpac-*

cio. Occasional Paper 4. Hertford: International Shakespeare Association, 1989.

Broich, U., and M. Pfister, eds. *Intertextualität: Formen, Funktionen, anglistische Fallstudien.* Tübingen: M. Niemeyer, 1985.

Brooks, H. F. "*Richard III,* Unhistorical Amplifications: The Women's Scenes and Seneca." *Modern Language Review* 75 (1980): 721–37.

Bruscagli, R. *G. B. Giraldi: drammaturgia ed esperienza teatrale.* Ferrara, 1972.

———. "G. B. Giraldi: comico, satirico, tragico." In *Il teatro italiano del Rinascimento,* edited by M. de Panizza Lorch, 261–83. Milan: Edizioni di Comunità, 1980.

———. *Stagioni della civiltà estense.* Pisa: Nistri-Lischi, 1983.

Bryson, N. "Intertextuality and Visual Poetics." *Style* 22/2 (1988): 183–93.

Budd, F. E. "Materials for a Study of the Sources of Shakespeare's *Measure for Measure.*" *Revue de littérature comparée* 11 (1931): 711–36.

Bullough, G., ed. *Narrative and Dramatic Sources of Shakespeare.* 8 vols. London: Routledge and Kegan Paul, 1957–75.

Burke, P. *Culture and Society in Renaissance Italy, 1420–1540.* London: Batsford, 1972.

———. *The Fortunes of the Courtier: The European Reception of Castiglione's Cortegiano.* Cambridge: Polity Press, 1995.

Bush, D. *Mythology and the Renaissance Tradition in English Poetry.* Minneapolis: University of Minneapolis Press, 1932.

Butler, L. E. "The Structural Uses of Incest in English Renaissance Drama." *Renaissance Drama,* n. s., 15 (1984): 115–45.

Cairncross, A. S. "Shakespeare and Ariosto: *Much Ado About Nothing, King Lear* and *Othello.*" *Renaissance Quarterly* 29 (1976): 178–82.

Cairns, C. *The Commedia dell'Arte from the Renaissance to Dario Fo.* New York: Edwin Mellen Press, 1989.

Calderwood, J. L. *The Properties of Othello.* Amherst: University of Massachusetts Press, 1989.

Caliumi, G. *Studi e ricerche sulle fonti italiane del teatro elisabettiano.* Rome: Edizioni di Storia e Letteratura, 1984.

——— ed., *Shakespeare e la sua eredità.* Parma: Zara Edizioni, 1993.

Campbell, O. J. "*Love's Labour's Lost* Re-studied." *University of Michigan Publications,* Language and Literature, 1 (1925): 3–45.

———. "The Relation of *Epicoene* to Aretino's *Il Marescalco.*" *PMLA* 46 (1931): 752–62.

———. "The Italianate Background of *The Merry Wives of Windsor.*" *University of Michigan Publications,* Language and Literature, 8 (1932): 81–117.

Candido, J. "Dining Out in Ephesus: Food in *The Comedy of Errors.*" *Studies in English Literature* 30 (spring, 1990): 217–41.

Canter, H. V. "Rhetorical Elements in the Tragedies of Seneca." *University of Illinois Studies in Language and Literature* 10 (1925): 1–185.

Carlson M. "Daniel Mesguich and Intertextual Shakespeare." In *Foreign Shakespeare: Contemporary Performance,* edited by Dennis Kennedy, 213–31. Cambridge: Cambridge University Press, 1993.

Carroll, W. C. *The Metamorphoses of Shakespearean Comedy*. Princeton: Princeton University Press, 1985.

Carron, J-C. "Imitation and Intertextuality in the Renaissance." *New Literary History* 19 (1988): 565–79.

Cartelli, T. "Shakespeare's *Merchant,* Marlowe's *Jew:* The Problem of Cultural Difference." *Shakespeare Studies* 20 (1988): 255–60.

Cassirer, E. *Individuum und Kosmos in der Philosophie der Renaissance*. Leipzig and Berlin: B. G. Teubner, 1927.

Castagno, P. C. *The Early Commedia dell'Arte (1550–1621): The Mannerist Context*. New York: P. Lang, 1994.

Cataldi, A. *La stirpe di Falstaff*. Florence: Le Monnier, 1989.

Cavalchini, M. "L'*Epitia* di Giraldi Cinzio e *Measure for Measure*." *Italica* 45 (1968): 59–69.

Celse, M. "Un Problème de structure théatrale: 'Beffa' et comédie dans le théâtre des Intronati de Sienne." *Revue des Etudes Italiennes* 15 (1969): 243–57.

Cerreta, F. V. "An Italian Source of Luzan's Theory of Tragedy." *Modern Language Notes* 72 (1957): 518–23.

Champion, L. S. "Ford's *'Tis a Pity* and the Jacobean Tragic Perspective." *PMLA* 90 (1975): 78–87.

Charlton, H. B. *Shakespearian Comedy*. London: Methuen, 1938.

———. *The Senecan Tradition in Renaissance Tragedy*. 2d edition. Manchester: Manchester University Press, 1946.

Clare, J. "'Greater Themes for Insurrection's Arguing:' Political Censorship of the Elizabethan and Jacobean Stage." *Review of English Studies,* n. s., 38 (1987): 169–83.

Clayton, J., and E. Rothstein, eds. *Influence and Intertextuality in Literary History*. Madison: University of Wisconsin Press, 1991.

Clemen W. *Die Tragödie vor Shakespeare: ihre Entwicklung im Spiegel der dramatischen Rede*. Heidelberg: Quelle and Meyer, 1955. Translated by T. S. Dorsch as *English Tragedy before Shakespeare: The Development of Dramatic Speech*. London: Methuen, 1961.

Clubb, L. G. "The 'Virgin Martyr' and the 'tragedia sacra.'" *Renaissance Drama* 7 (1964): 103–26.

———. *Giambattista Della Porta, Dramatist*. Princeton: Princeton University Press, 1965.

———. "Italian Comedy and *The Comedy of Errors*" *Comparative Literature* 19, no. 3 (1967): 240–51.

———. "The Arts of Genre: *Torrismondo* and *Hamlet*." *English Literary History* 47 (1980): 657–69.

———. "Introduction." In Giambattista Della Porta, *Gli duoi fratelli rival/The Two Rival Brothers,* edited and translated by Louise George Clubb, 1–40. Berkeley: University of California Press, 1980.

———. "Il teatro manieristico italiano e Shakespeare." In *Cultura e Società nel Rinascimento fra riforme e manierismi,* edited by Vittore Branca and Carlo Ossola, 427–48. Florence: Olscki, 1984.

———. "Ideologia e politica nel teatro dellaportiano." *Lettere italiane* 39 (1987): 229–45.

———. *Italian Drama in Shakespeare's Time.* New Haven: Yale University Press, 1989.

Clubb, L. G., and R. Black. *Romance and Aretine Humanism in Sienese Comedy.* Florence: La Nuova Italia, 1993.

Cody, R. *The Landscape of the Mind: Pastoralism and Platonic Theory in Tasso's 'Aminta' and Shakespeare's Early Comedies.* Oxford: Clarendon Press, 1969.

Cohen, D. *Shakespeare's Culture of Violence.* Basingstoke: Macmillan, 1993.

Cole, H. C. *The 'All's Well' Story from Boccaccio to Shakespeare.* Urbana: University of Illinois Press, 1981.

Comensoli, V. "Merchants and Madcaps: Dekker's *Honest Whore* Plays and the *Commedia dell'Arte.*" In *Shakespeare's Italy: Functions of Italian Locations in Renaissance Drama,* edited by Michele Marrapodi, et al., 125–39. Manchester: Manchester University Press, 1993.

Cope, J. I. *Dramaturgy of the Daemonic: Studies in Antigeneric Theater from Ruzante to Grimaldi.* Baltimore: Johns Hopkins University Press, 1984.

Corbey, R., and J. Leerssen. *Alterity, Identity, Image: Selves and Others in Society and Scholarship.* Amsterdam Studies on Cultural Identity. Amsterdam: Rodopi, 1991.

Cordner, M., P. Holland, and J. Kerrigan, eds. *English Comedy.* Cambridge: Cambridge University Press, 1994.

Corrigan, B. "*Il Capriccio:* An Unpublished Italian Renaissance Comedy and Its Analogues." *Studies in the Renaissance* 5 (1958): 74–86.

———. "Opportunities for Research in Italian Renaissance Drama 1967." *Research Opportunities in Renaissance Drama* 11 (1968): 9–20.

———. "Problems in Staging Renaissance Dramas." *Resarch Opportunities in Renaissance Drama* 12 (1969): 7–11.

Couliano, I. P. *Eros and Magic in the Renaissance.* Chicago: The University of Chicago Press, 1987.

Coulter, C. C. "The Plautine Tradition in Shakespeare." *Journal of English and Germanic Philology* 19 (1920): 66–83.

Cox, V. *The Renaissance Dialogue: Literary Dialogue in Its Social and Political Context.* Cambridge: Cambridge University Press, 1992.

Craig, H. "The Shackling of Accidents: A Study of Elizabethan Tragedy." *Philological Quarterly* 19 (1940): 1–19.

Croce, B. "La tragedia del Cinquecento." *La Critica* 28 (1930): 161–88.

Crockett, B. "'The wittiest partition': Pyramus and Thisbe in Ovid and Shakespeare." *Classical and Modern Literature* 12 (1991): 49–58.

Cronin, L. "A Source for John Ford's *Love's Sacrifice:* The Life of Carlo Gesualdo." *Notes & Queries,* n. s., 35 (March 1988): 66–67.

Cruciani, F., and D. Seragnoli, eds. *Il teatro italiano nel Rinascimento.* Bologna: Il Mulino, 1987.

Culler, J. "Presupposition and Intertextuality." *Modern Language Notes* 91 (1976): 1380–96.

———. *The Pursuit of Signs: Semiotics, Literature, Deconstruction.* London: Routledge and Kegan Paul, 1981.

Cunliffe, J. W. *The Influence of Seneca on Elizabethan Tragedy: An Essay.* London, 1893.

————. *Early English Classical Tragedies.* Oxford: Clarendon Press, 1912.

Cuvelier, E. "Horror and Cruelty in the Works of Three Elizabethan Novelists." *Cahiers Elisabéthains* 19 (1981): 39–51.

D'Ancona, A. *Origini del teatro italiano.* 3 vols. 2d ed. Turin: Bottega d'Erasmo, 1971.

D'Andrea, A. "Giraldi Cinthio and the Birth of the Machiavellian Hero on the Elizabethan Stage." In *Il Teatro Italiano del Rinascimento,* edited by M. de Panizza Lorch, 605–17. Milan: Edizioni di Comunità, 1980.

Dalla Valle, D. "Il tema della fortuna nella tragedia italiana rinascimentale e barocca." *Italica* 44 (1967): 180–208.

Dällenbach, L. "Intertexte et autotexte." *Poétique* 7/27 (1976): 282–96.

Dashwood, J. R., and J. E. Everson, eds. *Writers and Performers in Italian Drama from the Time of Dante to Pirandello.* New York: Edwin Mellen Press, 1991.

Davico Bonino, G. *La commedia italiana del cinquecento e altre note su letteratura e teatro.* Turin: Tirrenia Stampatori, 1989.

David, J. G., ed. *Studies in the Commedia dell'Arte.* Cardiff: University of Wales Press, 1993.

Davidson, C., et al., eds. *Drama in the Renaissance. Comparative and Critical Essays.* New York: AMS Press, 1984.

Davies, C. *Latin Writers of the Renaissance.* Cardiff: University of Wales Press, 1981.

Davies, S. *The Idea of Woman in Renaissance Literature. The Feminine Reclaimed.* Brighton: Harvester Press, 1986.

Dawe, R. D. "The Manuscript Sources of Robortello's Edition of Aeschylus." *Mnemosyne,* n. s., 4, 14 (1961): 111–15.

de Bruyn, L. *Woman and the Devil in Sixteenth-Century Literature.* Tisbury: The Compton Press, 1979.

de Grazia, S. *Machiavelli in Hell.* Princeton: Princeton University Press, 1989.

de Man, P. *The Resistance to Theory.* Minneapolis: University of Minnesota Press, 1986.

de Panizza Lorch, M., ed. *Il teatro italiano del Rinascimento.* Milan: Edizioni di Comunità, 1980.

Della Volpe, G. *La Poetica del Cinquecento.* Bari: Laterza, 1954.

Demetz, P., T. Greene, and L. Nelson, Jr., eds. *The Disciplines of Criticism: Essays in Literary Theory, Interpretation, and History.* New Haven: Yale University Press, 1968.

Delorme, J. "Le discours de l'intertextualité dans le discours exégétique." *Sémiotique & Bible* 15 (1979): 56–62.

Dembowski, P. "Intertextualité et critique des textes." *Littérature* 41 (1981): 17–29.

Derrida, J. *L'Ecriture et la différence.* Paris: Seuil, 1979. Translated by Alan Bass as *Writing and Difference.* London: Routledge and Kegan Paul, 1978.

Dessen, A. C. *Elizabethan Stage Conventions and Modern Interpreters.* Cambridge: Cambridge University Press, 1984.

Diamanti, D. "Il saggio e il folletto: Giraldi Cinzio in Shakespeare." In *Riscrit-*

tura, Intertestualità, Transcodificazione, edited by E. Scarano and D. Diamanti, 113–44. Pisa: ETS, 1992.

Diehl, Huston. "The Iconography of Violence in English Renaissance Tragedy." *Renaissance Drama,* n. s., 111 (1980): 27–44.

Dionisotti, C. *Machiavellerie. Storia e fortuna di Machiavelli.* Turin: Einaudi, 1980.

D'Ippolito, G. "Semiologia e *Quellenforschung:* origine, sviluppo, applicazioni del concetto di intertestualità." In *Semiotic Theory and Practice: Proceedings of the Third International Congress of the IASS Palermo, 1984,* edited by Michael Herzfeld and Lucio Melazzo, vol. 1, 441–53. Berlin: Mouton de Gruyter, 1988.

Dobijanka-Witczakowa, O. "*Hamlet* Gerharta Hauptmanna." *Germanica Wratislaviensia* 94 (1992): 135–52.

Dollimore, J. "Two Concepts of Mimesis: Renaissance Literary Theory and *The Revenger's Tragedy.*" In *Drama and Mimesis,* edited by James Redmond, 25–50. Cambridge: Cambridge University Press, 1980.

———. *Radical Tragedy. Religion, Ideology, and Power in the Drama of Shakespeare and His Contemporaries.* 2d ed. New York: Harvester Wheatsheaf, 1989.

Dondoni, L. "Un interprete di Seneca del '500: Giovan Battista Cinzio." In *Rendiconti dell'Istituto lombardo di lettere e scienze morali e storiche,* 93 (1959): 3–16.

Donno, E. S. "Introduction." In *Three Renaissance Pastorals: Tasso, Guarini, Daniel,* edited by Elizabeth Story Donno, xi–xxxiii. Binghamton, N.Y.: Center for Medieval and Early Renaissance Studies, 1993.

Doran, M. *Endeavors of Art: A Study of Form in Elizabethan Drama.* Madison: University of Wisconsin Press, 1954.

Drakakis, J., ed. *Alternative Shakespeares.* London: Methuen, 1985.

Draper, J. W. "Falstaff and the Plautine Parasite." *Classical Journal* 33 (1938): 390–401.

———. "Shakespeare and Florence and the Florentines." *Italica,* 23 (1946): 287–93.

DuBruk, E. E. *New Images of Medieval Women.* Lewiston: Edwin Mellen Press, 1989.

Ducharte, P. L. *The Italian Comedy.* Translated by Randolph T. Weaver. New York: Dover, 1966.

Durling, R. *The Figure of the Poet in the Renaissance.* Cambridge: Harvard University Press, 1965.

Dusinberre, J. *Shakespeare and the Nature of Women.* 2d ed. Basingstoke: Macmillan, 1996.

Dutton, R. *Mastering the Revels: The Regulation of Censorship of English Renaissance Drama.* London: Macmillan, 1991.

Dwora, G. "The Concept of the Bona Meretrix: A Study of Terence's Courtesans." *Rivista di Filologia e di Istruzione Classica* 108 (1980): 142–65.

Eco, U. *A Theory of Semiotics.* Bloomington: Indiana University Press, 1976.

———. *Lector in fabula. La cooperazione interpretativa nei testi narrativi.* Milan: Bompiani, 1979.

————. *The Role of the Reader: Explorations in the Semiotics of Texts.* London: Hutchison, 1981.

————. *I limiti dell'interpretazione.* Milan: Bompiani, 1990. English Translation, Bloomington: Indiana University Press, 1990.

Einstein, L. *The Italian Renaissance in England.* New York, Columbia University Press; London: Macmillan, 1902.

Elam, K. *The Semiotics of Theatre and Drama.* London: Methuen, 1980.

————. "The Fertile Eunuch: *Twelfth Night,* Early Modern Intercourse, and the Fruits of Castration." *Shakespeare Quarterly* 47 (1996): 1–36.

Eliot, T. S. "Shakespeare and the Stoicism of Seneca." In his *Selected Essays.* London: Faber, 1932.

Elton, W. R., and William B. Long, eds. *Shakespeare and Dramatic Tradition: Essays in Honor of S. F. Johnson.* Newark: University of Delaware Press, 1989.

Embiricos, A. "Critique comparée d''Erophile' et d''Orbecche.'" *L'Hellénisme contemporain* 10 (1958): 330–60.

Empson, W. *Some Versions of Pastoral.* 1935. Reprinted New York: New Direction, 1974.

Ette, O. "Intertextualität: Ein Forschungsbericht mit literatursoziologichen Anmerkungen" *Romanistische Zeitschrift für Literaturgeschichte* 9 (1985): 497–522.

Evans, R. C. *Habits of Mind: Evidence and Effects of Ben Jonson's Reading.* Lewisburg: Bucknell University Press, 1995.

Evans, J. X. "Erasmian Folly and Shakespeare's *King Lear:* A Study in Humanist Intertextuality." *Moreana,* vol. 27, no. 103 (1990): 3–23.

Faas, E. *Tragedy and After: Euripides, Shakespeare, Goethe.* Kingston: McGill-Queen's University Press, 1984.

Falletti, C. "Il comico non integrato e la frantumazione degli statuti." In *Il teatro italiano nel Rinascimento,* edited by Fabrizio Cruciani and Daniele Seragnoli, 275–96. Bologna: Il Mulino, 1987.

Farley-Hills, D. "The 'Argomento' of Bruno's *De gli eroici furori* and Sidney's *Astrophel and Stella.*" *Modern Language Review* 87 (1992): 1–17.

Farnham, W. *The Medieval Heritage of Elizabethan Tragedy.* Oxford: Blackwell, 1936.

Fatherty, T. J. "*Othello dell'Arte:* The Presence of *Commedia* in Shakespeare's Tragedy." *Theatre Journal* 43 (1991): 179–94.

Felver, S. "The *Commedia dell'Arte* and English Drama in the 16th and 17th Centuries." *Renaissance Drama* 6 (1963): 24–34.

Ferguson, M. V., M. Quilligan, and N. J. Vickers, eds. *Rewriting the Renaissance: The Discourses of Sexual Difference in Early Modern Europe.* Chicago: University of Chicago Press, 1986.

Fergusson, F. *The Idea of a Theater: A Study of Ten Plays.* Princeton: Princeton University Press, 1949.

Ferroni, G., *'Mutazione' e 'Riscontro' nel teatro di Machiavelli e altri saggi sulla commedia del Cinquecento.* Rome: Bulzoni Editore, 1972.

————. *Il testo e la scena. Saggi sul teatro del Cinquecento.* Rome: Bulzoni Editore, 1980.

Fitzpatrick, T. "*Commedia dell'arte* and Performance: The Scenarios of Flaminio Scala." *Renaissance Drama Newsletter,* supplement 5, University of Warwick, 1985.

Fleissner, R. F. "The Malleable Knight and the Unfettered Friar: *The Merry Wives of Windsor* and Boccaccio." *Shakespeare Studies* 11 (1978): 77–93.

Fonblanque, E. M. de. "The Italian Sources of *Othello.*" *The Fortnightly Review* 96 (1911): 907–18.

Forsythe, R. S. "*The Merry Wives of Windsor*: Two New Analogues." *Philological Quarterly* 7 (1928): 390–98.

Fowler, A. *Kinds of Literature: An Introduction to the Theory of Genres and Modes.* Cambridge: Harvard University Press, 1982.

Fraenkel, H. *Ovid: A Poet Between Two Worlds.* Berkeley: University of California Press, 1945.

Frantz, D. O. *Festum Voluptatis: A Study of Renaissance Erotica.* Columbus: Ohio State University Press, 1989.

Freedman, B. "Frame-up: Feminism, Psychonalysis, Theatre." *Theatre Journal* vol. 40, no. 3 (1988): 375–97.

———. *Staging the Gaze: Psychoanalysis and Shakespearean Comedy.* Ithaca: Cornell University Press, 1991.

Frieden, K. *Genius and Monologue.* Ithaca: Cornell University Press, 1985.

Frow, J. "Intertextuality and Ontology." In *Intertextuality: Theories and Practices,* edited by Michael Worton and Judith Still, 45–55. Manchester: Manchester University Press, 1990.

Frye, N. "The Argument of Comedy." *English Institute Essays 1948.* New York, 1949, 58–73.

———. "Characterization in Shakespearian Comedy." *Shakespeare Quarterly* 4 (1953): 271–77.

———. *Anatomy of Criticism. Four Essays.* Princeton: Princeton University Press, 1957.

———. *A Natural Perspective: The Development of Shakespearean Comedy and Romance.* San Diego: Harcourt Brace Jovanovich, 1965.

———. *Something Rich and Strange: Shakespeare's Approach to Romance.* Stratford, Ontario: Stratford Festival 1982.

Fuzier, J., and J.-M. Maguin. "Archetypal Patterns of Horror and Cruelty in Elizabethan Revenge Tragedy." *Cahiers Elisabéthains* 19 (1981): 9–25.

Gable, A. "Du Monin's Revenge Tragedy *Orbecche-Oronte* (1585): Its Debt to Garnier and Giraldi Cinthio." *Renaissance Drama,* n. s., 11 (1980): 3–25.

Gasparini, G., ed. *La tragedia classica dalle origini al Maffei.* Turin: Unione Tipografico-Editrice Torinese, 1976.

Gatti, H. *The Renaissance Drama of Knowledge: Giordano Bruno in England.* London: Routledge, 1989.

———. "Giordano Bruno and the Stuart Court Masques." *Renaissance Quarterly* 48 (winter, 1995): 809–42.

Gaudet, P. "'A little night music:' Intertextuality and Status in the Nocturnal Exchange of Jessica and Lorenzo." *Essays in Theatre/Etudes théâtrales* 13 (1994–95): 3–14.

Geckle, G. L. *John Marston's Drama: Themes, Images, Sources.* Cranbury, N. J.: Associated University Presses, 1980.

Genette, G. *Palimpsestes: La littérature au second degré*. Paris: Seuil, 1982.

———. "Transtextualités." *Magazine Littéraire* 192 (1983): 40–41.

———. "Structure and Functions of the Title in Literature." *Critical Inquiry* 14 (1988): 692–720.

Gentili, V. *La Roma antica degli elisabettiani*. Bologna: Il Mulino, 1991.

George, D. J., and C. J. Gossip, eds. *Studies in the Commedia dell'Arte*. Cardiff: University of Wales Press, 1993

Germanou, M. "Authorship, Textuality, and Intertextual Perspectives in the Theatre: The Case of Shakespeare." *Gramma: Periodiki Theorias kai Kritikes/Gramma: Journal of Theory and Criticism* 2 (1994): 61–76.

Gigliucci, R. *Lo spettacolo della morte*. Anzio: De Rubeis, 1994.

Gilbert, A. H. "Fortune in the Tragedies of Giraldi Cinthio." In *Renaissance Studies in Honor of Hardin Craig*, edited by B. Maxwell, et al., 32–43. Stanford: Stanford University Press, 1941.

———. *Literary Criticism: Plato to Dryden*. 1949. Reprinted Detroit: Wayne State University Press, 1962.

Gill, E. "A Comparison of the Characters in *The Comedy of Errors* with those in the *Menaechmi*." *Texas Studies in English* 5 (1925): 79–95.

———. The Plot-Structure of *The Comedy of Errors* in Relation to Its Sources." *Texas Studies in English* 10 (1930): 13–65.

Gillies, J. *Shakespeare and the Geography of Difference*. Cambridge: Cambridge University Press, 1994.

Giovannini, G. "Historical Realism and the Tragic Emotions in Renaissance Criticism" *Philological Quarterly* 32 (1953): 304–20.

Glasgow, R. D. V. *Madness, Masks and Laughter: An Essay on Comedy*. London and Toronto: Associated University Presses, 1995.

Goldberg, J. *James and the Politics of Literature*. Baltimore: Johns Hopkins University Press, 1983.

Goodman, A., and A. Mackay. *The Impact of Humanism on Western Europe*. London: Longman 1990.

Gordon, D. J. "Academicians Build a Theatre and Give a Play." In *The Renaissance Imagination,* edited by S. Orgel, 247–65. Berkeley: University of California Press, 1975.

Goudet, J. "La nature du tragique dans le *Torrismondo* de Tasso." *Revue des études italiennes* 8 (1961): 146–68.

Gould, T. "The Uses of Violence in Drama." In *Violence in Drama,* edited by James Redmond, 1–13. Cambridge: Cambridge University Press, 1991.

Goyet, F. "*Imitatio* ou intertextualité? (Riffaterre Revisited)." *Poétique* 18/71 (1987): 313–20.

Grabher, C. *Sul teatro dell'Ariosto*. Rome: Edizioni Italiane, 1946.

Grady, H. *The Modernist Shakespeare. Critical Texts in a Material World*. Oxford: Clarendon Press, 1991.

Grafton, A., and L. Jardine, eds. *From Humanism to the Humanities: Education and the Liberal Arts in Fifteenth- and Sixteenth-Century Europe*. London: Duckworth, 1986.

Gras, H. "*Twelfth Night, Every Man Out of His Humour,* and the Middle Temple Revels of 1597–98." *Modern Language Review* 84 (1989): 545–64.

Grassi, E. *Renaissance Humanism: Studies in Philosophy and Poetics*. Binghamton, N. Y.: Medieval and Renaissance Texts and Studies, 1988.

Greco, A. *L'istituzione del teatro comico nel Rinascimento*. Naples: Liguori, 1976.

Greenblatt, S. *Renaissance Self-Fashioning. From More to Shakespeare*. Chicago: University of Chicago Press, 1980.

———. *Shakespearean Negotiations. The Circulation of Social Energy in Renaissance England*. Oxford: Clarendon Press, 1988.

———. *Learning to Curse: Essays in Early Modern Culture*. London: Routledge, 1992.

———, ed. *The Power of Forms in the English Renaissance*. Norman, Okla., 1982.

Greene, E. J. H. *Menander to Marivaux: The History of a Comic Structure*. Edmonton: University of Alberta Press, 1977.

Greene, N. *Shakespeare, Jonson, Molière: The Comic Contract*. London: Macmillan, 1980.

Greene, T. M. *The Light in Troy: Imitation and Discovery in Renaissance Poetry*. New Haven: Yale University Press, 1982.

Greenfield, T. N. *The Induction in Elizabethan Drama*. Eugene: University of Oregon Books, 1969.

Greg, W. W. *Pastoral Poetry and Pastoral Drama: A Literary Inquiry, with Special Reference to the Pre-Restoration Stage in England*. London: Bullen, 1906.

Gregory Smith, G., ed. *Elizabethan Critical Essays*. 2 vols. Oxford: Oxford University Press, 1904.

Grendler, P. F. *Critics of the Italian World, 1530–1560*. Madison: The University of Wisconsin Press, 1969.

———. *Culture and Censorship in Late Renaissance Italy and France*. London: Variorum Reprints, 1981.

———. *Books and Schools in the Italian Renaissance*. Aldershot: Variorum, 1995.

Grewar, A. "The Clowning Zanies: Shakespeare and the Actors of the *Commedia dell'Arte*." *Shakespeare in Southern Africa: Journal of the Shakespeare Society of Southern Africa* 3 (1989): 9–32.

———. "Shakespeare and the Actors of the *Commedia dell'Arte*." In *Studies in the Commedia dell'Arte*, edited by David J. George and Christopher J. Gossip, 13–47. Cardiff: University of Wales Press, 1993.

Griffith, G. *Bandello's Fiction*. Oxford: Clarendon Press, 1955.

Grivel, C. "Les universaux de texte." *Littérature* 30 (1978): 25–50.

Groves, W. McDonald. "The *Commedia dell'Arte* and the Shakespearean Theatre: A Study of the Relevance of Applying *Commedia dell'Arte* Techniques to Shakespearean Production." *Dissertation Abstracts International* 44 (1984): 2626A. Ph.D. diss., University of Colorado, Boulder.

Guerrieri Crocetti, C. "Caratteri rilevanti della tragedia giraldiana." *Cultura e scuola* 39 (1971): 13–25.

———, ed. *G. B. Giraldi Cinzio, Scritti critici*. Milan: Marzorati, 1973.

Guidotti, A. *Il modello e la trasgressione: commedie del primo '500*. Rome: Bulzoni Editore, 1983.

Guillén, C. *Literature as System: Essays Toward the Theory of Literary History*. Princeton: Princeton University Press, 1971.

Gum, C. *The Aristophanic Comedies of Ben Jonson*. The Hague: Mouton, 1969.

Gurr, A. "Intertextuality at Windsor." *Shakespeare Quarterly* 38 (1987): 189–200.

———. "*The Tempest*'s Tempest at Blackfriars." *Shakespeare Survey* 41 (1989): 91–102.

Guttman, S. *The Foreign Sources of Shakespeare's Works* (New York: King's Crown Press, 1947).

Haber, J. *Pastoral and the Poetics of Self-Contradiction*. Cambridge: Cambridge University Press, 1994.

Habicht, W., D. J. Palmer, and R. Pringle, eds. *Images of Shakespeare: Proceedings of the Third Congress of the International Shakespeare Association, 1986*. Newark: University of Delaware Press, 1988.

Hainsworth, P., et al., eds. *The Languages of Literature in Renaissance Italy*. Oxford: Clarendon Press, 1988.

Hale, J. R. *England and the Italian Renaissance: The Growth of Interest in Its History and Art*. London: Faber, 1954.

———. *Machiavelli and Renaissance Italy*. London: English University Press, 1961.

———. *Florence and the Medici: The Pattern of Control*. London: Thames and Hudson, 1977.

———. *The Military Organization of a Renaissance State: Venice c. 1400 to 1617*. Cambridge: Cambridge University Press, 1984.

Handley, D. "'Amore' and 'Maestà:' Giambattista Giraldi's Magic Heroines." *Modern Language Review,* vol. 80, no. 2 (1985): 330–39.

Hanning, R. W., and D. Rostand, eds. *Castiglione: The Ideal and the Real in Renaissance Culture*. New Haven: Yale University Press, 1983.

Harbage, A. *As They Liked It: An Essay on Shakespeare and Morality*. New York: Macmillan, 1947. Reprinted Harper Torchbooks, 1961.

———. *Shakespeare and the Rival Traditions*. New York: Macmillan, 1952.

Hardison, O. B. "Three Types of Renaissance Catharsis." *Renaissance Drama,* n. s., 2 (1969): 3–22.

Harrold, W. E. "Shakespeare's Use of *Mostellaria* in *The Taming of the Shrew*." *Deutsche Shakespeare-Gesellschaft West* (1970): 188–94.

Hartman, G. "Literary Criticism and Its Discontents." *Critical Inquiry* 3 (1976): 203–20.

Harty, E. R. "Text, Context, Intertext." *Journal of Literary Studies* 1/2 (1985): 1–13.

Harvey, E. D., and K. Maus Eisaman. *Soliciting Interpretation*. Chicago: University of Chicago Press, 1990.

Hathaway, B. *The Age of Criticism: The Late Renaissance in Italy*. Ithaca: Cornell University Press, 1962.

Hebel, U. J. *Intertextuality, Allusion, and Quotation: An International Bibliography of Critical Studies*. Westport, Conn.: Greenwood Press, 1989.

Heck, T. F. *Commedia dell'Arte: A Guide to the Primary and Secondary Literature*. New York: Garland, 1988.

Heinemann, M. *Puritanism and Theatre: Middleton and Opposition Drama under the Early Stuarts.* Cambridge: Cambridge University Press, 1980.

Henke, R. "*The Winter's Tale* and Guarinian Dramaturgy." *Comparative Drama* 27 (1993): 197–217.

Herford, C. H. *Studies in the Literary Relations of England and Germany in the Sixteenth Century.* 1886. Reprinted London: Frank Cass & Co., 1966.

Herrick, M. T. *Comic Theory in the Sixteenth Century.* Urbana: University of Illinois Press, 1950.

———. *Tragicomedy: Its Origin and Development in Italy, France and England.* Urbana: University of Illinois Press, 1955.

———. *Italian Comedy in the Renaissance.* Urbana: University of Illinois Press, 1960.

———. "Trissino's Art of Poetry." In *Essays on Shakespeare and Elizabethan Drama in Honor of Hardin Craig,* edited by R. Hosley, 15–22. London: Routledge and Kegan Paul, 1963.

———. "Opportunities for Research in the Italian Drama of Renaissance." *Renaissance Drama* 6 (1963): 21–23.

———. "Hyrcanian Tigers in Renaissance Tragedy." In *The Classical Tradition: Literary and Historical Studies in Honor of Harry Caplan,* edited by L. Wallach, 559–71. Ithaca: Cornell University Press, 1966.

Higgins, L. A., and B. R. Silver, eds. *Rape and Representation.* New York: Columbia University Press, 1991.

Highet, G. *The Classical Tradition: Greek and Roman Influences on Western Literature.* New York: Oxford University Press, 1949.

Hill, E. D. "The First Elizabethan Tragedy: A Contextual Reading of *Cambises*." *SP* 84 (fall, 1992): 404–33.

Hilman, R. "La création du monde et *The Taming of the Shrew*: Du Bartas comme intertexte." *Renaissance et Reformation* 27 (1991): 249–58.

———. "Shakespeare's Romantic Innocents and the Misappropriation of the Romance Past: The Case of *The Two Noble Kinsmen*." *Shakespeare Survey* 43 (1991): 69–79.

———. *Intertextuality and Romance in Renaissance Drama: The Staging of Nostalgia.* Basingstoke, Macmillan, 1992.

———. "*Hamlet* et la Préface de Marie de Gournay." *Renaissance and Reformation* 18, 3 (1994): 29–42.

Hoenselaars, A. J. *Images of Englishmen and Foreigners in the Drama of Shakespeare and His Contemporaries: A Study of Stage Characters and National Identity in English Renaissance Drama, 1558–1642.* Rutherford, N.J.: Fairleigh Dickinson University Press, 1992.

———. ed. *Reclamations of Shakespeare.* Amsterdam: Rodopi, 1994.

Hoesle, J. *Das italienische Theater von der Renaissance bis zur Gegenreformation.* Darmstadt, 1984.

Holland, M. "De l'intertextualité: Métacritique." *Texte* 2 (1983): 177–92.

Holquist, M. *Dialogism: Bakhtin and His World.* London: Routledge, 1990.

Honigmann, E. A. J., ed. *Shakespeare and His Contemporaries: Essays in Comparison.* Manchester: Manchester University Press, 1986.

Horne, P. R. "Reformation and Counter-Reformation at Ferrara: Antonio Musa

Brasavola and Giambattista Cinthio Giraldi." *Italian Studies* 13 (1958): 62–82.

———. *The Tragedies of Giambattista Cinthio Giraldi.* Oxford: Oxford University Press, 1962.

Hosley, R. "Sources and Analogues of *The Taming of the Shrew.*" *The Huntington Library Quarterly* 27 (1964): 289–308.

Howard, D., ed. *Philip Massinger: A Critical Reassessment.* Cambridge: Cambridge University Press, 1985.

Howarth, D. *Lord Arundel and His Circle.* New Haven: Yale University Press, 1985.

Howarth, W. D. *Comic Drama: The European Heritage.* London: Methuen, 1978.

Howson, F. "Horror and Macabre in Four Elizabethan Tragedies." *Cahiers Elisabéthains* 10 (1976): 1–12.

Hunter, G. K. "English Folly and Italian Vice: the Moral Landscape of John Marston." In his *Dramatic Identities and Cultural Traditions: Studies in Shakespeare and His Contemporaries,* 103–32. Liverpool: Liverpool University Press, 1978.

———. "Italian Tragicomedy on the English Stage." In his *Dramatic Identities and Cultural Traditions: Studies in Shakespeare and His Contemporaries,* 133–56. Liverpool: Liverpool University Press, 1978.

———. "Seneca and English Tragedy." In his *Dramatic Identities and Cultural Traditions. Studies in Shakespeare and His Contemporaries,* 174–213. Liverpool: Liverpool University Press, 1978.

———. "Seneca and the Elizabethans: a Case-Study in 'Influence.'" In his *Dramatic Identities and Cultural Traditions. Studies in Shakespeare and His Contemporaries,* 159–73. Liverpool: Liverpool University Press, 1978.

———. "The Beginnings of Elizabethan Drama: Revolution and Continuity." *Renaissance Drama* 16 (1986): 29–52.

Hutcheon, L. "Literary Borrowing . . . and Stealing: Plagiarism, Sources, Influences, and Intertexts." *English Studies in Canada* 12 (1986): 229–39.

Hutton, E. *Pietro Aretino. The Scourge of Princes.* London: Constable, 1922.

Hyde, M. C. *Playwriting for Elizabethans, 1600–1605.* New York: Columbia University Press, 1949.

Il teatro classico italiano nel '500, Atti del *Convegno dell'Accademia Nazionale dei Lincei,* 9–12 February, 1969. Rome: Accademia Nazionale dei Lincei, 1971.

Iser, W. *Der implizite Leser.* English Translation. Baltimore: Johns Hopkins University Press, 1974.

———. *Shakespeares Historien.* English Translation. New York: Columbia University Press, 1993.

Jacobs, H. E. "Shakespeare, Revenge Tragedy, and the Ideology of the *Memento Mori.*" *Shakespeare Studies* 21 (1993): 96–108.

Jacomuzzi, A. "La citazione come procedimento letterario: Appunti e considerazioni." In *L'Arte dell'interpretare: Studi critici offerti a Giovanni Getto.* Cuneo: L'Arciere, 1984.

Jacquot, J. "Les tragédies de Sénèque et le théâtre élisabéthain." *Etudes Anglaises* 14 (1961): 343–44.

——, ed. *Les Tragédies de Sénèque et le théâtre de la Renaissance.* Paris: Editions du Centre National de la Recherche Scientifique, 1964.

Jardine, L. *Still Harping on Daughters: Women and Drama in the Age of Shakespeare.* Brighton: Harvester Press, 1983.

Javitch, D. *Poetry and Courtliness in Renaissance England.* Princeton: Princeton University Press, 1978.

——. "Pioneer Genre Theory and the Opening of the Humanist Canon." *Common Knowledge* 3 (1994): 54–66.

Jones, A. R. "Italians and Others: Venice and the Irish in *Coryat's Crudities* and *The White Devil.*" *Renaissance Drama* 18 (1987): 101–119.

Jones, E. *Othello's Countrymen: The African in English Renaissance Drama.* London: Oxford University Press, 1965.

——. *Scenic Form in Shakespeare.* Oxford: Clarendon Press, 1971.

——. *The Origins of Shakespeare.* Oxford: Clarendon Press, 1977.

Jones, R. C. "Italian Settings and the 'World' of Elizabethan Tragedy." *Studies in English Literature,* vol. 10, no. 2 (1970): 251–68.

Jones-Davies, M. T. "Paroles intertextuelles: Lecture intertextuelle de Parolles." In *'All's Well That Ends Well.' Nouvelles perspectives critiques,* 65–80. Montpellier: Publications de l'Université Paul Valéry, 1985.

——. "The End of Motion—The Ethics of *Romeo and Juliet.*" In *Roméo et Juliette: Nouvelles perspectives critiques,* edited by Jean-Marie Maguin and Charles Whitworth, 165–88. Montpellier: Publications de l'Université Paul Valéry—Montpellier III, 1993.

——, ed. *Diable, diables et diableries au temps de la renaissance.* S.I.R.I.R. 13. Paris: Jean Touzot, 1988.

Kahn, V. *Machiavellian Rhetoric: From the Counter-Reformation to Milton.* Princeton: Princeton University Press, 1994.

Karrer, W. "Titles and Mottoes as Intertextual Devices." In *Intertextuality,* edited by Heinrich F. Plett, 122–34. Berlin: de Gruyter, 1991.

Kastan, D. S., and P. Stallybrass, eds. *Staging the Renaissance: Reinterpretations of Elizabethan and Jacobean Drama.* London: Routledge, 1991.

Kawachi, Y. *Shakespeare and Cultural Exchange.* Seibido, 1995.

Kellet, E. E. *Literary Quotation and Allusion.* 1933. Reprinted London: Kennikart Press, 1969.

Kennard, J. S. *The Italian Theatre: From its Beginning to the Close of the Seventeenth Century.* 2 vols. New York: Blom, 1964.

Kennedy, G. "Ancient Antecedents of Modern Literary Theory." *American Journal of Philology,* vol. 110, no. 3 (1989): 492–98.

Kenneth, C. "Alberti and Shakespeare." *TLS,* 26 March 1931, 252.

Kerény, K. "Naissance et renaissance de la tragédie. L'origine de l'Opéra italienne et celle de la tragédie grecque." *Diogène* 28 (1959): 22–46.

Kerr, H. B. "Aaron's Letter and Acts of Reading: The Text as Evidence in *Titus Andronicus.*" *AULLA: Journal of the Australasian Universities Language and Literature Association* 77 (1992): 1–19.

Kerr, M. *Influence of Ben Jonson on English Comedy, 1598–1642.* New York: J. F. Tapley, 1912.

Kibédi, V. A. "Pour une histoire intertextuelle de la littérature." *Degrés,* vol. 12, no. 40 (1984): 1–10.

Kiefer, F. "Seneca Speaks in English: What the Elizabethan Translations Wrought." *Comparative Literature Studies* 15 (1978): 372–87.

———. "Seneca's Influence on Elizabethan Tragedy: An Annotated Bibliography." *Research Opportunities in Renaissance Drama* 21 (1978): 17–34, and 28 (1985): 129–42.

———. *Fortune and Elizabethan Tragedy.* San Marino, Ca.: Huntington Library, 1983.

Kirkpatrick, R. *English and Italian Literature from Dante to Shakespeare: A Study of Source, Analogue and Divergence.* London: Longman, 1995.

Kishi, T., R. Pringle, and S. Wells, eds. *Shakespeare and Cultural Traditions: The Selected Proceedings of the International Shakespeare Associaton World Congress, Tokyo, 1991.* Newark: University of Delaware Press, 1994.

Kistner, A. L. "The Senecan Background of Despair in *The Spanish Tragedy* and *Titus Andronicus.*" *Shakespeare Studies* 7 (1974): 1–9.

Kohler, R. C. "Vitruvian Proportions in Theater Design in the Sixteenth and Early Seventeenth Centuries in Italy and England." *Shakespeare Studies* 16 (1983): 265–325.

Krappe, A. H. "Une hypothèse sur la source de l'"Orbecca' de Giambattista Giraldi Cinthio." *Revue de littérature comparée* vol. 7, no. 2 (1927): 239–53.

Kristeva, J. "Bakhtine, le mot, le dialogue et le roman." *Critique,* vol. 33, no. 239 (1967): 438–65.

———. *Semeiotikè: Recherches pour une sémanalyse.* Paris: Seuil, 1969.

———. *Essays in Semiotics: Essais de sémiotique.* The Hague: Mouton, 1971.

———. "Word, dialogue, and novel." Translated as *Desire in Language* in *The Kristeva Reader,* edited by Toril Moi. Oxford: Blackwell, 1986.

Lanier, D. "Drowning the Book: *Prospero's Books* and the Textual Shakespeare." In *Shakespeare, Theory, and Performance,* edited by James C. Bulman, 187–209. London: Routledge, 1996.

Larivaille, P. *Pietro Aretino fra Rinascimento e Manierismo.* Rome: Bulzoni Editore, 1980.

Laroque, F. "Cannibalism in Shakespeare's Imagery." *Cahiers Elisabéthains* 19 (1981): 27–37.

Lawrence, W. W. "The Wager in *Cymbeline.*" *PMLA* 35 (1920): 391–431.

Lawton, H. W. "Sixteenth-Century Italian Criticism and Milton's Theory of Catharsis." *Studies in English Literature* 6 (1966): 139–50.

Lea, K. M. *Italian Popular Comedy: A Study in the Commedia dell'Arte, 1560–1620, with Special Reference to the English Stage.* 2 vols. Oxford: Clarendon Press, 1934. Reprinted New York, 1962.

Leavitt, S. E. "Scenes of Horror in Golden Age Drama." *Romance Notes* 10 (1968): 114–18.

Lebatteux, G. "La crise de la 'beffa' dans les *Diporti* et les *Ecatommiti.*" In *Formes et significations de la "beffa" dans la littérature italienne de la Renaissance.* Edited by A. Rochon, 179–201. Paris: Université de la Sorbonne Nouvelle, 1972.

Lee, A. C. "*Cymbeline:* The Source of the 'Wager Incident.'" *Notes & Queries,* series 12, vol. 1 (January-June, 1916): 342–43.

Leitch, V. B. "Versions of Textuality and Intertextuality: Contemporary Theories of Literature and Tradition." In *Deconstructive Criticism: An Advanced Introduction,* edited by V. B. Leitch, 55–163. New York: Columbia University Press, 1983.

Lenz, C., G. Greene, and C. Neely, eds. *The Woman's Part: Feminist Criticism of Shakespeare.* Urbana: University of Illinois Press, 1980.

Lepage, R. "A Study in Dramatic Transposition and Invention: Della Porta's *La Sorella,* Rotrou's *La Soeur,* and Middleton's *No Wit, No Help Like a Woman's.*" *Comparative Literature Studies* 24 (1987): 335–52.

Leps, M.-C. "For an Intertextual Method of Analyzing Discourse: A Case Study of Presuppositions." *Europa. A Journal of Interdisciplinary Studies,* vol. 3, no. 1 (1979–1980): 89–103.

Levi, C. "La fortuna di Medea." *Rivista d'Italia* 13 (1910): 117–32.

Levin, H. *The Myth of the Golden World in the Renaissance.* London: Faber, 1969.

Levin, R. *The Multiple Plot in English Renaissance Drama.* Chicago: Chicago University Press, 1971.

Levine, L. *Men in Women's Clothing: Anti-Theatricality and Effeminization, 1579–1642.* Cambridge: Cambridge University Press, 1994.

Levith, M. J. *Shakespeare's Italian Settings and Plays.* Basingstoke: Macmillan, 1989.

Lewalski, B. K., ed. *Renaissance Genres: Essays on Theory, History, and Interpretation.* Harvard English Studies, no. 14. Cambridge: Harvard University Press, 1986.

Lievsay, J. *Stefano Guazzo and the English Renaissance, 1575–1675.* Chapel Hill: University of North Carolina Press, 1961.

———. *The Elizabethan Image of Italy.* Folger Shakespeare Library Publications. Ithaca: Cornell University Press, 1964.

Lombardi, E. "La tragedia italiana del Cinquecento." *Il Propugnatore* 18, part 2 (1885): 202–17.

Lombardo, A. *Il dramma pre-shakespeariano: Studi sul teatro inglese dal Medioevo al Rinascimento.* Venice: Neri Pozza, 1957.

———, ed. *Shakespeare a Verona e nel Veneto.* Verona: Grafiche Fiorini, 1987.

Lombardo, G. *Hypsegoria. Studii sulla retorica del sublime.* Modena: Mucchi, 1988.

Long, J. H. *Shakespeare's Use of Music: The Histories and Tragedies.* Gainesville: University of Florida Press, 1971.

Lothian, J. M. "Shakespeare's Knowledge of Aretino's Plays." *Modern Language Review* 25 (1930): 415–24.

Lovejoy, A. O. *The Great Chain of Being: A Study of the History of an Idea.* Cambridge: Harvard University Press, 1936.

Lucas, F. L. *Seneca and Elizabethan Tragedy.* Cambridge: Cambridge University Press, 1922. Reprinted New York: Gordon Press, 1973.

Maestri, D. "Gli Ecatommiti del Giraldi Cinzio: una proposta di nuova lettura e interpretazione." *Lettere italiane* 23 (1971): 306–31.

Mammone, S. *Il teatro nella Firenze medicea.* Milan: Mursia, 1981.

Marcus, L. S. *Puzzling Shakespeare: Local Reading and Its Discontents.* Berkeley: University of California Press, 1988.

———. "The Shakespearean Editor as Shrew-Tamer." *English Literary Renaissance* 22 (1992): 177–200.

Margolin, J-C., and M.-M. Martinet, eds. *L'Europe de la renaissance, cultures et civilisations: Melanges offertes à Marie-Thérèse Jones-Davies.* Paris: Jean Touzot, 1988.

Mariti, L. *La commedia ridicolosa.* Rome: Bulzoni Editore, 1978.

Marotti, F. "Per una epistemologia del teatro nel Rinascimento: le teorie dello spazio teatrale." *Biblioteca teatrale* 1 (1971): 15–29.

———. *Storia documentaria del teatro italiano. Lo spettacolo dall'Umanesimo al Manierismo, Teoria e Tecnica.* Milan, 1974.

Marrapodi, M. "Carmagnola e Coriolano." *Annali della Facoltà di Magistero dell'Università di Messina,* vol. 3, no. 1 (1985): 505–25.

———. *La Sicilia nella drammaturgia giacomiana e carolina.* Rome: Herder, 1989.

———, et al. eds. *Shakespeare's Italy: Functions of Italian Locations in Renaissance Drama.* Manchester: Manchester University Press, 1993.

———. ed. *Il mondo italiano del teatro inglese del Rinascimento: relazioni culturali e intertestualità.* Palermo: Flaccovio Editore, 1995.

———. "Introduzione. Dalla cronaca al Boccaccio: il racconto dell'eros e il teatro." *Il mondo italiano del teatro inglese del Rinascimento: relazioni culturali e intertestualità,* edited by Michele Marrapodi, 11–32. Palermo: Flaccovio Editore, 1995.

Martin, C. "Retrieving Jonson's Petrarch." *Shakespeare Quarterly* 45 (1994): 89–92.

Martin, R. A. "Fate, Seneca, and Marlowe's *Dido, Queen of Carthage.*" *Renaissance Drama,* n.s., 11 (1980): 45–66.

Martindale, C. *Ovid Renewed.* Cambridge: Cambridge University Press, 1988.

Martinez, R. L. "The Pharmacy of Machiavelli: Roman Lucretia in *Mandragola.*" *Renaissance Drama,* n. s., 14 (1983): 1–43.

Mattioli, E. "Intertestualità e traduzione." *Testo a fronte* 5 (1991): 5–13.

McPherson, D. "Ben Jonson's Library and Marginalia: An Annotated Catalogue." *Studies in Philology* 71 (1974):

McPherson, D. C. *Shakespeare, Jonson and the Myth of Venice.* Newark: University of Delaware Press, 1990.

Melchiori, G. "'In fair Verona:' *Commedia erudita* into romantic comedy." In *Shakespeare's Italy: Functions of Italian Locations in Renaissance Drama,* edited by M. Marrapodi, et al., 100–11. Manchester: Manchester University Press, 1993.

———. "Falstaff's Ancestry: From Verona to Windsor." In *Shakespeare's Garter Plays. Edward III to Merry Wives of Windsor,* 77–91. Newark: University of Delaware Press, 1994.

Mellamphy, N. "Pantaloons and Zanies: Shakespeare's 'Apprenticeship' to Italian Professional Comedy Troupes." In *Shakespearean Comedy,* edited by Maurice Charney, 141–51. New York: New York Literary Forum, 1980.

Melzi, R. C. "*Gl'Ingannati* and its French Renaissance Translation." *Kentucky Foreign Language Quarterly* 12 (1965): 180–90.

———. "From Lelia to Viola." *Renaissance Drama* 9 (1966): 67–81.

Meyer, E. *Machiavelli and the Elizabethan Drama.* New York: Burt Franklin, 1969. Original edition, Weimar, 1897.

Miklashevskii, K. *La commedia dell'arte, o, il teatro dei commedianti italiani nei secoli XVI–XVII.* 2d ed. Venice: Marsilio, 1981.

Millar, E. A., ed. *Renaissance and Other Studies: Essays Presented to Peter M. Brown.* Glasgow: University of Glasgow, 1988.

Miller, O. "Intertextual Identity." In *Identity of the Literary Text,* edited by Mario J. Valdés and Owen Miller, 19–40. Toronto: University of Toronto Press, 1985.

Miola, R. S. *Shakespeare's Rome.* Cambridge: Cambridge University Press, 1983.

———. "*Julius Caesar* and the Tyrannicide Debate." *Renaissance Quarterly* 38 (1985): 271–89.

———. *Shakespeare and Classical Tragedy: The Influence of Seneca.* Oxford: Clarendon Press, 1992.

———. "New Comedy in *All's Well That Ends Well.*" *Renaissance Quarterly* 46 (1993): 23–43.

———. "*The Merry Wives of Windsor*: Classical and Italian Intertexts." *Comparative Drama* 27 (1993): 364–76.

———. *Shakespeare and Classical Comedy: The Influence of Plautus and Terence.* Oxford: Clarendon Press, 1994.

Molinari, C. "Scenografia e spettacolo nelle poetiche del '500." *Il Veltro* 8 (1964): 885–902.

———. *La commedia dell'arte.* Milan: Mondadori, 1985.

Montrose, L. A. "*A Midsummer Night's Dream* and the Shaping Fantasies of Elizabethan Culture: Gender, Power, Form." In *Rewriting the Renaissance: The Discourses of Sexual Difference in Early Modern Europe,* 67–87. Chicago: University of Chicago Press, 1986.

Moore, O. H. "Shakespeare's Deviations from *Romeus and Juliet.*" PMLA 52 (1937): 68–74.

Moretti, W. "La novella di Epitia e *Measure for Measure.*" In *Measure for Measure. Dal testo alla scena,* ed. Mariangela Tempera, 17–24. Bologna: Clueb, 1992.

Morgan, T. E. "Is there an Intertext in this Text?: Literary and Interdisciplinary Approaches to Intertextuality." *American Journal of Semiotics* 3 (1985): 1–40.

Morrison, M. "Some Aspects of the Treatment of the Theme of Antony and Cleopatra in the Tragedies of the Sixteenth Century." *Journal of European Studies* 4 (1974): 113–25.

Motto, A. L., and J. R. Clark. "Senecan Tragedy. A Critique of Scholarly Trends." *Renaissance Drama,* n. s., 6 (1973): 219–35.

Moyer, A. E. *Musica Scentia: Musical Scholarship in the Italian Renaissance.* Ithaca: Cornell Unversity Press, 1992.

Muecke, F. *Plautus "Menaechmi."* Bristol: Bristol Classic Press, 1987.

Muir, Kenneth. *The Sources of Shakespeare's Plays.* London: Methuen, 1977.

Mullini, R. 'Respublica': testo e intertesto nell'interludio per Mary Tudor.* Bologna: Clueb, 1984.

————. *La scena della memoria: intertestualità nel teatro Tudor.* Bologna: Clueb, 1988.

Mulryne, J. R., and M. Shewring, eds. *War, Literature and the Arts in Sixteenth-Century Europe.* Basingstoke and London: The Macmillan Press, 1989.

————, eds. *Theatre of the English and Italian Renaissance.* London: Macmillan, 1991.

Mulvey, L. "Visual Pleasure and Narrative Cinema." *Screen* vol. 16, no. 3 (1975): 6–18.

Mumford, I. L. "Relationships between Italian Renaissance Literature and Elizabethan Literature, 1557–1603." *Italian Studies* 9 (1954): 69–75.

Musarra, F. "Poesia e società in alcuni commentatori cinquecenteschi della 'Poetica' di Aristotele." *Il Contesto* 3 (1977): 33–78.

Musumarra, C. *La poesia tragica italiana nel Rinascimento.* Florence: Olschki, 1972.

Nencioni, G. "Agnizioni di lettura." *Strumenti Critici* vol. 1, no. 2 (1967): 191–98.

Net, M. "Towards a Pragmatics of Poetic Intertextuality." *Cahiers de Linguistique Théorique & Appliquée* 20 (1983): 159–62.

Neuhaus, H. J. "Shakespeare Hypertext." *Deutsche Shakespeare-Gesellschaft West* (1990): 78–93.

Neumeier, B. "Die Lust am Intertext: Robert Nyes Roman *Falstaff.*" *Deutsche Shakespeare-Gesellschaft West* (1988): 150–62.

Nevo, R. *Comic Transformations in Shakespeare.* London: Methuen, 1980.

Newman, J. O. "'And let mild women to him lose their mildness:' Philomela, Female Violence, and Shakespeare's *The Rape of Lucrece.*" *Shakespeare Quarterly,* vol. 45, no. 3 (1994): 319.

Nicoll, A. *The World of Harlequin: A Critical Study of the Commedia dell'Arte.* London: Cambridge University Press, 1963.

Nugent, E. M. *The Thought and Culture of the English Renaissance.* Cambridge: Cambridge University Press, 1956.

Ogawa, Y. "'This Forkèd Plague:' The Meaning of Comedy in *Othello.*" *Hokkaido University Gaikokugo Gaikokubungaku Kenkyu* 26 (1980): 273–311.

Ong, L. "Intertextuality and the Cultural Text in Recent Semiotics." *College English* 48 (1986): 811–23.

Oreglia, G. *La Commedia dell'Arte.* Translated by Lovett F. Edwards. London: Methuen, 1968.

Ornstein, R. *The Moral Vision of Jacobean Tragedy.* Westport, Conn.: Greenwood Press, 1977.

————. *Shakespeare's Comedies: From Roman Farce to Romantic Mystery.* Newark: University of Delaware Press, 1986.

Orr, D. *Italian Renaissance Drama in England Before 1625. The Influence of Erudite Tragedy, Comedy and Pastoral on Elizabethan and Jacobean Drama.* Chapel Hill: University of North Carolina Press, 1970.

Osborn, P. "'Fuor di quel costume antico': Innovation versus Tradition in the Prologues of Giraldi Cinthio's Tragedies." *Italian Studies* 37 (1982): 49–66.

Osborne, L. "Dramatic Play in *Much Ado About Nothing:* Wedding the Italian *Novella* and English Comedy." *Philological Quarterly* 69 (1990): 167–88.

Ostria, G. M. "Fundamentos linguisticos de la intertextualidad en el discurso literario." *Revista de Linguistica Teorica y Aplicada* 30 (1992): 219–29.

Paratore, E. *Dal Petrarca all'Alfieri: Saggi di letteratura comparata.* Florence: Olschki, 1975.

Parry, G. *The Seventeenth Century: The Intellectual and Cultural Context of English Literature, 1603–1700.* London: Longman, 1989.

Paster, G. K. "The City in Plautus and Middleton." *Renaissance Drama,* n. s., 6 (1973): 29–44.

Patey, C. "Beyond Aristotle: Giraldi Cinzio and Shakespeare." In *Italy and the English Renaissance,* edited by Sergio Rossi and Dianella Savoia, 167–85. Milan: Edizioni Unicopli, 1989.

Patterson, A. M. *Censorship and Interpretation: The Conditions of Writing and Reading in Early Modern England.* Madison: University of Wisconsin Press, 1984.

Pellegrini, G. *Dal Manierismo al barocco: studi sul teatro inglese del XVII secolo.* Florence: Olschki, 1985.

Perella, N. *The Critical Fortune of Battista Guarini's 'Il Pastor Fido.'* Florence: Olschki, 1973.

Pertusi, A. "Il ritorno alle fonti del teatro greco classico: Euripide nell'Umanesimo e nel Rinascimento." *Byzantion* 33 (1963): 391–426.

Perri, C. "On Alluding." *Poetics* 7 (1978): 289–307.

Perrone-Moisés, L. "L'intertextualité critique." *Poétique* vol. 7, no. 27 (1976): 372–84.

Pfister, M. "Comic Subversion: A Bakhtinian View of the Comic in Shakespeare." *Deutsche Shakespeare-Gesellschaft West* (1987): 27–43.

Pieri, M. "La *Rosmunda* del Rucellai e la tragedia fiorentina del primo Cinquecento." *Quaderni di teatro* vol. 2, no. 7 (1980): 96–113.

———. *La scena boschereccia nel rinascimento italiano.* Padua: Liviana Editrice, 1983.

Pietropaolo, D., ed. *The Science of Buffoonery: Theory and History of the Commedia dell'Arte.* Ottawa: Dovehouse Editions, 1989.

Pigman, G. W., III. "Versions of Imitation in the Renaissance." *Renaissance Quarterly* 33 (1980): 1–32.

Pinciss, G. M. *Literary Creations: Conventional Characters in the Drama of Shakespeare and His Contemporaries.* Wolfeboro, N. H.: Boydell & Brewer, 1988.

Pitkin, H. F. *Fortune is a Woman: Gender and Politics in the Thought of Niccolò Machiavelli.* Berkeley: University of Calfornia Press, 1984.

Plett, H. F. *Textwissenschaft und Textanalyse: Semiotik, Linguistik, Rhetorik.* Heidelberg: Quelle & Meyer, 1979.

———. "Intertextualities." In *Intertextuality,* edited by Heinrich F. Plett, 3–29. Berlin: de Gruyter, 1991.

———, ed. *Intertextuality.* Berlin: de Gruyter, 1991.

Pocock, J. G. A. *The Machiavellian Moment: Florentine Political Thought and the Atlantic Republican Tradition.* Princeton: Princeton University Press, 1975.

Poliziano, A. A. *La commedia antica e l'Andria di Terenzio: appunti inediti.* Florence: Sansoni, 1973.

Pool, A. *Tragedy: Shakespeare and the Greek Example.* Oxford: Blackwell, 1987.

Potter, L. "Fire in the Theater: A Cross-Cultural Code." In *Shakespeare and Cultural Tradition,* edited by T. Kishi, et al., 266–73. Newark: University of Delaware Press, 1994.

Pozzi, M. *Lingua e cultura del Cinquecento: Dolce, Aretino, Machiavelli, Guicciardini.* Padua: Liviana Editrice, 1975.

Praz, M. *Machiavelli e gl'Inglesi dell'epoca elisabettiana.* Florence, 1930.

———. *Machiavelli in Inghilterra ed altri saggi.* Rome: Tumminelli, 1942.

———. *Ricerche Anglo-italiane.* Rome: Edizioni di Storia e Letteratura, 1944.

———. "Shakespeare's Italy." *Shakespeare Survey* 7 (1954): 95–106.

———. *The Flaming Heart: Essays on Crashaw, Machiavelli, and Other Studies in the Relations between Italian and English Literature from Chaucer to T. S. Eliot.* Garden City, N.Y.: Doubleday, 1958. Reprinted, Gloucester, Mass.: Peter Smith, 1966; New York: Norton, 1973.

———, ed. *Tre drammi elisabettiani.* Naples: Edizioni Scientifiche Italiane, 1958.

Prescott, A. L. "Intertextual Topology: English Writers and Pantagruel's Hell." *English Literary Renaissance* 23 (1993): 244–66.

Presson, R. K. "Two Types of Dreams in the Elizabethan Drama and Their Heritage: Somnium Animale and the Prick-of-Conscience." *Studies in English Literature* 7 (1967): 239–56.

Pucci, P. "Decostruzione e intertestualità." *Nuova Corrente* 93–94 (1984): 283–301.

Pugliatti, P. *Shakespeare the Historian.* Basingstoke: Macmillan, 1996.

Quint, D. *Epic and Empire. Politics and Generic Form from Virgil to Milton.* Princeton: Princeton University Press, 1993.

Raab, F. *The English Face of Machiavelli: A Changing Interpretation, 1500–1700.* London: Routledge and Kegan Paul, 1964.

Radcliff-Umstead, D. *The Birth of Modern Comedy in Renaissance Italy.* Chicago: University of Chicago Press, 1969.

Raimondi, E. *Politica e commedia dal Beroaldo a Machiavelli.* Bologna: Il Mulino, 1972.

Ranke, W. "Adaptation und Intertextualität: Friedrich Dürrenmats *König Johann* und die Tradition der deutschen Shakespeare-Bearbeitung." *Jahrbuch für Internationale Germanistik* 24 (1992): 8–36.

Rebhorn, W. A. *Courtly Performances: Masking and Festivity in Castiglione's Book of the Courtier.* Detroit: Wayne State University Press, 1978.

Rewar, W. "Notes for a Typology of Culture." *Semiotica* 18 (1976): 361–77.

Rhu, L. "Agons of Interpretation: Ariostan Source and Elizabethan Meaning in Spenser, Harington, and Shakespeare." *Renaissance Drama,* n. s., 24 (1993): 171–88.

Riccoboni, L. *Discorso della commedia all'improvviso e scenari inediti.* Milan: Edizione Il Polifilo, 1973.

Rich, T. *Harington & Ariosto: A Study in Elizabethan Verse Translation.* New Haven: Yale University Press, 1940.

Richards, K. "The *Commedia dell'Arte* and the Caroline Stage." In *Italy and the English Renaissance,* edited by Sergio Rossi and Dianella Savoia, 241–51. Milan: Edizioni Unicopli, 1989.

Richmond, H. M. "Shaping a Dream." *Shakespeare Studies* 18 (1985): 49–60.

Richter, B. L. O. "Recent Studies in Renaissance Scenography." *Renaissance News* 19 (1966): 344–58.

Riehle, W. *Shakespeare, Plautus, and the Humanist Tradition.* Cambridge, Mass.: D. S. Brewer, 1990.

Riffaterre, M. *Semiotics of Poetry.* Bloomington: Indiana University Press, 1978.

————. "The Intertextual Unconscious." *Critical Inquiry* 13 (1986): 371–85.

Riggs, D. "'Plot' and 'Episode' in Early Neoclassical Criticism." *Renaissance Drama,* n. s., 6 (1973): 149–75.

Riposio, D. "Fra novella e tragedia: Giraldi Cinthio e Shakespeare." In *Metamorfosi della novella,* edited by G. Bàrberi Squarotti, 109–43. Foggia, 1985.

Robbins, E. W. *Dramatic Characterization in Printed Commentaries on Terence, 1473–1600.* Urbana: University of Illinois Press, 1951.

Roditi, E. "The Genesis of Neoclassical Tragedy." *South Atlantic Quarterly* 46 (1947): 93–108.

Rodway, A. *English Comedy: Its Role and Nature from Chaucer to the Present Day.* London: Chatto & Windus, 1975.

Rokem, F. "'What, has this thing appeared again tonight?'" *Theatre Research International* 19 (1994): 143–47.

Rolfs, D. "The Portrayal of Suicide in Italian Literature of the Counter-Reformation Era." *Forum Italicum,* vol. 9, no. 1 (1975):

Ronconi, A. "Prologhi 'plautini' e prologhi 'terenziani' nella commedia italiana del '500." In *Il teatro classico italiano nel '500. Atti del Convegno dell'Accademia Nazionale dei Lincei.* Quaderno no. 138. Rome: Accademia Nazionale dei Lincei, 1971.

Rose, M. B. *The Expense of Spirit: Love and Sexuality in English Renaissance Drama.* Ithaca: Cornell University Press, 1988.

Rossi, S., and D. Savoia, eds. *Italy and the English Renaissance.* Milan: Edizioni Unicopli, 1989.

Rothstein, E. *Influence and Intertextuality in Literary History.* Madison: Wisconsin University Press, 1991.

Rotonda, D. P. *Motif Index of the Italian Novella in Prose.* Bloomington, Indiana University Press Publications, 1942.

Rougé, B. "Ironie et répétition dans deux scènes de Shakespeare: Crise du *degree* ou tournant du *mischief?*" *Poétique* 87 (1991): 335–56.

Rouse, W. H. D. *Shakespeare's Ovid: Being Arthur Golding's Translation of the Metamorphoses.* London: Centaur Press, 1961.

Rudnytsky, P. L. "*A Woman Killed with Kindness* as a Subtext for *Othello.*" *Renaissance Drama,* n. s., 14 (1983): 103–24.

Ruffini, F. *Commedia e festa nel Rinascimento: la Calandria alla corte di Urbino.* Bologna: Il Mulino, 1986.

Ruggiero, G. *The Boundaries of Eros: Sex, Crime, and Sexuality in Renaissance Venice.* Oxford: Oxford University Press, 1985.

Ruprecht, H.-G. "Intertextualité." *Texte* 2 (1983): 13–22.

Rudd, N. *The Classical Tradition in Operation.* Toronto: University of Toronto Press, 1994.

Russo, L. "La tragedia nel '500 e nel '600." *Belfagor* 14 (1959): 14–22.

Ryan E. N. "Robortello and Maggi on Aristotle's Theory of Catharsis." *Rinascimento* 22 (1982): 263–73.

Salingar, L. *Shakespeare and the Traditions of Comedy.* Cambridge: Cambridge University Press, 1974.

———. "Postscript: Elizabethan Dramatists and Italy." In *Theatre of the English and Italian Renaissance,* edited by J. R. Mulryne and M. Shewring, 221–37. London: Macmillan, 1991.

Sanders, W. *The Dramatist and the Received Idea: Studies in the Plays of Marlowe and Shakespeare.* London: Cambridge University Press, 1968.

Sanesi, I. *Storia dei generi letterari italiani: La Commedia.* 2 vols. 2d ed. Milan: Vallardi, 1954.

Sarrazin, G. "Shakespeare und Orlando Pescetti." *Englische Studien* 46 (1913): 347–54.

Schalk, F. "Teoria del drama en las literaturas romànicas del Renascimiento." *Philologica Pragensia* 13 (1970): 203–13.

Schapira, E. *Der Einfluss des Euripides auf die Tragoedie des Cinquecento.* Inaugural-Dissertation zur Erlangung der Doktorwuerde der Philosophischen Fakultaet (I Sektion) der Ludwig-Maximilians-Universitaet zu Muenchen. Wuerzburg, Buchdruckerei Richard Mayr, 1935.

Schleiner, L. "Latinized Greek Drama in Shakespeare's Writing of *Hamlet.*" *Shakespeare Quarterly* 41 (1990): 29–48.

———. *Cultural Semiotics, Spenser, and the Captive Woman.* Bethlehem, Pa.: Lehigh University Press; London and Toronto Associated University Presses, 1995.

Schmitt-von-Muehlentels, F. "Die 'Cena Thyestea' als aestetisches Grenzproblem: Bemerkungen zur englischen Seneca-Rezeption." *Arcadia* 10 (1975): 65–72.

Schnierer, P. P. *Rekonventionalisierung im englischen Drama 1980–1990.* Tübingen: Niemeyer, 1994.

Schoeck, R. J. *Intertextuality and Renaissance Texts.* Bamberg: H. Kaiser, 1984.

Schwanitz, D. "Intertextualität und Äquivalenzfunktionalismus: Vorschläge zu einer vergleichenden Analytik von Geschichten." In *Dialog der Texte: Hamburger Kolloquium zur Intertextualität,* edited by Wolf Schmid and Stempel Wolf-Dieter, 27–51. Wien: Institut für Slawistik, Universität Wien, 1983.

Scott, M. "Machiavelli and the Machiavel." *Renaissance Drama,* n. s., 15 (1984): 147–74.

Scott, M. A. *Elizabethan Translations from the Italian.* Boston: Houghton Mifflin, 1916.

Scragg, Leah. *Shakespeare's 'Mouldy Tales': Recurrent Plot Motifs in Shakespearean Drama.* London: Longman, 1992.

Segre, C. "Intertestuale/interdiscorsivo: Appunti per una fenomenologia delle fonti." In *La parola ritrovata: Fonti e analisi letteraria,* edited by Costanzo Di Girolamo and Ivano Paccagnella, 15–28. Palermo: Sellerio, 1982. Reprinted as "Intertestualità e interdiscorsività nel romanzo e nella poesia," in

C. Segre, *Teatro e romanzo: due tipi di comunicazione letteraria,* 103–118. Turin: Einaudi, 1984.

———. ed. *Ludovico Ariosto: lingua stile e tradizione.* Milan: Feltrinelli, 1976.

Segré, C. *Relazioni letterarie fra Italia e Inghilterra.* Florence: Successori Le Monnier, 1911.

Sellers, H. "Italian Books Printed in England before 1640." *The Library,* 4th ser., 5 (1925): 105–28.

Sells, L. A. *The Italian Influence in English Poetry: From Chaucer to Southwell.* London, 1955.

Seragnoli, D. *Il teatro a Siena nel Cinquecento.* Rome: Bulzoni Editore, 1980.

Serpieri, A. "Reading the Signs: Towards a Semiotics of Shakespearean Drama." Translated by Keir Elam. In *Alternative Shakespeares,* edited by John Drakakis, 119–43. London, Methuen, 1985.

Serpieri, A. *Retorica e immaginario.* Parma: Pratiche, 1986.

———. et al. *Nel laboratorio di Shakespeare: dalle fonti ai drammi.* 4 vols. Parma: Pratiche, 1988.

Sewall, R. B. *The Vision of Tragedy.* New Haven: Yale Universty Press, 1959.

Shapiro, J. "'Which is *The Merchant* here, and which *The Jew?*': Shakespeare and the Economics of Influence." *Shakespeare Studies* 20 (1988): 269–79.

Sheen, E. "'The agent for his master:' Political Service and Professional Liberty in *Cymbeline.*" In *The Politics of Tragicomedy: Shakespeare and After,* edited by Gordon McMullan and Jonathan Hope, 55–76. London: Routledge, 1992.

Simon, J. *Education and Society in Tudor England.* Cambridge: Cambridge University Press, 1967.

Simonis, A. "Celan und Shakespeare: Zum Problem der Dialogizität in der Lyrik Paul Celans." *Orbis Litterarum* 49 (1994): 159–72.

Singer, D. W. *Giordano Bruno: His Life and Thought.* New York: Henry Schuman, 1950.

Smarr, J. *Renaissance Story-Teller.* Cambridge: Harvard University Press, 1973.

———. *Italian Renaissance Tales.* Rochester, Mi.: Solaris Press, 1983.

Smith, A. J. *The Metaphysics of Love: Studies in Renaissance Love Poetry from Dante to Milton.* Cambridge: Cambridge University Press, 1988.

Smith, B. R. "Sir Amorous Knight and the Indecorous Romans; or, Plautus and Terence Play Court in the Renaissance." *Renaissance Drama,* n. s., 6 (1973): 3–27.

———. "Toward the Rediscovery of Tragedy. Productions of Seneca's Plays on the English Renaissance Stage." *Renaissance Drama,* n. s., 9 (1978): 3–37.

———. *Ancient Scripts and Modern Experience on the English Stage, 1500–1700.* Princeton: Princeton University Press, 1988.

Smith, R. "Admirable Musicians: Women's Songs in *Othello* and *The Maid's Tragedy.*" *Comparative Drama* 28 (fall, 1994): 310–20.

Snyder, S. *The Comic Matrix of Shakespeare's Tragedies.* Princeton: Princeton University Press, 1979.

Sokol, B. J. "Figures of Repetition in Sidney's *Astrophel and Stella* and the Scenic Form of *Measure for Measure.*" *Rhetorica* 9 (1991): 131–46.

Sorelius, G. *Shakespeare's Early Comedies: Myth, Metamorphosis, Mannerism.* Studia Anglistica Upsliensia 83. Uppsala: Uppsala University, 1993.

Sorelius G., and M. Srigley, eds. *Cultural Exchange between European Nations during the Renaissance.* Uppsala: Uppsala University, 1994.

Sorella, A. *Magia, lingua e commedia nel Machiavelli.* Florence: Olschki, 1990.

Spingarn, J. E. *A History of Literary Criticism in the Renaissance.* New York: Columbia University Press, 1908. Reprinted, Westport, Conn.: Greenwood Press, 1976.

Spivack, B. *Shakespeare and the Allegory of Evil.* New York: Columbia University Press, 1958.

Spriet, P. "*The Winter's Tale* or the Staging of an Absence." In *The Show Within: Dramatic and Other Insets, English Renaissance Drama (1550–1642),* edited by François Laroque, 253–66. Montpellier: Publications de l'Université Paul-Valéry—Montpellier III, 1992.

Stanford, W. B. "Astute Hero and Ingenious Poet: Odysseus and Homer." *The Yearbook of English Studies* 12 (1982): 1–12.

Starobinski, J. "Le texte dans le texte." *Tel Quel* 37 (1969): 4–33.

Still, J., and M. Worton. "Introduction." In *Intertextuality: Theories and Practices,* edited by Judith Still and Michael Worton, 1–44. Manchester: Manchester Unversity Press, 1990.

Strong, R. *Henry, Prince of Wales and England's Lost Renaissance.* London: Thames and Hudson, 1986.

Styan, J. L. *The Dark Comedy. The Development of Modern Comic Tragedy.* Cambridge: Cambridge University Press, 1968.

Sutherland, J. M. "Shakespeare and Seneca: A Symbolic Language for Tragedy." University of Colorado, Boulder, Ph.D. diss., *Dissertation Abstracts International* 46 (1986): 3044A.

Sypher, W., ed. *Comedy.* New York: Doubleday, 1956.

Tarantino, E. *Le metamorfosi dell'amore: Lyly, Greene, Shakespeare e le origini della commedia romantica.* Rome: Bulzoni Editore, 1995.

Taviani, F. *La commedia dell'arte e la società barocca. La fascinazione del teatro.* Rome: Bulzoni Editore, 1970.

Taylor, M. M. "The Pastoral Reckoning in *Cymbeline.*" *Shakespeare Survey* 36 (1983): 97–106.

Tenenti, A. "Il concetto e la forma: il teatro in Italia fra '500 e '600." *Intersezioni* 1 (1981): 59-73.

Terpening, R. H. "Between Lord and Lady: The Tyrant's Captain in Rucellai's *Rosmunda* and Dolce's *Marianna.*" *Forum Italicum* vol. 15, nos. 2–3 (1981): 153–70.

Tessari, R. *La Commedia dell'Arte nel Seicento: 'Industria' e 'Arte Giocosa' della Civiltà barocca.* Florence: Olschki, 1969.

———. *Commedia dell'Arte: la maschera e l'ombra.* Milan: Mursia, 1981.

Thomas, K. *Religion and the Decline of Magic: Studies in Popular Beliefs in Sixteenth- and Seventeenth-Century England.* 1971. Reprinted, Harmondsworth: Penguin Books, 1973.

———. "The Place of Laughter in Tudor and Stuart England." *Times Literary Supplement,* 21 January 1977, 77–81.

Thompson, D. W. "Belphegor in *Grim the Collier* and Riché's *Farewell.*" *Modern Language Notes* 50 (1935): 99–102.

Thomson, J. A. K. *The Classical Background of English Literature.* London: Allen & Unwin, 1948.

———. *Shakespeare and the Classics.* 1952. Reprinted, London: Allen & Unwin, 1966.

Thrall, W. F. "*Cymbeline,* Boccaccio, and the Wager Story in England." *Studies in Philology* 28 (1931): 639–51.

Tomlinson, G. *Music in Renaissance Magic: Towards a Historiography of Others.* Chicago: University of Chicago Press, 1933.

Tomlinson, H., ed. *Before the Civil War: Essays on Early Stuart Politics and Government.* London: Macmillan, 1983.

Tonelli, F. "Machiavelli's *Mandragola* and the Signs of Power." In *Drama, Sex and Politics,* edited by James Redmond, 35–54. Cambridge: Cambridge University Press, 1985.

Toschi, P. *Le origini del teatro italiano.* Turin: Einaudi, 1976.

Townsend, R. *Harington & Ariosto.* New Haven: Yale University Press, 1940.

Tulip, J. "The Intertextualities of Ben Jonson's *Volpone.*" *Sydney Studies in Literature* 20 (1994–95): 20–35.

Turner J. G. *Sexuality and Gender in Early Modern Europe: Institutions, Texts, Images.* Cambridge: Cambridge University Press, 1993.

Ugolini, G. "Edipo e la 'Poetica' di Aristotele in alcuni trattati del Cinquecento." *Giornale italiano di Filologia,* vol. 38, no. 1 (1986): 67–83.

Varese, C. *Torquato Tasso. Epos—Parola—Scena.* Messina and Florence: D'Anna, 1976.

Vazzoler, F. "Approssimazioni critiche per la tragedia italiana del Cinquecento." *L'immagine riflessa* 2 (1978): 84–94.

Veltz, J. W. *Shakespeare and the Classical Tradition.* Minneapolis: Minnesota University Press, 1968.

———. "The Ovidian Soliloquy in Shakespeare." *Shakespeare Studies* 18 (1986): 1–24.

Veròn, E. "La place de l'intertextualité dans les théories de la réception du texte littéraire." *Cahiers Roumains d'Etudes Littéraires,* vol. 13, no. 3 (1986): 103–109.

Vickers, B., ed. *Shakespeare: The Critical Heritage.* 6 vols. London: Routledge and Kegan Paul, 1974–81.

Visconti, L. *La scena restaurata: Percorsi intertestuali del teatro inglese nel tardo seicento.* Pescara: Tracce, 1991.

Von Rosador, K. T. "Dekonstruktion." *Deutsch Shakespeare-Gesellschaft West* (1992): 92–106.

Vultur, S. "A propos des configurations intertextuelles." *Cahiers Roumains d'Etudes Littéraires,* vol. 11, no. 4 (1984): 72–78.

———. "La place de l'intertextualité dans les théories de la réception du texte littéraire." *Cahiers Roumains d'Etudes Littéraires,* vol. 13, no. 3 (1986): 103–109.

Waith, E. M. *The Pattern of Tragicomedy in Beaumont and Fletcher.* New Haven: Yale University Press, 1952.

———. "The Appeal of the Comic Deceiver." *The Yearbook of English Studies* 12 (1982): 13–23.

Watson, S. "Shakespeare's Problem Comedies: An Hegelian Approach to Genre." In *Drama and Philosophy,* edited by James Redmond, 61–71. Cambridge: Cambridge University Press, 1990.

Wayne, V., ed. *The Matter of Difference: Materialist Feminist Criticism of Shakespeare.* New York: Harvester Wheatsheaf, 1991.

Weimann, R. *Shakespeare and the Popular Tradition in the Theatre: Studies in the Social Dimension of Dramatic Form and Function,* edited by Robert Schwartz. Baltimore: Johns Hopkins Unversity Press, 1978.

———. "Textual Identity and Relationship: A Metacritical Excursion into History." In *Identity of the Literary Text,* edited by Mario J. Valdés and Owen Miller, 274–93. Toronto: University of Toronto Press, 1985.

———. "Subjekt und Diskurs in Shakespeares Charakterisierung: Menschendarstellung in neuer Sicht." *Shakespeare Jahrbuch* 126 (1990): 41–55.

Weinberg, B. *A History of Literary Criticism in the Italian Renaissance.* 2 vols. Chicago: University of Chicago Press, 1961.

Weiner, A. D. "Sidney/Spenser/Shakespeare: Influence/Intertextuality/Intention." In *Influence and Intertextuality in Literary History,* edited by Jay Clayton and Eric Rothstein, 245–70. Madison: University of Wisconsin Press, 1991.

Weinrich, H. "Füer eine Literaturgeschichte des Lesers." *Merkur* 21 (1967): 1026–38.

Wells, S., ed. *The Cambridge Companion to Shakespeare Studies.* Cambridge: Cambridge University Press, 1986.

———. ed. *Shakespeare and Cultural Exchange. Shakespeare Survey* 48. Cambridge: Cambridge University Press, 1995.

Welsford, E. *The Fool: His Social and Literary History.* London: Faber, 1935.

West, G. S. "Going by the Book: Classical Allusions in Shakespeare's *Titus Andronicus.*" *Studies in Philology,* vol. 79, no. 1 (1982): 62–77.

Whigham, F. *Ambition and Privilege: The Social Tropes of Elizabethan Courtesy Theory.* Berkeley: University of California Press, 1984.

Whitaker, V. K. "Shakespeare's Use of His Sources." *Philological Quarterly* 20 (1941): 378–87.

———. *Shakespeare's Use of Learning.* San Marino, Ca.: Huntington Library, 1953.

Wiggins, M. *Journeymen in Murder: The Assassin in English Renaissance Drama.* Oxford: Clarendon Press, 1991.

Wiles, D. *Shakespeare's Clown: Actor and Text in the Elizabethan Playhouse.* Cambridge: Cambridge University Press, 1987.

Wiles, D. "Marriage and Prostitution in Classical New Comedy." In *Women in Theatre,* edited by James Redmond, 31–48. Cambridge: Cambridge University Press, 1989.

Williamson, M. L. *Infinite Variety: Antony and Cleopatra in Renaissance Drama and Earlier Tradition.* Mystic, Conn.: Verry, 1974.

Woodbridge, L. *Women and the English Renaissance: Literature and the Nature of Womankind, 1540–1620.* Brighton: Harvester Press, 1984.

———. "Patchwork: Piecing the Early Modern Mind in England's First Century of Print Culture." *English Literary Renaissance* 23 (1993): 5–45.

Woolf, R. "The Influence of the Mystery Plays upon the Popular Tragedies of the 1560's." *Renaissance Drama*, n. s., 6 (1973): 89–105.

Worthen, W. B. "Disciplines of the Text/Sites of Performance." *The Drama Review,* vol. 39, no. 1 (1995): 13–44.

Worton, M. "Intertextuality: to inter textuality or to resurrect it?" In *Cross-References: Modern French Theory and the Practice of Criticism,* edited by David Kelley and Isabelle Llasera, 14–23. Leeds: Society for French Studies, 1986.

Wright, H. G. *Boccaccio in England from Chaucer to Tennyson.* London: The Athlone Press, 1957.

Wright, J. *Dancing in Chains: The Stylistic Unity of the Comoedia Palliata.* Rome, 1974.

Yates, F. A. *John Florio: The Life of an Italian in Shakespeare's England.* Cambridge: Cambridge University Press, 1934.

———. *Giordano Bruno and the Hermetic Tradition.* London: Routledge and Kegan Paul, 1964.

———. *The Art of Memory.* London: Routledge and Kegan Paul, 1966.

Young, D. *The Heart's Forest: A Study of Shakespeare's Pastoral Plays.* New Haven: Yale University Press, 1972.

Young, S. *Shakespeare Manipulated: The Use of the Dramatic Works of Shakespeare in* teatro di figura *in Italy.* London: Associated University Presses, 1996.

Zepp, E. H. "The Criticism of Julia Kristeva: A New Mode of Critical Thought." *Romanic Review* 73 (1982): 80–97.

Zeppa de Nolva, C. "Tragédie italienne et française au XVI siècle." *Revue des Etudes Italiennes* 2 (1937): 189–201.

Zima, P. "Der Text als Intertext." *Kritik der Literatursoziologie,* 103–112. Frankfurt: Suhrkamp, 1978.

———. "Intertextualität." *Textsoziologie: Eine kritische Einführung,* 81–86. Stuttgart: J. B. Metzler, 1980.

Zimmerman, S., ed. *Erotic Politics: Desire on the English Renaissance Stage.* London: Routledge, 1992.

Zorzi, L. *Il teatro e la città. Saggi sulla scena italiana.* 2d ed. Turin: Einaudi, 1977.

Zumthor, P. "Le carrefour des rhétoriqueurs: intertextualité et rhétorique." *Poétique* 27 (1976): 317–37.

———. "L'intertexte performanciel." *Texte* 2 (1983): 49–59.

Contributors

DAVID BEVINGTON is Professor of English and Comparative Literature at the University of Chicago. He has edited many plays by Shakespeare and other Elizabethan dramatists. His books include *From 'Mankind' to Marlowe* (1962), *Tudor Drama and Politics* (1968), and *Action is Eloquence* (1984).

ZARA BRUZZI is Lecturer in English Literature at Brunel College, London. She has published several articles on Renaissance drama and with A. A. Bromham is the author of *'The Changeling' and the Years of Crisis 1619–1624: A Hieroglyph of Britain* (1990).

LOUISE GEORGE CLUBB is Professor of Italian and Comparative Literature at Berkeley University. She has written an important monograph on Della Porta and edited *Gli duoi fratelli rivali*. She is the author of *Italian Drama in Shakespeare's Time* (1989) and of many other works on comparative drama.

VIVIANA COMENSOLI is Associate Professor and Chair of the Graduate Program in the Department of English at Wilfrid Laurier University in Waterloo, Ontario. She is the author of *'Household Business': Domestic Plays of Early Modern England* (1997) and coeditor of *Discontinuities: New Essays on Renaissance Literature and Criticism* (1997).

JULIET DUSINBERRE is a Fellow of Girton College, Cambridge. She is the author of *Shakespeare and the Nature of Women* (1975), *Alice to the Lighthouse* (1987), and *Virginia Woolf's Renaissance* (1997). She is editing *As You Like It* for Arden 3.

KEIR ELAM is Professor of English Drama at the University of Florence. His books include *The Semiotics of Theatre and Drama* (1980) and *Shakespeare's Universe of Discourse* (1984). He is currently completing a volume on the languages of contemporary drama and is editing *Twelfth Night* for Arden 3.

ROBERT HENKE is Assistant Professor of Drama and Comparative Literature at Washington University in St. Louis. He is the author of *Pastoral Transformations: Italian Tragicomedy and Shakespeare's Late Plays* (1997). He was a Fellow at Villa I Tatti in 1995–96, and is now writing a book on the *Commedia dell'Arte*.

A. J. HOENSELAARS is Associate Professor of English at the University of Utrecht. He is the author of *Images of Englishmen and Foreigners* (1992). His edited volumes include *Shakespeare's Italy* (with Michele Marrapodi, 1993), and *Reclamations of Shakespeare* (1994). He is Chairman of the Shakespeare Society of the Low Countries.

LISA HOPKINS is Associate Professor of English at Sheffield University. She is the author of *John Ford's Political Theatre* (1994) and of many articles and notes on Renaissance drama.

MICHELE MARRAPODI is Associate Professor of English at the University of Palermo. He is Associate Editor of *Cahiers Elisabéthains* and Assistant Editor of *Seventeenth-Century News*. He is the author of *'The Great Image'* (1984), and *La Sicilia nella drammaturgia giacomiana e carolina* (1989). His edited volumes include *Shakespeare's Italy* (1993), and *Il mondo italiano del teatro inglese del Rinascimento* (1995).

ROBERT S. MIOLA is Professor of English and Lecturer in Classics at Loyola College, Baltimore. He is the author of *Shakespeare's Rome* (1983), *Shakespeare and Classical Tragedy* (1992), *Shakespeare and Classical Comedy* (1994), and of many articles on Renaissance and comparative drama.

J. R. MULRYNE is Professor of English at the University of Warwick. He has edited a number of Renaissance plays and published several works on Shakespeare and Elizabethan drama. His edited volumes include *Theatre of the English and Italian Renaissance* (1991), *Theatre and Government under the Early Stuarts* (1993), and *Making Space for Theatre* (1995).

MICHAEL J. REDMOND is a Commonwealth Scholar at the University of Sussex, Brighton. His recent doctorial dissertation considers the representation of Italy in early modern English drama.

LEO SALINGAR is Senior Lecturer in English Literature at Trinity College, Cambridge. His books include *Shakespeare and the Traditions of Comedy* (1974), and *Dramatic Forms in Shakespeare and the Jacobeans* (1986).

MARIANGELA TEMPERA is Associate Professor of English at the University of Ferrara. She is the author of *The Lancashire Witches* (1981) and of many articles on Shakespeare and Renaissance drama. She is currently editing the series *Shakespeare: From Text to Stage* (1984–   ).

Index